THE
RESTLESS
CARIBBEAN

THE RESTLESS CARIBBEAN

Changing Patterns of International Relations

edited by
Richard Millett and W. Marvin Will

PRAEGER PUBLISHERS
Praeger Special Studies

New York • London • Sydney • Toronto

Library of Congress Cataloging in Publication Data

Main entry under title:

The Restless Caribbean.

   Includes bibliographical references.
   1. Caribbean area—Foreign relations—Addresses,
essays, lectures. 2. Caribbean area—Foreign
economic relations—Addresses, essays, lectures.
I. Millett, Richard. II. Will, W. Marvin.
F2177.R47   327.729   78-19764
ISBN 0-03-041806-2

PRAEGER PUBLISHERS, PRAEGER SPECIAL STUDIES
383 Madison Avenue, New York, N.Y., 10017, U.S.A.

Published in the United States of America in 1979
by Praeger Publishers,
A Division of Holt, Rinehart and Winston, CBS Inc.

0123456789 038 98765432

© 1979 by Praeger Publishers

Printed in the United States of America

To our families who empathized and sacrificed, our students who inspired, and Senora Castro de Link whose Maya Restaurant provided the atmosphere and sustenance for editorial coordination.

Foreword

William G. Demas

The underlying theme of this volume is the rapidly evolving patterns of Caribbean external relations, resulting primarily from the changing nature of the political and economic linkages of Caribbean countries and territories both within the Caribbean region and between the Caribbean and the metropoles or dominant powers. A work such as this, which sets out to analyze and place in perspective these rapidly evolving patterns, is both timely and valuable.

DEFINITIONS OF THE CARIBBEAN

At the outset it is necessary to define the "Caribbean." There are three separate conceptions of the Caribbean to be found among writers, commentators, and policymakers:

(a) the English-speaking Caribbean or Commonwealth Caribbean;
(b) the Caribbean archipelago which includes all the islands of the Caribbean Sea plus the mainland "extensions" of Guyana, Suriname, and Cayenne on the South American mainland and Belize on the Central American mainland; and
(c) the Caribbean basin, consisting of the countries of the Caribbean archipelago *plus* the littoral nations of Central and South America.

Thus, one may view the Caribbean as consisting of three concentric circles—the first or innermost one being the English-speaking Caribbean, the second or middle one being the Caribbean archipelago, and the third or outermost one being the Caribbean basin.

This book deals primarily with the English-speaking Caribbean and the rest of the Caribbean archipelago but places considerable emphasis on the external relations between these groups and the mainland nations of the Caribbean basin.

The English-speaking Caribbean

The Commonwealth Caribbean with a population of five million and a Gross National Product (GNP) of about $6 billion has for the last two

---

*The views expressed here are those of the author and do not reflect the official position of the Caribbean Development Bank. I wish, however, to acknowledge the useful assistance of my CDB colleague Herman Grant.

decades been groping to assert itself through attainment of independence and the creation of viable economies and societies. They first attempted political union in the form of the West Indies Federation which lasted from 1958 to 1962. This federal experiment failed for reasons which are not pertinent to analyse here. But certain bonds of functional cooperation were retained out of the wreckage—collaboration in university education, shipping and meteorology; joint collective bargaining over prices and access of the region's primary commodity exports to traditional developed country markets, mainly the United Kingdom, Canada, and the United States of America; and mutual consultation on a wide range of issues at annual meetings of the heads of government, at first of the so-called "Big Four"—Barbados, Guyana, Jamaica, Trinidad and Tobago—and later of all the other countries formerly in the Federation as well as Bahamas and Belize.[1]

The Caribbean Community

In 1968 the ten countries which participated in the defunct Federation plus Guyana[2] embarked on a process of formal economic integration, launching the Caribbean Free Trade Association (CARIFTA). Five years later CARIFTA developed and strengthened into the Caribbean Community. The Community covers three areas of activity: (1) Economic integration (pursued through the Caribbean Common Market and involving both free trade and cooperation in production); (2) Functional cooperation and common services in areas such as sea and air transport; university education; other aspects of education; health; labor relations; harmonisation of laws and legal systems; culture; information and broadcasting, etc.; and (3) The coordination of the foreign policies of the independent member states of the community.

The Community consists of two categories of member states: the relatively more developed countries (MDCs) of Barbados, Guyana, Jamaica and Trinidad and Tobago, which have all been independent for periods ranging from ten to sixteen years; and the relatively less developed countries (LDCs) consisting of Antigua, Belize, Dominica, Grenada, Montserrat, St. Kitts-Nevis-Anguilla, St. Lucia and St. Vincent. All of the countries in this second category are still politically tied to the U.K. and are not independent, with the exception of Grenada which achieved that status in 1974. However, all the others with the exception of Montserrat and Belize will soon achieve separate political independence. These relatively less developed countries are small, with populations ranging from 13,000 in the case of Montserrat to 110,000 in the case of Grenada and St. Lucia and all have rather narrow natural resource bases and limited cadres of trained human resources. In the Treaty of Chaguaramas establishing the Caribbean Community, a Special Regime for the Less Developed Countries seeks to provide the LDCs with opportunities for sharing equitably in the benefits of regional economic integration.

The English-speaking Commonwealth of the Bahamas, which achieved political independence in 1973, while not formally a member of the Community, cooperates with it in a number of noneconomic areas.

The Caribbean Archipelago

The second conception of the Caribbean, Caribbean archipelago, includes, in addition to the English-speaking Caribbean countries, Cuba, Haiti, Dominican Republic, Puerto Rico, U.S. Virgin islands, the Netherlands Antilles, the French Departments and Suriname. The area has a combined population of some 30 million people and combined G.N.P. of about $21 billion. The languages spoken in this second circle include Spanish, French, Dutch and English and the constitutional status of the states and territories varies considerably.

The French-speaking countries include independent Haiti as well as Martinique, Guadeloupe and Cayenne which are Departments of metropolitan France. The Spanish-speaking countries consist of independent Cuba and Dominican Republic as well as nonindependent Puerto Rico (which has free associated status with the U.S.A.). The U.S. Virgin Islands, are also not independent. The Dutch-speaking Caribbean includes Suriname which attained sovereignty in 1975 and the Netherlands Antilles (now contemplating independence) of which the largest are Aruba and Curacao.

There are considerable variations among the countries and territories in terms of levels of economic development, political and economic systems, and ideological paths to development.

In spite of the variations in language, constitutional status, political institutions, levels of economic development, and in developmental ideologies, the countries and territories of the Caribbean archipelago are characterised by many common features: a very long history of political colonialism, a heavy African element in the population, a long history of economic dependence on the metropolis, the legacy of slavery and indentureship, and the dominance of the sugar plantation in their economic history. It is this unity underlying so much diversity that makes the Caribbean Archipelago a "culture-area". It is my view that this "culture-area" is the "true" Caribbean.

The Caribbean Basin

Finally, there is the third conception of the Caribbean which also includes the mainland countries whose shores are washed by the Caribbean Sea: Mexico, the five Central American Republics, Panama, Colombia and Venezuela. The total population of these countries is 145 million and their total GNP is approximately $116 billion.

While the countries and territories of the Caribbean archipelago constitute a "culture-area", the Caribbean basin is a geopolitical concept. The basin can be viewed as a potential "diplomatic area" from the point of view of both the United States and the stronger Caribbean basin powers such as Mexico, Colombia and Venezuela and even by a non-Caribbean Basin country such as Brazil. It is within this framework of a potential geopolitical security or diplomatic zone that one should view many of the efforts to forge links of economic integration between the mainland and island countries.

NINE REASONS FOR INTEREST IN THE EXTERNAL RELATIONS OF THE CARIBBEAN

First, the Caribbean contains the last set of nonindependent territories in the Western Hemisphere (leaving aside the Falkland islands of Malvinas). In the English-, French- and Dutch-speaking Caribbean, several countries are yet to attain political independence although it is certain that nearly all the smaller English-speaking territories in the eastern Caribbean will soon attain this status. Indeed, in some cases there is doubt as to whether a majority of the people desire political independence, as in the French Departments of Martinique and Guadeloupe, in Puerto Rico and the U.S. Virgin Islands. Belize is being denied independence not because of the unwillingness of the metropolitan country concerned (the U.K.) or of the majority of its people but because it is threatened by its powerful neighbour, Guatemala.

Second, there is the question of the independent viability of many small island territories in the Caribbean.

Third, the region is of interest in that Cuba, the largest island in the Caribbean, has a centrally planned economy and close links with the Socialist bloc and is a full member of its Council for Mutual Economic Assistance (COMECON).

Fourth, partly as a consequence of the recent attainment of political independence, the foreign policy patterns of some of the independent Caribbean countries have been undergoing rapid change. Witness the desire of the part of Guyana and Jamaica to forge links of economic and technical cooperation with the centrally planned economies and with other Third World countries, particularly the more militant in the nonaligned group.

Fifth, potential middle-level powers in the Caribbean basin and Latin America are increasingly awakening to what they consider to be their new and legitimate role in the region, examples being Brazil, Venezuela, Colombia and Mexico.

Sixth, the French-, Dutch- and English-speaking Caribbean countries are the only parts of the hemisphere to have formal economic and trading relationships with the European Economic Community (EEC) through the Lomé Convention in the case of the independent countries and, in the case of the nonindependent countries or territories and departments, through an association with the EEC under Part IV of the Treaty of Rome.

Seventh, all the English-speaking Caribbean countries in the Caribbean, along with Canada, are the only members in the hemisphere of the British Commonwealth of Nations.

Eighth, the newly independent English-speaking and Dutch-speaking Caribbean countries have begun to form closer ties with Latin America as shown by their membership in organisations such as the Organisation of American States, the Inter-American Development Bank, the United Nations Economic Commission for Latin America (ECLA), and the Latin American Economic System (SELA).

Nine, English-speaking Caribbean countries, once bound together in political union under British colonial rule, are now groping toward meaningful economic integration as a means of overcoming the limits placed on their achieving more autonomous patterns of economic development in spite of their small size, extreme fragmentation, and external economic dependence, the legacy of their colonial history. As the smallest and most economically fragmented and externally dependent part of the hemisphere, the efforts of the English-speaking Caribbean at economic integration are deserving of close attention.

SIX CENTRAL ISSUES OF EXTERNAL RELATIONS OF THE CARIBBEAN STATES AND TERRITORIES

From the point of view of external political and economic relations, the central issues facing the countries and territories in the "culture-area" of the Caribbean Archipelago in today's world are: (1) The apparently internal question of the type, direction and pattern of economic and social transformation to be sought in order to provide for the basic needs of their peoples and to make them less externally dependent. This apparently internal question has farreaching implications for external linkages; (2) The economic and political relationships being created between individual English-speaking countries and territories; (3) The economic and political relationships between the English-speaking countries and territories and the other countries and territories of the Caribbean archipelago; (4) The relationship between the countries of the Archipelago and the larger and economically stronger Mainland countries; (5) The relationship between the English-speaking and other Caribbean countries and the wider Third World; and (6) The relationship between the English-speaking and other Caribbean archipelago countries and the developed Western and Socialist countries.

Ceasing to be the Third World's third world

It should be stressed that the issue of internal development strategies cannot be divorced from the other external issues. There is a definite relationship, although not always easily discernible, between development strategies pursued by countries and their external economic and political links.

Certain special features are most crucial in this context for the countries of the Caribbean, particularly from the point of view of the English-speaking Caribbean. This group is, historically, perhaps the most massively subordinated area of the world. Vidia Naipaul, the West Indian writer, with characteristically uncharitable wit, has referred to this part of the world as the "Third World's third world", meaning an area doomed to perpetual subordination, futility and even impotence even when all its constituent countries have attained political independence. He is speaking not only about political and economic subordination but also about lack of cultural identity and inability to become creative and authentic societies.

Unlike Naipaul, I contend that the Caribbean "culture-area", and particularly the English-speaking part, can achieve much greater economic strength, and hence genuine political independence and cultural identity than they now have. To achieve this there are four crucial preconditions: (1) The shaping of development objectives and strategies with a view to, first, converting the present massive external economic dependence into genuine interdependence with the rest of the world and, second, to satisfying the basic needs of the people for food and nutrition, shelter, health and educational facilities and, above all, productive employment; (2) The nature and kinds of links which they form with each other and with the outside world; (3) The achievement internationally of a more equitable international economic order; and (4) The degree of sucesss which they achieve in changing perceptions of themselves through seeking genuine self-reliance.

It is well-known that the economies of the Caribbean were created as appendages of the Western European economies in the early mercantilist phase of capitalism. In essence, this status still persists. Major decisions on investment, levels of production and technologies were all taken outside of the region. Historically, there were few if any production linkages between sectors at the national level, and little trade or production linkages at the regional level. They also were extremely dependent on preferential external markets for a narrow range of primary commodity exports, mainly sugar, which they increasingly tended to produce at relatively high costs of production; and, conversely, they always relied heavily on food imports. ⌈Unemployment and underemployment emerged as serious problems in the twentieth century with some relief being provided by emigration.⌋

The merchant company of the eighteenth century was replaced in the twentieth by the multinational corporation (MNC) as the prime mover and major decision-maker in many of the economies of the Caribbean. Today the legacy of economic dependence and underdevelopment (with unbalanced and fragile economies, large amounts of surplus labor, high-cost agricultural exports, heavy reliance on imported food, and lack of national and regional linkages in production) is still very much in force, in spite of attempts in a few of the countries to control the MNCs operating in sugar, insurance and banking, tourism, production of oil, bauxite and aluminum[3] and to change distorted structures of production and consumption.

Added to this legacy of extreme external dependence, most of the English-speaking Caribbean countries have to contend with the factor of small size and a narrow range of natural resources. Nevertheless, viewed as a region, the resource base of the English-speaking Caribbean countries is fairly adequate on a per capita basis. Resources include agricultural land, good climate for tourism, resources of fisheries, forestry, other building materials, oil and natural gas bauxite, hydroelectric and geothermal energy potential, and as yet undiscovered or unutilised natural resources.

With regard to size, two extreme views prevail in the region. One is that the countries are too small to ever achieve economic viability and independence. The second is that "small is beautiful" and that even the smallest island with a few thousand people can achieve economic viability through institutional and psychological changes brought about presumably by a certain type of highly idealistic political regime (and people). I would suggest that size, although important in many contexts, is not always of central or crucial importance, given appropriate national development strategies and schemes of integration among groups of neighbouring small countries. The valid point about reasonably large economic size so far as internal national development is concerned is that it facilitates the achievement of economies of scale in economic activities, in public administration and in Government-provided infrastructure and social services. The real point about reasonably large economic size so far as international relations are concerned is that it promotes greater bargaining power and independence of action. Of course, national development and patterns of international relations are closely interrelated. Coping with small size is possible through appropriate development objectives and strategies and through proper schemes of regional integration both economic and political.

Indeed, one can never separate the economic from the political aspects of integration. According to Bela Balassa,

> the conflict between national sovereignty and economic self-interest can be resolved only if there is a political interest and the political will to do so. Economic integration thus appears as part of a political process the final outcome of which is determined by essentially political factors.[4]

An important aspect of economic integration among groups of countries with weak and externally dependent economies is the need for coordination of all external relationships, both economic and political. This is why the Treaty of Chaguaramas establishing the Caribbean Community provides for the coordination of the foreign policies of the independent member states.[5] Perhaps the most important aspect of Caribbean integration[5] is the need for the closest possible unity of external policy and action among member countries. This key aspect does not usually receive as much emphasis as the nature, scope, and machinery for intraregional economic integration and "functional" cooperation.

Here the question arises, is it possible for Caribbean countries to unify or even effectively coordinate their external policies, postures, and actions? The answer is two-fold. First, in practice, wide divergence in development paths and strategies is not possible among small Caribbean states due to their common problems and similar historical legacies. Second, CARICOM members should not experience great difficulty perceiving the essentiality of increased unity of external policy and action to their survival as a people, whatever may be the ideological or rhetorical differences reflected in their national quests for development. As President Julius Nyerere has noted, "The United States is powerful not because it is capitalist but because it is united."

The moral here is that Caribbean countries have to make use of whatever latent geopolitical power they possess by joint external policies, positions, and actions. West Indian economist Havelock Brewster has pointed to the tremendous latent geopolitical strength of the eastern Caribbean islands by virtue of their constituting the eastern perimeter of the Caribbean Sea to approximately 20° latitude and the most important Caribbean access route to and from Europe and Africa.[6] As he puts it:

It is within the power of the smaller islandic countries to use their combined significance to get a better economic deal. The alternative is for Caribbean states to be consumed by Venezuela and Colombia, a possibility apparently already grasped by these countries. The political leaders of the more developed member countries would seem to be neither irrational nor moved by one-people notions for their engagement of the least developed countries.[7]

Accordingly, what is lacking in the smaller eastern Caribbean islands in terms of size and natural resource endowment could be more than fully compensated by joint and coordinated actions on the external front to realise their latent geopolitical power. And it should be noted that, if they act as a group, the English-speaking eastern Caribbean islands (the Leeward and Windward islands, Barbados and Trinidad and Tobago)[8] have more potential geopolitical power than the other member states of CARICOM. The english-speaking eastern Caribbean islands could use their geopolitical power to secure both for themselves and the other CARICOM countries a greater capacity for independent action and for more autonomous patterns of economic development. Thus we have the paradox that the relatively less developed countries can bring invaluable assets of a noneconomic but geopolitical nature to the entire Caribbean Community. It is this potential which would, for example, enable all the countries to negotiate a just share in the benefits to be gained from exploiting the resources of the Caribbean Sea as the concept of exclusive economic zone is applied by the bigger mainland countries of the Caribbean basin.

Toward New Caribbean Linkages

If this kind of cooperation is systematically pursued, it is possible that the eastern Caribbean members of CARICOM will develop a political union among themselves; for the dynamics of an integration scheme stressing external cohesion could in time overcome the massive obstacles of fragmentation, insularity and economic and political rivalries bred by centuries of metropolitan-imposed divisions.

What of the relations between CARICOM and the other countries and territories of the Caribbean? The answer is obvious. There is obvious need for growing economic cooperation. While over the next few years CARICOM should be further strengthened so as to produce benefits not only from trade liberalisation but also, and more importantly, from cooperation in production, parallel efforts should be made to develop closer economic links with the rest of the Caribbean archipelago.

These links will vary to an extent depending on the constitutional status of the countries and territories and the nature of their economic systems. For, unless the nonindependent constitutional status of Puerto Rico and the U.S. Virgin Islands and of Martinque, Guadeloupe and Cayenne changes (which at the moment is a very remote possibility, partly because of the high standard of living they somewhat artificially enjoy by virtue of their close relationship with their respective metropolitan countries) it would be impossible juridically for these countries to participate in the Caribbean Community either as full or associate members. Similarly, because Cuba has a centrally planned economy, it would also be difficult (for technical economic and not ideological reasons) for this country to become either a full or associate member of the Caribbean Community. Formal highly institutionalised links between CARICOM and the nonindependent territories must be ruled out, with trade and other economic cooperation links being developed on a rather informal basis. On the other hand, it should be possible for either associate or full membership of CARICOM (or formal Trade and Industrial Complementarity Agreements) to be extended to independent countries such as Haiti, Dominican Republic, Suriname and (shortly) the Netherlands Antilles. As the same time, since Cuba is fully sovereign, it should be possible for CARICOM to develop more formal Trade and Industrial Complementarity Agreements with this country.

These possibilities for closer economic cooperation at the level of the Caribbean archipelago have been recently recognised through the establishment of 1975 of the ECLA Caribbean Development and Cooperation Committee, on the initiative of the Prime Minister of Trinidad and Tobago. The CDCC has as full members all the independent countries of the Caribbean archipelago, while the smaller English-speaking islands in the eastern Caribbean, the Netherlands Antilles and Belize are associate members.

In the context of the mainland countries of the Caribbean basin and indeed of the wider Latin American area, it would be silly for the Caribbean Community to seek to isolate itself from its mainland neighbours in a small inward-looking bloc of five million persons. It should instead seek to develop closer economic relations with surrounding mainland Caribbean basin and Latin American countries, with whom geography has ordained close economic cooperation links.

The point here is not whether there should be economic cooperation with the larger nations in the basin but how. In facing up to this question of modalities, a moment's thought will indicate the answer: economic cooperation on a joint Caribbean Community basis. This answer is dictated by the fact that the economies of the English-speaking countries are among the weakest, smallest and possibly the most externally dependent in the Western Hemisphere. Hence the need to preserve the identity of their peoples and avoid (unwittingly) external domination in economic cooperation with the larger and stronger economies of neighbouring countries.

There is a strong parallel here with the rationale for the formation of the Andean Group of middle-sized South American countries[9] to deal more effectively with the bigger and stronger member countries of the Latin American Free Trade Association (LAFTA) namely, Argentina, Brazil and Mexico. The best hope of long-range stability in economic, diplomatic and political relationships between the individual newly independent, smaller and economically weaker English-speaking countries and the bigger countries on the mainland of the Caribbean basin and all the rest of Latin America lies in a strong united Caribbean Community, which has "externalised" itself. Ideally the Caribbean Community, widened to include other Archipelago countries, should as a community over time develop ever increasing links of economic and technical cooperation with the Central American Common Market, the Andean Common Market and with Brazil; as it is now trying to do under a Cooperation Agreement with Mexico.

Links With the Wider World?

As Third World countries, the Caribbean states need to cooperate economically and politically with as many other countries of the Third World as possible whether "globally" through membership of the non-aligned Movement, of the Group of 77 or through the growing movement for economic cooperation among developing countries or sectionally through commodity associations such as the International Bauxite Association (IBA) which Guyana and Jamaica did so much to bring about and of which the Dominican Republic and Haiti are also members. They must have a clear position and make their united voices heard on the growing confrontation over the future of Southern Africa. They also have a growing and obvious interest in the establishment of a new international economic order and on an equitable legal regime for the exploitation of the resources of the Caribbean Sea.

As an advocate of a "selective and partial delinking" strategy for Third World countries,[10] I see the need for a widening of Caribbean development options both through greater selectivity and greater geographical diversification in the trade and other economic relationships between Caribbean countries and both developed Western and Socialist countries. For the dominance of one or two great or middle powers is not compatible with a successful quest for genuine economic and political independence. It is in this context that closer economic and diplomatic relationships with the developed Western countries and the two super-powers, with China, and with other Socialist countries should be pursued.

The freedom of action to follow the kind of foreign policy broadly sketched out above, however, would depend on crucial factors in each Caribbean country as well as on the "externalisation" informed by a spirit of self-help and self-reliance within the framework of more selective and wider-ranging economic contacts with the outside world. The countries have to resolve such fundamental economic issues as the future role of transnational corporations in their economies; the problem of technology transfer, development and adaptation; the precise role of foreign aid in their economies; the kind of alternate international tourism which they should seek to promote; the acute and seemingly intractable problems of very heavy imports of food and weaknesses in the traditional commodity export sectors, arising from high costs and low productivity; the creation of national and regional linkages in production; the mobilisation of greater domestic savings and the changing of consumption patterns; and development of considerably greater volumes of exports of manufactures and non-traditional agricultural products to the outside world.

Above all, the ideology which helps shape development patterns must create a new self-image among the Caribbean people, a self-image which would reflect the latent West Indian creativity and ability to devise solutions to their own unique problems and to cast off their historically imposed attitude of mendicancy towards the metropolitan countries.

All of this is certainly a tall order; but not impossible if latent West Indian and Caribbean energies are harnessed!

NOTES

1. With the formation of the Caribbean Community in 1973/4, the Conference of Heads of Government was institutionalized as the supreme policy-making organ of the Community.

2. Belize became a member of CARIFTA in 1971.

3. Guyana has gone furthest in this direction; but both Jamaica and Trinidad and Tobago have been taking steps to bring key sectors of the national economy under local control and decision-making. Outside of the English-speaking Caribbean, Cuba has however embarked upon the most radical programme of restructuring the old economic and social relationships.

4. Bela Balasse, "Types of Economic Integration," *Economic Integration: Worldwide, Regional, Sectoral.* Macmillan, 1976, page 30.

5. To repeat, the Community aims at cooperation in three fundamental areas of activity: (a) Economic Integration, pursued through the Caribbean Common Market; (b) Cooperation and Common Services in "functional" areas such as Health, Education, Culture, Sea and Air Transportation, etc; and (c) The coordination of the foreign policies of the independent member states.

6. Inclusion of the Bahamas would add even greater strength to this island frontier of the Caribbean basin.

7. See Brewster's Letter to the Editor, *Caribbean Contact*, August 1977, page 15.

8. Brewster was, however, speaking mainly about the Leeward and Windward Islands and the Bahamas. He noted in this connection that Pureto Rico could also be an important part of this "shield," presumably on the assumption that it became independent.

9. Bolivia, Colombia, Ecuador, Peru and Venezuela. Chile, a founding member, withdrew from the Group in 1976.

10. For a brilliant exposition and sympathetic critique of the concept of Third World "delinking," see the contribution of Carlos Diaz-Alejandro on "Delinking North and South" in Fishlow, Diaz-Alejandro, Fagen and Hansen, *Rich and Poor Nations in the World Economy*, McGraw Hill, 1978.

Preface

The title of this volume, *The Restless Caribbean,* was chosen to reflect our view that the region is undergoing rapid, diffuse, and, at times, conflicting patterns of change in both its internal and external relations. New nations continue to emerge, political and economic ties both within and without the region experience constant alterations, and regional integration is apparently being sacrificed before the altar of national self-determination. States within the region represent almost every shade of political philosophy, ranging from Cuban communism and Jamaican and Guyanese socialism to Grenada's search for ties with Chile and Taiwan to the semimedieval rule of the Duvalier family in Haiti.

Even defining the region has become an increasing problem, with some restricting their definition of the Caribbean area to the islands, while others would include those mainland states which share a geographical proximity, such as Mexico, Panama, and Venezuela, or a cultural affinity, such as Guyana and Surinam, with the region. We have generally inclined toward this latter position, concentrating our attention upon the insular states, but devoting considerable attention to the mainland circum Caribbean as well.

The rapidity and scope of change within the region has influenced the international relations of both Caribbean and metropolitan states. In almost every area the old colonial relationships have broken down, but no stable pattern has emerged to replace them. The developed metropolitan nations have attempted numerous methods of maintaining their control or influence, varying from the French effort to incorporate its territories into the mother country through the variety of United States proposals for Puerto Rico to the less direct tactics of the United Kingdom and the Soviet Union. Caribbean states have sought to increase their own latitude in foreign affairs through an equally diverse set of arrangements, including efforts at federation, economic cooperation, identification with other Third World nations in international organizations, and internal reforms aimed at limiting the control exerted by external economic and political forces. These patterns of change continue.

International relations have been further complicated by the increased quantity and complexity of the issues involved. Within the Caribbean, such traditional sources of concern as external defense, boundary disputes, bilateral trade agreements, and cultural exchanges have declined in relative importance in recent years. Newer issues, involving world economic patterns, control of multinational corporations, law of the sea disputes, alternative patterns of postcolonial relations, the relationship of tourism to internal development, migration policy, and numerous other problems rarely considered a quarter of a century ago now complicate international relationships. New nations and new ideologies compete for influence with traditional forces. Solutions and proposals advanced for the region only a few years ago now often seem dated, if not irrelevant to the current situation.

While this pattern of complex change is by no means unique to the Caribbean, it is of special interest and concern there. Relatively compact in area and, if the major circum-Caribbean nations of Venezuela, Colombia, and Mexico are excluded, limited in population, it presents a manageable microcosm of the international problems of the developing world. In this one area four traditional colonial powers, the United States, the United Kingdom, France, and the Netherlands, compete for influence with the Soviet Union, with the oil-financed influence of Venezuela, and with the regional nations, new and old. The Caribbean is of vital security interest to the United States and is of significant economic interest to much of the developed world. Study of the region is facilitated by its general adherence to western political models and by the western elements in its cultural heritage. All of this combines to make the Caribbean a potentially important source of knowledge about the emerging problems and relationships between metropolitan nations and developing Third World states.

Most of the previous studies on the international relationships of the Caribbean have tended to emphasize either the Hispanic or the Commonwealth sector. Those written from the viewpoint of the United States have focused their attention upon the Latin Caribbean, often to the almost total exclusion of other areas. Studies produced by European or Commonwealth Caribbean scholars, on the other hand, have usually neglected the Latin Caribbean and have also often limited their focus to internal problems or to relationships with their former colonial overlords. We hope this volume combines the strengths of both these approaches with a sensitivity to the new and wider issues involved.

While we believe the essays contained in *The Restless Caribbean* make a significant contribution to understanding current international relations, we do not claim to have provided a definitive picture of the region. Space limitations forced us to drop projected studies of such problems as the influence of mass media, the Belizian dispute, and the impact of the debate over a new world economic order. After some consideration, we also decided that a single chapter on current U.S. Caribbean policy would probably prove both extremely difficult and diffuse and would also duplicate material contained in other sections. We did attempt to secure a chapter on Cuba's role in the Caribbean from a Cuban point of view, but we were unable to locate a Cuban scholar willing to undertake the task. A commissioned chapter on Afro-Caribbean links also failed to materialize. Within the space and time limitations imposed upon us, we have included the issues we felt most worthy of attention and most amenable to inclusion within the format of this volume. We have also sought a wide variety of ideological and national viewpoints, though we would hope for greater Commonwealth and Latin Caribbean representation among the authors of any future editions of this work. In many ways the problems we experienced in attempting to secure Caribbean contributors, and especially a Cuban perspective, reflect major problems within the region—divisions produced by transnational communication and differing ideologies.

The final responsibility for the composition of this volume is ours, of course, but the opinions expressed are those of the individual authors. We hope that our combined efforts will stimulate further research and writing on Caribbean international relations, helping to further our fragmentary understanding not only of the problems, but also of the possibilities for the future of this vital region.

The authors gratefully acknowledge the able assistance received in the preparation of this manuscript from Mrs. De Will; from the office staff of the SIUE History Department, Mrs. Julia Barton, Ms. Denice Taylor and Mr. Robert Bosworth; from Ms. Kimberley Coffee and Mr. Eugene Robinson, student assistants in the TU Political Science Department; from Drs. Courtney Blackman, Central Bank of Barbados, Robert W. Anderson, University of Puerto Rico, G.E.M. Mills, University of the West Indies-Jamaica, Edward Dew, Fairfield University, Kenneth Johnson and Edet Ituen, University of Missouri-St. Louis, Ms. Sheila Chen, Caribbean Community Secretariat, Guyana, Mr. J. Jasper, Foreign and Commonwealth Office, UK, from Ms. Phyliss Walker of Excelsior and from Prof. R. Noble Thompson of the SIUE Geography Department. Mr. Bruce Warshavsky of Praeger also merits our appreciation for his constant aid and encouragement with this project.

Contents

LIST OF TABLES

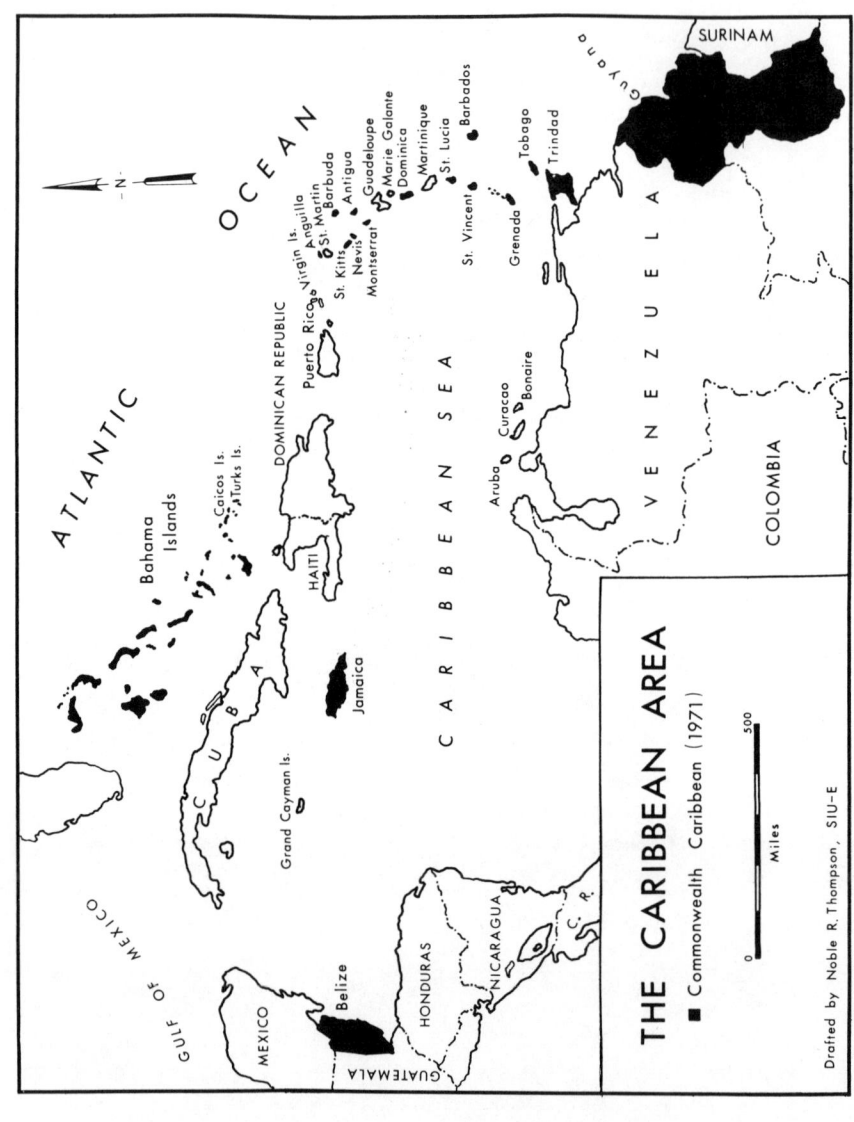

THE CARIBBEAN AREA

■ Commonwealth Caribbean (1971)

0 _____ 500
Miles

Drafted by Noble R. Thompson, SIU-E

Part I

The Context of Caribbean International Relations

1

Imperialism, Intervention, and Exploitation: The Historical Context of International Relations in the Caribbean

Richard Millett

INTRODUCTION

From the initial voyage of Columbus until the Cuban Revolution of 1959, international relations within the Caribbean area were characterized by overwhelming dominance and manipulation by nations external to the region. Before 1800, the Caribbean served largely as a stage upon which European powers performed, competing for political and economic control with little regard for the interests of those living in the area. The nineteenth century witnessed the emergence of the United States as a major regional power. The nations of the littoral as well as Haiti and the Dominican Republic also achieved political independence, but it was quickly made clear that in international political and economic matters they were still subject to the outside dominance they had endured throughout the colonial period.

The Spanish-American War represented the end of violent competition among outside powers for Caribbean territories, but force or the threat of force, now employed largely by the United States against the quasi-independent nations of the region, remained a prime factor in relations. External problems, such as the world wars and the Great Depression, served to divert or diminish the attention devoted to the area, providing at best a form of benign neglect. This gave the insular and littoral states a bit more freedom in determining area relationships, but basic rules remained unchanged until the post-World War II period. An examination of the historical development of relationships within the Caribbean will reveal ways in which this outside domination was created and maintained and should also show the causes of the changing patterns of international relations that have transformed this former colonial sea into today's restless Caribbean.

3

THE COLONIAL EPOCH: 1492–1783

The pattern for European relations within the Caribbean was set within the first few decades following the initial voyage of Columbus. Although there was debate within the Spanish court concerning Spain's right to rule in the Indies, basic operative policy always assumed this right.[1] Indigenous inhabitants were treated not as citizens of other nations, but as prime subjects for conversion to Christianity and subjection to the economic demands of Spain. This subjugation was pursued with such vigor that, within a few decades, the indigenous population of the Greater Antilles was virtually exterminated.

Conflicts among European powers over the Caribbean began immediately following the return of Columbus. The Portuguese king calmly announced that he held title to the areas visited by the Spanish, a claim which led Spain frantically to seek confirmation of its title from the Pope. The resultant papal demarcation line, modified in favor of the Portuguese in the 1494 Treaty of Tordesillas, divided the non-Christian world into Spanish and Portuguese spheres of influence, placing most of the Americas, including the Caribbean basin, within the Spanish sphere. Although they later engaged in smuggling slaves and other goods, the Portuguese accepted this treaty and never seriously challended Spanish Caribbean claims. Other European nations, however, were not so accommodating.

Open conflict within the Caribbean began with the 1521–22 raids upon Spanish commerce by the French-backed expedition of Giovanni de Verrazano. French attacks escalated through the 1550s, reaching a peak in 1555 when Jacques de Sores burned Havana.[2] The Treaty of Cateau-Cambresis in 1559 reduced the level of conflict, but also created the principle of the "Line of Amity" by which battles could be fought in the area south of the Tropic of Cancer and west of the thirtieth meridian without risking war in Europe.[3] As most of the Caribbean fell within this area the treaty did little to provide security for Spanish interests in the region.

Sporadic conflicts with the French continued for several decades, but in the last third of the sixteenth century the English emerged as the major threat within the region. Beginning with the voyages of John Hawkins in the 1560s and culminating in the raids of Sir Francis Drake on Santo Domingo, Cartegena, and Panama, English "sea devils" forced the Iberian government to divert considerable energy into defensive efforts, providing motivation for the disastrous voyage of the Spanish Armada. Until the seventeenth century, however, the Spanish monopoly of Caribbean trade and territory remained basically intact.[4]

By the start of the seventeenth century Spanish power was in decline, the Dutch had joined the French and English in attacks upon the Caribbean, and the stage was set for the creation of non-Spanish colonies. Initial British efforts in the Guianas failed, as did colonies on St. Lucia and Grenada. In 1624, however, a settlement established on St. Christopher (St. Kitts) marked the beginning of a permanent British presence in the Caribbean. At first the British had to share the island with the French, a problem they did not encounter when they settled on Barbados three years later.[5] Spain had failed to occupy the lesser Antilles and a rush soon ensued among other European nations to fill this vacuum. The Dutch devoted most of their energies to efforts in Brazil and the Guianas, resulting in the founding of Surinam, but they found time to settle Aruba, Curaçao, Saba, and St. Eustatius by the 1640s. Denmark, Sweden, and even Brandenburg Prussia joined in the territorial scramble, though the activities of the Danes were confined to the Virgin Islands and the presence of the Swedes and Brandenburgers was fleeting.

The British and French remained the main contenders for new Caribbean territories and, as Spain's power declined, they extended their ambitions to the greater Antilles. France took over the western third of Hispaniola (today the republic of Haiti), while Britain, in 1655, seized Jamaica. British penetration even extended to Central America with the beginnings of settlements at Belize and along the Mosquito Coast. The inevitable clash between British and French interests in the Caribeean soon began and, propelled by the power struggle in Europe, continued intermittently until 1814. The Dutch and Spanish were also involved in these conflicts, with the result that control of most of the islands of the lesser Antilles changed several times between 1650 and 1783. St. Lucia holds the record in this area, with some historians recording more than ten changes of sovereignty for that island, but even tiny St. Eustatius changed hands at least half a dozen times.[6]

The interests of the islands' inhabitants were largely ignored during these conflicts, but the period did witness a transformation of island life, with the rising dominance of sugar and of slavery. The pattern of a colonial monoculture, with wealth produced by a servile, nonwhite majority and enjoyed by a small, white minority, was firmly impressed upon the region. The culture of the governing powers was established in each island as were a multitude of commercial laws and regulations designed to insure that each colony developed along lines beneficial to the mother country.

THE DECLINE OF EUROPEAN HEGEMONY: 1783–1898

The achievement of United States independence in 1783 propelled an increasingly important actor into the arena of Caribbean relations.

Despite shared grievances, none of the British Caribbean territories had evidenced any serious desire to join with the rebellious mainland colonies and the end of the Revolution found them firmly under British control. The conflict, however, had influenced development in other areas. The Spanish regained Florida, but also acquired potentially dangerous trade and boundary disputes with the new North American republic. French West Indian troops had helped the revolution succeed, but took home with them disturbing ideas of colonial rights. The Dutch Caribbean possessions had played a vital role in the transshipment of supplies to North America, but had paid a heavy price for their actions, especially St. Eustatius, which was devastated by the British and never regained its former importance.

The French Revolution of 1789 and the subsequent series of international conflicts lasting until 1815 greatly complicated the situation in the Caribbean. The effects were most clearly felt in the colony of Saint Dominique where, by 1798, Toussaint Louverture had succeeded in driving the Spanish out of their half of Hispaniola and had then forced the French to withdraw militarily, leaving himself as head of a semiindependent state. For a few years both U.S. and British support was sent to Toussaint in an effort to prevent the return of French military influence and to gain a share of Hispaniola's trade. But, by 1801, the undeclared naval war between the U.S. and France had been resolved and Great Britain had even agreed to a brief period of peace. Being concerned with the effects of the example of a successful slave revolt, the Americans and the British dropped their support of Toussaint and offered no obstacles to the 1802 French reconquest of the island.[7] Yellow fever and Haitian resistance combined to force withdrawal from the French portion of the island in 1803, though it was not until 1809 that the French were forced out of Spanish Santo Domingo. Haitian independence was proclaimed and maintained by a succession of generals, who overran the Spanish side of Hispaniola in 1822, inaugurating twenty-one years of island unity which Dominicans characterize as the worst period in their history.[8] The United States, concerned with its slave problems, refused to recognize the Black republic, a situation which persisted until the Lincoln administration.

The Napoleonic Wars provided the opportunity for uprisings in Spain's mainland colonies and by the early 1820s Mexico, Central America, Colombia, and Venezuela had all gained independence. Simón Bolívar, leader of the Venezuelan and Colombian independence movements, had laid the basis for his later success during periods of exile in Jamaica and Haiti, receiving assistance from Haitian leader Alexandre Pétion in return for a promise to abolish slavery in areas he liberated.[9] Heavily garrisoned, isolated from liberation movements on the mainland, and fearful of internal slave uprisings, Cuba and Puerto Rico remained under Spanish control for another three-quarters of a century.

Both the United States and Great Britain anticipated economic and political advantages from the breakup of Spain's new world empire.[10] In 1822, under heavy congressional pressure, President Monroe began extending recognition to the new Latin American nations. The British hesitated briefly in this regard, but, in 1823, concerned about reported European efforts to reconquer Spain's American empire and hoping to forestall U.S. designs on Cuba, proposed a joint declaration opposing foreign support of Spanish efforts at reconquest or any transfer of the remaining colonies to a third party. The United States, while opposed to the transfer of Cuba or Puerto Rico to any European nation, had its own interests in the area and was reluctant to endorse the British proposal. Instead, with the guidance of Secretary of State John Quincy Adams, President Monroe, in December 1823, enunciated the famous Monroe Doctrine. Confident that his stance would be supported, however reluctantly, by British seapower, the president proclaimed American opposition to attempts to recognize those areas of the Western Hemisphere that had achieved their independence.[11] While its immediate impact was quite limited, this declaration of "America for the Americans" would be repeatedly cited in future decades as a foundation stone of American hemispheric policy.

Efforts to gain concrete support from this declaration, notably a Mexican move to arouse American opposition to 1825 French naval efforts in the Caribbean, produced little.[12] With the evaporation of any threat of reconquest by the Holy Alliance, the nations of the Caribbean littoral began to view the United States as more of a threat to than a guarantor of their sovereignty.

After the Napoleic Wars, intra-European conflicts over Caribbean possessions virtually ceased. The French, Dutch, and Spanish concentrated their energies on retaining the territories they still controlled. The struggle for dominance over the littoral was left largely to the United States and Great Britain.* France and Spain did retain an interest in the fate of Hispaniola with Spain actually reoccupying the Dominican Republic from 1861 to 1865, but in most other areas Anglo-American rivalry dominated the diplomatic scene.

Two major areas of potential conflict were efforts to abolish the slave trade and rivalry over transisthmian traffic across Central America. Both nations had banned the slave trade, but the British, possessed of dominant naval strength, made more aggressive efforts to enforce the ban. The abolition of slavery in the British West Indies in 1833 intensified and expanded these efforts as the government in London, concerned about

---

*The French effort to install the Archduke Maximillian as emperor of Mexico I consider to fall outside the scope of Caribbean relations.

the ability of West Indian sugar to complete economically with slave production, strove to cut off the slave trade to Cuba and other non-British areas. This led to interference with American shipping, providing a source of conflict in Anglo-American relations for nearly a quarter of a century.[13] U.S. interest in the acquisition of Cuba, spurred on by Southern efforts to acquire additional slave territory, complicated this dispute. This desire manifested itself in President Polk's project for purchasing the island, in U.S.-based filibustering expeditions designed to seize the island, and in the 1854 Ostend Manifesto in which American ambassadors to England, France, and Spain called upon their government to perhaps even force Spain into selling its prime Caribbean possession. Antislavery sentiment within the United States combined with determined British and Spanish opposition to negate these efforts.

Anglo-American rivalry in Central America was potentially even more serious. Representatives of both nations engaged in sharp struggles for influence in the area's five tiny republics. In addition, the British made a series of efforts to extend their control over the isolated Caribbean coast while the United States, especially following the discovery of gold in California, concentrated much of its energies on securing transition routes across the isthmus. A modus vivendi was arrived at in 1850 with the signing of the Clayton-Bulwer Treaty which sought to harmonize the interests of both nations in the area, pledging mutual cooperation in future canal construction and placing vague limits upon the possible expansionist plans of either state.[14] While not fully satisfactory to either party, the treaty endured for several decades, averting the possibility of an open clash in the area. A few years later, both the United States and British naval vessels helped frustrate the efforts of the Southern-backed filibuster of William Walker, to establish an American dominated regime in Nicaragua.

The U.S. vision of manifest destiny, so successfully demonstrated in the War with Mexico, had been halted in the Caribbean by the issue of slavery. That obstacle was removed by the Northern victory in the Civil War, but much of the desire for territorial aggrandizement also died with the South's defeat. Despite efforts by Secretary of State Seward and, later, by President Grant, U.S. expansionism in the Caribbean went into virtual hibernation until the 1890s. Grant actually submitted a treaty to the Senate annexing the Dominican Republic, but the Senate refused to ratify the agreement.

With no serious external challenges to their Caribbean possessions, the British enjoyed a relatively tranquil, but not uneventful, second half of the nineteenth century. During this period, migration patterns, which would have a strong influence on the region's future, were established. East Indians migrated in large numbers to Trinidad and to Guyana while

West Indian Blacks migrated out of their islands to the Netherland Antilles, the Central American mainland, and to Panama.[15]

Despite problems with Guatemala, the British consolidated their hold on Belize but were less successful in efforts to control Nicaragua's Mosquito Coast, conceding Nicaraguan sovereignty over that region following an armed confrontation in 1894.[16] Of greater significance, however, was the British dispute with Venezuela concerning the British boundary.

Unfortunately for the British, this dispute corresponded with a revival of United States interest in the Caribbean. James G. Blaine's creation of the Pan American Union, expanding commercial interests and Alfred Thayer Mahan's navalism combined to again direct American attention southward. President Grover Cleveland saw in the boundary dispute an opportunity to revive the Monroe Doctrine. The British modified their position in the face of Cleveland's pressure, although through arbitration they ultimately obtained most of the disputed territory.[17] The outcome of this confrontation, however, revealed the changing balance of forces within the area.

U.S. DOMINATION OF THE CARIBBEAN: 1898–1945

The addition of moral imperialism to the factors that precipitated the clash with England over the Venezuelan boundary set the stage for the Spanish-American War and the establishment of American hegemony in the Latin Caribbean. Internal uprisings in Cuba, the sinking of the Maine, as well as the other factors leading up to the war are too well known to need documenting here. The conflict itself was anticlimactic. In less than four months, the United States destroyed the Spanish fleet and occupied Cuba, Puerto Rico, Guam, and the Philippines.[18] Senator Henry Teller, believing that the Cubans would soon voluntarily request annexation, attached a rider to the Declaration of War, pledging the establishment of an independent Cuba.[19] As a result, the initial U.S. occupation of that island lasted only until 1901, but Puerto Rico has remained under American sovereignty ever since. While a Cuban government was installed and American troops withdrawn in 1901, it would hardly be accurate to say that Cuba was truly independent. As a price for American withdrawal, Cubans were forced to accept the Platt Amendment, leasing Guantanamo Bay to the U.S. Navy, giving the United States the right of military intervention, and placing crippling restrictions on their right to contract diplomatic or financial arrangements with other nations. The reality of this situation became clear in 1906 when civil strife erupted in Cuba. The American army promptly returned, installed a U.S. administration and governed the island until 1909.[20] Subsequent years saw numerous return visits by U.S. armed forces, although Cuban administrations remained at least nominally in power. In the case of Puerto Rico no pretence of self-rule was made. A military government was installed and the area was rapidly converted into a colonial possession.

Though not perceived as such at the time, an event whose long range impact on U.S.-Caribbean relations would rival that of the Spanish-American War occurred in 1899. This was the establishment of the United Fruit Company. Within a few years, the new company had extended its influence into railroad and steamship lines and communications systems throughout the Caribbean, wielding greater wealth and power than did the governments of many of the nations where it operated. Indeed, the company was often suspected of making and unmaking governments to suit its own interests.

Expanded U.S. political and economic interests in the region led to increased concern over a transisthmian canal. Reflecting British acceptance of dominant U.S. interest was the Hay-Pauncefote Treaty of 1901. With this agreement, England gave up its right to joint control over any future canal, conceding to the United States the right to construct, control, and defend such a waterway in return for a guarantee of the canal's permanent neutrality.[21]

The United States now proceeded rapidly to create a canal, selecting the Panama route over the Nicaraguan site and ratifying a treaty with Colombia providing construction rights. When Colombia balked at the proposed treaty, President Theodore Roosevelt promoted a Panamanian independence movement, expelling Colombia from the isthmus, then virtually forcing upon Panama the Hay-Bunau-Varilla Treaty which created the Canal Zone and stripped the new republic of much of its control over its own internal affairs.[22]

The opening of the canal profoundly influenced the whole area. Panama acquired an expanded West Indian presence as thousands of Jamaicans and other islanders arrived to help build the canal. The islands found themselves suddenly on a major route of world commerce when the canal opened, breaking down some of their previous isolation, but also making their political situation a matter of much greater concern to the United States. This was an important factor in the U.S. purchase of the Virgin Islands from Denmark in 1917.[23]

The construction of the canal, coupled with the outbreak of World War I, produced an American concern with Caribbean security that verged on the irrational. Between 1906 and 1917 American troops intervened in Cuba, Haiti, Honduras, Nicaragua, Mexico, and the Dominican Republic. This display of force was frequently justified by reference to what became known as the Roosevelt Corollary to the Monroe Doctrine.

It originated in response to the 1902 Anglo-German blockade of Venezuela. A threatened confrontation with the United States in this situation was narrowly averted through arbitration, but the incident left Roosevelt determined to gain European acceptance of the Monroe Doctrine while at the same time avoiding future confrontations over issues such as the Venezuelan debt default. Fearing the creation of a similar situation in the Dominican Republic, the president, in 1904, declared that, "in cases of wrongdoing or impotence" by other nations of the Western Hemisphere, the United States would have to exercise "international police power" in order to uphold the Monroe Doctrine.[24] This Roosevelt Corollary was translated into action the following year when the United States assumed control over Dominican customs to insure debt payments to international creditors.

Roosevelt's Caribbean diplomacy was expanded by Taft. His Dollar Diplomacy involved efforts to avoid intervention by promoting U.S., as opposed to European, bank loans to Caribbean nations, obtaining financial controls to insure that debts were paid, and promoting business interests within the area.[25] Taft preferred to avoid open intervention, but, as demonstrated in Nicaragua in 1912, he was willing to use this tactic when he felt it necessary to secure American interests.

The economic imperialism of the Taft administration produced considerable resentment, but the moral imperialism of his successor, Woodrow Wilson, would prove even more unpalatable. Determined to teach Latin Americans to "elect good men," President Wilson occupied Vera Cruz, Mexico, maintained limited military forces in Nicaragua and Cuba as a symbol of opposition to domestic political turmoil, and undertook major interventions in Haiti and the Dominican Republic. Unwilling to establish a colonial service, the United States left the administration of its Caribbean protectorates to the navy and Marine Corps, producing results which hardly corresponded with the professed aim of promoting democratic governments. The 1915 occupation of Haiti left a puppet regime in office, but gave all real power to the marines who controlled the armed forces, administered justice, built roads, and introduced Haitians to North American racism. During this intervention, which lasted until 1934, Haiti even acquired a new constitution, written in large part by Assistant Secretary of the Navy Franklin D. Roosevelt.[26] The Dominican intervention went even further. The national administration was removed and replaced by a succession of navy and marine officers.[27] Perhaps the ultimate expression of U.S. dominance over these two supposedly sovereign states came when the marines used the occupation to impose a boundary settlement on both nations.

The pattern of U.S. domination of the Caribbean established during the pre-World War I years was largely continued during the 1920s. A

Special Service Squadron of overage cruisers was based at Panama to enforce State Department policy and serve as a symbol of U.S. determination to maintain stability and protect economic interests in the area.[28] U.S. investments in the Caribbean continued to grow, as did the dependency of much of the area on the North American market. Marines withdrew from the Dominican Republic in 1924, but the Customs Receivership remained. From 1926 through 1932 another major intervention took place in Nicaragua. Official U.S. attitudes during this period were summed up in 1927 by Under Secretary of State Robert Olds. He wrote that the "area down to and including the Isthmus of Panama constitutes a legitimate sphere of influence for the United States if we are to have due regard for our own safety and protection. . . . There is no room for any outside influence other than ours in this region. We could not tolerate such a thing. . . ."[29]

Opposition to this attitude grew steadily in Latin America. Resentment also focused upon discriminatory trade practices. The Hoover administration made some effort to reduce this hostility, withdrawing the marines from Nicaragua and refusing to undertake new interventions, but the effects of the depression only aggravated economic discontent.

The Good Neighbor Policy is traditionally viewed as a positive change in U.S. policy toward Latin America in general and the Caribbean in particular. The Platt Amendment was abrogated, the United States ended its public defense of the right of intervention, the marines withdrew from Haiti and the obnoxious customs receiverships were ended. A new treaty with Panama modified the most objectionable features of the original canal treaty. Yet, although open interventions had ended, Washington's determinantion to dominate the Caribbean had not, as U.S. pressure to topple the regimes of Ramon Grau San Martín in Cuba and Arnulfo Arias in Panama made clear.[30]

Britain, France, and the Netherlands generally acquiesced in Washington's hegemony in the Caribbean. Their own attention turned inward with a resultant decline in regional power and influence. This was clearest in the case of the Dutch who, in 1929, had to endure the humiliating spectacle of having the governor of Curaçao kidnapped by a group of Venezuelan exiles.[31]

Growing internal discontent, manifested by everything from strikes and riots to Marcus Garvey's United Negro Improvement Association, characterized British rule in the Caribbean. By the 1930s, the effects of the depression, coupled with growing labor militancy and the emergence of domestic political leadership in the islands, forced Great Britain to allow increased internal self-government and to begin considering alternative patterns of political organization.[32] The idea of West Indies Federation found increasing support among groups, ranging from colonial administrators who saw it as a more efficient means of perpetuating the current system to bodies like the Caribbean Labour Congress who hoped it would provide an opening for the achievement of self-government.[33]

These trends were interrupted by the outbreak of World War II. The German conquest of the Netherlands and the defeat of France produced a crisis in the West Indies. In May 1940, British and French forces seized Aruba and Curaçao. Despite American protests, the British remained there until relieved by U.S. forces in February 1942.[34] Concerned about possible Nazi influence, Washington prepared an emergency plan to occupy French, Dutch, and even British new world possessions. Martinique, where French naval units were based, provided a special problem when it adhered to the Vichy regime. An invasion plan was seriously considered by the Roosevelt administration, but was ultimately dropped in favor of diplomatic and economic measures designed to insure the island's neutrality.[35]

This expansion of U.S. influence into the non-Hispanic Caribbean culminated in September 1940 with the Anglo-American Destroyer-Base Agreement. In return for 50 overage destroyers and other supplies, the United States obtained military bases in Trinidad, St. Lucia, Antigua, Jamaica, and other areas.[36] This involvement within the British West Indies would have economic and political repercussions for years to come.

U.S. influence in the Caribbean grew even more rapidly following Pearl Harbor. In 1942 the Anglo-American Caribbean Commission was created to coordinate nonmilitary aspects of Caribbean policy. Continued after the war, with French and Dutch participation, this became a major instrument of the metropolitan powers effort to advance their Caribbean interests.[37] In this, as in most other areas, the United States was, by 1945, clearly the dominant force.

THE MODERN ERA: 1945–1978

The complex changes which have characterized Caribbean international relations in the postwar period are the subject of the bulk of the essays in this volume. While this renders any detailed account of the period somewhat superfluous, it is worthwhile to attempt to delineate the major trends of the last three decades.

The most obvious change in the postwar Caribbean has been the decline of traditional colonialism. The political status of virtually every colonial territory has undergone major changes in recent decades. Jamaica, Trinidad and Tobago, Guyana, Barbados, and Surinam have all gained independence and Dominica, Belize, and the Netherland Antilles may soon join them. Puerto Rico's Commonwealth status represents some change, but the debate over its long range future is hardly resolved. Other British islands have received varying degrees of self-rule, while the French have tried to incorporate their territories into the metropolitan system of government. One of the final bastions of traditional colonialism, the Panama Canal Zone, is to be totally returned to Panama by the end of the century.

The wide variety of solutions that the metropolitan powers have adopted to end direct colonial rule reveals the complexity of the problem and the disadvantages of virtually every alternative solution. The multiplicity of newly independent states reflects, among other things, the divisive nature of the colonial heritage. This heritage helps explain the failure of the British sponsored West Indies Federation in the early 1960s.[38] The search for greater political unity continued, however, manifested in efforts like the Caribbean Free Trade Association and the Caribbean Community (CARICOM).

Efforts at economic development have been hampered not only by regional divisions, but also by the rapidly growing economic dominance of the United States and of multinational corporations. While some corporations, such as Reynolds Aluminum in Jamaica and Creole Petroleum in Venezuela, have recently been nationalized, others, like Gulf and Western in the Dominican Republic, continue to exercise inordinate economic and political influence. Even where nationalization has occurred, heavy dependence upon metropolitan markets, marketing facilities, and transport arrangements still remains. The bitter struggles involving allocation of the U.S. sugar quota provide effective examples of the power of this external economic influence.

The U.S. fear of communism, especially in an area as proximate as the Caribbean, has also played a major role in shaping international developments. Efforts to counter suspected Communist influence have involved a wide variety of tactics, including USIA activities, the distribution of development assistance, the use of economic pressure, and sub rosa support of favored political figures. When Washington policy makers have felt a threat sufficiently serious, they have used more direct and, at times, violent means. Cases in point would include the 1954 CIA sponsored overthrow of the Arbenz administration in Guatemala, the abortive 1961 Bay of Pigs invasion of Cuba, the more successful 1963 support of labor opposition to Chedi Jagan in Guyana, and the massive 1965 military intervention in the Dominican Republic.[39] Though strongly denied by the State Department, recent rumors of efforts to "destabilize" the Jamaican government may also fall into this category.

Despite the massive economic, political, and military influence of the United States, the influence of new forces and the ability of Caribbean nations to operate apart from and, at times, contrary to the interest of the metropolitan powers has increased in recent decades.* The major case in point, obviously, is Cuba. The impact of Castro's revolution, his ability to survive U.S. opposition, and his impressive domestic accomplishments have combined to produce growing influence in the Caribbean. Cuba has also provided the USSR with a greatly expanded presence in the area, but direct Soviet influence is less than that which can be indirectly exerted through Cuba.†

The increase in oil prices has made Venezuela, for the first time, a significant factor in Caribbean politics. To a lesser degree, Trinidad has also benefited from this increase and sought to translate its economic base into broader regional influence. While the role played by other newly independent states, such as Jamaica, Barbados, and Guyana, outside their own borders has been somewhat less, it has nevertheless contributed to the region's growing multipolarity, a development which complicates efforts at metropolitan domination.

Along with the host of new and emerging actors on the Caribbean scene have come new issues. These include those related to tourism, to the law of the seas, to the influence and potential cultural imperialism exercised by foreign-controlled mass media and to the search for a new economic order, superseding the metropole-dominated GATT and IMF system of international trade and finance. Conflicts over control of multinational corporations and efforts to establish producer nation controls over the prices paid for basic raw material exports also are important new issues.

CONCLUSION

The contemporary context of Caribbean international relations is determined, in many ways, by the region's historical heritage. Economic dependence, metropole domination, plus the internal constraints imposed by such factors as the heritage of slavery, monoculture, and colonial rule have obvious historical roots. The decline in European influence and the expanding role of the United States can also best be understood by examining its historic content. The extent to which the Carter adminis-

---

*The ability of Francois Duvalier of Haiti to withstand repeated Kennedy administration efforts to depose and then force the United States to renew foreign aid in order to obtain his vote for the expulsion of Cuba from the OAS is an example of this increased ability to function contrary to metropolitan interests.

†Since the Cuban missile crisis, the USSR has also been reluctant to risk direct confrontations with U.S. interests in the Caribbean.

tration will be bound by past precedents and the extent to which it will be able to pioneer new directions in U.S.-Caribbean policy is still an open question. In June 1977, then Assistant Secretary for Inter-American Affairs, Terence Todman, characterized our relations with the Caribbean as a "too often neglected subject," and added that "we need to devote more attention and more resources to the area—and we need to begin now."* Subsequent events, such as the visit by United Nations Ambassador Andrew Young to the region, seemed to give some credence to this statement. Perhaps the most hopeful sign has been the pressure exerted on the Balaquer regime to accept the victory of Antonio Guzman in the 1978 elections.

The United States, alone, however, is in no position to dictate the future of the Carribean. Historic trends towards greater multipolarity, increased complexity of issues and relations, growing economic and social frustrations, and increased nationalism with a constant potential for conflict will undoubtedly continue. The historic heritage will limit and shape, but not ultimately determine the future of Caribbean international developments. Perhaps the best lesson we can draw from the past is that, in coming decades, rapid and unpredictable change is the greatest certainty.

NOTES

1. For a discussion of this debate see Lewis Hanke, *The Spanish Struggle for Justice in the Conquest of America* (Philadelphia: University of Pennsylvania, 1949).

2. J. M. Parry and P. M. Sherlock, *A Short History of the West Indies* (New York: St. Martin's Press, 1968), pp. 32–33.

3. John Edwin Fagg, *Latin America: A General History,* 3rd ed. rev. (New York: Macmillan Co., 1977), p. 202.

4. Parry and Sherlock, op. cit., p. 43.

5. Cyril Hamshere, *The British in the Caribbean* (Cambridge, Mass.: Harvard University Press, 1972), pp. 27–31.

6. Ibid., p. 187.

7. Rayford W. Logan, *Haiti and the Dominican Republic* (New York: Oxford University Press, 1968), pp. 91–93.

8. Ibid., pp. 31–33.

9. For the best account of Bolivar's activities in the Caribbean see Gerhard Masur, *Simon Bolivar* (Albuquerque: University of New Mexico Press, (1948).

10. For accounts of the roles played by both nations in the independence movement see W. W. Kaufman, *British Policy and the Independence of Latin America* (New Haven: Yale University Press, 1951), and Arthur P. Whitaker, *The United States and the Independence of Latin America, 1800–1830* (Baltimore: Johns Hopkins Press, 1941).

---

*Statement by Assistant Secretary of State for Inter-American Affairs Terence A. Todman before the Subcommittee on Inter-American Affairs of the House of Representatives International Relations Committee, June 28, 1977.

11. Dexter Perkins, *A History of the Monroe Doctrine*, rev. ed. (Boston: Little, Brown & Co. 1955), pp. 28–64.

12. Dexter Perkins, *The Monroe Doctrine, 1823–1826* (Cambridge, Mass: Harvard University Press, 1927), pp. 200–03.

13. For a detailed discussion of this issue see Richard K. MacMaster, "The United States, Great Britain and the Suppression of the Cuban Slave Trade," (Ph.D. diss., Georgetown University, 1968).

14. Mary W. Williams, *Anglo-American Isthmian Diplomacy, 1815–1915* (Washington, D.C.: American Historical Association, 1916), pp. 67–109.

15. Parry and Sherlock, op. cit., pp. 237, 244.

16. Robert A. Humphreys, *The Diplomatic History of British Honduras, 1638–1901* (New York: Oxford University Press, 1961), pp. 151–66. For the Nicaraguan side of the Mosquito Coast issue see "Notable serie de documentos ineditos sobre las reincoporacion de la Mosquita," *Revista de la Academia de Geografía y Historia de Nicaragua* 12 (January–December 1953): 41–192.

17. Ernest R. May, *Imperial Democracy: The Emergence of America as a World Power* (New York: Harcourt, Brace and World, 1961), pp. 31–66.

18. For a history of this conflict see Frank Friedel, *The Splendid Little War* (Boston: Little Brown & Co., 1958).

19. Frederick Merk, *Manifest Destiny and Mission in American History* (New York: Alfred A. Knopf, 1963), pp. 257–58.

20. Dana G. Munro, *The United States and the Caribbean Area* (Boston: World Peace Foundation, 1934), pp. 1–34. For a detailed history of the second U.S. occupation of Cuba see Allan R. Millett, *The Politics of Intervention* (Columbus, Ohio: Ohio State University Press, 1968).

21. Williams, op. cit., pp. 300–10.

22. An excellent account of the United States' acquisition and construction of the Panama Canal is David McCullough's, *The Path Between the Seas* (New York: Simon and Schuster, 1977).

23. Wilfrid Hardy Callcott, *The Caribbean Policy of the United States, 1890–1920* (Baltimore: Johns Hopkins Press, 1942), pp. 426–29.

24. Dana G. Munro, *Intervention and Dollar Diplomacy in the Caribbean, 1900–1921* (Princeton: Princeton University Press, 1964), pp. 66–77. Edwin Lieuwen, *U.S. Policy in Latin America* (New York: Praeger Publishers, 1965), p. 42.

25. Callcott, op. cit., pp. 259–60.

26. For a detailed account of this intervention see Hans Schmidt, *The United States Occupation of Haiti, 1915–1934* (New Brunswick, N.J.: Rutgers University Press, 1971).

27. Richard Millett and G. Dale Gaddy, "Administering the Protectorates: The United States Occupation of Haiti and the Dominican Republic," *Revista/Review Interamericana* 6 (Fall, 1976), 392–99.

28. Richard Millett, "The State Department's Navy: A History of the Special Service Squadron, 1920–1940," *American Neptune* 35 (April 1975), 118–38.

29. Memorandum by Under Secretary of State Robert Olds, January 2, 1927, Record Group 59, "Records of the Department of State," Decimal File 817.00/4350, National Archives, Washington, D.C.

30. An excellent account of this period is Bryce Wood, *The Making of the Good Neighbor Policy* (New York: Columbia University Press, 1961).

31. F. A. Baptista, "The Seizure of the Dutch Authorities in Willemstad, Curacao by Venezuelan Political Exiles in June, 1929, Viewed in Relation to the Anglo-French Landings in Aruba and Curacao in May, 1940," *Caribbean Studies* 13 (April 1973), 37–41.

32. D. A. G. Waddell, *The West Indies and the Guianas* (Englewood Cliffs, N.J.: Prentice Hall, 1967), pp. 109–12.

33. Gordon Lewis, *The Growth of the Modern West Indies* (New York: Monthly Review Press, 1968), pp. 344–45.

34. Baptista, op. cit., p. 108. Stetson Conn and Byron Fairchild, *The Framework of Hemisphere Defense* (Washington, D.C.: Office of the Chief of Military History, 1960), p. 47.

35. Conn and Fairchild, op. cit., pp. 49–51, 85–87, 162–63.

36. Ibid., pp. 51–62. Much of the correspondence leading up to this agreement is published in *American State Papers.* Executive Department, *Papers Relating to the Foreign Relations of the United States, 1940* (Washington, D.C.: U.S. Government Printing Office, 1958), 3:49–77.

37. Lewis, op. cit., p. 350. William Sanders, "The Conference System in the Caribbean," in *The Caribbean: Current United States Relations,* ed. A. Curtis Wilgus (Gainesville: University of Florida Press, 1966), p. 203.

38. For details on this effort see Lewis, op. cit., pp. 343–86.

39. For a fuller discussion of many of these issues see F. Parkinson, *Latin America, the Cold War and the World Powers, 1945–1973* (Beverly Hills, Calif.: Sage Publications, 1974). Colin V. F. Henfrey, "Foreign Influence in Guyana: the Struggle for Independence," in *Patterns of Foreign Influence in the Caribbean,* ed. Emanuel de Kadt (New York: Oxford University Press, 1972), pp. 69–71, discusses the issue of CIA involvement in Guyana. British acquiescence in such an operation within one of their own colonies provides striking evidence of the extent to which they had conceded American hegemony in the Caribbean.

2

Caribbean International Politics:
External and Domestic Constraints

W. Marvin Will

International relations, broadly defined, represents the totality of interactions across national frontiers. For students and practitioners, however, it is more useful to concentrate on international goal setting and on interactions among sovereign governments in pursuit of mutual or exclusive goals. Such goal setting and goal seeking is shaped and constrained by the international system and regional subsystems in which national actors are environmentally linked and, as observers increasingly acknowledge, by national domestic environments as well. The impact of the external system is awesome for the majority of the world's nations which form the so-called developing or lesser-developed countries (LDCs) and especially for the relatively small, weak states of the Caribbean and circum-Caribbean region.[1]

THE EXTERNAL SYSTEM AND CARIBBEAN POLITICS

The prevailing international system, or more precisely the type of systemic equilibrium, is, according to Morton Kaplan, a major determinant of external impact. He identifies six systemic equilibrium configurations: (1) a universal "one world" system theoretically lacking the near-anarchical tendencies prevalent among sovereign actors that typify world politics; (2) a hierarchical system with an ordered gradation of state power; (3) a veto model emphasizing unbridled and unaligned competition among actors; (4) the balance-of-power system, a competitive multipolar check-and-balance configuration most closely identified with Euro-centered statecraft existent from the emergence of the modern state system in the mid-seventeenth century until World War I; (5) a tight or constricted bipolar system associated with the most intense phases of the cold war; and (6) looser or diffuse forms of bipolarity that accompanied decreased East-West tension. Only the latter three configurations have international historic precedents, according to Kaplan.[2] Each of the three has had a direct impact on the Caribbean region.

The Metropole: Power Balancing and Caribbean Colonization and Settlement

The multipolar balance-of-power configuration is generally perceived as the dominant international system in terms of impact and systemic persistence. Any attempt by a nation to expand its international influence or coercive ability "leads by necessity to this configuration . . . and to policies that aim at preserving it," asserts Hans Morgenthau. Individual or concerted attempts utilizing warfare, colonization, and other policies are made to check systemic offenders and to restore relative equiligrium.[3] Theoreticians argue whether such power balancing occurs as an automatic response process, as Morgenthau seems to suggest; as a purposeful arrangement, as British Foreign Secretary George Canning implied when he declared, "I resolved that if France had Spain, it should not be Spain 'with the Indies.' I called the New World into existence, to redress the balance of the Old";[4] or as a self-serving argument from hindsight, as Inis Claude concludes.[5] Most agree, however, that a multipolar systemic configuration called the balance of power prevailed in the seventeenth, eighteenth, and nineteenth centuries.

This was a period in which England, France, and the Netherlands vied with Spain and with each other to maximize their security, economic, and prestige goals in the previously Spanish-dominated Caribbean. This inter-power competition led to colonization of "unclaimed" islands such as St. Christopher (St. Kitts) and Barbados; protectorate status was accorded to the Mosquito Indians of the Central American coast; and lands were traded (a portion of present-day Guyana for Manhattan), nearly traded (Martinique and Guadeloupe for Canada), or purchased (the U.S. Virgin Islands). More frequently international power balances were adjusted via conquest (Jamaica, Haiti, Trinidad, Puerto Rico) from the Spanish Crown by major power "intruders" and by cession of lands as a result of numerous European wars which "caused critical disturbances in the Caribbean."[6]

Such external multipolar pressures had significant repercussions on domestic environments. St. Lucia, for example, alternated between French and English control at least twelve times and the aftereffect is a French-English-Creole cultural blend, as contrasted to the "Englishness" of neighboring "Bimshire" Barbados or the Spanish acculturation of the littoral.

An even greater impact on the externally-induced acculturation process was the introduction of slavery and indentured servitude to the area. This produced major influxes of such groups as exiled or indentured Englishmen, whose "red leg" descendants still reside in the Grenadines and Barbados; African slaves, whose numbers soared to massive preponderance in the seventeenth century following ascendancy of plantation agriculture and "King Sugar"; and indentured Asians, whom the Dutch and English brought from Java and the Indian subcontinent in the late nineteenth century to replace emancipated slaves.

These groups were exploited objects of the colonial plantation system but none were more deculturized, argues Rex Nettleford, cultural advisor to the Jamaican government, than the Afro-Caribbean.

> The Africans, of all the groups which came to the New World, came as individuals and not as part of a group which maintained identity through some great religion, or . . . through age-old recognizable customs.[7]

Unlike his European, Chinese, and Indian compatriots, the Afro-Caribbean does not psychologically possess a strong racial memory of great cultural achievement, Nettleford continues; even when the African presence in the Caribbean assumes a position of strength out of the sheer fact of numbers, "one finds that [the African] is really operating as a member of a cultural minority."[8]

Currently, blacks and racially-mixed West Indians dominate Caribbean populations, constituting over 90 percent in most islands and many mainland coastal areas, although East Indians possess majorities in Guyana and Suriname and a projected majority in Trinidad.

Colonial rule contributed to Caribbean disintegration, including

> political, linguistic, monetary and trade barriers. Cut off, with-drawing into themselves, the islands' "insularity" and . . . stagnation results. Even when attached to the same governing "mother country", their reciprocal contacts are very limited: they are poorly acquainted with each other.[9]

Additional unfavorable legacies attributable to external intrusions of the colonial era include patterns of socio-economic-political stratification, geographic parochialization, and societal and economic dependency.[10] Then, as now, the Caribbean was a metropolitan-dominated and penetrated subsystem, never a truly independent international actor on the world scene.

Polarized Cold War Politics: Constricted Bipolarity

The two remaining international configurations for which there are precedents reflect degrees of polarization since World War II. The impact of these constricted and diffuse bloc systems on the Caribbean was especially significant due to the region's proximity to its superpower neighbor and because historically the area has been in the U.S. economic and security interest sphere—in an American lake as it were.

Implementation of big stick and dollar diplomacy resulted in U.S. military involvement in the Caribbean area for thirty-six consecutive years following the Spanish-American War. This was rationalized officially as "the obligation of the [U.S.] Government under the spirit of the Monroe Doctrine."[11] U.S. policy became less interventionist during the Hoover and Roosevelt administrations, affording an opportunity for a cooperative front in World War II, but interventionist tendencies were revivified as a bulwark against perceived Communist expansion following the war.[12]

Cold war polarization had now entered the systemic spectrum and interventionist tendencies heightened in both the Eastern and Western blocs. In the United States it produced such policy rigidities as Secretary of State John Foster Dulles' view that if nations are not with us (not in the Western bloc) they are against us. The Soviets consistently expressed and exercised the right of forceful intervention during this period, most bluntly in the so-called Brezhnev Doctrine against Czechoslovakia. Melvin Gurtov argues that during the cold war era similar goals or "rules of the game" were established for the Caribbean area by the United States. The first is

> that access . . . by U.S. diplomats, public and private enterprise, and a range of other "contacts" . . . must be preserved to the broadest extent possible. A second is the obverse. . . . , access to the region by hostile influences should be limited or denied if they threaten (or appear to threaten) American security, political and economic paramountcy. . . . A third rule [is] that the independence of . . . governments is qualified to the extent they are unable to maintain political stability, promote public order against subversive forces, and protect [North] American lives and property. . . . Within this sphere of influence, like the U.S.S.R. in Eastern Europe, the United States claims the powers of chief arbiter and upholder of law and order.[13]

In 1954, U.S. sponsorship of the overthrow of Guatemala's Arbenz government provided the first major Caribbean area test of revised U.S. doctrine. It led former Guatemalan President Arévalo to term the policy an "international license to the United States to do . . . everything [it] pleases."[14]

Retarding Communist intrusion became an overriding U.S. goal. "The master plan of international communism," Dulles informed a Congressional committee, "is to gain a solid base in this hemisphere, a base that can be used to extend Communist penetration to the other peoples of the . . . America[s]."[15] Cuba and Cuban communism became the seminal issue for U.S. policy in the Caribbean. To combat real or imagined Communist threats, the United States initiated the Bay of Pigs military operation in Cuba in 1961, intervened to abort potential revolutionary development in the Dominican Republic in 1965, and intruded into Guyanese labor and independence politics during the mid-1960s.

There are many examples of more subtle expressions of external pressure on Caribbean states in the 1950s and 1960s. One incident, related by former Barbadian Prime Minister Errol Barrow, was the U.S. demand that Barbados abstain from inviting Cuba to its 1966 independence celebration under threat that the United States would apply pressure to dissuade other guests from attending. The island's leading newspaper termed submission to such a great power demand a major blot on Barbados' national honor.[16]

In addition, foreign aid programs of the era strongly reflected polarized politics, with principal U.S. support to the region extended to regimes supportive of its rules of the game. Major per capita aid recipients included Panama, the Dominican Republic, and Nicaragua.[17]

The Politics of Detente: Diffuse Bipolarity

Initiation of the constricted (tight) bipolar systemic configuration is relatively easy to document. It is more difficult, however, to pinpoint a precise beginning of the diffuse (loose) bloc international system which has been evidenced since the mid-1960s in numerous forms of inter-bloc dialogue and withdrawals from the "brink." President Nixon's journeys to China and the Soviet Union, plus initiation of the Strategic Arms Limitation Talks (SALT), are indicators of the system's more open approach to international interaction. East-West tensions do remain a persistent reality, with periodic junctures of confrontation and rhetorical stridency (as exemplified in the mid-1978 U.S.-Soviet imbroglio), yet it cannot be denied that diminished levels of inter-bloc confrontation and expanded degrees of intrabloc divergency did develop in the 1968–78 decade.[18] Such relaxations are reflected among both the Commonwealth and Hispanic nations in the Caribbean by the relative ease with which ideological shifts are now possible.

Nuclear parity, or the balance in Mutual Assured Destruction (MAD) capability, between East and West represents a major reinforcing element in development of the diffuse bipolar system. Former U.S. Ambassador Paul Kattenburg feels that MAD and its mutual destruction capacity has at least partially negated coercive or expansionistic tendencies of the opposing superpowers.[19] This, in turn, has contributed to elevated levels of intrabloc flexibility advantageous to Caribbean development.

This era has also produced shifts in metropole policy and goal-seeking actions toward the Caribbean states. However abhorrent the 1965 U.S. military action in support of conservative forces in the Dominican Republic may have been, it did demonstrate greater concern with the image of legality and openness than earlier CIA forays into Central American, Cuban, and Guyanese politics. In stark contrast to the 1965 action, the Carter administration in 1978 threatened withdrawal of aid and extended verbal support of fair ballot-counting procedures to the Dominican Revolutionary Party (PRD) in its election victory, thus, apparently indicating "support [of] the democratic process over . . . the forces of reaction."[20] The PRD leadership has termed President Carter's demand that Joaquin Balaguer and the military abide by open election rules "a new era in United States-Caribbean relations."[21]

Additional policy changes by the U.S. president and his Caribbean-conscious UN Ambassador Andrew Young appear to be both substantive and rhetorical, as noted elsewhere in this volume. While these actions may not be harbingers of the future, they appear to be a decided departure from the interventionist politics of the Johnson administration and the benign neglect and alleged destabilising policies implemented during the Nixon presidency.[22]

Other External Influences

Other aspects of the external system which impact on international goal-making and goal-seeking actions by the developing nations of the Caribbean include the proliferation of international actors—nation states, international organizations, and multinational corporations—and the acceleration of modernization influences.

New International Actors

The rapid expansion of nations since World War II, world-wide and regional, has created a major international environmental shift. There are presently approximately 160 sovereign states, the majority of which secured independence since World War II. Membership in the UN has experienced a nearly threefold increase since its organization in 1945, including a comparable percentage increase in new Caribbean states. More than half of the UN membership belongs to the bloc of non-aligned nations. The influx of former colonies has transformed the UN and has led to a proliferation of inter-governmental organizations (IGOs), especially regional and UN specialized agencies and organizations relating to Third World interests. As a result, the UN and other IGOs are no longer small, culturally-congruent European clubs. This change is positive, from a Caribbean perspective, since the increased participation of Third World and nonaligned nations ensures consideration of topics relevant to Third World and Caribbean interests. A recent evaluation in the West Indies has concluded that membership in inter-governmental international organizations is of enormous value to a new, small state, providing valuable technological and data services. Further, micro-states "in their search for economic assistance . . . tend to look to the multilateral agencies and the United Nations as a counterweight to dependency on bilateral arrangements."[23]

Conversely, the substantial accretion in nation states and the relatively weak status of these new majorities has contributed to global irresolution and, at times, to a diminution of support for international organizations and of international law itself. Failure to conclude treaties establishing a new economic order or a revamped law of the sea, both vital to Antillean interests, are notable cases in point.

The growth and spread of yet another new international actor, the multinational corporation (MNC), usually based in North America or Europe, presents a special problem for small, vulnerable states. Such transnational organizations are attracted to the Caribbean by availability of less costly labor, lucrative tax incentives, and the desire to penetrate regional or European markets or both.

Although MNCs may provide a necessary source of capital, the host country lacks adequate control over their operations and frequently fails to realize anticipated tax and employment benefits. It is not uncommon for MNCs in the Caribbean to shift profits to low-tax countries, to utilize the local economy for metropole profits, or to terminate operations upon expiration of their tax holiday, as has occurred in Jamaica and other Caribbean territories. The impact of these organizations on weak and relatively unintegrated states is momentous.[24] A more detailed critique of MNCs and other aspects of the international economic system will be explored in subsequent chapters.

Modernization Influences

The process of modernization, in the context of Caribbean politics, represents the penetration of developing states by the technological, communication, and value systems of "modern" or more developed countries (MDCs), and by individuals and organizations (including MNCs) based in such countries. Tourism is a major value peddler in this transferral process, together with the print and electronic media, and advertising pressures of the metropole.

Frequently such external influences are actively sought by the LDCs despite incongruity with local needs and values. A West Indian may view a range of metropole-produced films or TV episodes depicting crime, sex, and luxury, be everywhere bombarded by the consumerism, snob appeal, and style obsolescence solicitations of the Madison Avenue advertising approach. Such influences are prime contributors to the politics of discontent—a rising sense of relative deprivation—which frequently outstrips personal and governmental capacities to adapt.

Despite an ability for personal dollar elasticity that defies belief, West Indians are more and more experiencing the bitter frustration of "champagne tastes with mauby pocketbooks."[25] This quiet international systemic intrusion may well be the most insidious snare confronting Caribbean culture and development.

CARIBBEAN INTERNATIONAL POLITICS: DOMESTIC CONSTRAINTS

Although the enormity of external pressures on Caribbean politics is massive, the greatest immediate impact on the system is presented by internal demands and pressures. These include a constant need for decision-making political elites to adapt to demands and pursue support-generating policies if they and their regime are to survive. In the Caribbean, where alternatives for officeholders are extremely limited, survival assumes paramount importance, frequently forcing the decision-making elite to focus on short-run issues and internal domestic goals.[26]

Internal Determinants of International Politics

Human, material, and organizational resources are required to effectuate decision making and goal seeking in international politics. In the political lexicon these are customarily grouped as size, both territorial and demographic; natural resources, including mineral and agricultural; economic performance; and the political system.

Territorial and Demographic Size

Size, territorial and demographic, seems to represent the major factor or variable contributing to policy capability or potential national power capacity. The variety and quantity of raw material resources tend to be limited by the geographic confines of a nation, while small populations unduly restrict governmental performance and military defense capacity and tend to preclude markets of scale. Population pressures imposed by limited territorial space also curtail employment opportunities for potential entrepreneurs and cultural leaders, forcing their migration to metropole societies.

These problems are directly applicable to a large portion of the Caribbean and circum Caribbean where the five Central American states combined only approximate the U.S. state of California in geographic size and population. The largest Caribbean island, Cuba, is similar to the U.S. state of Pennsylvania in geographic size and its population of only 9.1 million is approximately twice that of the total Commonwealth Caribbean, or Haiti, or the Dominican Republic. Grenada, presently the most minuscule independent Caribbean state, has a population only slightly over 100,000. Even smaller states are on the verge of independence, leading the Commonwealth Secretary General S. S. Ramphal to speculate that by century's end the Caribbean could possess the world's highest per capita density of national governments.[27]

As Leopold Kohn, Courtney Blackman, and E. F. Schumacher point out, however, some positive benefits do accrue as a result of small geographic and demographic size.[28] A national plebiscite such as that conducted in Panama on the 1978 canal treaty issue is greatly facilitated by small population. And there is no doubt that geographic and demographic limitations in Barbados contribute positively to its elevated level of national integration and its superior communication facilities.

Natural Resources

Suriname and Guyana have major bauxite deposits while oil is a primary resource in Venezuela and Colombia. Among the Caribbean islands only Trinidad, Cuba, and Jamaica have substantial known mineral deposits—oil, nickel, and bauxite, respectively. Agriculture, though still vital to the region's economy, is in a serious state of decline due frequently to inappropriate government policies, negative cultural values, and more profitable employment in other sectors. In most of the Caribbean territories, therefore, primary natural resources are their people and their sea, sand, and sun. This combination has fostered a massive tourist industry which supplies much revenue and employment to the region, especially the Bahamas and the eastern Caribbean islands; however, it also represents an unstable and culturally disruptive force.

The educational level of the Caribbean peoples constitutes another important resource. Although educational levels vary enormously (from an illiteracy rate of more than 80 percent in Haiti to 96 percent literacy in Trinidad and Barbados), the peoples of the region reflect a high level of educational attainment as compared to other Third World areas. This is a positive factor in area development, but large numbers of relatively well-educated peoples frustrated by low levels of governmental policy response may also be destabilizing and stress-producing elements in these resource- and capability-restricted countries. Educational achievement frequently heightens individual expectations toward unattainable goals in local environs and, conversely, induces frustration when systemic failures reduce standards of living or eliminate jobs. When these factors occur simultaneously, a severe stress circumstance is created for governmental decision makers.[29]

Economic Performance

Such rising expectation and declining status factors appear to be present in several Caribbean countries. Jamaica, for example, is beset with the totality of problems associated with rising expectations, yet by virtue of its May 1978 agreement with the International Monetary Fund (IMF) its standard of living is expected to decrease significantly, fueled by a 30 to 40 percent inflationary spiral and a 30 percent unemployment rate. The post-1973 fourfold increase in energy costs plus a subsequent sharp decline in sugar prices and tourism revenues, combined with capital flight resulting from Prime Minister Michael Manley's expanded governmental programs, have so affected the island's economy that Jamaica now rests firmly in a debt trap with 75 percent of its foreign earnings expended for oil purchases and debt servicing.[30]

U.S. Assistant Secretary for Inter-American Affairs Terence A. Todman recently noted that unemployment averages 25 percent throughout the Caribbean, with rates reaching the 50 percent level in some of the smaller islands. Even higher unemployment and underemployment levels exist in many urban areas and among youth. Youth unemployment is an especially serious concern in the Caribbean since youth now represents a majority of the population—40 percent are age fifteen or younger.[31]

This places tremendous pressure on governments to provide services such as employment stimulation programs and educational and social service amenities. Such services represent a very basic aspect of economic development, therefore an added stress is placed on foreign policy goal-setting and goal-seeking processes.

Constraints from the National Political System

The national political system itself poses a major domestic constraint on the pursuit of Caribbean foreign policy. Such a system is composed of many facets of which competitive party systems are a primary component. The Caribbean area has more relatively open, competitive party systems than any other Third World region. Such parties impose major foreign policy constraints by serving as conduits for policy criticism and opposition and by keeping domestic goals, such as employment and other economic development issues, paramount. These systems also have the capability to compel change by effecting removal of incumbent regimes through the electoral process. Such opposition party victories occurred in the mid-to-late 1970s, in countries from Venezuela and Colombia to Puerto Rico and the Dominican Republic and from Surinam and Barbados to Jamaica and Costa Rica.

There are two additional phenomena which give impetus to closer linkage between policy maker and domestic issues: the development and growth of "pressure" or interest group movements; and the continued influence of personality politics emphasizing familial and geographic parochial politics. Both phenomena occur throughout the region, with the former more prevalent in the Commonwealth countries.

FOREIGN POLICY GOALS AND CONTEMPORARY POLICY

In addition to the seldom-avowed goal of political self-survival, there are at least four additional foreign policy goals, Donald Puchala generalizes, to which most governments attach at least a general level of support: national preservation, security, prestige, peace, and prosperity.[32] Although there is much overlap and ambiguity, most national foreign policies emphasize one or more of these interests with large, wealthy nations frequently stressing multiple goals.

In the Caribbean region, only Cuba and some states of the littoral commit major resources to security-related goals. During 1973, all Caribbean and circum-Caribbean states, with the exception of Venezuela and Cuba, recorded military expenditures less than 2 percent of Gross National Product (GNP); the Commonwealth island states and five additional area states were under 1 percent. During this period, the superpowers and Middle East confrontation states were spending approximately 10 percent of GNP on security and foreign policy.

There are major inducements in the Caribbean to emphasize the economic prosperity goal with its related employment or fiscal concerns. Poor, weak states usually cannot afford expansive security-oriented outlays, especially in the face of strong elite and mass demands for domestic policy outputs.[33] As a seasoned Caribbean foreign service officer explains:

Domestic constituency pressures impose on decision makers the necessity to give priority to the demands of the domestic environment. No
leader who consistently turns away from such demands could seriously
hope to have a long or peaceful tenure of office. The domestic environment, then, absorbs a high proportion of the state's total capabilities.
The extent to which the state can participate in external affairs is determined essentially by the size of its surplus capabilities. In very small
states, surplus capabilities are minimal. . . . The foreign policy issues
which stimulate the greatest amount of microstate concern are economic ones.[34] Stated another way, Guyana's UN Ambassador has defined that country's "foreign policy [as] an external component of a
national policy rooted firmly in domestic determinants." (*Christian
Science Monitor,* 11 April 1977.)

Diplomats from six Caribbean nations with whom this writer conferred
in early 1978 were in near accord with this basic assessment.

There are specific foreign policy goals in addition to those projected
by Puchala, to be sure, as Wendell Bell and others have generalized from
their studies of Caribbean elites. These include decolonization, antiracism, and increased Third World, especially African, linkages. Small
stress-impacted states, however, must limit their scarce human and fiscal
resources to carefully selected issues and forums. Such choices usually
relate to basic developmental needs. As Guyanese Chief of State Christopher Nascimento has noted, the Caribbean area is not unique in its
foreign policy approach; its goal seeking, too, is shaped by perceptions
of national self-interest.[35] Guyana's leadership in the nonaligned group
illustrates this; as does Jamaica's flirtation with the Soviet-dominated
Council for Mutual Economic Assistance (COMECON); Cuba's present
alignment within the Soviet sphere; Bahamian perception of their archipelago as an appendage of the U.S. mainland; or Grenada's "basic
survival" attempts which include flirtations with General Pinochet or any
other potential aid distributor.

As a result, Barbados' UN Ambassador Donald Blackman points out,
there presently is no unified Caribbean foreign policy—not even among
members of the Caribbean Community (CARICOM).[36] Although facing
essentially similar development problems and policy constraints, each
state attempts to shape its own development process and policy options.
A probable negative result is that each state now seems induced to
weaken regional integrative linkages in an attempt to seek its individual
"enlightened" interests;[37] a positive factor, however, is that most Caribbean states now seem sufficiently free from great power encumbrances
to pursue relatively diverse policy options.

In Derek Walcott's play, "T-Jean and His Brothers," the hero and
West Indian prototype, T-Jean, does just this. He borrows from each

system, takes from one, then the other; finesses his way among the powers; adapts, blends; but always he maintains a precarious balance, while simultaneously developing his Caribbean essence. He survives while both his hard-boiled and his compliant brothers are consumed by the system. In many ways, this is the status of Caribbean international politics at the close of the 1970s.

NOTES

1. See David J. Finlay and Thomas Hovet, Jr., *7304: International Relations on the Planet Earth* (New York: Harper and Row, 1975), pp. 15ff; Donald James Puchala, *International Politics Today* (New York: Dodd, Mead & Co., 1971), pp. 1–17; James N. Rosenau, ed., *Linkage Politics* (New York: The Free Press, 1969), pp. 49, 90–91, 330–40.

2. Morton Kaplan, *System and Process in International Politics* (New York: John Wiley and Sons, 1957), pp. 21, 60–74. The order of arrangement is changed and the descriptions have been added.

3. Hans Morgenthau, *Politics Among Nations: The Struggle for Power and Peace* (N.Y.: Alfred A. Knopf, 1961), pp. 167, 187–215.

4. Ibid., p. 191.

5. Inis Claude, Jr., *Power and International Relations* (New York: Random House, 1962). On this point, Morgenthau, op. cit., pp. 213–14, writes, "A nation seeking empire has often claimed that all it wanted was equilibrium."

6. A. Curtis Wilgus, "Editor's Foreward," in Albert Gastmann, *Dictionary of the French and Netherlands Antilles,* (Metuchen, N.J.: The Scarecrow Press, Inc., 1978), p. v; Eric Williams, *Documents of West Indian History: 1492–1655* (Trinidad: PNM Publishing Co., 1963), pp. 203–266. also see William Langer, *An Encyclopedia of World History* (Boston: Houghton Mifflin, 1948); Alan Burns, *History of the British West Indies* (London: George Allen and Unwin, 1965).

7. Rex M. Nettleford, *Identity, Race and Protest in Jamaica* (New York: William Morrow & Co., 1972), p. 35; W. Marvin Will, "Political Development in the Mini-State Caribbean" (Ph.D. diss., University of Missouri, Columbia, 1972), pp. 21–23.

8. Rex M. Nettleford, "Some Reflections on the Young," in *The Cultural and Environmental Impact of Tourism with Reference to the Caribbean,* vol. 2, *Tourism Impact* (Barbados: Caribbean Tourism Research Centre, 1977), p. 24.

9. Daniel Guérin, *The West Indies and Their Future,* trans. Austryn Wainhouse (London: Dennis Dobson, 1961), p. 15.

10. See Goerge L. Beckford, *Persistent Poverty* (New York: Oxford University Press, 1972).

11. *Small Wars Manual: United States Marine Corps* (Washington, D.C.: United States Printing Office, 1940), p. 2.

12. See Donald M. Dozer, *Are We Good Neighbors?* (Gainesville, Fla.: University of Florida Press, 1961).

13. Melvin Gurtov, *The United States Against the Third World* (New York: Praeger Publishers, 1974), pp. 82–83.

14. Juan José Arévalo, *The Shark and the Sardines,* trans. June Cobb and Paul Osequeda (New York: Lyle Stuart, 1961), p. 106.

15. Ydigoras Fuentes, *My War with Communism* (Englewood Cliffs, N.J.: Prentice-Hall, 1963), esp. pp. 50–51.

16. "Self-Respect and Our Nation's Independence," *Advocate-News* [Barbados], 30 November 1976.

17. These countries rank one, two, and four in per capita U.S. economic assistance to Latin America from 1962–1974: See Kenneth F. Johnson and Miles W. Williams, *Democracy, Power, and Intervention in Latin American Political Life: A Study of Scholarly Images* (Tempe, Ariz.: Center for Latin American Studies, Arizona State University, forthcoming).

18. Paul M. Kattenburg, *Observations on Some Forces of Change in the Contemporary World,* Institute of International Studies, Essay Series, no. 8 (Columbia, S.C.: University of South Carolina, 1978), pp. 1–14. On page 1, Kattenburg asserts that "by 1968 . . . the tight bipolarity of 1958 had effectively broken down". Also see Paul M. Kattenburg, Address to the St. Louis Council on Foreign Affairs, Chase-Park Plaza Hotel, St. Louis, Missouri, March 29, 1978.

19. Ibid.

20. "Carter Praised for Supporting Dominican Vote," *St. Louis Post-Dispatch,* 21 May 1978; see also St. Louis *Post-Dispatch,* 19–20, 24 May 1978.

21. "Carter Praised for Supporting Dominican Vote," op. cit. Similar praise from Caribbean leaders has resulted from President Carter's leadership regarding the Panama Canal treaties, although his congratulation to the Nicaraguan Somoza regime for its alleged "progress" in civil liberties dissipates much of the good will and suggests that Carter's Caribbean policy has not broken entirely with past patterns. See *St. Louis Post-Dispatch,* 8 June 1978 and the *Washington Post,* July 1978.

22. Led by Guyanese Minister of Foreign Affairs, Fred Wills, leaders of Guyana, Barbados, and Jamaica voiced frequent, heated, but usually unspecific criticism of the alleged U.S. "destabilisation" of their national politics during the mid-1970s; David Renwick, "Young—Gifted and Black," *West Indies Chronicle* 90 (September 1977): 4–5, commenting on the ambassador's visit to the Caribbean in 1977, noted that in prior administrations it would have been inconceivable that a representative of the U.S. president would have been so welcome in the Caribbean.

23. George L. Reid, *The Impact of Very Small Size on the International Behavior of Microstates,* Sage Professional Papers in International Studies (Beverly Hills, Calif.: Sage Publications, 1974), pp. 30–31; Ronald P. Barston, "The External Relations of Small States," in *Small States in International Relations,* eds. August Schou and Arne Olav Brundtland (Stockholm: Almgvist & Wiksell, 1971), pp. 48–49.

24. Direct metropolitan investment in the Commonwealth Caribbean alone is U.S. $5 billion, with a profit return of approximately 50 percent according to Ralph Gonsalvés, "Imperialism: The Monster of our Times," *The Nation* [Barbados], 12 October 1977, p. 23; see also North American Congress on Latin America, *Yanqui Dollar: The Contribution of U.S. Private Investment to Underdevelopment in Latin America* (New York: NACLA, 1971); David W. Ziegler, *War, Peace and International Politics* (Boston: Little, Brown & Co., 1977), pp. 401–12; Finlay and Hovet, op. cit., pp. 332–39; and Richard Cheltenham, Address, Annual Spring Conference, West Indian Association, Michigan State University, East Lansing, Michigan, May 9, 1978.

25. Attributed to Prime Minister Errol Barrow, as quoted in Will, op. cit., p. 23; also see Alan Wells, *Picture-Tube Imperialism?* (New York: Orbis Books, 1972).

26. Charles W. Yost, *The Conduct and Misconduct of Foreign Affairs* (New York: Random House, 1972), pp. 22 ff. As Yost observes, a major foreign policy goal is to "stay in power" even though it is usually not avowed.

27. For example, none of the five Associated States have populations in excess of 110,000 yet all but Antigua are actively seeking independence. In December 1978 St. Lucia plans to become the eighth Caribbean state to gain independence since 1962. Smallness is not unique to the Caribbean, however, since two-thirds of the world's nations are less

than five million in population. See *St. Louis Post-Dispatch*, 13 July 1978; and *West Indies & Caribbean Year Book, 1976/77* (Toronto: Caribook, [1976]).

28. See E. F. Schumacher, *Small is Beautiful*, Perennial Library (New York: Harper & Row, 1973); E. F. Schumacher, *Independence and Economic Development*, Sir Winston Scott Memorial Lectures (Barbados: Caribbean Graphics, 1976); and Norwell Harrington, ed., *Micro State Studies*, Caribbean Research Institute ([St. Thomas, V. I.]: College of the Virgin Islands, 1977), 1:1–2.

29. Ted Robert Gurr, *Why Men Rebel* (Princeton, N.J.: Princeton University Press, 1970); *West Indies & Caribbean Year Book*, 1976/77, op. cit.; J. M. G. M. (Tom) Adams, prime minister's Address to United Nations General Assembly, 31st sess., October 11, 1976, in *Barbados Bulletin* 2, no. 7 (October–December 1976): 2–9.

30. "Jamaica: Shock Treatment," *Latin American Political Report* 12, no. 19 (May 19, 1978): 149–50.

31. Terence Todman, Testimony before Subcommittee on Inter-American Affairs of U.S. House International Relations Committee, reprinted in U.S., *The Department of State*, June 28, 1977, pp. 1–4; similar statistics are given by David Renwick, op. cit.; however, Idris Hamid, "Unemployment—facts and faces," *Caribbean Contact* [Trinidad], April 1977, p. 19, sets the overall regional unemployment percentage as 15 to 25 percent, with a 40 percent upper limit. The percentage "does not include those who are paid miserable wages and who, at the end of the week and even a life-time, have little to show for their sweat and labour."

32. Puchala, op. cit., pp. 74–75. Puchala lists preservation and security goals separately; see also Yost, op. cit.

33. U.S. Arms Control and Disarmament Agency, *World Military Expenditures and Arms Trade, 1964–74* (Washington, D.C.: USACDA, 1976); Harold Sprout and Margaret Sprout, *Toward a Politics of the Planet Earth* (New York: Van Nostrand, Reinhold, 1971), pp. 356–61; Puchala, op. cit., pp. 176–78; Finlay and Hovet, p. cit., pp. 214–28.

34. Reid, op. cit., pp. 38–39. Patrick Bellegarde-Smith, "Haiti: Perspectives of Foreign Policy," *Caribbean Quarterly* 20, nos. 3–4 (September–December 1974): esp. 27 notes the Haitian tendency to "fuse" domestic and foreign policy goals. Also see David Vital, *The Inequality of States* (Oxford: Claredon Press, 1967), pp. 117–19.

35. Off-the-record interviews in the Bahamas, Barbados, Trinidad and Tobago, and the Dominican Republic, January 1978, and at Annual Spring Conference, West Indian Association, Michigan State University, May 1978. Guyanese Chief of State Kit Nacimento's comments were primarily in response to an address by UN Ambassador Donald Blackman; see also Wendell Bell and J. William Gibson, Jr., "Independent Jamaica Faces the Outside World: Attitudes of Elites After Twelve Years of Nationhood," *International Studies Quarterly* 22, no. 12 (March 1978): 5–45; Wendell Bell and Robert V. Robinson, "European Melody, African Rhythm, or West Indian Harmony? Changing Cultural Orientations of Jamaican Leaders" (Paper presented at Annual Convention, International Studies Association, St. Louis, Missouri, March 18, 1977).

36. Address by Ambassador Blackman, Annual Spring Conference, West Indian Association, op. cit.

37. Examples include recent failures to schedule Head of State Meetings among CARICOM governments and increased unilateral and bilateral actions inimical to regional integration including the "induced" removal of the only truly regional newspaper, *Caribbean Contact* from Trinidad to Barbados in April 1978. See "CARICOM Deserves a Decent Burial," *Trinidad Express*, 12 February 1978 and *Caribbean Contact*, March 1978.

Part II

Current Issues

3

Peoples on the Move: An International Perspective on Caribbean Migration

Elsa M. Chaney

Recent large-scale movements of people across international boundaries in search of greater economic opportunity are directly related to the disparity in growth between developed and developing countries. Such movements occur not only because of "push factors"—population pressures, land scarcity, un- and underemployment—but also because of marked wage differentials between the developed and developing world. An irony in the situation is that only dramatic improvement in employment opportunities in developing countries would reduce the outflow; moderate improvement probably would accelerate the movement since more could afford the journey. This anomaly is demonstrated by the fact that many migrants were employed in their homelands immediately prior to their departure.

During the 1960s, capital intensive development strategies in both agriculture and industry failed to generate sufficient employment opportunity for all those entering the labor force. In developing countries, millions have joined the ranks of permanent armies of the unemployed —or the "self-employed" who may, however, on many days have no work at all or who stay alive by inventing jobs in the interstices of the economy.

Rapid population growth, along with incomplete or aborted land reforms compound the problem and accelerate the rhythm of rural-to-urban migration. But many do not stop at their own frontiers. Small Caribbean islands and Central American countries, for example, have long regarded migration to neighboring or metropole countries as the normal solution to lack of economic opportunity at home. Paulo Singer, among others, has suggested that continuing to make distinctions between internal and international migration is artificial.[1] The same "push and pull" factors created by events in the international political and economic system impel millions of "surplus" people across their own borders.

Thus, energy problems, environmental concerns, and commodity agreements are not the only issues in the current North-South negotiations; in the long run, the exportation and importation of cheap laboring hands—like some new raw material—may pose even more serious political, economic, and ethical questions for both the sending and receiving societies. Indeed, the migration issue could well lead to political confrontations between the richer and poorer nations in the early or mid-1980s, particularly if economic recovery in the advanced nations continues to lag, or if there are new recessions—and if acute demographic pressures continue in the sending countries.

Movement across international borders was a key factor in the growth of today's advanced nations. In the sixteenth and seventeenth centuries, "the world as a whole [for the first time] began to be one migratory network dominated by a single group of technologically-advanced and culturally similar states."[2]

Today world migration has shifted direction: instead of flowing from the crowded, industrial European countries, it is flowing towards developed countries. Well-documented are the movements of West Indians and Surinamese to English and Dutch cities, and of contract laborers and others from Southern Europe and North Africa to Western and Northern Europe. We are only beginning, however, to connect to the same disparity-of-growth phenomenon the millions of Afro-Caribbean and Latin American migrants who are rapidly replacing the flow of European immigrants to the United States and Canada. Less noted and understood are the regional movements of Asian, African, and Latin American peoples seeking jobs in countries that may be only slightly better off then their own—another result of uneven growth.

Colombian migrants, for example, come not only to the United States, but go in even larger numbers to Venezuela. There Colombian *campesinos* (as well as workers skilled in the Colombian textile industry and other industries, who migrate legally) cross the long, permeable border, adding perhaps 1 million persons to—and accounting for about one-tenth of—the population of the neighboring republic. Steady, if not spectacular, numbers of Colombians have been going to Columbia's former territory of Panama since the end of the 1920s. More recently, perhaps 60,000 Colombians have gone to Ecuador because of jobs created by new petroleum enterprises.[3]

There are many implications of this movement of peoples for both sending and receiving countries. Major problems include the politically volatile issue of undocumented persons living within the borders of host countries; the relation of host country labor forces to imported laboring hands and the loss to the sending countries of so many trained men and women, producing a sort of "reverse aid" program from the less developed to the more developed countries. Moreover, research shows that the most energetic, ambitious, and capable among the unskilled also tend to migrate, at least in the initial stages.

The negative side of contemporary migration should be tempered by pointing out positive implications. The migration of peoples in search of a better life has been viewed historically as having positive social, cultural, and economic consequences, in contrast to the negative characterization of present-day movements. Sending societies gain seasonal or longer-term employment for their nationals. The loss of people is partly balanced by the remittances sent home and the safety valve that emigration provides for trained and untrained alike: the more skilled who may be frustrated at the lack of opportunity to practice their professions, and the less skilled who may not find any jobs at all. Host societies gain a flexible, often exploited, labor reserve.

There are two other considerations which have not been sufficiently examined from the host country perspective, and which may pose the most difficult questions for public policy:

1. The first issue concerns the nature of growth in industrialized nations, which apparently rests to an unacceptable degree on the availability of imported labor. Toleration of the new immigration groups in host societies has come about because "a continuous stream of migrants from economically backward areas is crucial to the process of economic growth, at least as it has occurred in the Western world."[4]

Industrial society always has tended to generate a set of jobs unacceptable to the native born, and many developed countries now solve this problem by importing contract labor or by tolerating illegal immigration.[5] Even in cases of those relatively privileged migrant workers who do factory work, imported labor is much more economical at times than opening a branch of a multinational concern (or locating an agribusiness) within the borders of a Third World country. In using migrants, the metropolitan center can take up existing slack capacity, rather than risk building and equipping new plants outside their boundaries.

But only a few migrants find work in factories. Typically they take on low-skilled, low-salaried jobs, such as restaurant workers, day laborers, street cleaners, janitors and custodians, parking lot attendants, and particularly for the women, domestic servants.

There are other advantages to the advanced nations in such an arrangement. Laboring hands go home when they are no longer needed, and in most work-contract systems, are not allowed to bring their families along. Thus, host countries can avoid paying most of the social costs of the new, flexible labor reserve (social security and pensions, health and unemployment insurance, schools, welfare provisions, and the like). Moreover, imported labor hands can be paid less and are far less likely to organize in demand of their rights.

Thus, for advanced countries, the questions that must be asked include: Can the kind of growth that depends upon a new international reserve army of labor lead to equitable societies in either the host or the sending countries? What kinds of regulatory policies might be introduced which would protect the foreign workers? Might there be, in international justice, some argument that there is an obligation to accept some foreign workers since many of the presently less-developed countries received substantial numbers of Europeans because of Europe's earlier industrialization?

2. A second issue concerns the distinct character of the new immigrants. These new immigrants differ from the settler-immigrants of another era who left their homelands never to return. Today's Third World migrants by and large intend one day to return to their own countries. Even if they never actually do go back, they intend to return. Circumstances may cause repatriation to be repeatedly postponed—until they can educate their children, accumulate certain consumer goods or save to buy a piece of land, but the desire to go back remains in the immigrants' thoughts and calculations, with implications for their adjustment to the host society.

Even though these persons cluster in low-paid, low-prestige jobs that nobody else will do, they nevertheless are often resented because they are viewed as "taking jobs away" from host country nationals. Often, too, they are racially distinct; many times, even if they speak the language of the host country, they do so in the particular accent and lilt of the homeland, often a former colony of the host society. In times of recession, the outcry against immigrants becomes particularly vociferous. According to one North American who was refused employment,

> the real reasons the growers don't want us is that they can pay those wetbacks [sic] less and they dog them around. Those Jamaicans don't stop cutting; they run all day. If they stop running, they are sent back to the islands. The growers know they can't dog Americans around like that.[6]

Again, policy makers in the host society must ask what are the consequences of the presence of so many groups that appear determined to remain with their "feet in two societies"? Will the contemporary search for "roots," the latest twist in the accentuation of Hispanic and Black cultural values in the United States mean that the second generation will also remain alienated and will adjust in quite different, as yet unpredictable ways, to the dominant culture? It may be that the extent to which metropolitan countries succeed in preventing a second generation from growing up and being socialized to the host country's norms will determine whether they will avoid the explosive class and racial clashes experienced in many host country urban centers in recent times.[7]

In the meantime, the question of international migration has entered the political discourse among nations. One long-range solution lies in the advanced nations beginning to allow the Third World an autonomous development through a new world economic system of just prices for raw materials, generous transfer of technology (particularly intermediate scale) and political and material support for those societies that are attempting to attain a more equitable distribution of income and a better standard of living for their poor. To absorb more of their own populations at home is, of course, one long-range solution although some international migration doubtless will continue.

Unless and until population pressures abate, international movement of peoples probably will continue on a large scale, governed by necessity in both the sending and receiving societies. Against the background of mutual necessity, there will be a jockeying to turn international migration to the best possible advantage. Factors in the international political system will no doubt generally favor the receiving countries. These factors include the state of the economy of the world, as well as of the sending and host countries; the political situation of the receiving countries and the extent to which users of migrant labor can influence the political situation; and the extent to which both sending and receiving countries wish migration, acknowledged and regulated or unacknowledged and unregulated, to continue.

NOTES

1. Paulo Singer, "International Migration and Employment," in *International Migration, World Population Year* (Paris: CICRED, 1974), p. 128.

2. Kingsley Davis, "The Migration of Human Populations," in *The Human Population: A Scientific American Book* (San Francisco: W. H. Freeman, 1974), pp. 55–65, esp. p. 56.

3. Ramiro Cardona, et al., *Elements for a Comprehensive Model of International Migration: The Case of Colombian Migration to the United States* (Bogotá: Corporación Centro Regional de Población, 1976), pp. 75–78.

4. U.S. Department of Labor, "The Role of Immigration in Industrial Growth: A Case Study of the Origins and Character of Puerto Rican Migration to Boston," Report prepared for the Manpower Administration by Michael J. Piore, 1973, mimeographed, p. 25; see also Michael J. Piore, Speech at Fordham University, Department of Sociology, 1976.

5. Ibid.

6. Philip Shabecoff, "Florida Cane Cutters: Alien, Poor, Afraid," New York *Times,* 12 March, 1973, quoted in *NACLA Report on the Americas* 11, no. 8 (November–December 1977):12.

7. Piore, "The Role of Immigration in Industrial Growth," op. cit., pp. 25–31.

4

The International Politics of Caribbean Migration

Dawn Marshall

The title of this book, *The Restless Caribbean,* is a very apt one for the peoples of the region. Ever since emancipation, the West Indian has been moving from limited opportunities, chronic poverty, and deprivation to what are perceived as better conditions, both within and without the Caribbean. It is surprising that migration has not received more attention in the literature on Caribbean international relations. Migration has been an issue that has concerned both the Caribbean countries and those countries with which they jockey in the international arena, but those who analyze the region's foreign relations have seldom included migration in their discussion.

Discussions on foreign relations have been concerned mainly with the Caribbean as a sphere of influence for metropolitan powers. In a very real sense migration is the result or consequence of influence already exerted on, or existing in, the region. For example, potential migrants who wish to go to the United States wish to go not only because of the limited opportunities at home, but because they perceive the United States to embody the attitudes, values, and opportunities to which they aspire. And they aspire to this way of life because of the variety of influences exerted on the Caribbean by the United States.

In most discussions of international relations the focus of attention is the Caribbean itself. This is not true of migration. With migration, the major concern becomes the impact on the host country rather than increased influence within the Caribbean. Thus it seems that analysts of international relations have considered migration as an issue different in "kind" from their usual concerns, and for that reason have neglected it. Where the issue has been raised, it has been considered in the context of assistance, with the Caribbean arguing that receiving countries should consider allowing immigration as a form of aid.[1]

Despite the developed world's continuing need for migrant labor, metropolitan countries have begun to impose such restrictions on the movement of the Caribbean peoples that Caribbean governments will be forced to look more critically at emigration and its role in the development process. Although it is likely that Caribbean area countries will continue to regard emigration as a safety valve, there are indications that, viewed through the lens of nationalism, both political and economic, migration will have to be perceived differently.

MIGRATION AS AN EXPRESSION OF MUTUAL NECESSITY

International migration takes place against a background of mutual necessity by both the sending and receiving countries. This background of movement from countries with a surplus of labor to countries with an abundance of capital is becoming accepted as an economic framework for international migration that lends itself to a variety of both capitalist and marxist interpretations. The main element of this framework is that labor shortages represent a constraint on the economic growth of countries with an abundance of capital. In order to alleviate this constraint, governments of receiving countries permit immigration of workers attracted by the wage differential. This differential is such that these migrants are willing to work for lower wages and at less desirable jobs. Migrants therefore introduce an element of flexibility into the labor market: they can be recruited in times of labor shortage, then dismissed and expelled from the country in times of recession. If migrant workers have either entered the country illegally, or are working illegally, the degree of flexibility increases as, of course, does the profit level. This may be a reason why receiving countries often seem unduly tolerant of illegal migrants.

Although it is tempting to see this process as operating only between the Third World and the metropolitan countries, it should be recognized that it does take place at many levels. The current migrations of Colombians to Venezuela, of down islanders from the Eastern Caribbean to the U.S. Virgins, or of Haitians to the Bahamas can all be explained within this broad framework of development diferentials.[2] It is more difficult, however, to fit some past Caribbean movements into this mold. Movements to the banana republics of Central America, to the sugar plantations of Cuba, or to the refineries of Curaçao were different, in that the demand for labor was created by the expansion of a specific economic sector. With the completion of a project, or with depression in the sugar or banana industry, some migrants returned home while others moved on to other countries.

Against this background of mutual necessity which leads to migration there is a jockeying for advantages. This jockeying is influenced by a number of factors (the state of the world economy or the political situation in either country), none constant, that places the advantage mainly in the court of the receiving countries. Governments of developed countries have found it politically expedient to allow immigration and argue that in this way they provide friendly Caribbean governments with a much needed safety valve for population and employment pressures. They have even facilitated the movement by devising institutional arrangements like the official recruiting procedures for farm labor designed by both the U.S. and Canadian governments.

Despite such efforts toward a New International Economic Order, it is likely that the inequalities and disparities of growth between the receiving and sending countries will persist—and the mutual necessity for migration will continue. There is of course an alternative, that of allowing excess capital to flow to the countries with surplus labor, but this also has its shortcomings.

EMIGRATION AS AN ESCAPE VALVE

Although West Indians have been migrating ever since they have been free to do so, movement was mainly within the Caribbean until the 1880s.[3] Emigration was actively promoted by the governments of the islands. In Barbados, for instance, eight Emigration Acts, or amendments thereto, were passed by the legislature between 1881 and 1929. Most of these approved financial assistance for dependents left behind. In comparison, only two Immigration Acts were passed during this period, both of which were concerned with restricting the immigration of paupers. By the 1920s, despite some objections to emigration from planters in Jamaica (1884), St. Lucia (1887), and Barbados (1906–12),[4] on the grounds that it reduced the labor force available for sugar production, West Indian administrators had come to perceive emigration as a means of alleviating hardship and distress caused by economic depression, unemployment, or natural hazards.[5] This perception was reinforced when these outlets for migration were closed in the 1920s by U.S. quota restrictions and by depressions in both the sugar and banana industries. This cessation of emigration coincided with drastic reductions in the levels of mortality in most islands. The resultant increase in island populations was not relieved until the emigration to Britain in the 1950s.

Population pressure has manifested itself in the islands mainly as chronic unemployment. In Barbados, for example, "unemployment remains chronic and presents the single biggest economic and social problem in the community,"[6] and the reduction or elimination of unemployment has been among the aims and objectives of each of the eight Development Plans devised since 1946. Even after the British government slammed its door on West Indian migration in 1962[7], the Barbados government could restate its policy of continuing efforts to persuade countries to accept its citizens and, wherever practicable, to provide them with the skills acquired by other countries.[8] While West Indian governments have acknowledged the loss of their more highly trained people by migration, the consensus has been that because of remittances, reductions in population growth, and skills brought back by any returning migrants, gains to the Commonwealth Caribbean have far outweighed the losses.[9]

In their pursuit of these policies, however, West Indian governments have shown some concern for the welfare of their nationals abroad. At first emigration from the islands was unrestricted and no legislation existed to control the conditions under which it took place.[10] However, reports from the British Vice Consul in Panama soon revealed physical conditions which engendered disease and sickness, lack of concern by employers for ill laborers, and requests by laborers for assistance or even repatriation. Concern over the situation in Panama was bolstered by the inadequacy of provisions made by migrants for their dependents, and by the overcrowding of ships going to Panama. Control of migrant recruiting and of transport were embodied in some of the Emigration Acts such as the Barbadian Emigration Act of 1891 or the St. Lucian Emigrant Protection Ordinance of 1911. These restrictions probably represented an attempt to avoid public expense for the relief of emigrants and were motivated by the costs of repatriation and the impossibility of finding jobs for returning migrants.

West Indian Governments continue to express interest in their nationals abroad. In 1971, the U.S. Immigration Service waged a systematic campaign to expel illegal aliens from the U.S. Virgins. Seven percent of the population were expelled. The Premiers of St. Kitts and Antigua visited the Virgin islands to investigate the charges of brutal treatment and it was announced that the Commonwealth Caribbean was sending a joint mission to Washington to formally protest the deportations.[11] While such protests were not expected to reverse the policy, they were expected to influence the conditions under which the deportations were made and to indicate that the migrants had not been abandoned by their national governments. West Indian governments, however, generally failed to take any active steps to organize or supervise the large migration to Britain in the 1950s, and gave little thought to the social problems created in the West Indies by the movement.[12] Given the very positive perception of the impact of migration by West Indian governments since the nineteenth century, the difficulties these governments have in dealing with economic problems in the islands even with migration, and their constant fear of having to provide for large numbers of returning migrants, it is not surprising that their migration policies, though predominantly motivated by narrow self-interest, exhibit a certain amount of ambivalence.

THE NEED FOR CONTROL

Traditionally the need for restricting or curtailing Caribbean migration has been felt by the receiving countries—in particular the United States, the United Kingdom, and Canada. Unfortunately, these restrictions have at times embodied strong racial discrimination. Initially the United States had no significant restrictions on migration. But after finding its first legal expression in the Chinese Exclusion Act of 1882, a racial bias continued to manifest itself. Organizations such as the Immigration Restriction League agitated for tighter controls on immigration. Strong social and political pressures led to the Immigration Act of 1924, which imposed a ceiling of 150,000 for all migrants except close relatives of U.S. citizens and refugees, and devised "complicated formulas to restrict immigrants from certain countries in order to retain the racial and ethnic composition of the U.S. population."[13] During World War II, the United States relaxed its stand on Caribbean migration because of its need for labor, admitting substantial numbers of West Indians. However, this relaxation, which had continued after the war, came to an end with the McCarran [Immigration] Act of 1952 which, because of its discriminatory bias, again effectively ended Caribbean migration to the United States.

The West Indian movement to the United Kingdom also had its origin in World War II. West Indians who went to Britain to support the war effort were exposed to British conditions and opportunities. Disappointed by postwar opportunities available in the Caribbean and refused entry to the United States after 1952, West Indians viewed the expansion of economic opportunities in the United Kingdom in the 1950s as a godsend. Because of their status as British subjects, they were confident of unrestricted entry into the mother country. But as Ceri Peach generalizes, while "the shortage of workers made West Indians economically acceptable, the shortage of housing made them socially undesirable."[14]

This movement to Britain was far greater than any previous movement to the United States and was the first experience with what happens when large numbers of blacks enter a predominantly European environment. The results were not favorable, and in 1962 Britain passed the Commonwealth Immigrants Act, which, although designed to stipulate the conditions under which all Commonwealth citizens could enter the United Kingdom, was in fact drafted for the specific purpose of controlling colored immigration. Levitt and McIntyre argue quite forcibly that the British experience is a useful lesson in what happens when no organized effort is made by either the sending or receiving countries to establish an apparatus for dealing with the inevitable social problems.[15]

Until 1962 the discriminatory bias of Canadian immigration laws was explicit. Canadian immigration regulations were designed to attract European immigrants. Fortuitously for the West Indies, at the time that Britain was slamming its door on colored immigrants in 1962, revisions to the Canadian Immigration Act were made to eliminate the racial bias. At that time, Canada still maintained its need for continued immigration to sustain its high rate of economic growth but articulated the need to limit immigration to skilled personnel. The 1965 Immigration Act of the United States allowed additional West Indians to enter the United States and increased immigration to both Canada and the United States, therefore, compensated for British restrictions.

In the late 1960s and the 1970s, immigration from the Third World into both Canada and the United States increased as a result of less restrictive policies. But this period of relatively free migration is coming to an end. In 1972, the U.S. Commission on Population Growth and the American Future recommended that immigration levels should not be increased and that the nation's population should be stabilized.[16] Canada also began to recognize that a basic weakness of its selection and admission system was its lack of control over the total volume of immigration.[17] This does not mean that immigration from the Caribbean is going to be curtailed. Both countries still see a need for skilled people, and the current immigration policies of the Caribbean's traditional receiving countries—the United States, the United Kingdom, and Canada—increasingly favor the immigration of skilled and professional people.

But Levitt and McIntyre have shown that, because of the substantial discretionary powers of Canadian immigration officials in administering the law, this criterion of skill has resulted in the selection of West Indian immigrants who, as a group, are more highly qualified than other migrants.[18] While Canada has made gestures towards unskilled Caribbean migrants in the domestic servant scheme and the seasonal farm laborers scheme, as has the United States, it is clear that the two biases—against black immigrants and in favor of skilled personnel—are important criteria that will form the future migration policies of the metropolitan countries. The immigration controls devised for Third World peoples will inevitably foster the interests of the receiving countries.

THE ALTERNATIVE

Instead of moving workers to countries with an abundance of capital, there exists the alternative of allowing excess capital to flow to the countries with a surplus of workers. This is not a new idea; in 1954 Britain and the United States recognized, in a joint statement about the economic development of the Commonwealth Caribbean, that "migration of industry to the area should be encouraged when appropriately adapted to the labor and other conditions in the area."[19] Exacerbated by illegal or undocumented migrants, the idea is being stated more positively now: "Only through the achievement of relative economic parity between the sending countries and the United States can the flow of illegal immigration be stemmed."[20] The objective now is economic parity to eradicate the developmental differentials within which the mutual necessity of migration has evolved, and the United States, at least, sees this as being achieved "only through massive infusions of foreign aid and economic development."[21] The question is, How is such economic development to be achieved?

Past experience does not engender confidence in the idea that economic development, of the type Caribbeanists perceive relevant to their area, can be achieved by massive infusions of foreign aid; while the necessity of foreign assistance is acknowledged, this has seldom come without strings. Further, the concept of balanced economic development accepted by most Caribbeanists involves the material welfare of all the people of the region. Given the existing disparities of wealth and privilege in the Caribbean, the attainment of this concept must involve some redistribution. This has often been articulated in socialist terms, and some of the islands have begun to look outside the Western Hemisphere for infusions of aid. The maintenance of the United States as the dominant Western Hemisphere power has been the core of U.S.–Caribbean policy "from the time it was formulated until the present day."[22] and it is unlikely that the United States will approve of any economic development that may threaten that hegemony.

While economic parity is unlikely in the near future, there will of necessity be some response from the sending countries in the Caribbean, at both an individual and an official level. Past experience does not produce expectations of a very positive response. As early as 1840, two years after Emancipation, Barbadian workers were insisting on "their undoubted right to carry their labor to the best market."[23] More than a century of emigration has reinforced the West Indians' strong propensity to migrate and the people of the Caribbean perceive the receiving countries as part of the system of opportunities available to them. If they desire an opportunity that is not available at home, they automatically extend their search to other countries, mainly in the developed world. Such a reflexive action, as much a result of the influence in the Caribbean of countries such as Canada, the United Kingdom, and the United States as it is a result of kinship ties with Caribbean migrants in these countries, is not likely to disappear, and clandestine movement is often the response to restrictive immigration measures.

West Indians have been fortunate in that, as one outlet for migration closed, another has opened. Thus, chance has seemed to absolve West Indian governments from the obligation to reexamine the basic tenet of their migration policy: that emigration is an escape valve. When the British outlet for emigration closed, Knox observed that the manner in which the West Indies responded would determine whether they were to be "perpetual knockers-at-the-door of others."[24] There are no indications that any new doors are likely to open, so perhaps West Indian governments will be forced into that vital reexamination. The need for skilled personnel in the process of economic development, together with the loss of skills due to the migration policies of the receiving countries, may cause some West Indian governments to modify their positive assessments of the effects of emigration. But if we accept the U.S. view that the only alternative to migration is economic parity, then even this reassessment will not change the short-term necessity for migration, for economic development is a long and painful process. It seems that for some time to come the people of the Caribbean are destined to be knockers-at-doors. It is hoped that receiving countries will acknowledge the need for careful, sensitive, and successful negotiations between countries on migration possibilities, but at the same time will both allow and actively support the Third World's quest for economic parity.

NOTES

1. Kari Levitt and Aliister McIntyre, *Canada-West Indies Economic Relations* ([Montreal]: McGill University, Centre for Developing-Area Studies, 1967), p. 81.

2. Roy S. Bryce-Laporte, "Caribbean Migration to the United States: Some Tentative Conclusions," in *Caribbean Immigration to the United States,* ed. Roy S. Bryce-Laporte and Delores M. Mortimer (Washington, D.C.: Smithsonian Institution, Research Institute on Immigration and Ethnic Studies, 1976) p. 196.

3. G. W. Roberts, *Fertility and Mating in Four West Indian Populations* (Jamaica: Institute of Social and Economic Research, 1975), pp. 2–18.

4. Velma E. Newton, "Aspects of British West Indian Emigration to the Isthmus of Panama, 1850–1914," Mimeographed (Paper presented at the Ninth Conference of Caribbean Historians, University of the West Indies, Barbados, April 1977), p. 30.

5. Roberts, op. cit., p. 5.

6. *Barbados Development Plan 1969–1972,* (Bridgetown, Barbados: Government Printing Office, 1969).

7. This phrase was adapted from the book by Robert Moore and Tina Wallace, *Slamming the Door: The Administration of Immigration Control* (London: Robertson and Co., 1975).

8. *Barbados Development Plan 1965–1968,* (Bridgetown, Barbados: Government Printing Office, 1965), p. 23.

9. Hilborne A. Watson, "International Migration and the Political Economy of Underdevelopment: Aspects of the Commonwealth Caribbean Situation," in Bryce-Laporte and Mortimer, op. cit., p. 18.

10. Velma E. Newton, *British West Indian Immigration to the Isthmus of Panama 1850–1914,* (M.A. thesis, Department of History, University of the West Indies, Jamaica, 1973), chap. 3.

11. The *Advocate-News* (Barbados), issues between 23 March and 10 May 1971.

12. A. D. Knox, "Foreword," in R. B. Davison, *West Indian Migrants: Social and Economic Facts of Migration from the West Indies,* (London: Oxford University Press, Institute of Race Relations, 1962).

13. U. S., Commission on Population Growth and the American Future, *Report: Population and the American Future,* (Washington, D.C.: Government Printing Office, 1972), p. 114.

14. Ceri Peach, *West Indian Migration to Britain: A Social Geography* (London: Oxford University Press, Institute of Race Relations, 1968), p. 100.

15. Levitt and McIntyre, op. cit., p. 103.

16. U.S. Population Commission, op. cit., pp. 116–18.

17. Freda Hawkins, "Canadian Immigration: A New Law and a New Approach to Management," *International Migration Review* 11, no. 1 (1977): 80–81.

18. Levitt and McIntyre, op. cit., pp. 95–101.

19. Roy Preiswerk, ed., *Documents on International Relations in the Caribbean,* (Rio Piedras, Puerto Rico: Institute of Caribbean Studies, 1970), p. 143.

20. Austin T. Fragomen Jr., "Legislative and Judicial Developments: President Carter's Amnesty and Sanctions Proposal," *International Migration Review* 11, no. 4 (1977): 529.

21. Ibid., p. 530.

22. Gordon Connell-Smith, *The United States and Latin America: An Historical Analysis of Inter-American Relations* (London: Heinemann, 1974), p. 267.

23. G. W. Roberts, "Emigration from Barbados," *Social and Economic Studies* 4, no. 3 (September 1955): 248.

24. Knox, op. cit., p. xiii.

5

Tourism: Development or Dependence?

Herbert L. Hiller

For many years it has been said that the Caribbean is dependent on tourism. In the shorthand of conventional development theory, this refers to the significant employment and foreign exchange spurred by overseas travel into the area—between four and five million air visitors annually during the 1970s who have steadily generated double digit contributions to both employment and Gross National Product (GNP).[1]

Yet tourism is more than just jobs based on leisure spending. It represents the way that powerful nations, such as the United States, perceive and relate to the rest of the world. Places are categorized in ways that assign status in the global order. Therefore, if we wish to examine the international implications of Caribbean tourism, we need to understand how tourism fits into American life, and how the Caribbean has been organized to take part.

Basically, tourism results from paid vacations, long-range communications and transportation, plus an induced propensity to travel. Tourism has become an integral part of an affluent society. High status is accorded leisure travel. Everyone is encouraged to participate, and probably a majority already does. From the ads that entice us, through the transport, lodgings, and food that we buy, to the bills that keep coming in later, tourism is a systematized approach to industrial leisure.

Two aspects are noteworthy—one, that travel generally popularizes taste and experience thought of as fabulous, terrific, exotic. By and large, these are qualities missing from workaday lives. Two, tourism nevertheless connotes waiting in lines, noise, and anxiety—more or less everyday matters.

Such is the dual nature of tourism, for even as it is meant to get us "away from it all," it remains organized by the institutional forces that govern our work. The emphasis on escape from the humdrum must still conform to satisfy industrial priorities of volume, standardization, and predictability. ITT owns Sheraton. Gulf & Western runs factories at home and resorts abroad. The communications technology, accounting systems, and bureaucratization of management are the same in tourism as in manufacturing, education, and government. This is not to say that people don't have a good time on holiday. They usually do, utilizing the popularized options the vacation industry favors.

Tourism is packaged, wholesaled, computerized. Its workers refer to themselves as part of "the travel industry." Local, state, and national governments are beginning to regulate tourism as they do business in general. Trade associations and the trade press join with airlines and hotel chains for industrywide lobbying. Other features in common with business include emphases on packaging and marketing, discount selling, built-in obsolescence, and underworld connections.

As consumers, the affluent are meant to get away from it all. Henry Ford explained that we need the time off to consume what we produce. Technology has made it possible for us to go far away, so now it is morally acceptable to be enticed as far and as often as we desire, to consume as tourists our escape from workaday lives. The study of how to induce travel has become part of industrial management science, taught at many universities. There is a future in it.

In the Caribbean, tourism occurs against a background of political decolonization: the withdrawal of Westminster and The Hague, the incorporation of the French territories into a metropolitan union, and rising national aspirations in the U.S. colonial legacy—Puerto Rico and the Virgin Islands. In the devolution of empire, a common definition of development remains: for Caribbean peoples to achieve the status of industrial consumers. This model steadily makes clear who in the world is developed and who still has to be brought along.

Development in tourism is measured much the same as in industry generally: the more scaled up, the more advanced. During the early 1970s, one government policy maker declared that his country was leaving the era of the corner grocery store and entering the Supermarket Age.[2] By this he acknowledged that Jamaica had developed a modern hotel plant scaled to fit the jumbo jets. Tourism would be the leverage to push the country into the future.

This scenario makes sense to tourism policy makers. After all, no one disputes that tourism "belongs" to industrial society, that the apparatus of airlines, chain hotels, wholesalers, and retailers is authoritative, and that, since the vacation is an act of discretion, the vacationer has the right to determine where and how to spend it. The attitude toward visitors is properly fostered that "you gotta give 'em what they want." And "what they want," according to the travel industry, is something out of this world.

Those in the Caribbean proficient at tourism know that the name of the game is to make it easy for travel agents to sell The Product. Since all agents are authorized to sell more or less every vacation in the world and can only be familiar with a fraction, the agents' attention is most easily attracted to mainstream products, vacations which, even though extending over thousands of miles into foreign countries, will still be predictable. Best of all, even if one's product is not personally known to the agent, the name of it will be—hence, the proliferation of standardized hotel systems and corporate image making behind packaged tours.

It takes a particular history to accept that the external manifestations of one's culture are valuable chiefly as ornamentation for hotels designed, constructed, and managed in the interest of overseas profit. In time, however, all successful Caribbean tourism administrators come to accept this about mass tourism, and few can resist giving in. Indeed, they are chosen for their ability to organize the national tourism sector in response to overseas priorities, even if these remain at odds with genuine development, with such objectives as self-resourcefulness, energy conservation, and import restrictions.

At the core of the process has been the shift from locally integrated guest houses and small hotels to the scale and pace of cosmopolitan life reflected in the modern resorts that are either set apart from local communities or that overwhelm them. The process was spurred after World War II when international development agencies conceptualized that Americans on vacation would motivate backward Caribbeans by giving them a glimpse of life as it is meant to be. A U.S. foreign aid consultant argued the ruling theory that "new hotels and motels provide front parlors for countries to meet visitors and appropriate environments for doing business as a member of modern society."[3]

Authoritative voices joined in support of tourism's economic and social benefits to underdeveloped peoples. Pan Am foresaw "tourist waves surging ever higher,"[4] that would leave island populations with "eighty cents or more of every dollar a tourist spends."[5] The Organization of American States (OAS) lauded the prospect of "millions of tourists traveling from country to country not only help[ing] raise the standard of living of the host country but encourag[ing] integration of peoples through the interchange of ideas, drinking and eating habits, and styles of clothing."[6]

However, even such "integration," which would inevitably cast the visitor as model and the local as novice, was less and less likely, given the rationalization of resort development in favor of self-serving trade assumptions about tourist behavior. Through most of the 1970s the World Bank policy took the industry position that

> the development of well-planned resort areas at priority sites to serve relatively large concentrations of visitors is likely to be much more economical than more scattered development which would require infrastructure to be provided over wide areas. Moreover, the former type of development is likely to be more in accord with market preferences as the tourists can enjoy a wider variety of activities and services.[7]

Many West Indians had long foreseen how "giving 'em what they want" would lead to reordering sensitive areas of their lives, that scale, pace, and mood would lapse, behavior and events would come to be staged. In the era between the two world wars, a critic of Jamaican tourism observed the adulation of tourists already "seemed to many people fraught with adverse social implications for the black masses of the population. There was, in their view, every likelihood that the interests of black Jamaicans might as a consequence be completely subordinated to that of itinerants from overseas."[8]

This presentiment was confirmed a half century later by another Jamaican, Peter Goffe, who observed the "far-reaching repercussions on the developing national psyche [that came from the] significant visible reward of servile, obsequious behavior, of those with a talent for flattery, and the withholding of reward from and therefore the effective punishment of those demonstrating no such talent."[9] Not only did island tourism officials not resist the trend, he pointed out in the *Cornell Hotel & Restaurant Assn. Quarterly,* but they took their cues from overseas to foster it, so that

> even after political independence, the Jamaican tourism establishment has remained a bastion of last resistance to social change in the direction of the country's self-interest. . . . The assumption of a need-for-fantasy as the fundamental buyer motivation behind the purchase of a Jamaican tourism experience has dominated the character of international tourism in Jamaica.[10]

Official U.S. and Caribbean tourism policies continued to dovetail (except in Cuba). The famous Zinder Report on the future of tourism in the Eastern Caribbean was one of a series of studies by overseas consultants and financed by donor nations—this, in 1969, by the U.S. Agency for International Development.[11] Like most of the others, it projected a bright future for tourism in the region, basically conditioned on the natives' continued good service. Even though its economic arguments were later discredited,[12] the report set Caribbean governments throughout the region—both independent and still colonial—vying for overseas investors by exempting their operations from tax, import, and employment policies.

Correspondingly, the United States, through its Overseas Private Investment Insurance Corporation and other bilateral, hemispheric, and global agencies, offered necessary inducements for hotel investors and airlines to enter the region. As they began to exploit their opportunities, the hotel chains concerned themselves almost solely with investment and operational considerations, inflating reports of their local economic contribution, while essentially ignoring the effects of what they were doing on the social, cultural, and physical environments.[13]

The Supermarket Age was dawning. Along with frozen foods, tv, and packaged baby formula, the islands were getting modern hotels and jetports. The travel industry had progressed from custom trade to mass marketing. Most tourists were already organized to travel on "packages." This was the result of a two-pronged strategy to attract the new travelers needed to make jumbo jet investments pay off. Packaged tours allowed wholesalers to work with discounted airfares authorized by the Civil Aeronautics Board. Meanwhile, the airlines were authorized by the U.S. Air Traffic Conference, an agency of the CAB, to pay travel agents 40 percent bonuses on air tickets packaged with hotels (and often rental cars and local attractions as well). This had the added advantage of benefiting airline hotel subsidiaries overseas which proliferated with the advent of jet travel.[14]

In 1970, when Christian Action for Development in the Caribbean convened an ecumenical consultation on tourism, the wide variance was noted between the growth of tourism in the region and the values of more self-resourceful development.[15] Tourism was judged an extension of the plantation system with its hierarchical control overseas effected through island cadres—"local representatives who conform to American standards and whom they can understand," wrote Gordon Lewis of the North American multinationals.[16]

The system juxtaposed affluent whites at leisure with poor blacks at work in their service. Development through tourism demanded subordination of the native. As the former travel editor of the New York *Times* observed: "The islands need tourism to survive; that means the tourists, with all their demands and occasional paranoia, will continue to call the shots. The visitors are not going to change, therefore the islanders must."[17]

Moreover, the vaunted economic benefits were only meagerly realized. In his authoritative investigation into tourism economics of the Commonwealth Caribbean, John Bryden noted that imports from overseas to service the industry heavily siphoned off the capitalization tourism was meant to support.[18] Even employment did not measure up to expectations as hotel properties became increasingly capital-intensive.[19] Bryden concluded that insofar as they depended on tourism, many of the smaller islands of the region would find "that progress towards higher real incomes for the bulk of the population is likely to be slow, much slower than is suggested by most previous studies in the region."[20] He added, "that to achieve such progress considerable change will be required in the structure of the tourist industry, as well as elsewhere in the economy."[21]

As charges mounted that tourism was failing the region, industry officials rallied. Members of the Caribbean Hotel Association were assured by the trade press as they lobbied against greater government control that their leadership could "rely on strong support for its position from the American hotel chains and other U.S. hotel interests in the Caribbean."[22] One spokesman remonstrated that "people who speak against the chain hotels are just not viewing the situation objectively. Without the large hotels," he declared, "most of the islands would dry up and blow away.... Hilton is probably doing more to further local island cultures than anyone else, including the islanders themselves."[23]

In a rare speech critical of industry posturing, however, a prominent Caribbean tour wholesaler summed up the post-war experience by referring to "the conquistadores of Caribbean tourism," who, he said

> just as they had done in Atlantic City and Miami Beach and Honolulu, redesigned the natural beauty of the islands and made it ugly. They rearranged the environmental harmonies and left the stink of pollution and decay. They bombarded an innocent people with unrealistic promises of a new standard of living, and plunged them deeper than ever into ill-tempered privation.... Viewing the wreckage of the seventies, we can assess the crimes of the sixties in two equally disparaging ways: They were committed either by fools or by thieves....[24]

Nevertheless, efforts have been made throughout the 1970s to better integrate tourism into national life. This course has prevailed over largely rhetorical calls to give up on tourism altogether, and even Cuba has eagerly reentered the international tourist sweepstakes. The efforts, although sporadic, have coalesced around promoting what its proponents call "indigenous tourism." Its attitude toward tourists challenges conventional doctrine that vacationers will come only for imported fantasy, and organizes instead around the concept that "We gotta give 'em what we have—and make what we have what they want."

The chief difficulty in establishing this alternate position has not been dispute over the greater local efficacy of indigenous emphases.

Analysts throughout the Caribbean and elsewhere have long made the case in favor of greater use of local materials, adaptation to local scale, taking much of the cues and substance for the travel experience from island life, without having to sacrifice comfort or service—indeed, with all at a lower cost and making the region more competitive in worldwide tourism.[25] Rather, the chief stumbling block has been the unwillingness of regional tourism policy makers to consider that there might be a market for this more authentic Caribbean expression.*

A notable effort toward making tourism more supportive of self-resourceful development has been the establishment of the Caribbean Tourism Research Center, funded by governments of the region and the Inter-American Foundation, an agency of the U.S. government. Since its founding in 1973, the center has steered an erratic course. Although conceived to help regional tourism officials come to grips with the failures of conventional tourism and to research the availability of alternate markets for more indigenous vacations, the center has steadily become influenced by industry interests to provide conventional marketing services. By mid-1978, the OAS had become a working partner of the center, with uncertain prospects for the center's founding purposes.

Steadily, more authoritative voices within the region have begun to speak in favor of alternatives to conventional tourism, but none is heard yet within tourism itself.[26] Supporters have come from the Caribbean Development Bank,† the University of the West Indies,[27] Caribbean Community Secretariat,[28] Caribbean Conservation Association,[29] and elsewhere. The most notable government spokesman has been James F. Mitchell, when he served briefly as premier of St. Vincent. A small hotelier from Bequia in the Grenadines, Mitchell forthrightly declared a policy of indigenous tourism he called "To Hell With Paradise."[30] The policy, which would have linked tourism with local agriculture, architecture, cooling technology, recreation, and so forth, was never implemented, however. Mitchell's government was replaced by another which ignored his thrust and instead chose casino gambling to help put the island on the tourist map. Mitchell later observed that "my tourism policy, along with others, failed. For the people themselves," he said, "are so oriented to un-natural, and non-indigenous values that is is difficult to translate this into novel permanent policy."[31]

The irony is that developments in North America in the late 1970s indicate the existence of a vast and growing market for authentic experi-

---

*As of mid-1978, however, Jamaican tourism policy was coming to favor self-resourcefulness, but still more motivated by severe foreign exchange constraints than by philosophical commitment.

†Current CDB policy on hotel loans exclusively favors properties of not more than 40 rooms, part of a policy to stimulate local entrepreneurships.

ence. A broad swing of the pendulum has peaked near the limits of industrialization, and an unexpected constituency of conservatives, liberals, and radicals seems bound by common dissatisfaction with the centralization of American life, the morbid dependence on styling over substance, the rule of indulgence, and the excessive cost of it all.

Although Caribbean tourism remains largely set in the industrial mold, alternatives gain adherents elsewhere. Growing numbers of vacations seek out the small city hotels and rural inns of Western Europe. Vast numbers hike, bike, and boat on their own and with kindred groups, to savor the wilderness and civilized places alike. Advocates of indigenous tourism urge a link between what the islands have to offer and the market for local experiences. It is apparent, however, that little is likely to happen unless regional tourism policy makers are convinced such markets exist.

By and large, the Caribbean today has become off limits for those who seek greater authenticity. For them the Caribbean is reflected in travel industry images as a place where everything seems subordinated to the background din of boozing, casinos, swinging nightlife, and general dissipation. A cartoon in *The New Yorker* in 1978 shows a middle-aged couple talking over drinks: "Let's go to the Caribbean or someplace," says one, "and give our brains a rest."[32]

An earlier generation of Caribbean experts declared the islands fit only for "sun-lust" tourism.[33] Reflecting on tourism's course in his region, a retired Barbados diplomat observed that

> in the fifties and early sixties you could hardly get a hotelier to understand the significance to economic development of what he was doing. Outside of his then narrowly conceived interests there was no contact with the motivating elements of the society. . . .[34]

The region was compared unfavorably to Disney Land by a prominent instructor at one of the industry training schools.[35] The islanders have absorbed their negative self-image. "We welcome foreigners, we ape foreigners, we give away our national patrimony for a pittance to foreigners, and, what is worse, we vie among ourselves in doing all of these things," lamented the president of the Caribbean Development Bank.[36] The historical legacy is "a lack of awareness of their own potential," William Demas says of Caribbean peoples.[37] "It is their state of psychological, cultural, and intellectual dependence on the outside world."[38] It is enough, he says, to "make the angels weep."[39]

It is likely that only as Caribbean economies sink further will alternate modes of tourism be seriously considered. Still higher fuel costs may force a change as the hotels using heavy technology become steadily more impractical. As in the Bahamas, Jamaica, Puerto Rico, and elsewhere, governments will be pressured to take over failing hotels to protect the jobs of nationals. Massive overseas assistance, such as the World Bank is organizing through its Caribbean Group for Economic Co-operation, may allow some properties to continue.*

Tourism has already become the "sick man" of Caribbean economies, kept alive primarily by modern support systems controlled overseas. However, it is not dependence on overseas markets that has failed the region, but catering to the escapist urge. For in this way the region abets America's wasteful aggrandizement of global resources. The region cannot hope to use tourism in its own interest until it begins to market an indigenous mode and to align its marketing with those forces in American life that seek to reduce the prepossession of industrial values within that country itself. For the Caribbean, bound to redress a history of metropolitan privilege, tourism must become an act of intervention in the debate over the American future.

NOTES

1. *Report of Tourist Travel to the Caribbean* (New York: Caribbean Tourism Assn., annual reports from 1970 through 1976); Theodore Stanger and Martin Baron, "Stability in Caribbean Depends on U.S. Largesse," The Miami *Herald,* 27 January 1978.

2. Remarks of Moses Matalon on the state of Jamaican tourism at First Specialized Conference on Caribbean Tourism, Caracas, January 1975, organized by Caribbean Tourism Research Center. Matalon spoke as Chairman of Jamaica's Urban Development Corp., principle architect of the nation's tourism policy.

3. U.S., Department of State, Irving G. Tragen, *Case Study: Tourism: Resource for development. A Study of Benefits to Developing Countries from Investments in Hotels and Motels* (Washington, D.C., Department of State, 1968–1969), p. 6.

4. Pan American World Airways public relations handout, "How the Tourist Dollar is Spent" (Miami, n.d.), p. 1.

5. Ibid.

6. O.A.S., *Tourism in the Americas: Road to a Better Life* (Washington, D.C.: Organization of American States, 1973), p. 1.

7. World Bank, *Tourism Sector Working Paper* (Washington, D.C.: International Bank for Reconstruction & Development, 1972), p. 17.

8. Frank F. Taylor, "The Tourist Industry in Jamaica, 1919 to 1939," *Social and Economic Studies* 22, no. 2 (1973): 212.

9. Peter Goffe, "Development Potential of International Tourism; How Developing Nations View Tourism," *The Cornell Hotel and Restaurant Assn. Quarterly,* November 1975, p. 27.

10. Ibid.

11. H. Zinder and Associates, *The Future of Tourism in the Eastern Caribbean* (Washington, D.C.: H. Zinder and Associates, Inc., 1969).

---

*Ironically, the bank itself in mid-1978 was preparing to get out of tourism lending as part of a shift toward rural and agricultural development and small-scale industrial projects.

12. Kari Levitt and Iqbal Gulati, "Income Effect of Tourist Spending; Mystification Multiplied: A Critical Comment on the Zinder Report," *Social and Economic Studies* 19, no. 3 (1970): 326.

13. The attitude was typified in remarks to trade professionals by the president of Inter-Continental Hotels who, while outlining industry criteria for evaluating overseas hotel sites, relegated his comments on local sensibilities to this: that for tourists especially, the hotel should "develop the country's native themes in at least one restaurant," then concluding that "[hotel] operators gain a broad viewpoint of the world and its people. They help develop better understanding among nations, and they gain the satisfaction of helping under-developed nations get on their feet financially."

14. See also "World Airlines Plunge Deeper Into Hotel Business," *Service World* (London) (September–October 1974), for a recapitulation of airlines and their subsidiary properties.

15. See report of the conference, *The Role of Tourism in Caribbean Development: Report of Ecumenical Consultation* (Barbados: Christian Action for Development in the Eastern Caribbean, 1971).

16. Gordon K. Lewis, *Notes on the Puerto Rico Revolution,* (New York: Monthly Review Press, 1974) pp. 69–70.

17. Robert W. Stock, "Of Tourism and the Soul: The Caribbean Dilemma," The New York *Times,* 13 June 1976, p. 18.

18. John M. Bryden, *Tourism & Development: A Case Study of the Commonwealth Caribbean* (London: Cambridge University Press, 1973), p. 221.

19. Ibid., p. 132.

20. Ibid., p. 221.

21. Ibid.

22. Patrick Arton, "The Challenge in the Caribbean," *Travel Trade,* June 19, 1972, p. 3.

23. Fred Ruoff, then in charge of Caribbean marketing for Hilton International, quoted in Joel A. Glass, "Chain Hoteliers Air Dismay Over Criticism in Caribbean," *Travel Weekly,* October 6, 1972, p. 1.

24. John Keller, President, Caribbean Holidays, New York, "Keller Blasts Caribbean Greed Merchants—Cites Cayman Islands as Good Tourism Example," press release by Michael Finn Associates, New York, November 19, 1975.

25. See, among writings of the author, Herbert Hiller, Introduction to Information Document, *Seminar "To Secure a Lasting Tourism,"* San Juan, Puerto Rico, January 6–9, 1972 (Washington, D.C.: Organization of American States, n.d.); and Herbert Hiller, "Industrialism, Tourism, Island Nations, and Changing Values," in *The Social and Economic Impact of Tourism on Pacific Communities,* ed. Bryan H. Farrell (Santa Cruz, California: Center for South Pacific Studies, University of California, July 1977), p. 115.

26. For typical academic discussions—and a good statement by the industry when among academics—see "Tourism," *Caribbean Issues* (St. Augustine, Trinidad) 2, no. 1 (April 1976).

27. "Tourism," op. cit.

28. Edwin Carrington and Byron Blake, among others, at the CARICOM Secretariat, have made studies on self-resouceful tourism. Sometimes these have received Caribbean-wide dissemination, as in the case of one that defined an overall scaled down secenario, presented at the Tourism Impact Seminar in the Bahamas, November 1975.

29. See, for example, paper by R. Bouret, p. 25 and comments of H. L. Hiller, p. 39 in *An Environmental Newsletter* (St. Thomas, V.I.) 2, no. 3 (October 1971).

30. Policy statement read at Caribbean Tourism Assn. Annual General Meeting, Port-au-Prince, Haiti, 1972, reprinted in *LKHH Accountant* (Philadelphia) 53, no. 4 (Winter 1974).

31. James F. Michell, Bequia, St. Vincent, May 3, 1975.

32. *The New Yorker,* February 27, 1978, p. 29.

33. H. Peter Gray, "Towards an Economic Analysis of Tourism Policy," *Social and Economic Studies:* 394.

34. J. Cameron Tudor, former Barbados High Commissioner to the United Kingdom, address to annual meeting of Caribbean Tourism Association, Barbados, September 11, 1975.

35. Donald E. Lundberg, *The Tourist Business* (Boston: Cahners Books, 1974), p. 218.

36. William Demas, "The Road to West Indian Nationhood," in *West Indian Nationhood and Caribbean Integration,* ed. David I. Mitchell (Barbados: CCC Publishing House, 1974), p. 10.

37. William Demas, "Development, Identity and Unity in the Caribbean," in *West Indian Nationhood and Caribbean Integration,* op. cit., p. 2.

38. Ibid.

39. Ibid.

6

The Multinational Corporations, External Control, and the Problem of Development: The Case of Trinidad and Tobago

Ken I. Boodhoo

INTRODUCTION

The multinational corporation (MNC) "is one of the most powerful impediments to Third World development" since it siphons off the natural wealth of developing countries to the metropole, "first as plunder and then in the more respectable form of dividends, fees, etc."[1] Thus, domestic development of Third World countries is sacrificed at the expense of Western industrial expansion. This chapter will analyze the implications of MNC activity for the development process with respect to the Caribbean, by examining MNC activity and attempted state control in Trinidad and Tobago.

MNC operations are guided by two basic principles. The first is centralized control by the metropole-based parent corporation, generally located in the United States. Secondly, such corporate integration and centralized decision making give rise to global maximization of profits.

The recent rise to independence of Third World states, particularly in the Caribbean, has generally led to conflict with MNCs. While independence bestows "legal" authority to control national destiny, Third World status connotes an underdeveloped nature of the state, especially in the economic sphere. The demand for economic development requires considerable local control over economic decision making which, in turn, conflicts with centralized decision making by the MNC. In most cases, global needs of a company conflict with development objectives of the state in which a subsidiary is located. Prime Minister Eric Williams of Trinidad notes that "decisions of these corporations . . . can make nonsense of economic plans in developing countries."[2] The rationale for controlling activities of the MNC within a host country, therefore, is not motivated purely by a desire to exercise sovereignty but, more fundamentally, lies in the promotion of the process of national development.

MNCs AND DEVELOPMENT

Since "development" is a normative term, it is not easily defined. Dudley Seers generalizes that the development process includes "the realization of the potential of human personality." At a more basic level, in terms of income distribution, he believes that enough food, a job, and equality all contribute to the realization of development and that if all three of these have improved, "then beyond doubt this has been a period of development for the country concerned."[3] If, however, the gap in income distribution widens and the level of employment decreases, even though the Gross National Product (GNP) and per capita income may have increased, the converse of development transpires and the process of underdevelopment accelerates. Increases in GNP and average per capita income are more directly related to growth than development. This distinction is summarized succinctly by Mahbub Haq:

> The most unforgivable sin of development planners is to become mesmerized by high growth rates in the Gross National Product and to forget the real objective of development. In country after country, economic growth is being accompanied by rising disparities. . . . economic growth has meant very little social justice. It has been accompanied by rising unemployment, worsening social services and increasing absolute and relative poverty.[4]

The primary developmental objective, he continues, must be a "selective attack on the worst forms of poverty." Rather than taking care of GNP and assuming this will take care of poverty, Haq concludes, "let us reverse this and take care of poverty, and this will take care of the GNP."[5]

Defenders of MNCs argue that their activities promote positive change in three major areas of Third World weakness: technology deficiency, foreign investment scarcity, and the balance of payments difficulties. Recent studies of MNCs, however, have not demonstrated that it is precisely in these three crucial areas of Third World economies that MNC operations have had implications for underdevelopment rather than development.[6]

An important factor contributing to economic development, the corporations claim, is their introduction of more efficient technology and management skills which allegedly create new productive facilities, increase output, and increase employment. The introduction of this technology, partly as a consequence of its efficiency, does increase output; however, such increased output in most cases is accompanied by reduced employment.

THE CASE OF TRINIDAD AND TOBAGO

The petroleum industry dominates the economy of Trinidad and Tobago and Texaco's operations stand supreme. More than 80 percent of total refining capacity and approximately 20 percent of crude production is owned by Texaco, with approximately 5 to 10 percent of the company's total assets invested in this subsidiary. In recent years, Shell Trinidad sold its assets to the state and was reorganized as the Trinidad Oil Company (TRINTOC), while British Petroleum's relatively minor operations in Trinidad were purchased in 1969 by the Trinidad Tesoro Company, a joint venture between the government of Trinidad and the Tesoro Petroleum Corporation of the United States. Each of these companies hold a one-third share in Trinidad Northern Areas Ltd. (TNA), an exploration and production company. AMOCO (Trinidad), an entirely foreign-owned subsidiary, is the most recent major oil company to operate in Trinidad and produces more than 50 percent of all crude. It is also involved in natural gas operations.

The industry's domination over Trinidad's economy has continued to increase in recent years, with petroleum accounting for 87.7 percent of all exports in 1975 and 90.2 percent in 1976. Petroleum dominates imports as well, since processing of imported crude is a major part of the industry. Petroleum imports as a proportion of total imports increased from 50.6 percent in 1975 to 57.3 percent in 1976. Petroleum's contribution to Gross Domestic Product (GDP), particularly in the past five years, is most significant, growing at an estimated rate of 245 percent between 1970 and 1976 and increasing its contribution to the GDP from 22 percent in 1970 to 48 percent in 1976.[7]

The industry's steady growth has not been matched by employment figures in the industry, however, as Table 6.1 indicates. On a percentage basis, between 1960 and 1968 the value of output in the petroleum sector increased by 88 percent, while employment in the industry fell by 24 percent.

Since 1968, the value of output in the petroleum industry has increased about tenfold, yet employment has continued to decrease and was less than 10,000 in 1977. Texaco Trinidad's employment fell from 6,830 in 1974 to 6,360 in 1977. Unemployment in Trinidad increased from 13.0 percent in 1971 to 15.2 percent in 1975, with an increase in the labor force of 25,000 or 8 percent during that period.[8] Thus, while

TABLE 6.1: Exports and Employment in the Petroleum Industry

Year	Petroleum Exports (millions of TT dollars)	Employment in the Petroleum Industry
1960	392.91	15,540
1963	525.91	14,200
1966	580.95	14,300
1968	737.83	11,800

Source: Overseas Trade Reports (Trinidad: Central Statistical Office, 1961–68); Annual Statistical Digest (Trinidad: Central Statistical Office, 1960–68).

the annual growth rate of GDP between 1970 and 1976 was a regional high of 23.1 percent, stimulated largely by the expansion of the petroleum sector, unemployment also increased, due primarily to weak linkages with other economic sectors.[9]

Necessarily, productivity of the petroleum worker has increased rapidly. In 1972 productivity was TT$24,350; in 1974 TT$73,619; and in 1977 TT$126,427.[10] While productivity between 1972 and 1974 increased by a little more than 200 percent, during the period 1974–77 this figure was 68 percent. Since wage rates between 1972 and 1974 increased by 24 percent, and a new wage rate is under arbitration, it is not surprising that the industry profits have skyrocketed. In 1972, Texaco (Trinidad) showed a net profit of TT$19.7 million; by 1974 this rose to TT$101.5 million, or an increase of 500 percent.[11] These figures reflect profits only in crude production.

The introduction of technology utilized by the MNC contributes further to widening the income distribution gap and consequently to inequality. A study of Mexico and Brazil—two countries where MNCs have been most active—demonstrates that, from

> 1950 to 1965 in Mexico, the ration of income of the richest 20% to the poorest 20% went from 10.1 to 17.1. . . . In Brazil from 1963 to 1973 the share of income of the richest 5% went from roughly 28 to 37%, while the share of some 40 million other Brazilian people (the poorest 40%) dropped from 10.6 to 8.1% of the nation's total output.[12]

Not only, therefore, is this technology displacing employment, but just as important, it also appears to contribute to inequality of income distribution and hence to inquality within the developing country.

MNCs present themselves as benevolent agencies for the introduction of much-needed investment capital in the capital deficient Third World. Initially, of course, the introduction of foreign investment stimulates development within such economies. Eventually, however, foreign investment changes from a stimulant to a retarding agent. It ceases being complementary to local factors and becomes competitive with them. Additionally, development is not stimulated when foreign investment dominates rather than advances local factors of production. The feed-milling industry in Trinidad is illustrative of this situation.

Originally, Trinidad's major feed-milling company was Trinidad Stock Feed Ltd., an entirely locally owned and controlled enterprise. Today, three additional and larger firms have loose associations with U.S. firms, while the largest three are entirely U.S. dominated. Local firms, as a consequence of external linkages, are increasingly dependent upon U.S. suppliers for raw materials. Indeed, some of these firms are not permitted to purchase on the cheaper open market.

The goals of foreign investment of the MNC, particularly profit maximization, may conflict with the development goals and policies of the state. At that point, foreign investment contributes to underdevelopment. Thus, while Shell and British Petroleum operated in Trinidad for close to half a century, their sudden decisions to phase out operations were motivated by increased profitability elsewhere—for example, the North Sea oil discoveries.

In the case of Trinidad,

> direct investment is centered in some of the more profitable sectors of the economy, investment income outflows are large, averaging TT$106.5m per annum between 1956 and 1967. . . . In only one year of the 1957–65 peak period of foreign investment did direct investment exceed income outflows. In that period direct investment averaged (TT) $85.7m per annum and outflows of investment income were 30% higher—at TT$111.2m per annum. In the post-peak period (1966 and 1967) income outflows were over two and a half times the capital inflows. This is more indicative of the gap that is likely to persist in the near future.[13]

As a consequence of the foregoing, foreign investment over a long period, without any significant degree of local control, becomes a dubious factor in the promotion of national economic development.

Finally, there is the question of the balance of payments input of the MNC upon national economies: MNCs claim that they alleviate balance of payment deficits of their host countries through the finance capital they bring in addition to their production of items that were formerly imported.[14] However, historically, experiences with MNCs indicate that, particularly in the area of product pricing, with regard to both the inputs and the outputs, there are adverse implications for the host's balance of payments. Export restrictions placed by the parent companies, as is the case of Unilever regarding its Jamaica and Trinidad subsidiaries, have a similar adverse effect. When a subsidiary of an MNC exports to another subsidiary, in effect, what has really taken place is an intracompany transfer, with price not necessarily related to cost. By manipulating prices, the MNC is able to maximize profits if, for instance, export tariffs are high.

With regard to pricing within multinational corporations, Dudley Seers has written:

> many of the prices used by companies in drawing up accounts are meaningless, because transactions are between departments of the same company, or between closely associated companies . . . the price shown on export declarations, or quoted to tax officials, really . . . reflects primarily the company's preference as to where it wants to pay its taxes.[15]

A study of export pricing among MNCs in some selected Latin American states showed that 75 percent was sold to other subsidiaries of the same company. Most important, the firms "on the average underpriced their exports by some 40 percent relative to prices received by local firms."[16] Underpricing obviously reduced the level of export tax revenues, and does not contribute to a positive balance of payments situation.

In Trinidad, foreign crude petroleum accounts for 75 to 80 percent of total crude refined at Texaco (Trinidad's) plant. Texaco Inc. pays Texaco (Trinidad) a processing fee for each barrel of crude refined locally. This fee bears no relation to the value added. Indeed, it was deliberately reduced, permitting the local company to show operation cost losses, thereby reducing local taxes paid. In 1970, local refining costs per barrel were TT$.62, yet Texaco Inc. paid a processing "fee" of TT$.59.[17] Federated Chemicals Trinidad Ltd., as well, underpriced ammonia sold to its parent, W. R. Grace.

It is clear that the rhetoric of the MNC does not match the reality of its presence. Thus, whereas the MNC claims the stimulation of development, its practices usually lead to the reverse. Some controls on the MNCs' operations appear necessary.

The production of sugar is the most important agricultural activity in the Caribbean. Sugar's contribution to Trinidad's economy, in terms of exports—about 10 percent—is second only to petroleum. It, however, is the largest private employer of labor. Approximately 10,000 to 12,000 workers are employed on sugar estates. There are over 10,000 sugar cane farmers, a minority of whom are also sugar workers.* Caroni Ltd., for-

---

*Whereas local employment in sugar is high, it may be rightly argued that wages and working conditions are poor.

merly a wholly-owned subsidiary of the multinational Tate and Lyle Group of Companies, dominates the industry. It controls the majority of land and over 80 percent of milling facilities.*

Through Caroni Ltd., Tate and Lyle maintain linkages with other subsidiaries located both within and outside Trinidad. All these linkages have implications for the structure of marketing, pricing, and costs of the product, yet such factors are not controlled locally. Tate and Lyle, through Caroni Ltd., handles the transportation and marketing of the entire Trinidad sugar output. Shipping is carried on by Sugar Lines and Anchor Lines Ltd., both subsidiaries of Tate and Lyle. All of Trinidad's sugar sold on the preferential markets of the United Kingdom and Canada goes to either Tate and Lyle Refineries Ltd., or to Canada and Dominion Sugar Company Ltd., both subsidiaries of Tate and Lyle. Within Trinidad, too, the sugar industry is fully integrated. In 1965, Sugar Lines Terminals Ltd., a Tate and Lyle subsidiary, built bulk-loading facilities from which all export sugar is loaded. United Molasses Company, another subsidiary, buys its molasses from Caroni Ltd., yet it owns 20 percent of Caroni's shares.

In 1970, during a period of civil unrest, the state purchased 51 percent of Caroni's shares.† A vital aspect of this new arrangement was the question of the localization of decision making in the industry. The government claimed that its purchase of 51 percent of Caroni's shares transferred the center of decision making for the industry from Tate and Lyle's head offices in London to Trinidad.[18] However, this transfer is clouded by two related transfers.

Caroni Ltd. was never an autonomous enterprise. The company was a wholly-owned subsidiary of Tate and Lyle. It is essentially a plant. It is not a firm. The nature of multinational corporations like Tate and Lyle demands a total integration of worldwide operations with the center of decision making located in the metropolitcan country. By the government's purchase, then, of 51 percent of Caroni Ltd., the former is merely one shareholder out of many in the assets of a multinational enterprise —albeit the majority shareholder in one of its subsidiaries. And because fundamental decisions for the enterprise as a whole have always been made at the head office, it can be expected that these decisions will continue to be made at that center.

---

*Caroni's two minor competitors are state-owned Orange Grove National Sugar Company and the formerly foreign-owned Forres Park Ltd., recently purchased by the state.

†In 1975, during another period of unrest, the state increased its share participation to 55 percent.

Secondly, the linkage between Caroni Ltd. and the parent enterprise continued after the purchase of 51 percent shares by the negotiation of three agreements between Tate and Lyle and the Trinidad government concerning Caroni's operations. The first is a management contract, for Tate and Lyle's management of Caroni Ltd.[19] The second concerns a services and consultancy agreement by which Tate and Lyle in London oversees the day-to-day commercial negotiations, provides accountancy services in the United Kingdom, and other minor functions. The fee is approximately $216,000.[20] The third agreement is the purchasing and technical services agreement, at a fee of 5 percent of the cif value of order.

The result of these agreements, of the integrated nature of the operations of Tate and Lyle, is that 51 percent participation by the Trinidad government in Caroni Ltd. has not been sufficient to stimulate meaningful control over that enterprise.*

Attempts to promote national development of necessity demand some control over activities and policies guiding foreign investment within host nations. Such efforts are further hindered because much of the banking systems of small Third World countries are still dominated by foreign-owned banking MNCs, which themselves have close ties with industrial MNCs. Hence, these latter MNCs are able to borrow locally and repatriate capital without restrictions. The absence of local legislation to inhibit capital outflows permits reinvestment of profits elsewhere at higher returns. The balance of payments situation, then, may be exacerbated, not alleviated.

CONCLUSION

Some states, in their haste to "take over" foreign enterprises, almost unwittingly create new forms of external control, the most common of which is the device of the management contract. As the case of local ownership of the sugar industry of Trinidad demonstrates, ownership over the enterprise does not necessarily result in domestic control. It is recognized that such forms of local ownership may meet the emotional aspirations of the electorate and also of a government not concerned with effective control. In the absence of effective national or regional controls over MNC penetration, the development process appears retarded. This has inevitable implications for social and political stability in the Caribbean area.

---

*One may now rightly argue that Tate and Lyle is able to obtain a substantial annual sum of money from their operations without the risks of ownership.

NOTES

1. Richard Barnet and Ronald Mueller, " A Reporter at Large: Global Reach-1," *New Yorker*, 2 December 1974, p. 62; also see Ronald Mueller, "The Multinational Corporation and the Exercise of Power: Latin America," in *The New Sovereigns*, Abdul Aziz Said and Luiz Simmons (Englewood Cliffs, N.J.: Prentice-Hall, 1975), p. 155.

2. Speech by Dr. Eric Williams, United Nations Petroleum Seminar, *Nation*, Oil Supplement, 19 April 1968, pp. 6–7.

3. Dudley Seers, "The Meaning of Development," in *The Political Economy of Development and Underdevelopment*, ed. C. K. Wilber (New York: Random House, 1973), pp. 6–7.

4. Mahbub Haq, *The Poverty Curtain*, (New York: Columbia University Press, 1976), pp. 24–25.

5. Ibid., p. 35.

6. See Albert Hirschman, "How to Divest in Latin America, and Why," in *The Widening Gap*, ed. Barbara Ward (New York: Columbia University Press, 1971), pp. 252–274; Mueller, "Multinational Corporations," op. cit.; Ronald Mueller and Richard Barnet, *Global Reach* (New York: Simon and Schuster, 1974); and N. Girvan, *Foreign Capital and Economic Underdevelopment in Jamaica*, (Institute for Social and Economic Research, 1971).

7. Republic of Trinidad and Tobago, *Review of the Economy 1977* (Trinidad: Central Statistical Office, n.d.), pp. 22, 58–59.

8. Trinidad *Guardian*, 1 April 1978, p. 6; Inter American Development Bank, *Economic and Social Progress in Latin America, 1976 Report.* (Washington, D.C., 1977), p. 357.

9. *Review of the Economy 1977*, op. cit., esp. p. 14.

10. O. Baptiste, ed., *CRISIS* (Trinidad: Imprint Caribbean, 1976), p. 256. See also Trinidad *Guardian*, op. cit.

11. Ibid., p. 257.

12. As quoted by Mueller in "Multinational Corporation," op. cit., p. 62.

13. A. McIntyre and B. Watson, *Trinidad and Tobago*, Studies in Foreign Investment in the Commonwealth Caribbean, no. 1 (Jamaica)

14. Mueller, "Multinational Corporation," op. cit., p. 60.

15. Dudley Seers, "Big Companies and Small Countries: A Practical Proposal," *Kyklos* 16 (1963), fasc. 4:599–600.

16. Mueller C. K. Wilber ed., op. cit., p. 142.

17. Baptiste, op. cit., p. 258.

18. Editorial, Trinidad *Guardian*, 1 August 1970.

19. Ibid., 13 July 1971. Reputed to cost TT $200,000.

20. As reported in the *Cane Farmer*, July 1971, p. 236.

7

The New International Economic Order and the Caribbean: The External/Internal Nexus

Harald M. Sandstrom

INTRODUCTION

It is probably no exaggeration to label as a great debate the verbal joustings, official declarations, and frustrating negotiations that have been used to improve the position of the developing countries within the context of a New International Economic Order (NIEO). This debate has concentrated almost exclusively on external economic relations between North and South, rich and poor. Yet there is an important corollary to the NIEO-type restructuring of the international order, the New *Internal* Economic Order—decolonization of the economy, focusing especially on the restructing of plantation agriculture and the redistribution of wealth. These are the demands increasingly articulated by nationalist movements.

The organic relationship between these two NIEOs is the major concern of this chapter. This focus is sustained by two observations: (1) that with small nations, it is almost impossible to distinguish between external and internal economic relations; and (2) that the development process—however that concept is interpreted—so dominates the agendas of Third World nations that their foreign policies are bound to reflect that priority. These points, in turn, are buttressed by (1) the ubiquitous presence and enormous growth of multinational corporations (MNCs) in the Third World, resulting in such an interpenetration of domestic and international economies that traditional conceptions of sovereignty must be reexamined; and (2) the recent trend toward commodity cartelization, initiated by the dramatic success of the Organization of Petroleum Exporting Countries (OPEC) in quadrupling oil prices since 1973–74, ushering in an era of international cooperation among raw material exporters. Both MNCs and cartels—especially the International Bauxite Association (IBA)—are enormously important in Caribbean political economy. However, as they are dealt with elsewhere in this volume, this chapter will concentrate on selected aspects of Caribbean trade in the context of the twin NIEOs. We must first cover two pieces of essential background: (1) the origin and meaning of the New International Economic Order, and (2) dependency theory as the mode of analysis increasingly used by Third World scholars and political leaders.

Dignitas

In 1975, UN Secretary-General Kurt Waldheim argued that "the international system of economic and trade relations which was devised 30 years ago is now manifestly inadequate for the needs of the world community as a whole."[1] In 1974, the Sixth Special Session of the UN General Assembly issued a Declaration and Action Programme on the Establishment of a New International Order,[2] following increased Third World agitation for such action in the early 1970s. Against the backdrop of détente, the OPEC success, growing multipolarity in the world economy (Japan, West Germany), transition from commodity surpluses to shortages, and increasingly volatile internal situations, the leaders of the Third World decided to use their rising economic power in pursuit of both economic and political objectives. Among the major economic objectives are change in the developing countries' trade in primary products and manufactures, the latter having difficulty gaining access to the markets of the more developed countries; change in monetary and financial arrangements to accommodate Third World countries' need for resources and for frameworks to regulate their external debt; the access to and transfer of technology; and change in the primarily bipolar pattern of trade with former metropolitan countries. Seen as a whole, this constitutes major structural change by Third World countries. The proposed means include collective self-reliance, modeled on OPEC. The political objectives of Third World leaders focus on being treated as first-class members of the world order and gaining a greater decision-making role in the world economy.[3]

Writing before the expression "a New International Economic Order" had been coined, Wilson McWilliams came up with a perspective that, in view of recent developments, should have been given great attention.

> The index of political development is ... the *capacity to command dignity,*
> to escape the "cultural shame" of a people forced to change regardless

of their own will. The ability to command dignity is not simply the ability to command attention. . . . *Dignitas,* as the Romans knew, implies the ability to control in part the actions of others.[4]

This concept of *dignitas* is a one-word summary of what the NIEO is about.

Third World Dependency

Jagdish Bhagwati has pinned the label of "benign neglect" on the previous orthodoxy, according to which an invisible hand would see to it that all shared equally in the gains from trade. Otherwise known as the standard or diffusion model, this orthodoxy views underdevelopment as an original condition, sees a trickle effect development resulting from capital and modernizing moving from industrial centers to the Third World periphery, and welcomes import-substituting industrialization and regional integration in that periphery. And an expanding national bourgeoisie is seen as a leadership cadre capable of securing national development in this evolutionary fashion.[5]

In contrast, we now have a doctrine of "malign neglect" according to which relations between rich and poor nations are viewed as detrimental to the latter. Latin American and Caribbean dependency theory represents the most coherent and elaborate version of this proposition. Underdevelopment, far from being an original condition, is seen as created and maintained by the very international capitalist system seen by diffusionists as the source of escape from underdevelopment. The importation of so-called modernizing ideas is seen as cultural imperialism —the imposition of alien tastes and life styles. Import substitution and regional integration are viewed as new and more efficient ways through which the international capitalist system can exploit the Third World. The prime beneficiaries of these policies are huge multinational corporations, who send Third World countries into deeper and deeper trouble by using such methods as repatriation of profits, debt service, costs of patents, and technical services. There is little doubt that the dominant thrust in dependency literature is that the litmus test of "full-fledged" dependency theory is its emphasis on the interrelationship of foreign economic control (mostly referred to by the more emotionally satisfying term "imperialism") which promotes class dominance by an indigenous clientele bourgeoisie, which facilitates external control for the price of being maintained in power.[6] We cannot emphasize this point enough. The external/internal nexus of the NIEO dovetails exactly with the imperialism/class dominance thrust of dependency theory.

THE NIEO AND CARIBBEAN POLITICAL ECONOMY

Regardless of the truth of dependency theory, the point about the foreign economic control and class dominance relationship is particularly important, as it clearly establishes that dependency theory and its close West Indian relative, Black Power ideology, are theories of revolution.[7] Throughout the Caribbean, strong and growing opposition movements are embracing these theories and demanding control of the "commanding heights" of their economies in order to rid their nations of what they perceive as foreign exploitation and government complicity.[8] Governments have responded variously. Forbes Burnham of Guyana and Michael Manley of Jamaica have employed strategies of cooptation, Burnham placing himself at the head of Guyana's Black Power movement and Manley adopting the slogans and symbols of the radical opposition. In Trinidad, Dr. Eric Williams has resorted to some repression in the face of an election boycott, a resulting constitutional crisis, and continual rumbling from a Black Power opposition still not reconciled to having been denied the fruits of victory in the near-successful February 1970 uprising. With such pressures, the area's leaders come before the forums of international economic negotiations designed to restructure the international order with an important "or else" to buttress their negotiating positions.

The Lomé Convention

With this background in mind, let us look at the Lomé Convention, at which representatives from forty-six African, Caribbean, and Pacific (ACP) countries met with representatives from the European Economic Community (EEC) to hammer out a new pattern of economic relations. Their agreement, signed in February 1975, is considered a first step in the direction of implementing a new international economic order, and was hailed as "revolutionary," "a turning point in history," "a new relationship of solidarity," and "a New Marshall Plan"—except this one negotiated new links "with all participants on an equal footing."[9] (Dignitas?) In the face of this euphoria and excitement, it is necessary to pin down, in matters relating to the Caribbean, precisely what was achieved. First, the convention does not apply to the whole Caribbean, only to four independent members of the Caribbean Community (CARICOM)—Barbados, Guyana, Jamaica, and Trinidad and Tobago. One official account summarizes the main features of the convention as follows: "free access to the biggest market in the world; trade promotion measures; industrialization incentives; financial and technical assistance for infrastructure, the productive sector and training, the system of stabilization of export earnings, an innovation in international trade relations which is to act as a guarantee against bad years for commodity-exporting countries."[10] This certainly sounds like a substantial accomplishment.

Two sober analyses, however, conclude that the Lomé Convention will not contribute significantly to Caribbean development. Anthony Gonzales indicates that the agreement on sugar represents a comedown from the former Commonwealth sugar agreement, under which the Caribbean had a 50 percent quota compared to the 31 percent under Lomé. Moreover, diversification of market structure—that is, selling to a larger number of buyers—was achieved at the expense of a basic price for sugar that did not meet the rather high cost of West Indian production. Further still, market diversification was achieved at the expense of placing limits on diversification of agriculture: the land cannot be freed for alternative production (as it needs to be in view of large-scale food imports at rising prices) if you tie it down to producing cash crops against a quota. Such commodity arrangements (including one on bananas) were therefore not undertaken because of the favorable terms; they were concluded because of the high unemployment in banana and sugar cultivation and the need to have guaranteed short-run income to ease that unemployment.[11]

Why, then, is the Lomé Convention important? A major analytical study contains the answer right in the title: "The Lomé Convention: Inching towards Interdependence." The rather meager economic benefits are less significant than the political, organizational, and psychological impact.[12] A substantial portion of the Third World, including the Commonwealth Caribbean nations, displayed a remarkable unity in their common negotiating front and the experience was apparently a heady one, generating confidence that dependence can be negotiated into interdependence.

Dependence in trade constitutes an important aspect of the larger dependency syndrome. The question is whether significant exports in more than one commodity exist, the costs of production, the kinds of marketing arrangements (diversified or not?), whether preferential shelter in the metropolitan market (for example, sugar in the EEC) is required, and the level of imports: food, manufactured goods, or both? Much of this is affected by the size of the economy. If the domestic market is small, production cannot benefit from economies of scale, unless regional integration is pursued, or unless there is specialization in a small number of commodities for the world market. The latter was, of course, the pattern brought about through colonialism. Specialization requires reliance on foreign demand (over which there is little control) in order to gain the resources to purchase the products that must be imported. Small economies, therefore, became much more heavily reliant on international trade than larger economies and consequently more dependent on "decisions and tastes of foreign consumers and producers, and on foreign technology and technical change."[13] Size also makes it hard to change production structures and to pursue self-generated development. Furthermore, technology available from the more industrialized states tends to require large-scale production in order to become efficient, and is therefore frequently inappropriate for small economies.[14] One final difficulty is the pattern of protection in the export markets that limit access for Third World light manufactured goods and processed agricultural goods. Given the other constraints on small economies, such tariff structures provide further impetus to continue a well-established specialization in agricultural goods or raw materials.

This syndrome helps explain why the Lomé sugar arrangement reinforces dependence, though access to the ECC market for Third World manufactured goods counterbalances that dependence somewhat. The above discussion also provides a theoretical background for understanding why Caribbean trade patterns tend to perpetuate dependence, for while Caribbean economies do not rely exclusively on one crop, they are heavily concentrated on one major commodity (see Table 7.1). All this means that Caribbean economies remain relatively vulnerable to fluctuations in world market price and world demand. Much of that market and demand is provided by the United States, whose market size and proximity give it a considerable edge over other would-be trading partners. Indeed, we find that over half of the countries—Costa Rica, Dominican Republic, El Salvador, Guatemala, Honduras, Nicaragua, Panama (though her pattern changes from 1974 on) Trinidad and Tobago, and Venezuela (and discounting Cuba because of its special relationship with the USSR)—rely extremely heavily upon the United States as purchaser of their major commodity, while the figures are not nearly as heavy, though still quite substantial, for U.S. exports of machinery and transport equipment to the Caribbean. The relative share accounted for by the major import and export appears to be remarkably stable over the decade.[15]

Diversification of market structure was achieved at the expense of low return (though a stable and certain return) for certain key commodity exports. This suggests that market diversification is a matter of considerable priority to Third World nations, presumably because greater diversity of markets reduces reliance (dependence?) on any one trading partner. It is presumed further that such reduced reliance or dependence is desirable in order to, inter alia, maximize flexibility and minimize vulnerability to politically inspired boycotts and embargoes, such as the one the United States implemented against Cuba. It appears that if diver-

TABLE 7.1: Major Export as Proportion of Total Export (in percentage)

	1970	1971	1972	1973	1974	1975	1976	Export
Barbados	37.1	32.8	32.0	31.1	30.2	43.8	26.5	sugar
Colombia	60.1	53.5	44.0	47.1	38.5	37.2	49.0	coffee
Costa Rica	31.6	26.3	27.7	27.2	28.3	19.6	27.6	coffee
Cuba (N.A.)								
Dominican Republic	44.4	57.2	48.3	44.7	53.4	64.5	37.5	sugar
El Salvador	51.1	43.6	43.1	43.7	41.5	32.7	52.0	coffee
Guatemala	34.4	33.7	31.5	32.9	30.0	25.9	31.2	coffee
Guyana	28.4	27.0	33.6	30.4	48.5	50.2	34.0	sugar
	34.4	32.1	33.5	36.8	25.4	23.7	33.8	bauxite
Haiti	34.9	41.4	37.9	38.4	25.4	23.7	33.8	coffee
Honduras	14.2	11.9	12.9	18.2	16.2	19.4	25.5	coffee
Jamaica	44.6	36.8	39.9	43.9	48.3	46.8	41.2	alumina
Mexico	2.0	2.0	1.2	1.0	4.0	15.0	16.3	petrol.
	6.0	6.7	6.6	5.4	7.6	5.5	.5	sugar
	6.1	5.3	5.0	6.9	5.1	6.3	9.8	coffee
Netherlands Antilles	96.4	94.5	91.2	87.0	80.2	94.1	88.8	petrol.
Nicaragua	17.9	15.6	13.2	15.8	12.1	12.6	22.0	coffee
Panama	19.4	25.1	17.6	16.9	41.0	45.0	28.0	refined petrol
Surinam	41.4	46.7	48.8	45.0	35.5	42.8	—	alumina
Trinidad and Tobago	77.3	77.1	77.6	81.4	86.1	86.7	91.0	petrol.
Venezuela	90.2	92.2	91.3	88.6	95.1	94.5	94.2	petrol.

Source: International Monetary Fund, *International Financial Statistics*, January-April 1978 (Washington, D.C., 1978). Calculated from the raw data.

sification of trade partners has been an objective for the Caribbean nations in the years from 1967 to 1976, it has been an elusive target.

One final point—Caribbean leaders such as P.J. Patterson, Jamaican minister of industry, trade and tourism, have been in the forefront of the Third World push for indexing the price of primary products to the average price of manufactured goods so that they may rise commensurately. This argument is premised on declining terms of trade for primary products relative to manufactured goods. Yet recent evidence strongly suggests that this premise is invalid. While Stauffer supports the theory, Johnson and Bhagwati cast doubt upon it, Powelson is emphatic in his rejection, and Walsh points to the fallacies of the UN measures usually cited by indexation proponents, and concludes that the case for indexation is less than convincing.[16] It would seem that the time has come for Caribbean leaders to assess this new evidence and to assure themselves that they are not undermining their credibility by rhetorical repetition of the indexation demand.

CONCLUSION

This chapter attempts to show, through a blend of theory and application, the internal and external linkages of the twin NIEOs in the Caribbean. Caribbean trade problems tend to demonstrate the difficulty of breaking dependency patterns. Dependency theory is becoming prevalent as a mode of analysis within the Caribbean, *dignitas* is a major goal pursued in international negotiations and confrontations, and primary product producers are making common cause in Lomé-type conventions and in cartels. What implications can we draw from all this for international relations in the Caribbean?

There appears to be cause for gloom. Whatever the objective merits of dependency theory and Black Power ideology—and Third World and metropolitan scholars have a great deal of trouble trusting each other's objectivity in such matters—it seems abundantly clear that these revolutionary critiques of the prevailing order voice a theme with deep resonance in Caribbean societies. As area political leaders face increasing pressure from below, they cannot be ignored: they will be projected onto the international stage in order to promote legitimacy back home. The NIEO has a solid political home base. It will not go away. Nor will it necessarily assure solidarity among Caribbean nations, as witness the prediction by the Economist Intelligence Unit that the Caribbean Common Market will not survive 1978.[17] It is hoped that the peoples of the Caribbean will be able to deal with each other with a common understanding that political systems with high dependence on energy and resources tend to become increasingly conflict prone in times of scarcity, and with the common realization that restructuring the area's "plantation societies" into a new internal economic order will require extreme sensitivity on all parts. The twin NIEOs contain volatile issues, and they will shape Caribbean international relations for the foreseeable future.

NOTES

1. *Reshaping the International Order: A Report to the Club of Rome,* Jan Tinbergen, coordinator (New York: E. P. Dutton, 1976), p. 9.

2. Reprinted in Guy F. Erb and Valeriana Kallab, eds., *Beyond Dependency: The Developing World Speaks Out,* (New York: Praeger Publishers, (1975), pp. 185–202.

3. The foregoing has been drawn from Gamani Corea, "North-South Dialogue at the United Nations: UNCTAD and the New International Economic Order," *International Affairs* (London) 53 (1977): 178–79, and the following works by prolific NIEO analyst C. Fred Bergsten: "Introduction" and "The International Economic Framework to 1980," in *Toward a New International Economic Order: Selected Papers of C. Fred Bergsten, 1972–1974* (Lexington, Mass.: D.C. Heath, 1975), pp. xiii, [3]-4, 11; his contribution to panel discussion, and his "Access to Supplies and the New International Order," in *The International Economic Order: The North-South Debate,* ed. Jagdish N. Bhagwati (Cambridge, Mass.: The MIT Press, 1977), pp. 199, 347. It is worth noting that if the NIEO depends in part on détente, as Bergsten suggests, it may be facing difficulties as the cold war appears to be picking up over Angola; Zaire and Shaba; and Ethiopia and Somaliland.

4. Wilson C. McWilliams, "The Developing Nations and the International Order," in *Garrisons and Government: Politics and the Military in New States,* ed. Wilson C. McWilliams (San Francisco: Chandler, 1967), pp. 307–8, emphasis in original. On the concept of dignity, McWilliams cites R. E. Gahringer, "On the Moral Importance of Status and Position," *Ethics* 67 (1957): 200–202; on the concept of cultural shame, Pierre van den Berghe, *Caneville: The Social Structure of a South African Town* (Middletown, Conn.: Wesleyan University Press, 1963), pp. 46–59. For a similar perspective, see *Reshaping the International Order,* op. cit.

5. Bhagwati, *The New,* op. cit., p. 2, and Harald M. Sandstrom, chapter on "Diffusion Theory" in "West Indian and Latin American Dependency Theories: A Comparative Study" (Ph.D. diss., University of Pennsylvania, 1975).

6. Bhagwati, op. cit., and Sandstrom, op. cit., chapter on "Latin American Dependency Theory." While international relations literature for a long time remained insensitive to the importance of dependency theory, some excellent and quite sensitive work has been published recently. See especially the outstanding collection of essays, edited and most competently commented upon by James A. Caporaso in the Winter 1978 number of *International Organization* (32:1) entitled "Dependence and Dependency in the Global System."

7. For further elaboration, see Sandstrom, op. cit., "Introduction" and "Conclusion."

8. See, for instance, the major article by Clive Thomas on "Guyanese Sugar: Why We Must Nationalize," *Caribbean Contact,* August 1975, pp. 14–15. Significantly, it is followed by an article about Guyanese Prime Minister Forbes Burnham calling for a Socialist Caribbean.

9. Hans-Joerg Geiser, "The Lomé Convention and Caribbean Integration: A First Assessment," *Revista/Review Interamericana* 6 (Spring 1976): 24; Marion Bywater, "The Lomé Convention: Community Concludes 'Historic and Revolutionary' Trade and Aid Pact With 46 Developing Countries," *European Community,* no. 184 (March 1975), p. 8.

10. *Ninth General Report on the Activities of the European Communities in 1975* (Brussels and Luxembourg, February 1976, #474), p. 262.

11. See Anthony Gonzales, "International Economic Relations of the Caribbean. Trade Strategies of the Commonwealth Caribbean in a Changing World Economic Order: Special Reference to the Lomé Convention and Caribbean Economic Integration," in *The Caribbean Yearbook of International Relations, 1975,* ed. Leslie F. Manigat (Groningen, The Netherlands: Sijthoff & Noordhoff, 1976), pp. 357, 367.

12. Isebill V. Gruhn, "The Lomé Convention: Inching Towards Interdependence," *International Organization* 30 (1976): #241–62.

13. The foregoing was heavily dependent on import of ideas from William G. Demas, "How to be Independent," *Caribbean Review,* October–November–December 1974, p. 11, and Norman Girvan, "The Development of Dependency Economics in the Caribbean and Latin America: Review and Comparison," *Social and Economic Studies* 22 (1973): 6

14. On this point, see E. F. Schumacher's important work, *Small is Beautiful: Economics as if People Mattered* (New York: Harper & Row, 1973).

15. Data from U.S., Bureau of the Census, *U.S. General Imports, World Areas by Schedule A Commodity Groupings,* Report FT 155, Annuals 1967–76, and *U.S. Exports, World Area by Schedule B Commodity Groupings,* Robert FT 455, Annuals 1967–76 (Washington, D.C.: US Government Printing Office).

16. See Robert B. Stauffer, *Nation-Building in a Global Economy: The Role of the Multinational Corporation,* vol. 4, no. 01–039 1973, p. 39; fn. 6, Harry G. Johnson, "Commodities: Less Developed Countries' Demands and Developed Countries' Responses," in *The New International Economic Order & The North-South Debate,* ed. Jagdish N. Bhagwati (Cambridge, Mass.: The MIT Press, 1977), pp. 240–51, followed by "Comment" by I.M.D. Little, pp. 252–53; and Ghagwati's own comment, p. 9 and p. 21 n. 7, citing Ian Little, "Economic Relations with the Third World—Old Myths and New Prospects," *Scottish Journal of Political Economy,* November 1975, p. 227; John P. Powelson, "The Strange Persistence of the 'Terms of Trade,' " *Inter-American Economic Affairs* 30 (Spring 1977): 17; and James I. Walsh, "Can Indexation Help Chronic Trade Deficits?," *Inter-American Economic Affairs* 28 (Winter 1974): 96.

17. *Quarterly Economic Review of The West Indies, Belize, Bahamas, Bermuda, Guyana,* 1st Quarter 1978, p. 2.

8

The Caribbean and the Law of the Sea: New Occasion for Discord

Judith Ewell

In 1967, the United Nations convoked a new Law of the Sea Conference in order to write a modern and comprehensive international treaty on maritime law.[1] Rapid improvements in the technology of offshore oil drilling and deep sea mining and increased competition in the harvesting of fish and crustaceans had prompted nations to regard the seas as sources of wealth. Existing international law, largely written by great maritime nations such as the United States and Great Britain, had treated the seas only as passageways, a concept that inadequately served the new situation. Rich and poor nations debated treaty language for over a decade in the United Nations without reaching agreement on laws for resource exploitation. Developing nations at the same time competed with one another for the control of maritime resources in their regions. The Caribbean, a semienclosed sea bordered by eighteen sovereign states and twenty-nine territories that have varying degrees of autonomy, became an especially sensitive area.[2] Regional rivalries, unsettled land boundaries, ideological conflicts, domestic tensions, and strained relations between mainland countries and their island dependencies caused nations to be obdurate on maritime delimitations; in effect, they extended their existing disagreements into the sea.

Most of the resources in the Caribbean, both real and projected, lie close to the mainland, some islands, and banks. Consequently, conflicts between nations most often concern delimitation of the territorial seas, recently extended from three miles to twelve. Some of the issues that must be resolved include how to divide territorial seas in shared bays, the amount of territorial seas to be allotted to an island that lies within the territorial sea of another state, the extent of the territorial sea that an

81

archipelago may claim, the division of claims to the seas that wash upon disputed land, and the readjustment of maritime boundaries when the shoreline, or base line, has shifted. Obviously, these questions do not necessarily affect all states equally. The issues have been and will continue to be negotiated bilaterally and will offer few incentives to develop regional agreements on resource sharing.

Some of the oldest and most bitter disputes in the Caribbean involve countries located on the southern rim. Originating in the inaccurately drawn boundaries of the Spanish colonial period and intensified by prospects of offshore oil, conflicts between Venezuela and her neighbors have multiplied.

The Gulf of Venezuela is bounded on the east by Venezuela's Paraguaná Peninsula, on the south by the Strait of Tablazo leading into Lake Maracaibo, and on the west by the Guajira Peninsula, where the boundary between Colombia and Venezuela has been drawn. On the north, the tiny uninhabited archipelago of Los Monjes, only nineteen miles from the Colombian section of the Guajira, guards the entrance to the Gulf. The boundary line and the ownership of the islands had long been contested, although Colombia's cession of the archipelago to Venezuela in 1952 temporarily ended the controversy.[3] In 1952, however, both Venezuela and Colombia claimed only three miles of territorial sea and had expressed little interest in exploiting the offshore areas of the gulf.[4] Venezuela unilaterally extended her territorial seas to twelve miles in 1956, but Colombia waited until 1970 to do so. The changes in maritime jurisdiction reflected both changes in international law and Colombia's relatively recent effort to obtain a share of the offshore petroleum in the region.

Two legal issues have been at stake in the gulf. First—and simplest —Venezuela has argued that Los Monjes is entitled to twelve miles of territorial sea; Colombia protested that uninhabited islands were not entitled to such rights. If the islands receive a territorial sea within the nineteen-mile strip that separates them from Colombia, Colombia's jurisdiction would be reduced to a point equidistant from both coasts, or nine and one-half miles.[5] Second—and more important—Colombia has claimed that her 6 percent of coastline along the gulf entitles her to an equivalent share of the territorial seas in the gulf. Venezuela refuses to acknowledge the claim. When Venezuela signed the Geneva Convention on the Territorial Sea and the Contiguous Zone in 1961, she specifically rejected the principle that shared bodies of water should be divided by a line equidistant from both boasts. Colombia's claim asserts the equidistance principle, but Venezuela counters that historically she has exercised jurisdiction and sovereignity over the entire gulf and should continue to do so.[6]

Negotiations between Venezuela and Colombia on the gulf issues became particularly stormy in the 1970s and have been made even more so by the sensitivity of the issue in domestic politics. For example, in 1974 a group of Venezuelan retired military officers issued a manifesto insisting that Venezuela not cede "one square millimeter of land or sea beyond Castilletes."[7] Colombian President Alfonso López Michelsen subsequently suggested in 1975 that the gulf be denoted a historic bay under the ownership of Venezuela and Colombia.[8] Venezuela was cool to the compromise and refused to discuss cooperative management of the gulf's resources until after the delimitation of territorial waters had been decided.[9]

Venezuela also has a long-standing dispute with Guyana, located on her eastern frontier. Citing Spanish colonial sources, Venezuela claims that her boundary extends to the Essequibo River, about 160 miles south of the present border. If honored, Venezuela's claim would deprive Guyana of about three-fifths of her coastline and 60,000 square miles of territory. The continental shelf area in the disputed region reaches to 90 miles in some areas and contains valuable bauxite deposits; the shrimp grounds off the coast are also rich, and there is a good possibility that offshore oil deposits exist. Venezuela had accepted the 1899 arbitration of the boundary until 1962, when she declared the arbitration decision to be null and void.[10] Then, on the eve of Guyanan independence in 1966, Venezuela, Great Britain, and Guyana agreed to a new commission that would adjudicate the disputed boundary. The work of the commission was to be secret, and disputes were to cease until a decision was reached.

In the midst of a hotly contested presidential election in 1968, however, the Venezuelan government violated the 1966 agreement by claiming the territorial seas of the disputed territory. Concern for offshore resources as well as domestic politics prompted the gesture, and Venezuelan spokesmen stated that the move was intended "to take concrete steps of dominion in relation . . . to the oil concessions that the State of Guyana have conceded in this zone."[11] Guyanna Prime Minister Forbes Burnham deplored Venezuela's bad faith in the boundary negotiations and rejected the neighboring state's claim.[12] In 1970, the two nations signed the Protocol of Port-of-Spain, and agreed to eschew further territorial claims for twelve years.

Venezuela has used historic precedent and Spanish boundary lines to bolster her claim to jurisdiction in the Gulf of Venezuela and the Guyana territory. Looking to the north and northeast, however, Venezuelan spokesmen have argued on the basis of ecological and geological unity of the Venezuelan mainland, adjoining islands, shelves, and archipelagoes.[13] Great Britain accepted the ecological arguments in the

Gulf of Paria Treaty in 1942 and Venezuela received about two-thirds of the shelf in the gulf that faces Trinidad-Tobago; the equidistance principle, specifically rejected by Venezuela in 1961, was not evoked in 1952. The settlement satisfied the Venezuelan government and was not renegotiated in 1956 when Venezuela extended her territorial seas to twelve miles. The 1956 law did, however, broaden Venezuela's interpretation of "ecological unity" when it asserted that "channels, depressions or irregularities in the seabed of the continental shelf shall not constitute a break in the continuity of the shelf."[14]

Nature has provided yet another opportunity to disagree on the Gulf of Paria. The boundary line fixed by the language of the 1942 treaty and that indicated by more recent hydrographic charts are different. Venezuela's coastline in the western channel and Serpent's Mouth is composed of mud flats, which have been moving seaward. The base line from which Venezuela's territorial waters have been measured has thus moved closer to Trinidad, with the result that the territorial seas of the two countries now overlap in one small area.[15] Disputes over fishing rights and jurisdiction over three small islands in the gulf have disturbed Trinidadian-Venezuelan relations in the 1970s.[16] Eric Williams, prime minister of Trinidad-Tobago, called for a special regime for the Gulf of Paria at the Law of the Sea Conference in Caracas in 1974. Venezuelan spokesmen responded to Williams's proposal for regional management no more enthusiastically than they had to Colombia's similar suggestion for the Gulf of Venezuela.[17] Logically, Venezuela can see no benefits in surrendering resource rights in either gulf to regional or binational management.

Venezuelans have also remarked on the ecological unity of the Venezuelan mainland and the chain of archipelagoes to the north "only interrupted in the section in which Aruba, Bonaire, and Curacao are located."[18] A specific problem to be resolved is the division of the continental shelf between Venezuela and the Netherlands Antilles. The shelf drops off drastically into several deep basins, but Venezuela does not recognize that such channels constitute limits to her continental shelf. Holland and Venezuela have discussed the delimitation of the shelf several times, but have been slow to resolve the question.

As long as the Netherlands maintains control of the Antilles and does not extend her territorial seas beyond 3 miles, the territorial seas between Venezuela and the islands need not be negotiated. If and when Holland (or an independent Antillian government) extends the territorial seas to 12 miles, the 15-mile-wide strip of water between Aruba and Venezuela could be difficult to adjudicate. Venezuela probably would not voluntarily accept a reduction of her seas to the 7½ miles that the equidistance principle requires.

Future agreement between Venezuela and the islands on maritime issues will probably depend on domestic politics in the independent Antilles. When The Hague grants independence to the Antilles, Venezuela expects that the islands will be drawn automatically into her orbit. Both Holland and the island elite would in fact like to see Venezuela assume responsibility for the economic and military protection of the islands.[19] Island nationalists object to the possibility of a Venezuelan protectorate and would be less likely to try to placate Venezuela in maritime negotiations.[20]

Along the western rim of the Caribbean, the most serious conflict over sea issues is that between Guatemala and Belize, formerly British Honduras. Like some of the Venezuelan disputes, this one originated in vague concessions dating from the Spanish colonial period. Guatemala asserts that the British never had legal sovereignty over the area, but only began to press the issue when Great Britain granted Belize internal self-government in 1964, with full independence to follow.[21] Of course, if Guatemalan claims to all of Belize succeed, the issue of the division of waters between them will be moot.

If, as seems more likely, the two states continue to exist as neighbors, Guatemala has considerable incentive to press her claim to the Amatique Bay, which is located off the Gulf of Honduras and divided by the boundary between Belize and Guatemala. Belize has a total Caribbean coastline of 200 miles, while Guatemala has only 70. The barrier reef off Belize's coast, the world's second largest, is a rich fishing ground. Furthermore, offshore areas promise to yield oil, and several oil companies hold exploration licenses for the Belize shelf, where Exxon had begun drilling by 1977.[22] Great Britain further complicated the relations between the two states by her efforts to guarantee Belize's independence through agreements negotiated with Guatemala in order to avoid a commitment of armed forces to the new nation. In January 1978, journalists in Belize revealed that Great Britain had been discussing the cession of an oil-rich corridor on Amatique Bay to Guatemala in exchange for assurances that the latter country would not invade Belize. Publicity given the discussions between Guatemala and Great Britain probably forestalled the cession and surely aroused suspicions of Belize nationalists.[23] Although a shared jurisdiction over the waters and shelves of Amatique Bay is attractive in theory, friction between the two countries would seem to preclude such an arrangement in the near future.

The Caribbean islands have also become more concerned with insuring marine resources. Most of them are, or have been, the possessions of maritime powers that have been slow to extend their territorial seas beyond the 3-mile limit. As the former territories become independent, they look to the seas to provide economic resources that their barren lands often cannot. The archipelago principle, as outlined in a working draft of the UN Law of the Sea Treaty (1975), promises greater protection of island resources while it has the potential to provoke new conflicts; the draft defines an archipelago as "a group of islands . . . interconnecting waters and other natural features which are so closely interrelated that such islands, waters, and other natural features form an intrinsic geographic, economic, and political entity, or which historically have been regarded as such."[24] Archipelagic states such as the Bahamas have proposed a unique treatment of their base lines and territorial waters: they will draw their base lines around the outer perimeter of their islands, cays, reefs, and banks and proclaim that the connecting waters are internal waters, although neutral ships will probably be allowed to pass through designated channels. All parts of the Bahamas, which extend for over 500 miles, are more than 24 miles from their nearest neighbors, so international boundary delimitations will not be affected.

The greatest conflicts created by the Bahamas government's assertion of the archipelagic principle have involved access to the rich fishing grounds off the Bahamas banks. In August 1975, the Bahamas declared the spiny lobster to be a creature of the Bahamian continental shelf, and foreigners were forbidden to fish for it even beyond the twelve miles of territorial sea. Regional politics heightened the issue, since the Bahamas granted concessions to some foreigners who wanted to harvest the lobsters. The concessions were, however, valid only for nationals of the contracting country and, as a practical matter, the law excluded the large number of exiled Cubans who fished the banks from Miami. Tempers flared over the issue, and several incidents of armed attacks on or by fishing vessels in the Bahamas waters occurred.[25]

Most of the other archipelagoes in the Caribbean lack the autonomy to effect an aggressive interpretation of the archipelago principle. The many island groups that still remain tied to extraregional nations may experience considerable frustration in attempting to secure the rights to their surrounding marine resources. Puerto Rico is an example.

In July 1976, Puerto Rican Governor Rafael Hernández Colon requested that Puerto Rico be allowed to attend the UN Law of the Sea Conference as an observer and be included among the signatories of the forthcoming treaty. The governor referred to language in the draft treaty that guaranteed the rights to surrounding resources to the inhabitants of colonies or territories under foreign domination. There was no explicit mention in the draft of "free associated states," and the Puerto Ricans feared that the island's resources might accrue to the United States.[26] The U.S. State Department denied the Puerto Rican request in September 1976, claiming that the island's rights were being protected by the U.S. negotiating team.[27]

The resources at stake are those that lie between the 3-mile and the 12-mile limit. United States law reserves to the federal government the rights to resources beyond the 3-mile limit and permits states to exploit the marine areas up to 3 miles. Treaties and legislation governing U.S.-Puerto Rican relations have explicitly preserved the island's rights beyond the 3-mile limit;[28] moreover, since Puerto Rico is not a state, the legislation relating to federal-state relations does not apply. Some Puerto Ricans fear, however, that the application of the new 12 miles of territorial sea and the 200-mile resource zone may cloud the laws currently governing U.S.-Puerto Rican resource exploitation. Recent finds of significant oil reserves off Puerto Rico's north shore intensify concern. In addition, island nationalists interpreted ex-President Gerald Ford's call for statehood for Puerto Rico as an ominous sign that the United States intended to insure federal control of the surrounding resources.[29]

In sum, changing views of the sea, heightened and popularized by the Law of the Sea Conferences, are provoking new tensions in the Caribbean. As the maritime nations grant independence to their Caribbean territories, the leaders of the new nations desperately seek some new sources of income for their governments. Aggressive claims to potential maritime resources areas frequently earn political capital at home while keeping alive hopes of a petroleum bonanza to secure the future. Older ex-Spanish nations like Venezuela and Guatemala struggle to retain the areas they currently control and attempt to extend them, if possible, at the expense of the weaker new nations. The stronger nations hope to fill the political vacuum left by the departing colonial powers in the region while they gain control of resources to further their economic development.

Since the greatest potential for wealth lies along the shelves near the coasts, most of the specific disputes are likely to continue to involve the 12 miles of territorial sea rather than the 200-mile resource zone tentatively accepted by the Law of the Sea Conference. Multinational oil companies have the potential to encourage these binational resource disputes to escalate into full-fledged conflicts. Ironically, the tensions thus engendered may ease only if and when further exploration reveals that there is nothing to fight about.

NOTES

1. For Latin American contributions to the Conference, see Francis T. Christy et al., *Law of the Sea: Caracas and Beyond* (Cambridge, Ma.: Ballantine, 1975); F. V. García Amador, *América Latina y el derecho del mar* (Santiago, Chile: Instituto de Estudios Internationales, Universidad de Chile, 1976); Karin Hjertonsson, *The New Law of the Sea: Influence of the Latin*

American States on Recent Developments of the Law of the Sea (Leiden: Sijthoff, 1973); and Ralph Zacklin, ed., *The Changing Law of the Sea; Western Hemisphere Perspectives* (Leiden: Sijthoff, 1974).

2. Some of the specific problems are discussed in Lewis M. Alexander, ed., *Gulf and Caribbean Maritime Problems* (Kingston, R. I.: University of Rhode Island Press, 1973).

3. Arthur M. Birken, "Gulf of Venezuela: A Border Dispute," *Lawyer of the Americas* 6 (February 1974): 53–54; also Gordon Ireland, *Boundaries, Possessions, and Conflicts in South America* (Cambirdge, Ma.: Harvard University Press, 1938; reprinted, New York: Octagon Books, 1971), pp. 206–15.

4. Birkin, op. cit., p. 54.

5. For a discussion of the territorial seas around islands and archipelagoes, see Robert D. Hodgson, "Islands: Normal and Special Circumstances," in *Law of the Sea: The Emerging Regime of the Oceans,* ed. John King Gamble, Jr., and Guilio Pontecorvo (Cambridge: Ballinger, 1974), pp. 137–200; and C. F. Amerasinghe, "The Problems of Archipelagoes in the International Law of the Sea," *The International and Comparative Law Quarterly* 23 (July 1974): 539–75.

6. Isidro Morales Paul, "Venezuela: The Country in the Caribbean," in Zacklin, op. cit., p. 29; Kaldone G. Nweihed, *La Vigencia del Mar: una investigación acerca de la soberanía marítima y la plataforma continental de Venezeula dentro del marco internacional del derecho del mar* (Caracas: Equinoccio, Univ. Simón Bolívar, 1973), pp. 459–469.

7. "The Oceans," *Lawyer of the Americas* 7 (February 1975): 217

8. Ibid., (October 1975): 776.

9. I am indebted to Dr. Juan Pablo Gómez-Pradilla, Ambassador of Colombia to the Organization of American States, for his explanation of the Venezuelan and Colombian positions in regard to the gulf. Interview with Juan Pablo Gómez-Pradilla, Washington, D.C., February 17, 1977.

10. For background on the origins of the boundary controversy see Ireland, op. cit.

11. U.S., Department of State, Bureau of Intelligence and Research, The Geographer, *Limits in the Seas: Straight Baselines—Venezuela,* International Boundary Study no. 21 (11 June 1970), p. 2.

12. "Statement on Guyana-Venezuela Relations by the Prime Minister of Guyana, The Hon. L. F. S. Burnham to the National Assembly, July 12, 1968," in *Documents on International Relations in the Caribbean,* ed. Roy Preiswerk (Río Piedras, Puerto Rico: Univ. of Puerto Rico Press, 1970), pp. 720–23.

13. Eric Williams, "The Threat to the Caribbean Community: Political Leader's Speech at the Special Convention of the People's National Movement, Sunday, June 15, 1975," *Caribbean Monthly Bulletin* (Supplement), 15 July 1975, pp. 29, 40–44.

14. Quoted in Morales Paul, op. cit., p. 127.

15. U.S., Department of State, Bureau of Intelligence and Research, The Geographer, *Limits in the Seas: Continental Shelf Boundary: Venezuela-Trinidad,* International Boundary Study no. 11 (6 March 1970), pp. 1–2.

16. Williams, op. cit., pp. 29, 40–44.

17. Ibid.

18. Ibid., p. 29.

19. *Latin America,* 19 January 1973, p. 22; 29 June 1973, p. 206.

20. Ibid.

21. "Statements by the Representative of Guatemala, Mr. Castillo-Arriola, to the Fourth Committee of the General Assembly of the United Nations, November 15 and December 12, 1967," in Preiswerk, op. cit., pp. 672–78.

22. *Latin America: Political Report,* December 16, 1977, p. 390.

23. Ibid., 27 January 1978, p. 25.

24. United Nations, Third Conference on the Law of the Sea, "Informal Single Negotiating Text," *International Legal Materials* 14 (May 1975): 737

25. "The Oceans," *Lawyer of the Americas* 5 (February 1973): 186–87.

26. Governor Rafael Hernández Colon to Secretary of State Henry A. Kissinger, July 3, 1976. Copy supplied by Richard D. Copaken, Counsel for Puerto Rico. In personal files of Judith Ewell, Williamsburg, Va.

27. Acting Secretary of State Charles W. Robinson to Governor Rafael Hernandez Colon, September 14, 1976. Copy Supplied by Richard D. Copaken. In personal files of Judith Ewell.

28. Richard D. Copaken, Jan Schneider, Alexander Kress, "Continental Shelf Rights of Puerto Rico Under Domestic Law," Memorandum to Governor Rafael Hernández Colon, December 30, 1976, pp. 63–70. In personal files of Judith Ewell.

29. The Washington Post, 2 January 1977, p. 2; *Latin America: Political Report,* 24 June 1977, p. 189.

9

The Canal and the Caribbean

Jan Black

INTRODUCTION

The concept embraced by United States military strategists that the Caribbean area constitutes the "soft underbelly" of the United States has been a very important determining factor in the history of most Caribbean nations. American concern in this area was considerably increased early in this century with the acquisition of the Panama Canal Zone and the subsequent opening of the transisthmian canal route. The influence of these developments and the concurrent increase in the United States' strategic interests were felt throughout the Caribbean. The area suddenly became a major path for world commerce. Economic, political, and even cultural patterns, such as those produced by the migration of thousands of Jamaicans and other West Indians to Panama to work on canal construction, were sharply affected. The opening of the canal may well have provided the final impetus for the U.S. decision to purchase the Virgin Islands from Denmark. No country, however, has been more strongly influenced by this concept and the actions that have flowed from it than Panama. It accounts for Panama's nationhood, for the canal that has been its economic base, and for the North American presence that has been its major source of frustration.

The primary factors conditioning Panama's national development and its external relations have always been its size and strategic location and its economic dependence upon the canal and international trade. Provisions of the 1903 Hay-Bunau-Varilla Treaty, under which the United States was granted the Canal Zone "in perpetuity," made Panama a virtual protectorate of the United States until 1936. Relations with the United States in general, and the status of the canal zone in particular, have continued to be the overriding concerns of foreign policy makers, and have strongly influenced domestic political contests as well as relations with all other countries.

Despite the negotiation of additional treaties in 1936 and 1955, plus several lesser concessions by the United States, various aspects of the relationship have continued to generate resentment among Panamanians. Aside from the large issue of jurisdiction over the zone, which bisects the territory of the republic, Panamanians have complained that they have not received their fair share of the receipts from the canal, that commissaries in the zone have damaged commercial interests in the Republic, that Panamanian workers in the zone have been discriminated against in economic and social matters, and that the large-scale presence of the U.S. military in the zone and in bases outside the zone casts a long shadow over national sovereignty.

After serious rioting in 1964, which indicated the intensity of nationalistic aspirations concerning the status of the zone, the United States agreed to enter into negotiations for a new treaty. Meanwhile, studies relating to the construction of a new canal were undertaken. In 1971, after a four-year interlude, negotiations were renewed, but it was not until 1977 that two new treaties, one providing for Panamanian assumption of control over the canal in the year 2000 and the other for a permanent joint guarantee of the canal's neutrality, were signed. The treaties were ratified by a Panamanian plebiscite in October 1977 and by the U.S. Senate in March and April 1978. The treaties may have launched a new era in Panamanian national life and in U.S.-Panamanian relations, but it is not likely that it will be an era free of serious discord.

THE CANAL AND THE ZONE

The geopolitical significance of the Isthmus of Panama has been recognized at least since its discovery by the Spanish Conquistadores, who contemplated digging a canal across it. The discovery of gold in California in the 1850s aroused U.S. interest and resulted in the construction of a transisthmian railroad. In 1879, a French company under the direction of Ferdinand de Lesseps, builder of the Suez Canal, undertook the construction of a canal across the isthmus, but the project fell victim to disease, faulty design, and, ultimately, bankruptcy, and was abandoned in 1889.

Naval operations during the Spanish-American War at the end of the nineteenth century served to convince President Theodore Roosevelt of the necessity of a U.S.-controlled canal somewhere in the area. This interest led to the Spooner Act of June 29, 1902, providing for a canal through the Isthmus of Panama, and the Hay-Herran Treaty of January 22, 1903, under which Colombia gave its consent to such a project in the form of a 100-year lease on a zone ten kilometers wide. This treaty, however, was not ratified in Bogotá, and the United States, determined to construct an isthmian canal, intensified its interest in the Panamanian separatist movement.

With financial assistance arranged by Philippe Bunau-Varilla, a French national representing the interests of de Lesseps' company, native Panamanian leaders conspired to take advantage of Washington's interest in a new regime on the isthmus. In October and November 1903, the revolutionary junta, with the protection of United States naval forces, carried out a successful uprising against the Colombian Government. Acting, paradoxically, under the Bidlack-Mallarino Treaty of 1846 between the United States and Colombia, which provided that U.S. forces could intervene in the event of disorder on the isthmus to guarantee Colombian sovereignty and an open transit route on the isthmus, the United States prevented a Colombian force—sent to suppress the insurrection—from moving across the isthmus to Panama City, the site of the rebellion.

President Roosevelt recognized the new Panamanian junta as the de facto government on November 6; de jure recognition followed on November 13. Five days later, Bunau-Varilla, as the diplomatic representative of Panama, concluded an isthmian canal treaty with Secretary of State John Hay in Washington. (Bunau-Varilla had not lived in Panama for seventeen years before the incident, and he never returned. Nevertheless, while residing in the Waldorf-Astoria Hotel in New York, he wrote the Panamanian declaration of independence and constitution and designed the Panamanian flag.) Isthmian patriots were particularly to resent the haste with which Bunau-Varilla concluded the treaty, an effort partially designed to preclude the objections an arriving Panamanian delegation might raise to its provisions. Nonetheless, the Panamanians, having no apparent alternative, ratified the treaty on December 2, and approval by the U.S. Senate followed on February 23, 1904.

The rights granted to the United States in the Hay-Bunau-Varilla Treaty were extensive. They included a grant "in perpetuity [of] the use, occupation and control" of a ten-mile strip of territory along with three nautical-mile extensions into the sea from each terminal "for the construction, maintenance, operation, sanitation and protection" of an isthmian canal.*

---

*A reconciliatory treaty with Colombia, providing an indemnity of US$25 million, was finally concluded in 1921.

Furthermore, the United States was entitled to acquire additional areas of land or water necessary for canal operations and held the option of exercising eminent domain in Panama City. Within this territory, Washington gained "all the rights, power and authority . . . which the United States would possess and exercise if it were the sovereign . . . to the entire exclusion" of Panama.

The republic became a de facto protectorate of the larger country through two provisions whereby the United States guaranteed the independence of Panama and received in return the right to intervene in its domestic affairs. For the rights it obtained, the United States was to pay the sum of $10 million, and a yearly annuity, beginning nine years after ratification, of $250,000 in gold coin. The United States also purchased the rights and properties of the French canal company for $40 million.

At a cost of more than $300 million and some 4,000 lives (most were immigrants from the British West Indies), the canal was completed in 1914. The canal consists of two sets of locks raising and lowering ships from the artificial Gatun Lake in an eight to ten-hour passage.

Subsequent agreements modified the 1903 treaty. The treaty of 1936 terminated Panama's protectorate status and rescinded the U.S. right of eminent domain. A 1955 treaty abolished the discriminatory wage differential in the Canal Zone that favored U.S. citizens over Panamanians, but provided for a 15-year rent-free lease of 25,000 acres of the republic's territory to the United States for military maneuvers. Meanwhile, Panama's annuity was increased to $430,000 in 1936, to $1.9 million in 1955, and was later adjusted for inflation to $2.3 million.[1]

Twenty to thirty ships daily, accounting for about 5 percent of world trade, by volume, pass through the canal. Tolls have been kept artifically low, averaging a little more than $10,000 per vessel in the 1970s. Nevertheless, use of the canal is declining as a result of competition from alternate routes and the increasing use of vessels, such as supertankers and aircraft carriers, too large to transit the canal.

Under the 1903 treaty, the governor of the Canal Zone was appointed by the president of the United States and reported to the secretary of the army. He served also as president of the Canal Zone Company, in which capacity he reported to a board of directors appointed by the secretary of the army. U.S. jurisdiction in the zone was complete and residence was restricted to employees of the U.S. government and their families. In the 1970s residents included some 40,000 U.S. citizens, two-thirds of whom were military personnel and their dependents, and about 7,500 Panamanians. The zone was, in effect, an outpost of U.S. military socialism, and the comfortable life style of its residents stood in stark contrast to the poverty on the other side of its guards and fences.

Military activities in the zone have been under the direction of the U.S. Southern Command (SOUTHCOM). Under the terms of the 1903 treaty, the primary mission of SOUTHCOM was to have been the defense of the canal. In fact, however, SOUTHCOM has served as the nerve center for the wide range of U.S. military activities in the Caribbean and South America, including communications, training of military and paramilitary personnel, overseeing of U.S. military assistance advisory groups, the conduct of joint military exercises with Latin American armed forces, and the implementation of contingency plans to ensure "internal security" in the hemisphere.

Among the most controversial of U.S. military activities in the zone has been the maintenance of institutions wherein military personnel from the Americas have been trained in counterinsurgency and guerrilla warfare. The training complex in the Canal Zone has included the School of the Americas (Army) at Fort Gulick, the Inter-American Air Force Academy at Albrook AFB, the smaller Inter-American Geodetic Survey School at Fort Clayton, operated jointly by the three service branches, and the U.S. Army Jungle Warfare School at Fort Sherman.

The best known of these schools, the School of the Americas, was officially opened in 1949 and by 1956 was offering courses exclusively in Spanish and Portuguese. The school counts so many political leaders among its alumni that it is known throughout Latin America as the "escuela de golpes" (coup d'etat school). Among its graduates is Panama's current leader General Omar Torrijos, yet one of the issues in the treaty negotiations was the possible closing of the school.*

PANAMANIAN POLITICS AND THE CANAL ISSUE

The focal point of consensus in Panamanian political life, cutting across both social and partisan cleavages, has been nationalism. Nationalistic sentiments, directed primarily against U.S. operations in the Canal Zone, have been catered to in varying degrees by all who held positions of leadership or who sought popular support. Public demonstrations and riots, which occurred in 1927, 1947, 1959, and 1964, have been effective in influencing policy, especially in relation to the country's stance vis-à-vis the United States. National leaders have alternately responded to and

---

*This led to considerable debate within the U.S. military establishment as to the value of the institution and possible alternative locations in Puerto Rico or other areas. Despite considerable pressure within Panama to force its closure, it now seems that the school will remain in the Canal Zone for at least a few more years, but its long-range future remains in doubt.

contributed to an explosive climate of public opinion, but they have had to take care to keep popular resentment narrowly focused on the North Americans in the Canal Zone, lest it turn on themselves, the Panamanian elite.

Until the coup d'état of 1968, which resulted in a moratorium on organized civilian political activity, power had been wielded almost exclusively by a small number of aristocratic families. The middle class, or sector, generally aspiring to upper-class status, had not developed a distinctive set of values or goals. Persons of middle-class background had occasionally gained political prominence, but this was acquired through a process of coöptation by the upper class rather than through a middle-class movement. The middle class was constrained from challenging the system by the dependence of most of its members upon government jobs, and the slow pace of industrialization had limited the political role of urban labor.

The lower classes in general lacked organization and leadership and had been distracted from a recognition of common problems by the ethnic antagonisms between those of Spanish or mestizo background and the more recent immigrants from the West Indies. Students, both university and secondary, attempted, on occasion, to fill the vacuum by serving as spokesmen of lower-class interests and frustrations.

The multiparty system that existed before the coup d'état served as a means of regulating competition for political power among the leading families. Individual parties characteristically served as the personal machines of leaders and clients, who anticipated jobs or other advantages if their candidates were successful. The country was generally governed through shifting coalitions of several such parties.

The National Guard, the country's combined police and armed forces, had begun to expand its domestic political role in the 1930s, and since the late 1940s served as the final arbiter of political controversies. Since deposing elected President Arnulfo Arias and seizing control of the government in October 1968, it has consolidated its authoritative position by exercising strict control over the press and educational institutions and through arrests and banishments of actual or potenetial political leaders. By 1970, effective executive authority was being exercised by Brigadier General Omar Torrijos Herrera, Commander of the National Guard, although Demetrio Lakas served as president for ceremonial purposes. The National Assembly was dissolved after the coup and half of its membership accompanied Arias into exile. Political parties were officially declared "extinct" in March 1969. Subsequently, a commission appointed by Torrijos drafted a new constitution, which was duly ratified in 1972 by a newly constituted National Assembly.

The coup d'état of 1968 precipitated rioting in a few urban slum areas, demonstrations by students, and an insurgent movement among peasants in Chiriquí Province that persisted for several months. Since med-1969, however, there has been little evidence of concerted opposition, and a sharp upturn in investments has indicated that the initial discomfiture of the business community has been overcome.

Torrijos has enjoyed considerable support from Cuban Premier Fidel Castro on the canal issue, but he has been careful to distance himself from the Marxist Left. The political label he appears to wear most comfortably is "populist." His domestic program has emphasized public works, especially the construction of roads, bridges, schools, and low-cost public housing, and an agrarian reform program based to some extent on the model of the Israeli kibbutz. On the other hand, he has been most generous in his dealings with the banking community and foreign investors, and, incidentally, with his relatives, who appear in large numbers on the public payroll.[2]

During the first two years after the overthrow of Arias, while the guard sought to consolidate its control of the government and Torrijos sought to disestablish his competitors within the guard, the canal issue was generally held in abeyance. By 1971, however, the negotiation of new treaties had reemerged as the primary goal of the regime. Like other leaders before him, he had to walk the tightrope of taking a strong enough stand on the issue to maintain popular support while keeping popular manifestations of frustration within controllable limits. A measure of his success is that by the time the new treaties were signed in 1977, Torrijos had held power longer than any other leader in Panama's history.

THE 1964 RIOTS AND THE NEGOTIATION OF NEW TREATIES

Public demonstrations and riots arising from popular resentment over U.S. policies have not been uncommon, but the rioting that occurred in January 1964 was uncommonly serious. A symbolic dispute over the flying of the Panamanian flag in the zone escalated into rioting that persisted for three days and resulted in the deaths of twenty Panamanians and four U.S. citizens, as well as serious injuries to several hundred persons and more than $2 million worth of property damage.

At the outbreak of the fighting, Panama charged the United States with aggression, severed relations, and appealed to both the OAS and the UN. A joint declaration recommended by an OAS investigating committee was signed by the two countries in April and diplomatic relations were restored, but the controversy smoldered for almost a year, until President Johnson announced that plans for a new canal would be drawn up and that an entirely new treaty would replace the 1903 treaty governing the Canal Zone.

Negotiations were carried on until 1967, but when the terms of three draft treaties were revealed, Panamanian public reaction was strongly adverse. The new treaties would have abolished the resented "in perpetuity" clause in favor of an expiration date of December 31, 1999, or the date of the completion of a new sea-level canal if that were earlier.

Panamanian nationalists, however, were incensed by provisions for the continuance of U.S. military bases in the canal area, U.S. deployment of troops and armaments anywhere in the republic, and for a U.S.-appointed majority on the joint board of nine governors for the zone. Thus, Panamanian President Marcos Robles announced that further negotiations were necessary.[3]

One of Arnulfo Arias' first statements after assuming the presidency in October 1968 asserted Panamanian sovereignty over the Canal Zone, but after twelve days in office he was deposed by the National Guard. Commander Omar Torrijos maintained that Panama had no desire to take operating control of the canal away from the United States. By 1970, however, Torrijos controlled the National Guard, the country had been consolidated, and Torrijos had begun to move toward identifying his government with Panamanian nationalistic aspirations.

Negotiations for a new set of treaties were resumed in June 1971, but they dragged on, accomplishing little, until March 1973 when, at the urging of Panama, the United Nations Security Council called a special meeting in Panama City. A resolution calling on the United States to negotiate a "just and equitable" treaty was vetoed by the United States on the grounds that the disposition of the canal was a bilateral matter. But Panama had succeeded in calling attention to the support of the Latin American states in particular and the international community in general for its position. Of the fourteen Security Council members not from the United States, thirteen had voted in favor of the resolution and one abstained.[4]

The United States signaled renewed interest in the negotiations in late 1973, when Ellsworth Bunker was dispatched to Panama as a special U.S. envoy. In early 1974, U.S. Secretary of State Henry Kissinger and Panamanian Foreign Minister Juan Antonio Tack announced their agreement on a set of principles. Prominent among them were: recognition of Panamanian sovereignty in the Canal Zone; immediate enhancement of economic benefits to Panama; a fixed expiration date for U.S. control of the canal itself; increasing Panamanian participation in the operation and defence of the canal; and continuation of U.S. participation in the defense of the canal. The strong resemblance between these principles and the rejected treaty drafts of 1967 went virtually unnoticed, and these principles guided the continuing negotiation.

U.S. attention was distracted later in 1974 by the Watergate scandal and the resignation of President Nixon. Negotiations were accelerated by President Ford in mid-1975, but faltered on U.S. insistence upon, and Panamanian rejection of, U.S. defense rights for an indefinite period and on sharp disagreements as to the portion of the Canal Zone and the number of military installations the United States would retain.

Negotiations lagged again in 1976 as the canal became an issue in the U.S. presidential campaign, but shortly after assuming office, President Carter appointed former Ambassador to the OAS Sol Linowitz as conegotiator and talks were resumed in earnest.

Meanwhile, the disposition of the canal and the zone had become a prominent issue in the OAS and in virtually all forums in which the United States confronted Latin Americans. Latin American governments had been unanimous in their support of the proposition that a new treaty more equitable to Panama was in order, although some were considerably more adamant about it than others. Most dependent upon the canal in terms of the percentage of their total trade passing through it were Central American countries and countries on the west coast of South America. All of these, with the exception of Chile, had taken positions supportive of the Panamanian position. But Panama's strongest support had come from those relatively open systems most responsive to public opinion. The government of Venezuela, in particular, had made the conclusion of more equitable treaties a major foreign policy goal.

Although to the Caribbean island states the disposition of the canal was of lesser economic consequence, it was an issue highly charged with political symbolism. The governments of Cuba and Jamaica were particularly supportive of the Panamanian position. In January 1976, General Torrijos spent a week in Cuba, where Castro publicly counseled him that the Panamanian struggle called not for radicalism, but rather for moderation. The Cuban leader thus contributed to insulating Torrijos against domestic opposition from the Left. Torrijos was subsequently an official guest of Jamaican Prime Minister Michael Manley, and in August 1977 Jamaica joined Venezuela, Colombia, Costa Rica, and Mexico in issuing a communiqué supporting Panama's claims, praising President Carter's efforts, and urging the conclusion of new treaties.

Agreement on two new treaties was announced on August 10, and the treaties were signed by Carter and Torrijos, with much fanfare and with most hemispheric heads of state in attendance, on September 7, 1977, in Washington, D.C. The new Panama Canal Treaty abrogates the treaty of 1903 and all other previous treaties dealing with the canal and the Canal Zone. The treaty expires on December 31, 1999, after which Panama is to assume full ownership and control of the canal.

As soon as the treaty comes into effect, Panama assumes jurisdiction over the Canal Zone, although the United States retains the use of all land and water areas and installations necessary to the operation, maintenance, and defense of the canal. For the duration of the treaty, the canal is to be operated by a new U.S. government agency, the Panama Canal Commission, supervised by a board of five North Americans and four Panamanians, all appointed by the United States. Panamanians, however, are to participate increasingly in the operation of the canal, and for the decade of the 1990s, the U.S. administrator and Panamanian deputy administrator will be replaced by a Panamanian administrator with a U.S. deputy. The treaty does not call for a reduction in the U.S. military presence, but does pledge that Panamanians will participate increasingly in defense activity.

Panama's annual share of the tolls is to amount to $.30 per ton, or about $40 to $50 million. Panama is also to be compensated with $10 million annually from canal tolls for the provision of public services in the canal operating areas, and an additional $10 million annually will be awarded to Panama if canal revenues are sufficient.

The number of U.S. nationals employed by the new commission is to be 20 percent less in five years than the number employed by the Panama Canal Company immediately before the treaty took force. However, those already employed by the company are to be protected against deterioration in the terms and conditions of employment.

Finally, for the duration of the treaty Panama will not contract with any other country for the construction of a sea-level canal without U.S. consent and the United States will not seek rights to construct such a canal on the territory of any country in the Western Hemisphere other than Panama.

In an accompanying document, the treaty concerning the Permanent Neutrality and Operation of the Panama Canal, the Republic of Panama declares that in times of peace or war the canal shall remain "open to peaceful transit by the vessels of all nations on terms of entire equality" and the United States and Panama agree to maintain the "regime of neutrality." Another article of the treaty, however, states that U.S. and Panamanian "vessels of war and auxiliary vessels will be entitled to transit the Canal expeditiously."[5]

The vagueness of the neutrality treaty gave rise to consternation among U.S. conservatives, and led to the issuance on October 14, 1977, of a joint statement of understanding between President Carter and General Torrijos. This statement affirmed that each country was to "defend the Canal against any threat to the regime of neutrality," but that such provision was not to be interpreted as "a right of intervention of the United States into the internal affairs of Panama." It also assured that in case of need, U.S. vessels could "go to the head of the line."

U.S. DEBATE AND RATIFICATION

Although a plebiscite on the treaties in Panama on October 23, 1977, which drew a large turnout and returned a vote of 2 to 1 in favor, served as a reminder to North Americans that the Panama Canal issue was not strictly a domestic one, the campaigns for and against ratification by the U.S. Senate raised such a furor that bilateral issues and international implications were almost lost from view.

For the most adamant proponents of the new treaties, such as Senator Frank Church, the basic argument was obvious. The maintenance of a colony, bisecting another sovereign state, is unbecoming for a supposedly enlightened great power in the late twentieth century. For the most adamant opponents, the argument was equally simple. In the words of former Governor Ronald Reagan, "We bought it, we paid for it, and they can't have it." Senator S. I. Hayakawa put the issue more clearly in perspective with his quip, "We stole it fair and square."

For many members of the Senate and other interested parties, however, the debate centered on whether or not the canal was vital to U.S. commerce or defense or both and on the political reliability of Panamanian leadership.

The canal, proponents argued, is clearly vital to Panama. Thirty percent of its foreign trade transits the canal, and canal traffic generates, directly or indirectly, some 25 percent of its foreign exchange earnings and 13 percent of its gross national product. Thus, Panama's stake in keeping the canal open and operating efficiently is far greater than that of the United States. As for a supposed U.S. obligation to other nations that use the canal, proponents noted that Panama's strongest supporters on this issue have included those nations most dependent on the canal for their own commerce.[6]

Opponents of the treaties argued that the canal is vital to the U.S. defense posture, and that only with a fully equipped U.S. garrison in the zone can it be fully protected. Proponents argued that in the nuclear era the canal is not of great strategic value. But to the extent that it is of value, they argued, the best way to protect it from the clearest immediate threat —sabotage—is through ensuring the cooperation rather than the enmity of Panamanians.

Early public opinion polls and head counts in the Senate were discouraging to the treaties' proponents, but prospects for ratification took a turn for the better in January 1978, when Senate Minority Leader Howard Baker announced that he would support ratification and public opinion polls showed markedly increased support after President Carter addressed the issue in a fireside chat on February 1. The neutrality treaty was ratified by the Senate on March 16 by a vote of 68 to 32, one vote more than the two-thirds required. But it passed only after the adoption of a reservation severely crippling to the original intent of the treaty— at least as understood by Panamanians. An eleventh hour compromise between the sponsor of that reservation, Senator Dennis DeConcini, the Carter administration, and the Panamanian government, on the wording of a similar reservation to be attached to the Panama Canal Treaty, made possible the ratification of that treaty by a vote of 68 to 32 on April 18.

PROSPECTS FOR THE FUTURE

The treaty provisions for the transfer of proprietorship of the canal in the long term, and for the implementation of Panamanian jurisdiction in the Canal Zone, and sharply increased revenues for Panama, in the short term represent no small achievement. It should not be assumed, however, that with the new treaties all sources of friction have been eliminated.

The long term—until the year 2000—appears very long indeed to a great many Panamanians. Furthermore, a great many matters of serious concern are not dealt with at all in the treaties or are dealt with in a manner sufficiently vague as to give rise to conflicting interpretations.

Even though the extensive U.S. military presence has been highly offensive to Panamanians, the United States promises no reduction before the year 2000. It promises only to "endeavor to maintain its armed forces in the Republic of Panama in normal times at a level not in excess of that of the Armed forces of the United States of America in the territory of the former Canal Zone immediately prior to the entry into force of this treaty." And the provision of the permanent neutrality treaty that after the year 2000 "only the Republic of Panama shall operate the Canal and maintain military forces, defense sites and military installations within its national territory," is contradicted by the U.S. Senate's reservation allowing for bilateral agreements on the stationing of U.S. military forces in Panama after that date.

The neutrality treaty is self-contradictory in that it guarantees transit to vessels of all nations on terms of "entire equality" but, as subsequently interpreted by President Carter and General Torrijos and amended by the U.S. Senate, guarantees that U.S. vessels may, if necessary, go "to the head of the line." A reservation attached by the U.S. Senate to the Canal

Treaty nullifies that treaty's provisions for bilateral accord on the construction of a sea-level canal.

Despite prohibition against intervention in the internal affairs of Panama, the meaning of the U.S. guarantee of the canal's neutrality remains unclear. In fact, the so-called DeConcini reservation, legitimatizing U.S. military intervention in the event of interference with the operation of the canal, smacks of the protectorate status from which Panama supposedly emerged in 1936. Although the compromise wording in the reservation to the Canal Treaty, to the effect that the U.S. right to keep the canal open shall not be "interpreted" as a right to intervene in Panama's domestic affairs, was accepted by Torrijos, it will be less than reassuring to many Panamanians. At any rate, power disparities remain, and many Latin American states can attest to the fact that when the United States believes that its interests are threatened, treaty commitments to nonintervention are easily overlooked.

NOTES

1. Donald Barr Chidsey, *The Panama Canal: An Informal History* (New York: Crown Publishers, 1970); Sheldon B. Liss, *The Canal: Aspects of United States-Panamanian Relations* (Notre Dame: University of Notre Dame Press, 1967); David Howarth, *Panama; Four Hundred Years of Dreams and Cruelty* (New York: McGraw-Hill, 1966); G. A. Mellander, *The United States in Panamanian Politics: The Intriguing Formative Years* (Danville, Illinois: Interstate Printers and Publishers, 1971); David McCullough, *The Path Between the Seas; The Creation of the Panama Canal, 1870–1914* (New York: Simon and Schuster, 1977).

2. Martin C. Needler, "Omar Torrijos: The Panamanian Enigma," *Intellect* 105, no. 2381 (February 1977): 242–43.

3. L. D. Langley, "U.S.-Panamanian Relations Since 1941," *Journal of Inter-American Studies* (Coral Gables) 12, no. 3 (July 1970): 339–66; Eugene H. Methvin, "The Anatomy of a Riot: Panama 1964," *Orbis* 14, no. 2 (Summer 1970): 463–89; Peggy Poor, "A View From the Canal," *The New Republic,* 22 February 1964 pp. 13–14.

4. U.S., Congress, Senate, Committee on Foreign Relations, *A Chronology of Events Relating to the Panama Canal,* 95th Congress, 1st sess., December 1977.

5. U.S., Department of State, Bureau of Public Affairs, *Texts of Treaties Relating to the Panama Canal,* Selected Documents, no. 6A (Washington D.C.: Government Printing Office, 1977).

6. U.S., The Library of Congress, Congressional Research Service, Foreign Affairs and National Defense Division, Larry Storrs, *Panama Canal Treaties,* Issue Brief no. IB77042, 1977

10

Puerto Rico: The Unsettled Question

Roberta Ann Johnson

Puerto Rico, part of the Greater Antilles, was, in a sense, removed from the Caribbean community by the United States who integrated her people, her economy, and her political life with that of the North American mainland. That the fate of an island was determined by a faraway colonizer was not unusual in the Caribbean. That the situation continues to be Puerto Rico's fate does make her unusual in a decolonized world.

Because of the United States connection, Puerto Rico is not a free actor in the Caribbean; on the contrary, Washington determines her foreign relations. The role Puerto Rico plays is that of "U.S. agent in the Caribbean" and she has even been called "the United States' southernmost border."[1] Puerto Rico's lack of autonomy was condemned by the United Nations in 1973 and has been decried by all three status positions on the island: independentists, who want full autonomy with full-fledged nationhood; commonwealthers, who want more autonomy with a New Pact; and statehooders, who want at least to legitimize the lack of autonomy with increased representation and participation. U.S. influence has been so pervasive in many aspects of Puerto Rican society that it was not until 1972 that the first course on Caribbean politics was taught at the University of Puerto Rico.[2]

ECONOMIC INTEGRATION

Economically, Puerto Rico's depressions and prosperity were determined by the United States. During the first part of this century most of the island's income was derived from sugar and its products; the jíbaro's rice from Louisiana and Texas, its bacalao from Newfoundland, and its machetes from Hartford, Connecticut were bought with "sugar money" and the Puerto Rican population was described as being in a state of virtual peonage to the "big plantation."[3] In the Depression of the 1930s Puerto Rico was referred to as the United States "poorhouse." *Harper's* reported that nowhere under the American flag was there such a concentration of squalor, disease, and chronic starvation, and Puerto Rican Governor Theodore Roosevelt Jr.'s personal accounts of island suffering included descriptions of "babies like skeletons" and "pathetic little groups carrying home-made coffins." Because Puerto Rico's major products were sugar, coffee, and tobacco, Luis Muñoz Marín, the island's first elected governor, described the economy as "providing all the after-dinner benefits without the dinner."[4]

"Operation Bootstrap" started in 1951, and by the 1960s the island was referred to as a United States "showcase." American tourists and industries were flying south. In 1960 new hotel construction was adding 500 rooms each year;[5] and in 1961, factories were going up at the rate of five per week.[6]

By the early 1970s economic investments had taken another direction, tying tighter the fate of island and mainland. Petrochemical companies moved in with a total capital investment of over $1.2 billion. Today, even with an economic recession, a soaring unemployment rate, and a shaky petrocomplex,[7] Puerto Rico is economically well off compared to her Caribbean neighbors, and was classified as a "developed economy" by the World Bank in 1967 (the only Latin American state to be officially given that designation).[8] In 1976, the island's per capita income was $2,328, contrasted to the other nations of the Greater Antilles: Jamaica, $1,070, Cuba, $860; Dominican Republic, $780; Haiti, $200.[9]

This increased income helped mainland business. By 1959, although Puerto Rico was sixth among the world's purchasers of U.S. goods, it led in per capita purchases.[10] Today, $3 billion of the $5 billion in Puerto Rican imports comes from the United States, and 85 percent of its $2.7 billion exports goes to the United States.[11] The two countries' economies are intertwined.

Another kind of economic system has worked to integrate the island and mainland: the welfare system. Puerto Rico receives $2 billion anually in United States aid, which includes housing subsidies, grants for education, welfare, and food stamps.[12] According to Rubén Berríos, 71 percent of all Puerto Rican households depend on the U.S. food stamp program.[13] Economic dependency holds the island in a strong grip.

Not only U.S. money but Puerto Rican emigrants bind the two countries. Emigration intertwined the fate of the island and the mainland and resulted in a situation where, today, out of 5 million Puerto Ricans, 1.8 million live on the mainland.[14] This out-migration was encouraged by the

Puerto Rican government and was economically motivated.[15] Many Puerto Ricans return to the island to retire.[16]

Thus, Puerto Rico was integrated into the United States system as the movement of money, industry, and people created and fed mutual needs.

POLITICAL INTEGRATION

Politically, the symbol of a "freely chosen union" was Estado Libre Asociado (ELA) or Commonwealth. In the 1940s its architect, Luis Muñoz Marín, envisioned commonwealth merely as an interim solution; but by 1952 he was arguing that commonwealth status was "a new alternative, equal in dignity, although different in nature, to independence or federated statehood."

Although heralded as a status alternative, in fact Public Law 600, which provided Puerto Rico with a commonwealth constitution, produced little change in the relationship between Puerto Rico and the United States. What the law did, however, was add to the relationship the symbolic dimension of Joint action.[17]

Public Law 600 was "in the nature of a compact." The phrase has never been clarified. The United States has not treated the commonwealth relationship as the agreement between equals that Puerto Rican commonwealthers have argued it is. In fact, three times since the 1952 commonwealth "contract" Puerto Rico tried unsuccessfully to initiate a change in the relationship. Perhaps Robert Anderson is correct when he writes that commonwealth merely gave Puerto Rico a "slightly longer leash."[18]

Cuba's description of commonwealth status was not so mild. In 1977, she characterized commonwealth as a "juridical monster which meant that Puerto Ricans had no citizenship of their own, no rights to decide on matters of foreign policy, no rights in matters of defense and no rights to decide on how their economy or their country should be run."[19]

UNITED NATIONS

Regardless of how little it really changed the relationship between Puerto Rico and the United States, the Commonwealth Constitution did involve an important change in the United Nations. According to the UN Charter, the United States was obliged periodically to submit information concerning economic, social, and educational conditions in its non-self-governing territories. Since 1946 this had been done for Puerto Rico. However, in March 1953, the United States announced that such reports were no longer necessary because Puerto Rico's new commonwealth status removed it from the non-self-governing category.[20]

Official Puerto Rican support for this view was provided by Resident Commissioner Fernos-Isern who, as alternate delegate, appeared in the UN on behalf of the United States, "representing a free people with a voluntary government." During the hearings held by the Fourth Committee on Trusteeships, he defined Public Law 600 as a basic status change. In November 1953, the U.S. position was approved and the United States no longer had to submit periodic reports on Puerto Rico to the United Nations. According to Tugwell, the argument would not have prevailed if Muñoz had not pressed the issue and made it a United States victory.[21]

Thus in 1953, the countries were officially politically bound "in the nature of a contract." With the approval of the world forum, the people of Puerto Rico continued to be cast as irreversibly American. As the island was being integrated into the mainland economy, Muñoz was engineering and legitimizing commonwealth status to insure continued close ties with the United States. The real commitment to integrate politically was symbolized, not by a Puerto Rican Commonwealth Constitution, but by the Puerto Rican effort in the United Nations to convince the world she was no longer a colony.

THE COMMITTEE ON DECOLONIZATION AND EL PLEBISCITO

But the United Nations was changing and, as a forum, was reflecting a different world view. Hollis Barber suggests 1960 as the turning point, "when the General Assembly passed the 'Declaration on the Granting of Independence to Colonial Countries and Peoples,' " conferring "on all peoples the fundamental human right of independence. . . ."[22]

In 1961, the General Assembly created the Committee on Decolonization, a Committee of Seventeen (soon to expand to twenty-four) to act as a watchdog on these matters. There is no question that the very existence of this committee was, in part, responsible for the 1967 plebiscite held to settle the question of Puerto Rican status.

In 1964, the UN Committee on Decolonization got its first requests from Puerto Rican independentist groups, and the Cuban delegation, to consider the case of Puerto Rico. Action was delayed until April 1967 when part of the committee, a nine-member working group, considered the case of Puerto Rico in closed session. At the same time, officials in the U.S. and Puerto Rican governments were working to further legitimize the relationship between the two countries by plebiscite.[23]

Following a 1962 exchange of letters between Governor Luis Muñoz Marín and President John F. Kennedy, a United States-Puerto Rico Commission on the Status of Puerto Rico was established. Its task was to "study all factors which may have a bearing on the present and future relationship between the United States and Puerto Rico."[24] The Commission's major conclusion was that all three forms of political status—commonwealth, statehood, and independence—were valid, and the Commission recommended a status plebiscite, "an expression of the will of the citizens of Puerto Rico. . . ."[25] The Puerto Rican legislature voted to hold such a plebiscite on July 23, 1967.

The Puerto Rican organizations that brought the status issue to the United Nations claimed "the U.S. had gotten the Puerto Rican government to set up the plebiscite to forestall UN action. . . ."[26] According to Independence Party President Concepción de Gracia, the plebiscite was "nothing but an effort to stop the negotiations in the UN to have the Puerto Rico case reexamined."[27] This claim was supported by the fact that UN action was forestalled until after the plebiscite.

Only 65.8 percent of those eligible—fewer than the number who usually vote in island general elections (80 percent)—participated in the July 23 plebiscite. The 702,512 who went to the polls voted overwhelmingly for continued relations with the United States. They cast 425,079 votes (60.5 percent) for commonwealth and 273,315 (38.9 percent) for statehood. Fewer than 1 percent voted for independence.

Independentist forces on the island opposed the plebiscite and had united in an antiplebiscite group called *Concentración Soberanista Antiplebiscitaria.* A rally against the plebiscite had over 30,000 in attendance. There is no doubt that independentists were responsible for the boycott of many voters (perhaps 15 percent of the eligible population). Nevertheless, a commonwealth spokesperson could claim with some force that "it is absolutely clear that the big majority of people of Puerto Rico want permanent association with the United States."[28] The plebiscite seemed to legitimize in the world forum the formal ties between island and mainland, and stopped a condemning statement from the Committee of Twenty-four. Once again, as with Public Law 600 in 1953, without really changing United States-Puerto Rico relations the two countries managed temporarily to affect the UN view of their relationship. Then, in 1973, after hearing representatives from Puerto Rican independentist groups, the Committee of Twenty-four adopted a resolution reaffiring the Puerto Rican people's right to self-determination and independence and asking the United States to refrain from any interference with the exercise of this right.

Cuba has been a prime mover in the United Nations on behalf of Puerto Rican independence. Furthermore, there is some evidence that the United States has been trying to link improved U.S.-Cuban relations with Cuba's stand on Puerto Rico. For example, at the Algiers conference of non-aligned nations, Cuba made it clear in September, 1975, that Puerto Rican independence is "non-negotiable, especially in the context of *bi-lateral discussions with the United States.*"[29] And two years later, 1977, GRANMA, the Cuban weekly, linked the two issues explicitly:

> On August 17, Cuba asked the U.N. Special Committee on Decolonization to reaffirm the Puerto Rican people's inalienable right to independence and self-determination.... In presenting the draft resolution, Cuban Ambassador to the U.N. Ricardo Alarcón pointed out that it "was in keeping with the principles of Cuba's foreign policy, and those principles cannot be negotiated with anybody."
> The above statement had to do with speculations made before the Committee by Severo Colberg, a spokesman for the People's Democratic Party of Puerto Rico, to the effect that Cuba and the United States might make a deal over the Puerto Rican case.[30]

The 1977 Cuban resolution on Puerto Rico was tabled and, so far, UN declarations have merely embarrassed the United States but have fallen short of changing the official classification of Puerto Rico by again requiring periodic reports from the United States. Yet, as Anderson suggests, "Puerto Rico with or without the formal [UN] declaration, will continue to be a symbol of remaining colonialism in the Third and Socialist worlds at least."[31]

It is in that arena—in the Third and Socialist worlds—that Puerto Rican independentist leaders are treated like leaders of a government in exile. Representatives are granted official status and compensated from UN funds for their expenses in attending UN meetings.[32] Unlike commonwealthers and statehooders, the independentists are involved in international relations, petitioning the United Nations and attending conferences and meetings. In 1975, Cuba recognized the Puerto Rican Independence Movement as the sole representative of the Puerto Rican nation.[33] "Delegations of the Puerto Rican National Liberation Movement have visited governments, mass organizations, parties and peoples in various countrues of Africa, Asia, Latin America, North America and Europe."[34] Independentist are changing a commonwealth reality captured by Concepción de Gracia: ". . . we live with our windows closed to the world."[35] Under the present commonwealth status, it is in Washington D.C., after all, that all of Puerto Rico's foreign affairs and most of Puerto Rico's internal affairs are decided. It was this situation that the "New Pact" was designed to change.

NEW PACT

On April 28, 1974, *The San Juan Star* headlines announced, "Governor Proposes Plan of Near Total Autonomy." The plan was the result of the work of the Ad Hoc Advisory Group on Puerto Rico, created the year before.[36] The results of this study to improve Commonwealth in the four areas (pillars) of association—common defense, common market, common currency, common citizenship—included a proposal for more island autonomy in international affairs. The Compact of Permanent Union Between Puerto Rico and the United States (HR 11200) proposed that "The Free Associated State may participate in international organizations and make educational, cultural, health, sporting, professional, industrial, agricultural, financial, commercial, scientific, or technical agreements with other countries consistent with the functions of the United States, as determined by the president of the United States and the governor of the Free Associated State on a case-by-case basis."[37]

It was a clear attempt at barter: in exchange for permanent union, Puerto Rico was asking for the freedom to have independent relationships. There were other areas in which the *Ad Hoc Report* asked for increased autonomy. Proposed changes in shipping and commerce, for example, would affect Puerto Rico on the international scene. But symbolically, the proposal to open the windows to the currents of international relations was most important.

The U.S. response to the *Report* tells us more about Puerto Rican-United States relations than even the list of changes proposed in the *Report* itself. The Interior Department, in its written response, stated that the requested name change to "Free Associated State" might be "impermissible under the U.S. Constitution" and rejected the idea of bilateral contract between two countries asserting "Puerto Rico remains a territory of the United States . . .";[38] they had "serious doubts" about Puerto Rican participation in international organizations but deferred to the Department of State; they had "serious problems" with Puerto Rico's proposal to acquire property ceded to the U.S. from Spain; they rejected the tariff proposal but deferred to the Department of Commerce and the Treasury; they "had a problem" with Puerto Rico controlling her flow of aliens but deferred to the Departments of State and Justice; and Puerto Rican representation in both Houses of Congress would, according to Interior, require a constitutional amendment.[39] It was a strong bureaucratic rejection of practically every committee proposal with an especially loud "no" to the idea that the Puerto Rican-United States agreement could be anything like a contract between sovereigns. An earnest proposal met with a callous reception—it was the pattern of Puerto Rican-United States relations for nearly three-quarters of a century.[40]

Luis Muñoz Marín, in an interview on January 4, 1978, insisted that the New Pact proposals had interest and support in the U.S. Congress. Nevertheless, during congressional hearings on these proposed New Pack changes, the irreverent banter between the Co-Chair of the Ad Hoc Committee, Marlowe Cook, and the Chair of the Congressional Subcommittee on Territorial and Insular Affairs, Phillip Burton, seemed to reveal a kind of indifference to the serious problems Puerto Rico faces.[41]

PRESIDENT FORD AND PUERTO RICAN STATEHOOD

Nothing shows the insensitivity of Washington to Puerto Rico's needs quite so well, however, as President Gerald Ford's New Year's Eve Statement recommending Puerto Rican Statehood. It surprised, embarrassed and shocked Puerto Rican leaders and knowledgeable statesiders. Even the newly elected statehood governor of Puerto Rico, Carlos Romero Barcelo, claimed he had no advanced knowledge of Ford's statehood proposition.[42]

The Ford statehood bill was hastily put together by the Solicitor's Office at the Interior department. The president's press secretary, Ron Nessen, claimed that the president's statement and bill were a response to the work of the New Pact Ad Hoc Committee;[43] Muñoz Marín, however, suggested that President Ford had "some kind of deal with the Republicans of Puerto Rico who voted for him at the Republican Convention."[44]

"Radio Havana, in reporting Ford's push for statehood, called the President 'a frantic annexationist.' "[45] Whatever his motivation Ford's statehood bill does reveal two things about the United States' Puerto Rican policy: its whimsical, almost arbitrary nature, and its colonial quality. Described as "abrupt, ill-timed and harmful . . . ,"[46] the bill provided procedures for statehood before even asking the Puerto Rican people what they wanted.[47]

Criticized for this omission, the president did amend his bill to include an early referendum and transmitted a draft to Congress on January 17, 1977.[48]

Ford's bill might have been merely a gesture from an outgoing president, but a former Statehood resident commissioner, Jorge Cordova Diaz, was referring to it as the "Grito de Vail," and the new Statehood governor was vowing to educate the people on the advantages and desirability of statehood, believing that Ford's statements would probably improve the investment climate and tourist industry.[49]

What with the Statehood party victory in 1976,[50] with the Statehood governor's 1977 tax reform plan to whittle away Commonwealth tax exemptions,[51] with the well-publicized activity of the Carter-linked pro-statehood faction in the Commonwealth party,[52] with the increased island participation in the federal electoral process, characterized as "the front end of a train whose last coach is statehood,"[53] and with 59 percent of mainland Americans favoring statehood for Puerto Rico,[54] there may well be a commission established to study the possibility of Puerto Rico's becoming a state. But like the Ad Hoc Commission which studied the commonwealth status, there is no guarantee that its recommendations will be treated seriously, let alone be the basis of a change in policy. The United States and Puerto Rico are not, after all, equal partners.

It is the present blatant inequality between the "partners" in commonwealth which explains the appeal of independence and statehood. The United States, by its inaction, is killing commonwealth. Too often commonwealth, according to Matthews, is looked upon as a "half-way station,"[55] it has lost the support of mainland liberals,[56] and for Anderson, it is "bankrupt as an idea."[57] The "joint striving for a nobler more worthwhile relationship," which Jaime Benitez points to as an essential ingredient of commonwealth, seems to be one-sided. Puerto Rico, alone, continues to strive to eliminate the "colonial-type vestiges."

By 1977, it was not only the independentists who were petitioning the United Nations for a change in the Puerto Rican situation. Statehood-ers, as well as representatives of the Puerto Rican Bar Association, made statements to the Committee of Twenty-four. "For the first time," said the *Washington Post,* "virtually the whole spectrum of political opinion in Puerto Rico has appeared before a U.N. committee . . . criticiz[ing] the island's commonwealth status. . . ."[58] One of the more dramatic statements was made by Juan Garcia Passalacqua, representing Americans for Democratic Action; formerly a supporter of commonwealth, he pointed to the 1976 election in which 57 percent of the vote was statehood or independence, and argued:

> The people of Puerto Rico represented here by its new anti-colonial majority, awaits your endorsement of these simple principles for decolonization. There will then be the final decisive struggle for state-hood and independence—never again a colony.[59]

CONCLUSION

Political status continues to be the most important unsettled question for Puerto Rico. Status determines the kind of relationship the island can have with its Caribbean neighbors as well as with the other countries of the world. The status issue divides the island's people like no other issue.

As divisive as the status issue is, there is one thing that unites all three status positions. What they share is the strong desire to rid the island of its colonial vestiges: independentists, by throwing out the colonizer; statehooders, by merging with the colonizer; and commonwealthers, by becoming more equal to the colonizer with a New Pact. All three positions, regardless of sympbols and slogans, share the common insight that Puerto Rico is still a non-self-governing territory. This is a fact regardless of petrocomplexes, high per capita income, and food stamps.

NOTES

1. See Robert W. Anderson, "Puerto Rico Between the United States and the Caribbean" (Paper presented at the Conference of Contemporary Trends and Issues in Caribbean International Affairs, Port of Spain, Trinidad, May 23–27, 1977), p. 11.

2. Kenneth R. Farr, *Personalism and Party Politics* (Hato Rey, Puerto Rico: Inter-American University Press, 1973), p. 118.

3. Roberta Ann Johnson, "The 'Failure' of Independence in Puerto Rico," *Civilizations* 25, No. ¾ (1975): 239.

4. Roberta Ann Johnson, "The Puerto Rican Independence Movement: 1898–1967" (Ph.D. diss., Department of Government, Harvard University, Cambridge, Mass., 1971), pp. 64, 65.

5. Ralph Hancock, *Puerto Rico: A Success Story* (Princeton, N.J.: D. Van Nostrand Co., 1960), p. 116.

6. Earl Parker Hanson, *Puerto Rico: Ally for Progress* (Princeton, N.J.: D. Van Nostrand Co., 1962), p. 103.

7. "Tesoro's $130 Million Burden," *Business Week*, May 9, 1977, pp. 93–94.

8. John Bartlow Martin, "A Commonwealth's Choice," *Harper's*, December 1977, p. 18.

9. By comparison, Puerto Rico's per capita income in 1940 was $121; in 1965, $900. *U.S. News and World Report*, January 17, 1977, p. 73; see also International Bank for Reconstruction and Development, *World Bank Atlas, Population, Per Capita Product, and Growth Rates* (Washington: IBRD, 1977).

10. Hanson, op. cit., p. 76.

11. U.S. News and World Report, op. cit. See also Henry Pelham Burn, "Two Faces of Development: Puerto Rico," *Vista* 9, No. 3 (December 1973): 31–34.

12. *U.S. News, and World Report* op. cit.

13. Rubén Berríos Martínez, "Independence for Puerto Rico: The Only Solution," *Foreign Affairs* 55 (April 1977): 562.

14. *U.S. News and World Report*, op. cit., p. 73.

15. Berríos, op. cit., p. 569.

16. By 1960, of all Puerto Ricans who had come to the mainland, one-fourth had returned to the island. Hancock, op. cit., p. 142.

17. Ralph Nader, "The Commonwealth Status of Puerto Rico," *Harvard Law Record* 23, No. 12 (December 13, 1956): 2–8

18. Anderson, op. cit., p. 8.

19. *Granma, Weekly Review,* Year 12, Number 34, Havana, Cuba (August 21, 1977): 10.

20. The best history of the United Nations proceedings is in Jesus de Galindez, "Government and Politics in Puerto Rico: New Formulas for Self-Government," *International Affairs* 30 (1954): 340–41; see also, "Puerto Rico's New Self Governing Status Transmitted to Secretary General," *U.S. Department of State Bulletin* 28 (April 30, 1953): 587; United Nations General Assembly, Official Record, Eight Session, Plenary at 311; Rubén Berríos Martínez, "The Commonwealth of Puerto Rico: Its Reality in the National and World Community" (Divisional Thesis, Yale Law School, New Haven, Conn., 1964), p. 179.

21. Rexford G. Tugwell, *The Art of Politics as Practiced by Three Great Americans: Franklin Delano Roosevelt, Luis Munoz Marin, and Fiorello H. LaGuardia* (Garden City, N.Y.: Doubleday and Co., 1958), pp. 226, 227.

22. Hollis W. Barber, "Decolonization: The Committee of Twenty-four," *World Affairs* 38, No. 2 (Fall 1975): 129.

23. See Roberta Ann Johnson, "The 1967 Puerto Rican Plebiscite: The People Decide Their Destiny," *Revista/Review Interamericana* 5, No. 1 (Spring 1975).

23. Public Law 88–271, February 20, 1964; 78 Stat. 17, quoted in *Status of Puerto Rico. Report of the United States-Puerto Rico Commission on the Status of Puerto Rico,* August 1966, p. 3.

25. *Ibid.,* p. 8.

26. *The San Juan Star,* April 8, 1967, p. 6.

27. *The San Juan Star,* March 16, 1967, p. 6.

28. *The San Juan Star,* April 11, 1967, p. 1.

29. *Puerto Rico Libre: Bulletin of The Puerto Rican Solidarity Committee,* Vol. III, No. 2, (September 15, 1975): 1.

30. *GRANMA, Weekly Review,* Year 12, Number 35, Havana, Cuba (August 28, 1977): 10.

31. Anderson, op. cit., p. 15.

32. Barber, op. cit., p. 128.

33. *Puerto Rico Libre* (September 15, 1975) op. cit.

34. Juan Mari Bras, in an article based on a speech given before the UN Special Committee on Decolonization on September 2, 1976, *Black Scholar* 8 (December 1976): 19.

35. Concepción de Gracia, quoted in "A Talk with the Candidates," *San Juan Review* L:9 (October 1964): 14.

36. U.S., Congress, Senate, Committee on Interior and Insular Affairs, Hearing, 94th Cong., First Sess., December 3, 1975, pp. 41, 42.

37. U.S. Congress, House, Committee on Interior and Insular Affairs, Subcommittee on Territorial and Insular Affairs, Hearings, 94th Cong., Second Sess. on Hr 11200 and HR 11201, January 20, February 9, 1976, pp. 4, 5.

38. A territory "in a new form of political relationship—not as an independent State but linked to a broader political system in a Federal association without an independent and separate existence." *Ibid.,* pp. 49, 50.

39. *Ibid.,* pp. 50–53.

40. Johnson, "The Puerto Rican Independence Movement," op. cit., pp. 39–44.

41. Hearings, House of Representatives, op. cit., p. 195.

42. Manny Suarez, "CBR Disagrees with Statehood Steps Outlined in Ford Bill," *The San Juan Star,* January 14, 1977, p. 1; "Romero: Accion Ford Prueba EU Daria Estadidad," *El Mundo,* January 2, 1977, p. 1.

43. "Nessen: 14-Month Study Preceded Ford Statement," *The San Juan Star,* January 6, 1977, p. 1.

44. Interview with Luis Muñoz Marín, January 4, 1978, Trujillo Alto.

45. *Miami Herald,* January 2, 1977.

46. Harold J. Lidin, "Gordova, Benitcz Speak Minds on Status Tizzy," *The San Juan Star,* January 11, 1977, p. 11.

47. Harry Turner, "Draft Bill Sets Convention Before Plebiscite on State," *The San Juan Star,* January 13, 1977, p. 13; "Ford Proposal is senseless Says Jackson," *The San Juan Star,* January 4, 1977, p. 1.

48. "Communication from the President of the United States transmitting A Draft of Proposed Legislation to enable the People of Puerto Rico to Form a Constitution and State Government, to Be Admitted into the Union, and for Other Purposes," January 17, 1977 (Washington, D.C.: U.S. Government Printing Office, 1977).

49. Liden, op. cit.; see also Suarez, "Romero Vows," op. cit., p. 1.

50. The Statehood party got 48.3 percent of the vote, Commonwealth, 45.4 percent;

51. *Latin America: Political Report,* Vol. XII, No. 8, (24 February, 1978): 63.

52. *Latin America: Political Report,* Vol. XII, No. 19, (19 May, 1978): 146.

53. *Ibid.,* p. 148.

54. "59% On Mainland Favor State in Gallup Inc. Poll," *The San Juan Star,* January 5, 1977, p. 1.

55. Thomas Matthews, "Problems and Leaders in the Caribbean," in *The Caribbean: Its Hemispheric Role,* ed. A. Curtis Wilgus, vol. 17, series 1 (Gainesville, Florida: Center for Latin American Studies, University of Florida Press, 1967), p. 29.

56. Martin, op. cit., p. 19.

57. Anderson, op. cit., pp. 6, 7.

58. *Washington Post,* August 19, 1977.

59. *Puerto Rico Libre: Bulletin of The Puerto Rican Solidarity Committee,* Vol. V, No. 6 (October/November, 1977): 12.

Part III

National Policies

11

The United States and Cuba: Cooperation, Coexistence, or Conflict?

John N. Plank

For almost two centuries, Cuba has preoccupied leaders of the United States, principally because of its strategically important geographic location. As a glance at a map reveals, Cuba lies 90 miles across the Florida Straits from U.S. territory. This largest of the Caribbean islands arcs for 760 miles from northwest to southeast, dominating both the Windward Passage (which links the Atlantic and the Caribbean) and the Straits of Yucatan (which give access to the Gulf of Mexico.)

Historically, the primary concern has been to insure that Cuba not fall under the control of an extrahemispheric power that could use the island as a base for actions inimical to the interests of the United States. Spain's continued sovereignty during the nineteenth century was acceptable, for Spain was weak. What could not be tolerated was the possibility that Spain might be replaced in its imperial role by another more dynamic and aggressive European state. Primarily to prevent that contingency, the United States participated in the last stages of Cuba's struggle for independence and secured the incorporation of the Platt Amendment in the Cuban constitution of 1901. The amendment allowed the United States to construct its major navel base at Guantánamo; it also gave the United States an assured right to intervene militarily at its discretion. Thereby the United States safeguarded its conventionally defined security interests in Cuba and the Caribbean.

In its relations with Cuba, however, the United States involved itself far more intensively and extensively than would have been required to meet its defense needs in the Caribbean and the Gulf of Mexico. It came to play an assertive, tutelary role in almost all aspects of the country's development. From the Spanish-American War until the collapse of

Batista's regime in 1959, the presence and influence of the United States were overwhelming.

With the wisdom that retrospect provides, it is easy to judge that the United States erred grievously in fashioning its relationship with Cuba. But during the period of U.S. dominance, policy makers believed they were behaving responsibly and constructively, serving the best interests of both Cuba and the United States.

After 1948, the United States came to view Cuba through the prism of the Cold War, thereby risking very serious distortion of judgment. The presumed omnipresence of the Communist menace and the great exaggeration of Communist capabilities in the Western Hemisphere led the United States to construct its policy upon faulty information, to depend upon doubtful Cuban allies, to discount indications of grave disharmonies in Cuban society, economy and polity, and to distrust those who with any degree of stridency or urgency called for revolution or radical reform. When the dictatorship of Batista collapsed, the United States was ill-prepared to deal with the successor regime of Fidel Castro.

In any event, no sooner had Castro assumed power than it became evident that he was not interested in prepetuating the special U.S.-Cuba relationship that had been such a dominating feature of Cuba's life as an independent state. Nor did Castro seem eager to engage in the construction of a new, more wholesome association. His objective was to attain almost complete independence from the United States as rapidly as possible; and his driving pursuit of that goal was to carry him and the country he ruled into the Soviet orbit. That was the outcome, of course, that U.S. policy makers had most dreaded, but they found themselves incapable of preventing it.

Since 1959, official preoccupation with Cuba has been intense, at times nearly obsessive. Concern for national security has been a major cause of that preoccupation. There is more involved here than that, however. With Castro's turn toward Marxism-Leninism, the United States suffered a major setback in the cold war, and a gaping breach appeared in the ideological defenses of the Western Hemisphere. Castro's Cuba has challenged the United States at a more profound level than it has ever been challenged before in this hemisphere. And that it should be Cuba, of all the hemispheric states, that abandoned the United States was cause for additional distress. Small wonder that it has proved almost impossible for the United States to accept with equanimity the presence of a Communist Cuba in the region. Since 1959, the United States has tried to devise a Cuban policy that would adequately reflect this country's displeasure and would enable it effectively to "deal with Castro." To date that policy has not emerged, nor is it soon likely to. Reflection reveals the reasons.

In theory, four conceivable U.S. foreign policy approaches toward Castro's Cuba can be distinguished. One is based upon thorough and unremitting hostility toward Castro's regime, looking toward its overthrow and supersession by one more acceptable to the United States. A second would be acceptance of Castro's government as an unfortunate fact of international life that must be grudgingly tolerated. A third assumes Castro's susceptibility to the technique of the carrot and the stick: through judicious use of rewards and penalties by the United States, Castro can be induced to modify his behavior in ways the United States finds more acceptable. A fourth, entailing a radical about face for the United States, depends upon not only the acceptance of Castro's continuing dominance in Cuba, but also an affirmative recognition of the achievements of the Cuban revolution.

In practice, neither the first nor the fourth of these alternatives is realistic at the present time. The second and third have been followed by this country in recent years, but the second is intrinsically unappealing (and is thought by many in the United States to be unbecoming in a great power), while the third has achieved little success. In short, our government cannot get rid of Castro and cannot embrace him. Therefore, it must coexist with him, either sullenly tolerating him, or attempting alternately to cajole and bully him.

Recently, to be sure, there has been some relaxation of official constraints—citizens, for instance, no longer are impeded by the United States from travelling to Cuba—and understandings between the United States and Cuba have been reached regarding such issues as fishing rights and hijacking. Also there are now interest sections in both Havana and Washington, providing direct representation for the United States and Cuba in the two countries for the handling of some routine matters. But the impact of this loosening has been very modest, and there is small prospect of a substantial improvement in U.S.-Cuban relations.

As the situation is defined at present in both Washington and Havana, there is no readily apparent way out for the United States from this unattractive and unrewarding situation. As long as Fidel Castro remains in power, as long as he can count upon the support of the Cuban people, as long as the Soviet Union is prepared to subsidize "the first socialist state in the Americas," Cuba will continue to be an unresolved —and probably unresolvable—problem for the United States.

But can we in the United States look at the situation with fresh perspective? Is there a prospect that we can make Castro's presence in the Caribbean, taking him as he is now and is likely to remain, a presence that is acceptable to us? Can we reevaluate our security interests in the Caribbean and the hemisphere to discount substantially the significance of Cuba? Can we reassess, profoundly and dispassionately, our relationships not only with Cuba and the Caribbean, but with Latin America as a whole? Most important, can we probe deeply and critically into our own values and institutions, our own premises and prejudices, in an effort to determine their bearing upon our present difficulties? It would be only after such a thorough questioning, reassessment, and reorientation, that the United States could come to constructive terms with Castro's Cuba and what it represents.

Such a reexamination is difficult and painful because the roots of our hemispheric policies—and, our policy towards Cuba—lie deep in our past, deriving from a conception of ourselves and our mission that first began to take form in the seventeenth century. Our task then was an exemplary one: "For we must consider that we shall be as a city upon a hill," said John Winthrop, "and the eyes of all peoples are upon us."[1] In the Americas, which we and others came also to call the New World, we later assumed a special responsibility. As announced in the Monroe Doctrine of 1823, it was to do what we were capable of doing to insure that the newly independent states to our south had their opportunity to develop, free from the interventions of the former colonial powers and their allies. We assumed then that those states, left to their own devices, would evolve haltingly and ineptly toward an approximation of what we had already become, and that our own continuing development would mark the course that they, at their own pace and in their own fashion, would follow. Toward the end of the nineteenth century, and particularly with the Spanish-American War and the subsequent accession of Theodore Roosevelt to the presidency, we redefined our hemispheric role. No longer was it to be almost exclusively an exemplary one. We deliberately took upon ourselves responsibility for the political and economic tutelage of the Caribbean and Central American peoples.

As for Cuba, its relationship to the United States between the Spanish-American War and the collapse of the Batista regime was an anomalous one. If Cuba was not a possession of the United States (as was Puerto Rico), neither was it independent even to the extent that the states of Central America, the Dominican Republic and Haiti were independent. Not only did the Platt Amendment, as embedded in the Cuban constitution, allow the United States to intervene militarily in the country, thereby depriving the Cubans both *de jure* and *de facto* of ultimate self-determination; also, through an elaborate set of trade and tariff arrangements, Cuba's economy was tied and effectively subordinated to that of the United States. The abrogation of the Platt Amendment in 1934 and the movement toward "Cubanization" of the sugar industry and other enterprise during the 1930s, 1940s, and 1950s, did not substantially change the pattern of U.S. domination and Cuban dependence in both the political and the economic spheres. Moreover, so strong were emanations from the United States in other areas (the communications media, entertainment, sports, and the arts), that Cuba had scant opportunity to develop an indigenous culture that could provide a core of national identity for the Cuban people.

As for the United States, those citizens who determined foreign policy were, on balance, well-pleased with the Cuban relationship, as it had evolved. It was, of course, fully compatible with Theodore Roosevelt's interpretation of the Monroe Doctrine:

> Chronic wrongdoing, or an impotence which results in a general loosening of the ties of civilized society, may in America, as elsewhere, ultimately require intervention by some civilized nation, and in the Western Hemisphere the adherence of the United States to the Monroe Doctrine may force the United States, however reluctantly, in flagrant cases of such wrongdoing or impotence, to the exercise of an international police power. *If every country washed by the Caribbean Sea would show the progress in stable and just civilization which with the aid of the Platt Amendment Cuba has shown since our troops left the island* ... all question of interference by this Nation with their affairs would be at an end.[2]

The special trade and tariff arrangements between the United States and Cuba effectively prevented major economic incursions by other powers, and the special defense arrangements presumably insured that Cuba could never become a security threat to this country. In addition to these considerations was the assumption that Cuba could be counted an unswerving ally of the United States in the latter's dealings with the wider, extra-Caribbean, extrahemispheric world.

The benefits of the U.S.-Cuban relationship were not perceived as accruing only to the United States. As President Roosevelt had said elsewhere in his message enunciating the Roosevelt Corollary to the Monroe Doctrine, "Our interests and those of our southern neighbors are in reality identical."[3] And it is undeniable that a great number of Cubans, including those with whom U.S. citizens regularly associated, evidently profited from the association. These included Cuba's diplomats, its successful politicians, its military men, businessmen and many of its landowners. These people apparently shared the values of U.S. leaders and shared, at least formally, their commitment to constitutional democracy and to free enterprise and the market economy. It was regrettable if understandable that U.S. leaders overlooked the deplorable social and economic situation of less-privileged Cubans and that they underestimated or misinterpreted demands from within Cuba for radical change, not only in the internal dispensation but in the relationship with the United States.

Cuba cooperated with the United States during the Second World War; but it was not lost upon the Cuban people that the ideological purpose of the Allied effort was to protect and advance the causes of self-determination and freedom in an all-out struggle against authoritarian tyranny and totalitarianism. Franklin Roosevelt's Four Freedoms —freedom from want and fear, freedom of speech and religion—came to be viewed by many Cubans, particularly younger ones, as goals actively to be pursued within their own country. Both the corrupt, oppressive, and distributively unjust internal Cuban political system and the unwholesome connection with the United States which supported that system came under increasing challenge. Unfortunately, the United States was unable to evaluate these developments properly.

Severely complicating the picture was the eruption of the cold war. For a decade, beginning in 1948, any voices that were raised in Cuba condemning the established political and economic structure or questioning the desirability of the U.S.-Cuba relationship were suspected of being those of conscious or unconscious agents of the international Communist conspiracy. This unreasoned response on the part of those charged with responsibility for U.S. policy played automatically into the hands of those supporting the Cuban status quo, whether in Cuba or the United States.

The cold war also introduced a marked change of tone, of mood, into U.S.-Latin American (and therefore U.S.-Cuban) relations. Whereas in earlier periods, the United States had conducted its hemispheric affairs in a spirit of robust optimism and self-confidence (as during the administrations of Theodore Roosevelt, Woodrow Wilson, and Franklin Roosevelt), after 1948 the prevailing mood was one of anxiety and fear. Change in Latin America, particularly planned and substantial change of a socially and economically radical kind, was inherently to be feared on the ground that, of all elements in Latin America, only Communists had the skill, the discipline, and the fervor that would enable them to profit from the unrest engendered by such radical change. From 1948 until the overthrow of Batista, and indeed down to the present, the United States has conducted a defensive, reactive, and fundamentally unenthusiastic policy in this hemisphere.

The events of 1954 in Guatemala are illustrative of this policy. There, an inept Guatemalan government dominated by a collection of inexpert and frequently confused Marxists embarked upon a program of land reform and settlement. The United States engineered an invasion by proxy, overthrew the Arbenz regime, and saw to the installation of a military dictatorship that would insure—at least for the short term—the perpetuation of the status quo ante Arbenz. To this day, Guatemala has not seen fundamental reform of either its land or its tax structures, and Guatemala's political and economic development has been severely hindered in consequence.

The Guatemalan case has particular point, of course, in that the successful invasion by proxy served as a precedent for the United States in its ill-starred effort to overthrow Fidel Castro in 1961 by means of the Bay of Pigs adventure. Beyond that, it is probably correct to say that the objective of the U.S. government in 1961 was also a return in Cuba to something approximating the status quo ante Castro, albeit a political and economic dispensation less corrupt and brutal and somewhat more open and egalitarian, more concerned with distributive justice. What can be said with assurance about the episode is that the United States had only one clear objective in 1961: Cuba and the hemisphere were to be rid of Fidel Castro.

Castro entered Havana triumphantly in January 1959; most of those Cubans with whom the U.S. leadership was accustomed to deal and who were known, understood and trusted—whether in the public or the private sector—either had already fled the island or were to depart shortly. This country was badly out of phase with contemporary Cuban realities and was unable either to empathize with Castro's revolution or to establish credibly its good faith in dealing with the new regime.

It is sometimes asserted that the United States drove Castro into the arms of the Soviet Union, the implication being that had this government behaved differently toward him, he might have come to terms with us and avoided his suffocating alliance with the Kremlin. That is very dubious. Leaving aside speculation about what might have been Castro's original intentions, whether or not he had "always been a Marxist" (as he later claimed to have been),[4] there can be little doubt that the gulf in understanding between the U.S. leadership and Fidel Castro was unbridgeable.

First, it must be acknowledged that the initial inclination of the United States establishment was not to treat Castro in full seriousness. Historically, Latin American leaders in general have never been accorded the same respect and status in Washington that European leaders have received, and Cuban leaders in particular have ranked among those least esteemed. Washington believed that Castro, like his predecessors, could be brought around to an accommodation readily enough or, if that should prove difficult, he could easily be deposed. There was never anywhere in the highest official circles a disposition to deal with Castro on terms of real equality and respect.

Second, U.S. leaders had never before encountered a Latin American like Fidel Castro. Charisma is a much overworked term; but if it is applicable to any contemporary political figure, it is applicable to Castro.

The sheer power of his personality cannot be denied; and U.S. leaders underestimated that power. He was not a simple Latin American *caudillo* although he had many of the *caudillo's* attributes.

Third, Castro enjoyed at home—as he did to some extent outside Cuba—a Robin Hood image: he was the vindicator of wrongs and injustices perpetrated by Batista and his cohorts in collusion with the U.S. establishment. Cuba and its problems were perceived by Castro and his supporters very differently from the way they were perceived in the United States. For months and years after Batista's collapse, Washington continued to try to persuade the rest of the world that Cuba before Castro had really been among Latin America's most "highly developed" societies, enjoying one of the region's highest per capita incomes, one of its most advanced welfare systems, one of its highest literacy rates. The Cuba which Castro promised to transform, and the Cuba the United States wished to see maintained, could not have been less congruent.

Finally, Castro gave every appearance of being supremely self-confident, absolutely secure in his conviction that he possessed the wisdom, power, and ability to remake Cuban society. He felt himself to be in charge, in control of events. To U.S. leaders, accustomed as they were to working within institutional and other constraints, this mood of buoyant confidence and disregard for conventional and established limits was interpreted as sheer arrogance and was intensely disliked and distrusted. The personalism of Castro's rule presumably was not in itself so objectionable, as the United States was used to dealing with dictators in Latin America. It was, however, used to dealing with "its own" dictators, like Nicaragua's Somoza, or the Dominican Republic's Trujillo, or Venezuela's Pérez Jiménez.

What is particularly unusual about the Cuban situation at the time of Castro's assumption of power was the disintegration of established political institutions and the absence of legitimate authority structures and forms. Because of the total discrediting of the preceding regime, Castro was able to consolidate his control and orient his administration within what was almost a political vacuum. There is good reason to suppose that Castro himself was surprised at the extent and plenitude of the opportunity that presented itself to him upon his accession. As for U.S. leaders, the vacuum attendant upon revolutionary situations is something to be prevented at almost any cost. If and when it emerges, it is greeted with great uneasiness, and efforts are made to fill it with institutions and men acceptable to the United States. In the Cuban case, the United States was unable either to prevent the emergence of the vacuum or to fill it with actors acceptable to U.S. leaders.

From the time of his assumption of power, Castro moved in ways that made effective communication and cooperation with the United States increasingly difficult. The summary executions of some of Batista's more notorious lieutenants were a case in point. From Castro's point of view, these procedures were justified and indeed necessary, not only for the purposes of consolidating his control but also in order to satisfy a vengeful spirit among his followers: no doubt the number of executions would have been very substantially greater had the United States and other countries not opened themselves to the political refugees. From the point of view of the United States, on the other hand, the executions reflected a fundamental departure from the rule of law.

Castro did not try to legitimize his assumption of power by holding elections, presumably asking himself and the Cuban people, Who or what could stand against him? It was a good and appropriate question, for whatever opposition there might have been to Castro was either discredited or cowed. The United States claimed that it wished to see Castro's regime legitimized via the electoral process; however, if he had followed the plebiscitary route—the only electoral route that realistically was open to him at the time—the United States would have done its best to discredit the result, which would of course have been overwhelmingly favorable to Castro.

Underlying many of the early difficulties that the United States had in dealing with Castro was this country's inability or unwillingness to recognize that Castro simply was not in the mold of earlier Cuban leaders. He did not acknowledge the superior status and wisdom of the United States, or the condition of real dependency in which Cuba presumably found itself via-à-vis the United States. That being so, the hostility of the United States appears to have been almost inevitable. As is well known, members of the Eisenhower administration began earnestly in 1960 to plan for his overthrow.

Was the U.S. leadership aware of how its policy strengthened Castro's power? Evidently not, for the United States continued to operate on the assumption that Castro was viewed inside Cuba as a hated usurper and betrayer, a tyrant and oppressor, and that the Cuban people yearned to return to a regime not radically unlike that which Castro had destroyed, a regime purged of the worst abuses of the old system, and marked by modest reforms in the areas of taxation and land distribution, but basically a political and economic dispensation patterned after the U.S. model.

Not only did the United States err in its assessment of the Cuban public's evaluation of Castro, but also through providing a safe haven for the regime's most vociferous and determined enemies, it enabled Castro to export a large part of his opposition. Few revolutions have been given comparable social and political assistance. Also, the presence of the exiles —eventually some 600,000 in the United States alone—enabled Castro to point with alarm at the threat to revolutionary Cuba emanating from the United States.

A comprehensive and systematic review of the course of U.S. policy toward Cuba between 1959 and today is unnecessary here. The policy has been uninspired, unimaginative, and negative. Much more significant is the fact that concern about Cuba has affected and distorted our policy toward the Caribbean and Latin America ever since Castro's triumph. The Alliance for Progress, for instance, was aborted almost from its conception by its inherent ambiguity: was it designed principally to stop Castro-like and Castro-supported revolutions elsewhere in Latin America, or was its purpose to help Latin American societies pass through, with a minimum of disruption, a period of rapid social, economic, and political change, seen to be essential for balanced development? The two assessments are not necessarily incompatible, although they comport only awkwardly with one another. But whenever risk of Castro-like revolution appeared in Latin America, the United States abandoned its commitment to change and chose stability. Better that the objectives of the alliance be abandoned, than that the hemisphere witness the emergence of another Castro. Established Latin American elites knew very well how to use the fear of Castro and communism that motivated U.S. hemispheric behavior, and they did so.

Case after case could be cited: the role of the United States in the overthrow of President Goulart in Brazil in 1964, the Dominican intervention of 1965, the subversion of the regime of Salvador Allende in Chile in 1973. It may be recalled that opponents of the 1978 Panama Canal treaties cited their concern that Castro or elements allied with him might disrupt, or even come to control, the waterway.

Also, the United States expended an inordinate amount of energy in striving to gain the support of its Latin American neighbors in a policy designed to exclude Castro's Cuba from all participation, economic and political, in the affairs of the hemisphere. That policy, finally imposed by collective decision in 1964, began to erode almost at once. Today, the exclusionary policy is no longer collective at all, it being left to each individual hemispheric state to devise its own Cuba policy, and frequently enough the state has decided to reestablish full relations with the island.

Since 1968, in a process initiated by President Nixon and Secretary of State Kissinger, there has been a fundamental change in U.S. relations with the Western Hemisphere; and it is now appropriate to say that U.S. policy makers think of Latin America and the Caribbean not as a region with which the United States has a geographically and historically sanctioned "special relationship," but rather as a collection of disparate states, some small, some large, some comparatively advanced, some still quite underdeveloped, some of strategic importance to the United States, others of scant significance. To the extent that region is thought of as a bloc, it is thought of as part of the South in the North-South encounter. The "Western Hemisphere idea," so important during the first 175 years of this country's independent life, has largely ceased to play a substantial role in policy formulation.

As for Cuba itself, U.S. policy has remained largely static. There is no longer frenetic concern about Cuba, but there is no strong drive to fully normalize relations. Cuba is no longer perceived as a major threat to other mainland Latin American countries, and even concern about neighboring Caribbean lands is reduced, in part because the counterinsurgency capabilities of the states of the region are now presumably adequate to deal with incipient, Castro-inspired insurrection, in part because Castro has redirected his energies away from this hemisphere toward domestic Cuban problems and also toward involvement, military and otherwise, elsewhere in the world.

The preponderance of evidence indicates that Castro is firmly in control in Cuba, despite nearly two decades of effort by the United States and some other entities to topple or at least to embarrass him mightily; and Washington now appears prepared to acknowledge that Castro is likely to continue as Cuba's unchallengeable leader as long as he chooses to do so. The Cuban economy is in difficulty, when it is assessed by the conventional instruments of Western economics and against Western indicators; but the Cuban people do not appear to be either suffering or restive because of economic shortcomings. The rest of the world, not only the Socialist countries or the nonaligned, but also the developed countries of the West, have come to terms with Cuba. Some United States politicians are advocating an end to U.S.-Cuban hostility, while U.S. businessmen are beginning to inquire after the potentialities of the Cuban market, and artists, sport figures, scholars, students and ordinary tourists are becoming acquainted with Cuba.

In light of the changing international roles of the United States and Cuba, why does not the United States adjust its Cuba policy more dramatically? Why does it not move toward full diplomatic recognition of the Castro regime or seek a China-like rapprochement? One important reason is also simple: there is little demand for such a change. From a political point of view, as President Kennedy was the first president to discover, the political costs of moves toward a rapprochement with Cuba can be considerable, but the political gains from such a move are very small.

Beyond such political considerations, several ostensible reasons have been advanced for U.S. intransigence. One is that the United States cannot reestablish full relations until Castro has agreed to make restitution to expropriated U.S. property owners that is "adequate, prompt and effective." But that condition need not be controlling, as it has not been historically in other situations, where the United States leadership concluded that the best interests of the country would be served by renewing relations. Another ostensible reason is that Cuba's military alliance with the Soviet Union poses an insuperable obstacle to normal relations. But in this era, the real military threat to the United States comes directly from the Soviet Union, not from Cuba; and as was demonstrated as long ago as 1962 in the missiles crisis, in a major crisis the United States will choose to deal directly with the Soviet Union.

Finally, an announced reason for the unwillingness of the United States to renew relations is that Castro had steadfastly refused to commit himself to halting the export of his revolution. This reason deserves serious consideration.

Historically, in the conduct of foreign relations, the leaders of the United States have based their policies upon two very different sets of premises. One set derives from a strong ideological component in this country's national tradition. It gives rise to a strain of policy that has been labelled "idealistic," and its practitioners include such presidents as Woodrow Wilson who led this country in a struggle to "make the world safe for democracy," but who also intervened in Mexico to "teach the Mexicans to elect good men." Another practitioner was President Eisenhower, who conducted the military side of a "Crusade in Europe,"* and who also, with his Secretary of State John Foster Dulles, conducted a crusade against international communism.

The other set of foreign policy premises has been called "realistic"; and policy derived on its terms presumably takes account only of national interest defined in terms of power and power relationships, to adopt the language of its principal theorist, Hans J. Morgenthau. Richard Nixon and Henry Kissinger gave priority to this strain in the American tradition. Evidently, neither those who may be called "idealists" nor those called "realists" operate on the basis of one strain alone; but one or the other has been dominant.

The ordinary citizens of the United States, like the country's leaders, feel the tension between these two orientations. On the one hand, the United States is a nation that is based upon an ideology derived from values embodied in the documents prepared by the founding fathers. These are truths that are held to be self-evident, and they are held to pertain to all men. The mission of the United States is to bear these truths, to exemplify them, and to help spread them among all mankind.

On the other hand, the United States is a great power in the accepted sense: it is capable of exerting massive force in the surrounding world

---

*This is the title Dwight Eisenhower gave to his wartime memoirs written in 1948.

environment; and it shares space in this world with other powers which also have massive force to exert, either alone or in coalition. Power is a factor that must be taken into account in the conduct of foreign affairs; but so also is the ideology of the United States if the United States is to maintain its national identity and integrity.

As far as U.S. relations with Cuba are concerned, the policy implication of the idealistic-realistic tension is clear enough. The United States can afford to adhere to a fairly rigid ideological line against Fidel Castro's regime because Cuba is of relatively little importance to U.S. interests today. The United States does not feel itself obliged to come to terms with Cuba, as it feels itself obliged to come to terms with the Soviet Union and the Peoples Republic of China, two regimes with which the United States has no more ideological affinity than it does with Cuba. (The same kind of observation, of course, can be made regarding strong United States expressions of concern about human rights violations in Latin American countries and comparatively muted expressions where countries of greater strategic importance are concerned, such as Iran, Saudi Arabia, the Philippines, South Korea, etc.)

It is well to be clear about what is ideologically at issue between the United States and Cuba, because real ideological division prevents compromise. Most important, Cuba is the first avowedly Marxist-Leninist state in the Western Hemisphere. In Cuba, as in the Soviet Union or the Peoples Republic of China, the distinction, so important in pluralistic, constitutionally democratic political systems, between society and state is blurred: in Cuba, Castro is not only in charge of the governmental apparatus, he is also the heart, will, and mind of the Cuban people, presuming to guide Cubans in numerous aspects of their activity and development.

The obliteration of the distinction between society and state has far-reaching consequences. Law, for instance, is no longer to be regarded as an impartial instrument, available to members of a society not only for the handling of disputes among themselves but also for defense of their fundamental rights vis-à-vis the state itself. Such conceptions are incompatible with regimes like Castro's, where "Socialist legality" requires that all citizens behave in ways supportive of the Revolution.

There is no need to dwell further upon ideological incompatabilities. If individual freedom is the underlying ideological premise of the U.S. system, then social and economic equality is the orienting value in Cuba. For Castro, individual freedom which occupies such a high place in the scale of values of the United States is deprecated as having little or no worth in a society characterized by harsh class divisions, and gross inequities in the distribution of goods and the access to opportunity. From the U.S. perspective, on the other hand, the loss of political freedoms is far too high a price to pay for the attainment of relative equality of opportunity and reward.

We may return now to the question raised at the beginning of this chapter, Can the situation that obtains between the United States and Cuba be redefined so as to allow a relationship more constructive than the present one to emerge? The redefinition would require two very substantial changes on the part of the United States.

First, the U.S. would have to acknowledge that its experience with constitutional democracy is accountable to special circumstances of geography, history and good fortune that have only remote analogues in Latin America and this experience is not applicable to Cuba. Secondly, it must be admitted that the political freedom prized in the United States is worth substantially less in the eyes of Cubans and many others in the Caribbean region, not only because historically they have seldom enjoyed the benefits of these freedoms, but also because those peoples are prepared to assign an even higher worth to the attainment of decent material and social conditions. It seems unlikely, however, that American leaders will soon publicly accept these propositions and without such acceptance prospects for a policy of cooperation rather than conflict with Cuba remain poor.

There is, therefore, almost no prospect of radical change in our evaluation of the respective roles of the United States and Cuba in the hemisphere and the world. Even if the Carter administration was disposed to move toward conciliation and cooperation with Cuba, Castro's own recent pronouncements and behavior make such a shift domestically hazardous if not impossible. The Cuban chief of state continues to make clear that he is contemptuous of United States values and institutions and that he has no intention of compromising his revolution for the sake of an accomodation. Moreover, his activities in supporting armed struggle in Africa, in opposition to the declared interests of the United States, make any direct United States approach to him at this time extremely difficult.

Castro aspires to a role of leadership among the peoples of the third world and a prominant position among those who govern the nonaligned states. While his protestations of nonalignment are at times questioned even within that bloc of states, he does think of himself as as independent figure leading an ideologically independent Cuba. He is most unlikely to take any action which might be viewed as capitulation to the United States. Quite to the contrary, he apparently would like to see the United States come to him as a supplicant. No president of the United States, however is likely soon to come contritely to Havana. For the forseeable future, then, we shall probably have to endure the continuation of the present relationship that is neither peace nor war, neither accomodation nor violent hostility.

NOTES

1. John Winthrop, "A Model of Christian Charity," *The Papers of John Winthrop,* (Boston: Massachusetts Historical Society, 1931), II, p. 295.

2. From President Theodore Roosevelt's Annual Message to Congress, December 6, 1904, in Ruhl J. Bartlett ed., *The Record of American Diplomacy: Documents and Readings in the History of American Foreign Relations,* 3rd ed. (New York: Alfred A. Knopf, 1954), p. 539.

3. Ibid.

4. See Loree Wilkerson, "I Am a Marxist," in James Nelson Goodsell ed., *Fidel Castro's Personal Revolution in Cuba, 1959–1973* (New York: Alfred A. Knopf, 1975), pp. 41–54.

12

Soviet and Cuban
Interests in
the Caribbean

W. Raymond Duncan

Soviet and Cuban goal seeking in the Caribbean merits serious study because of the confusion and debate that surround Soviet and Cuban foreign policy today, generated largely by the close economic dependency of Havana on Moscow. The dual roles followed by these countries during the Angolan civil war of 1975–76, and later in support of Ethiopia against Somalia, complicate understanding of their roles in international relations. Soviet and Cuban interests, as a result of these conditions, are frequently perceived as working globally in tandem, with Havana construed essentially as a satellite state.[1] Given this easy tendency to interpret Cuban foreign policy as a by-product of Soviet influence rather than as a unique actor, it is useful to focus on the Caribbean. For here is a kind of laboratory in which to inquire more deeply into the extent of congruence in Soviet and Cuban diplomacy in one major arena of international politics.

The purpose of this chapter is to examine, first, Soviet thought about the Caribbean as delineated, secondly, from the Cuban perspective. Focus on each country's reasons for pursuing a Caribbean posture suggests the degree to which Soviet and Cuban expectations are identical, how they are different, and the potentially distinct directions they can take in the long run. One overall conclusion is that Soviet and Cuban roles in the Caribbean, despite their Marxist similarities and close economic association, are best understood as emanating from two culturally and historically different countries, each pursuing their own national interests, albeit in some respects parallel, and which are operating in a volatile region of the world noted for its divisive insularity and independent frame of mind.

But it is nevertheless a region in quest of maximum opportunities to solve enormous economic and social development problems which condition Caribbean countries to Soviet and Cuban overtures.

SOVIET PERCEPTIONS OF THE CARIBBEAN

Now that Cuba seems to be working in tandem with the Soviet Union —in Africa and Latin America—it is quite natural to blur one's vision of their foreign policies into a single thread rather than analyzing them as distinct strands of diplomacy. This tendency seems especially true of the Caribbean which, in fact, is of distinct interest to both Moscow and Havana, and where the activities of each have been on the increase during the 1970s, as depicted in Tables 12.1 and 12.2. Moscow and Havana's special flirtations with socialist Guyana and Jamaica during the mid-1970s even more encourage us to believe there is a perceptual fusion of their foreign policies, with the frequent generalization that Cuba is a proxy or, in effect, satellite state of the USSR. Moscow and Havana's foreign policies today do converge in the Caribbean and certainly the Soviet Union and Cuba are locked in tight economic embrace. Yet the absolute permanence of this wedding and the total commonality of Soviet and Cuban interests in and perceptions of the Caribbean may be more shadow than substance. Interpretating contemporary Soviet and Cuban policy can be sharpened by showing not only their aspects of similarity, but also by probing the distinct underlying conceptual models of the world operating from Moscow and Havana.

From Soviet perceptions, the Caribbean leaped into significance with the coming of the Cuban Revolution in 1959 and its subsequent turn toward radical nationalism and Marxist-Leninism.[2] This event gave Moscow its first major toehold in North America's "strategic rear," and marked another major event in the expansion of the "world socialist system" in its continuing struggle with capitalism and imperialism.[3] Cuba, geographically located in the backyard of imperialism's power center—the United States—became the fulcrum on which Moscow's Latin American policy began its renaissance period from the early 1960s onward. As the Latin American link on which the world socialist system seems most securely tied, notably after the 1973 demise of Marxist leader Salvador Allende in Chile, Cuba cannot help but be of enormous importance to the Soviets as a channel for affecting the rest of Latin America in its relationships with the "capitalist" and "imperialist" United States. Located in the Caribbean, moreover, Cuba directs Soviet attention to other Caribbean countries such as Puerto Rico and Panama where the

TABLE 12.1: Diplomatic, Consular, and Trade Representation of Communist Countries in Latin America and the Caribbean, June 30, 1971

	Albania	Bulgaria	People's Republic of China	Cuba	Czechoslovakia	East Germany	Hungary	Mongolia	North Korea	North Vietnam	Poland	Romania	USSR	Yugoslavia
Argentina		E			E, T		E, T				E, T	E	E, T	E
Bahamas														
Barbados														
Bolivia		NRA			E(NRA)		E(NRA)				NRA		E, T	E
Brazil	NRM	L, T	E, T	E, T	E, C, T	T	L, T				E, C	L, T	E, T	E
Chile		E, T	E, T	E, T	E, T	E, T	E(NRA), T		T	T	E, T	E, T	E, T	E
Colombia		C			C, T	T	C				NRA, C, T	NRA, T		NRA
Costa Rica		T			C, T						NRM			
Dominican Republic														
Ecuador					E, T	T	NRA				E(NRA), T	NRA	E, T	NRA
El Salvador														

134

Grenada						
Guatemala						
Guyana					NRA	
Haiti			NRM, T			
Honduras	NRA		NRM			
Jamaica					C	
Mexico	E	E, T	E, T		E, C	E, T
						T
Nicaragua			NRM			
Panama	NRA		NRM, T			
Paraguay	NRA					
Peru	E	E, T	E(NRA)	E	E	E
Surinam						
Trinidad and Tobago						
Uruguay	E	E, T	T, E(NRA)	E(NRA), T	E, T	E
Venezuela	E	E, T	E	NRA	E, T	E

Note: E—Embassy; L—Legation; E(NRA)—Embassy (non-resident Ambassador); C—Consulate; T—Trade Office; NRA—Non-resident Ambassador; NRM—Non-resident Minister

Source: Compiled by the author.

TABLE 12.2: Diplomatic, Consular, and Trade Representation of Communist Countries in Latin America and the Caribbean, December 31, 1976

	Albania	Bulgaria	People's Republic of China	Cuba	Czechoslovakia	East Germany	Hungary	Mongolia	North Korea	North Vietnam	Poland	Romania	USSR	Yugoslavia
Argentina	E	E,C,T	E,C,T	E,C,T	E,C,T	E,C,T	E,C,T	NRA	E	R	E,C,T	E,C,T	E,C,T	E,C,T
Bahamas				NRA										
Barbados				NRA										
Bolivia		NRA			E(NRA)	R	E(NRA)				E(NRA)	E(NRA)	E,T	E
Brazil	L	E,T	E,T		E,C,T	E,C,T	E,T				E,C,T	E,T	E,T	E,C,T
Chile			E,T									E,T		C
Colombia		E,C,T		E,C,T	E,C,T	E,C,T	E(NRA, C, T				E,C,T	E,C,T	E,C,T	E
Costa Rica	R	T			E(NRA),T	NRA	NRA		R	R	NRA	E,C,T	E,C,T	NRA
Dominican Republic														
Ecuador		E(NRA)			E,T	E	E(NRA)				E	E(NRA)	E,T	E(NRA)
El Salvador		T			T							T	T	T

Grenada		R								
Guatemala										
Guyana	E, T	E	R	NRA, T	NRA	NRA	NRA	E	E	
Haiti					L					
Honduras		NRA	NRA		NRA	NRA	NRA			
Jamaica	E	R	R	R	NRA	R	NRA	R	E	
Mexico	E, C	E, T	E, T	R	E	E, T	E	R	E, T	E
Nicaragua					NRA					
Panama	E	NRA	R	R	E(NRA)	E(NRA)	NRA	E		
Paraguay							NRA	NRA		
Peru	E, T	E, T	E, T	T	E, T	E, T	E, T	E, C, T	E	
Surinam	R		R			R	R	R		
Trinidad and Tobago	E	NRA	R				NRA	NRA		
Uruguay	E, T	E, T	E(NRA)		E(NRA), T	E	E, T	E, T	E	
Venezuela	E	E, T	R	R	E	E	E	E	E	

Note: E—Embassy; L—Legation; E(NRA)—Embassy (non-resident Ambassador); C—Consulate; T—Trade Office; NRA—Non-resident Ambassador; NRM—Non-resident Minister; R—Relations, but no representatives exchanged

Source: Compiled by the author.

"imperialist" United States faces a variety of problems. The Cuban Revolution gave the Caribbean region significance in Soviet ideological and national perceptions.

To prove the significance of Cuba and the Caribbean more deeply requires a a brief commentary on the impact of Marxist-Leninist ideology on the formation and execution of Moscow's foreign policy. The nature of the present epoch, as Soviets see it through the Marxist dialectic and inevitable historical evolution, is one of the growing might of the world socialist system stimulated by the power of the Soviet Union itself.[4] Capitalism is in the midst of a "general and unsurmountable crisis" leading toward less ability for imperialism—the highest stage of capitalism—to impose its will in the world and equally toward the ultimate transition to socialism.[5] And Moscow tends to view the general growing strength of the socialist system specifically in the success of the Cuban Revolution next door to "imperialist" North America and also in the contemporary events within the Caribbean that make it an area of special concern.[6]

The present epoch is characterized in Soviet terminology by the struggle between the forces of socialism and the forces of imperialism, which they term the "correlation of forces." The Caribbean is a region where the Soviets envision this correlation tilting favorably toward the socialist trend.[7] In effect, this correlation of forces and the growth of the socialist system means a Soviet view of weakened United States economic strength and political power in the world generally, and directly in its own Caribbean backyard. Cuba and the Caribbean, then, are seen as part of a major global pattern rather than as isolated regions.

Soviet ideology presents Moscow's leaders with a built-in tendency to view events in Cuba and the Caribbean in terms of their impact on the power distribution between socialism and imperialism—more directly on power distributed between Moscow and Washington. Marxism-Leninism posits a bipolar (correlation of forces) world of socialism versus capitalism-imperialism, a perpetual conflict, in which weakened United States power automatically weakens imperialism and strengthens world socialism—and the Soviet Union. The correlation of forces analysis stresses the importance of power to Moscow, and this predisposes Moscow's leaders to encourage favorable situations, especially in regions that are strategically important. It is a fluid and dynamic conceptualization of power—quite unlike the Western and U.S. views of "balance of power" with the built-in tendency toward maintenance of the status quo around the world.[8] The important points here are that Moscow appears to see the correlation of forces moving favorably in the Caribbean, that the Caribbean is part of the United States' "strategic rear," and that it is potentially a fruitful area for encouraging anticapitalism and antiimperialism indirectly through Cuban diplomacy and directly through Moscow's bilateral relations with Caribbean countries, or through the Soviet-controlled Council for Mutual Economic Assistance (CMEA or COMECON).

In the Soviet view, the Cuban Revolution ranks high in promoting radical departures from traditional Latin American dependency on and subservience to the United States. Cuba, in the words of one Soviet spokesman, has become a "shining example of what might be achieved by a people who have rejected the capitalist path of development and embraced the road to building socialism."[9] The Soviets see Cuba as a catalyst for restructuring inter-American relations and generally reducing the role played by U.S.-based multinational monopolies.[10]

This assessment is based in part on the progressive reentry of Havana into Caribbean and Latin American diplomacy following a period of sharp isolation between 1966 and 1968. The acceptance of Cuba back into the Caribbean region is illustrated by growing diplomatic and trade relations, notably with Barbados, Guyana, Jamaica, and Trinidad and Tobago, but including other Caribbean and Latin American countries, as shown in Tables 12.1 and 12.2.[11] This growing fraternity of Cuba and its Caribbean neighbors undoubtedly helped bring an end to the formal embargo of Cuba which had been sanctioned by the Organization of American States (OAS). The Soviets see the July 1975 vote as one example of weakening U.S. power in the inter-American system, since Washington had for so long opposed lifting the embargo.

The diminished role of the United States in the inter-American system is underscored by other recent events, which the Soviets interpret as part of the anticapitalist and antiimperialist trend in the Caribbean. The formation of the new Latin American economic system (SELA) in October 1975, under the initiatives of Mexico and Venezuela, and strongly supported by Cuba and several Caribbean states, provides one illustration. The Soviets are quick to point out the conspicuous presence of Cuba and the absence of the United States in SELA, and its impact on the weakening of the U.S.-dominated OAS. They see this as an example of a trend toward "unity and solidarity founded on the realization by the peoples of the continent that they have a common historical destiny and must act in a united front against imperialist expansion."[12]

Other Soviet-cited evidence of this type includes the formation of the joint Caribbean Shipping Company of eight countries (NAMUCAR), which is seen as further evidence of a successful "integrational trend" in Latin America leading toward accelerated weakening of "imperialism's position."[13] Of major prominence in the Soviet literature today is Caribbean and Latin American raw materials diplomacy which is opposed to United States private business control. Guyana's nationalization of the Reynolds Guyana Mines in January 1975, thus bringing the country's bauxite mining industry fully under state control, is one example of this trend.* The formation of the Caribbean Free Trade Association (CARIFTA), Mexico's new link-up with the Soviet-East European Council for Mutual Economic Assistance (CMEA), and the steady growth of relations between the Latin American states and the East European countries can be added to the positive events from the Soviet point of view.

Two other aspects of the favorable correlation of forces in Latin America merit Soviet attention. One is the desire of some Caribbean leaders to adopt socialist models of economic change and to borrow from the Cuban experiment.[14] Guyana and Jamaica are singled out for special attention, given the increasingly close ties between Cuba, Guyana, and Jamaica from the early 1970s onwards, and the increasing links between the Soviet Union and Eastern European countries with the Caribbean states.[15] A second positive feature of contemporary Caribbean affairs is the continued role played by Cuba as the major critic of U.S. diplomacy in Latin America, despite the détente-thawing of Soviet-American relations since 1972.[16] Cuba and the United States appear to be moving more closely toward restored diplomatic relations, yet the Cuban government remains a strong verbal opponent of Washington's Caribbean diplomacy. This is clearly demonstrated in Havana's support for an independent Puerto Rico.

While these events are interpreted favorably relative to global development of the world socialist system in Moscow's ideological prism, they also bear upon Soviet national interests. The Kremlin, as several scholars emphasize today, is playing a traditional game of great power politics, having telescoped their hopes for revolutionary transformations far into the future. They seek to affirm the reality of Soviet power in the Third World with its vital raw materials and strategic role in sea communications. Cuba and the Caribbean offer one fruitful area in which to seek such goals with the concomitant result of reduced U.S. power.

The Soviets probably perceive their maritime interests expanded in the Caribbean by continued attention to this area with its important geographic location relative to the United States and the insular nature of its states with their sea-space relationships. Soviet maritime interests are significant in Cuba as a naval port of call and as a base for merchant marine trade activities, fishing fleet operations, and oceanographic work.[17]

---

*Jamaica also signed an agreement in November 1974 with the Kaiser Aluminum and Chemical Corporation for a 51 percent shareholding by the Jamaican government. And, in 1973, Australia, Guinea, Guyana, Jamaica, Sierra Leone, Surinam, and Yugoslavia formed the International Bauxite Association (IBA) in an effort to gain more leverage in international bauxite operations.

CUBAN POWER POLITICS, REALISM, AND
DECISION-MAKING ELITES IN CARIBBEAN AFFAIRS

Cuban perceptions of the Caribbean flow from operating principles in foreign policy held by Havana's decision-making elite. The first principle appears to be recognition of the essential role played by power in world politics and in securing Cuba's own national interests. The underlying assumption here is that the Castro government has learned much about power politics through its conflicts with the United States since 1959, as well as from its experiences gained with the Soviet Union, Latin America, and recently in Africa, especially Angola. The Castro brothers and their 26th of July supporters in power today are natural inheritors of power through their Sierra Maestra days as guerrilla fighters and in the building of radical nationalism and socialism inside Cuba since the early 1960s.[18] Fidel is, as numerous commentators report, the consummate *político* in domestic politics, a person keenly attuned to domestic power politics that can be translated into foreign policy.

In pursuance of power politics in foreign policy, the decision-making elite in Castro's government—be they the new generation of pragmatic technocrats under Carlos Rafael Rodríguez, the revolutionary antiimperialists who follow Fidel, or the military mission proponents behind Raúl, can be characterized as basically realist in their perceptions of the external world.[19] This means that Cuba, like many another country, is acutely aware of the importance of increasing its own capabilities as a basis for securing its own long-term interests. These interests include, in their minimum parameters, preserving Cuba's territorial security, political independence, cultural uniqueness, and national identity while pressing for its economic development through the accumulation and application of power in its diplomatic, economic, political, technological, and other forms. While different elites within the Cuban government tend to view the acquisition and application of power in different terms from region to region, they are aware of the pitfalls of relying strictly upon the goodwill or morality of other countries or upon international organizations such as the UN to preserve Cuba's key interests. Cuba is not prepared to follow an idealistic foreign policy devoid of power politics.

Havana's conceptualizations are shaped and conditioned by its island's history. One influence is the experience with dependence on and domination by the United States, following many centuries of dependency on Spain. Since Cuba's geopolitical location in the Caribbean is still the same, this experience urges the Cuban leadership to significant sensitivity to North American power and its bearing upon Havana's future. If, as the Soviets argue, the Caribbean is located in Washington's strategic backyard, it is equally true that North America lies in Cuba's strategic front yard, a point Havana can never forget. It should be stressed that past dependency on the United States and all the interference in Cuban internal economics and politics that dependence spawned, undoubtedly also shape Cuban perceptions of the relationship with the USSR. It is one reason that Cubans may indeed wish to minimize their client-state relationship with Moscow without jeopardizing fraternal Soviet-Cuban ties, which some scholars note as a key goal in current Cuban foreign policy.[20] Fraternal ties are required in the short run if Cuba's economic capacity to extend its power in world politics is to increase during the last century of this century.

Castro's government is sensitive to Cuba's past wounded nationalist sentiments, coupled with the dependency relationship and overpowering culture of North America. In Cuban power politics, then, there is a determination to accentuate a Cuban national imprint on Caribbean, Latin American, and African affairs—as if to somehow compensate for the past, to dramatize the enormous significance of the Cuban Revolution, and to give the Cuban people new sources of national pride in their past and future destiny. Building national identity inside Cuba would appear to have found expression in certain aspects of Cuban foreign policy since the early 1960s. This is certainly true in the Caribbean where Cuba can take pride in growing acceptance and diplomatic ties.[21]

If power politics—conditioned by past dependency and frustrated nationalism—are one key to Cuban interests in the Caribbean, the adoption of Marxism is another. Marxist ideology brings with it certain guiding norms about class struggle, inevitable conflict as long as captitalism coexists with socialism, and ultimate long-range victory for socialism. In some respects the Cubans mirror Soviet assessments about the correlation of forces in world politics, specifically that the world balance is tipping toward socialism.[22] Yet Cuba frequently points out that the battle with imperialism in the Caribbean and Latin America is far from won, and that the struggle will be long.[23]

Marxism also provides a ready made list of friends and enemies within Cuba's immediate proximity and in distant lands. Friends are those who are waging the anticapitalist and antiimperialist struggles, hopefully even adopting socialism, and enemies are those who are not. This is an ideology that works for the Cubans as it does for the Soviets, to accentuate again the key role of power in world politics and foreign policy, defined in terms of a central Marxist enemy—the United States. The United States also happens to be the principle enemy evolving out of Cuba's past dependency and frustrated nationalism. The upshot is that Marxism reinforces the Cuban decision-making elites' sensitivity to U.S. power, expecially in the Caribbean, which is so imperative in the geopolitics of Cuban national interests. At the same time it directs Cuban power politics globally to those groups waging militant revolutionary struggles throughout the Third World.

CUBAN POLICIES IN THE CARIBBEAN

Given the requirements of power politics, realism, and Marxist-Leninism as underlying principles in Cuban foreign policy, what interests do they shape and condition relative to Havana's neighbors? First the Caribbean, given the threatening shadow cast by Washington, is of prime importance. Where Washington's power can be reduced, all the better, for it strengthens Cuban security. Just how Washington's power can be reduced—while at the same time keeping open the channels for restored diplomatic relations and the potential flow of needed sophisticated technology—varies from country to country, yet entails a number of common variables. These range from reducing the power of multinational corporations where possible (bauxite companies being nationalized in Guyana and Jamaica), to stopping the technological brain drain from the Caribbean and Latin America to North America, to turning the Panama Canal back to Panama, to pressing for independence for Puerto Rico—all projects which the Cubans actively support.[24]

Secondly, supporting countries that appear interested in socialist models of change well befits Cuba's Marxist predilections. So much the better if these countries, in this case Guyana and Jamaica, show a willingness to adopt parts of the Cuban model and, in a variety of ways, act to reinforce Cuban national pride. Signing cultural, educational, medical, sports, and technical agreements with Caribbean countries helps build pride among the Cuban people in their revolution, while at the same time gaining diplomatic allies in a proximate and critical geopolitical region. Throughout the 1970s, medical teams went out to Guyana and Jamaica, school buildings and mini-dams were constructed in Jamaica with Cuban help, and sports scholarships were given to Jamaica as another means to bind the two countries together. Fidel Castro visited Kingston in October 1977, following Prime Minister Manley's earlier visit to Havana, and Mrs. Beverly Manley, on another visit in December 1977, cited Cuba as "pointing the path to development" and as a "source of hope for the future."[25] The stakes can of course go beyond the Caribbean. Cuban involvement in the Angolan civil war of 1975–76 brought air stopover privileges from Guyana for Cuban planes enroute to Angola, and both Guyana and Jamaica have become supportive of Cuba's involvement in Africa.

Third, in building Cuban power in the Caribbean and weakening that of the United States, Cuba has pressed for the independence of Puerto Rico, Belize, and Dominica. While such pressures can be interpreted as natural for a Marxist nation pushing for national liberation movements, they can also be seen as logical to a Caribbean state trying to increase its power by weakening that of other strong states, in this case by breaking up their holdings in areas geographically close to Cuba and leaving smaller independent states with which Cuba might play a more influential role.

Fourth, Cubans are critically aware of the constraints imposed upon their future potential for economic growth by global interdependence. As one scholar has argued, the Cubans have been sheltered from the energy crisis and the rising price of oil by the assistance of the USSR—but this has bound the Cubans more closely with the Soviet Union, a situation with which they do not always feel at ease.[26] This uneasiness is easily understandable, given the long-term effects of the energy crisis on future Soviet oil deliveries and on the Soviet capacity to supply advanced technology and other skills which the Cubans need. Constraints imposed on the Cubans by international economic relationships bring them back to the Caribbean in several respects. Mexico and Venezuela, also key actors in Caribbean affairs, are potential oil suppliers, and Havana's relations with Caracas and Mexico City are laying potential, albeit not explicit, connections with these suppliers should the need for their petroleum arise. Second, Washington is a potential supplier of future capital and advanced technology, which means that Havana's Caribbean posture must be tempered with the understanding of North America's long-term role as a trade partner. These considerations bear upon the style in which Havana must conduct its relations in the Caribbean—looking to a future of less dependency upon the Soviet Union and a return to improved trade relations in Latin America and with the United States. As if to underscore this point, Carlos Rafael Rodríguez has stated that "by virtue of its historical development and geographical location, Cuba belongs to the Latin American community. We have never renounced and never shall renounce these ties."[27]

A fifth interest in the Caribbean that naturally flows from Havana's central operating principles is that of gaining increased flexibility in its own foreign affairs. Stated in other terms, this means reducing the dependency syndrome felt in Havana's ties with Moscow, and doing so in the short run, rather than waiting for some future date when Moscow's supplier role may become less dominant. Developing an active Caribbean policy allows Havana to gain flexibility vis-à-vis the Soviet Union and, in fact, to augment its power. Havana's Caribbean diplomacy demonstrates an independence in foreign policy perhaps not found in its African ventures, which seem to reflect a satellite or proxy status relative to Moscow. The Caribbean posture also extends Cuban power; it provides Havana with one avenue in which to gain prestige and to influence Washington's backyard—a power which can be measured against that of Washington and counterpoised to the Soviets—while providing a base for playing a more active role in world affairs. Translated into specific terms, the Caribbean diplomacy has produced a number of new trends favorable to a Cuban sui generis concept of power.

What did the Caribbean diplomacy produce? It helped to end the OAS embargo against Cuba, despite United States opposition. It allowed Cuba to join the new economic system of Latin America (SELA), cosponsored by Mexico and Venezuela in October 1975. The new role of Cuba in the inter-American states system also promoted a further weakening of the OAS, which Havana publically decries as an outdated instrument of American capitalism and imperialism. Cuba's ties in the Caribbean community also helped build bridges leading to the new Caribbean Multinational Shipping Enterprise (NAMUCAR), in which Cuba stands to play a powerful role given its astronomical rise in maritime strength.*

These trends are important considerations from Cuba's point of view about the crucial role played by power in regional and global affairs. They are all distinctly supportive of Cuban national interests and national pride, and encourage Havana to be more self-confident about its diplomacy. The extent to which these trends encourage the Cubans to seek more flexibility in world affairs at a time of increased economic dependency on the Soviet Union, or the extent to which Cuba can be more flexible beyond the Caribbean and Latin American (its traditional and natural geopolitical area of interest), or the degree in which success in the Caribbean may ameliorate frustrations felt in the close Soviet embrace are perhaps additional important considerations, but ones about which no definitive conclusions are yet possible.

Sixth, Caribbean interests are clearly a part of the more broad spectrum of Third World affairs in which Cuba aspires to play a leading role. The Caribbean countries, as part of the Latin American Third World—with which the Caribbean and Latin American countries now identify (having moved away from older concepts of Pan Americanism)—are speaking out with increasing demands on the developed world (including the USSR at times). Their aspirations for a New International Economic Order (NIEO) provide one case in point. As Cuba's role in the Caribbean

---

*Cuba's merchant fleet consisted of only fourteen vessels prior to the 1959 Revolution, with an overall dead weight of 57,715 tons. In just eighteen years of revolution, the number of ocean-going freighters and coastal freighters increased to eighty, with an overall dead weight of more than 700,000 tons.

is enhanced, as it has been during the past three years as a supplier of aid and technical information to Guyana and Jamaica, then its general prestige in Third World forums may also increase. In this context it is not surprising to learn that Havana will be the site of the Sixth Summit Conference of Non-Aligned Countries and of the Eleventh World Festival of Youth and Students in 1979.[28]

CONCLUSIONS

While Soviet and Cuban interests in the Caribbean converge on a number of issues, they also reflect distinct foreign policy perceptions. There is a degree of unity in views on ideology, the role of power in world politics, acceptance of peaceful policies over violent ones, and generally gearing foreign policy to fit emerging Caribbean leftism in countries like Guyana and Jamaica. Yet the divergence of Moscow and Havana in the Caribbean is also clear. Cuba appears more active than the Soviets, given logistical and geographical facts. Havana also more easily identifies with the region's cultural and historical legacy of colonialism and African ancestry—and for this reason is capable of forging a Caribbean link to its Third World leadership role. Finally, Cuba has developed several small island development skills in cultural affairs, education, housing, medicine, and sports—to identify only a few of the areas—which may be suitable to other Caribbean countries.

Moscow and Havana both face a number of constraints to their Caribbean postures. Most Caribbean states are intensely independent, not likely to form a chain of homogeneous Communist states. Furthermore, Washington's renewed interest in the Caribbean during President Carter's administration, if translated into aid and improved trade relations, could offset Caribbean attraction to limited Cuban and Soviet aid.

Finally, Caribbean countries are deeply divided by ethnic differences and by distinct political groups vying for power. Some of these groups view Cuba as an attractive model to solve their country's difficulties; for other groups Cuba is to be feared. The Cuban and Soviet presence, especially the more geographically proximate Cuba, therefore tends to perform a politically divisive function in the region—as the case of Jamaica illustrates. The impact of this situation in the long-run is difficult to measure, but could take at least three forms: (1) right wing conservative reactions, (2) increasing drift toward leftist solutions to development problems, or (3) high rates of political destabilization with no clear resolution of leadership friction over how to develop during the last quarter of the twentieth century. In any case, the development needs of the Caribbean countries, combined with the dynamics of international relations in this area, clearly call for a consistent Caribbean focus in U.S. foreign policy.

NOTES

1. A number of works tend to take the "satellite" view of Cuban foreign policy. See, for example, Hugh Thomas, "Cuba's Military Adventures," *The Christian Science Monitor,* 17 March 1978, pp. 14–15; Peter Vanneman and Martin James, "The Soviet Intervention in Angola: Intentions and Implications," *Strategic Review* (Summer 1976), pp. 92–103. For a balanced view of Cuban foreign policy, emphasizing the role of internal decision-making elites, see Edward Gonzalez, "Complexities of Cuban Foreign Policy," *Problems of Communism* 26 (November–December 1977): 1–15.

2. Moscow regularly praises the Cuban Revolution of 1959 as a milestone in Latin American history that weakened imperialism and increased the liberation struggle of the Latin American people. See, for example, S. Mishin, "Latin America: Current Trends of Development," *International Affairs* (Moscow), no. 5 (May 1975): 54–55. For incisive treatment of this early period, see Andrés Suárez, *Cuba: Castroism and Communism 1959–1966* (Cambridge, Mass.: M.I.T. Press, 1967). Also Edward Gonzalez, *Cuba Under Castro: The Limits of Charisma* (Boston: Houghton Mifflin Co., 1974), pp. 121 ff.

3. See Leon Gauré and Morris Rothenberg, *Soviet Penetration of Latin America* (Miami: Center for Advanced International Study, University of Miami, 1975), pp. 1–7.

4. On the consolidation of the position of socialism and its relationship to the liberation struggle in Latin America, see D. Lozinov, "The Liberation Struggle in Latin America," *International Affairs* no. 9 (August 1977): 39–45.

5. B. Gafurov, "The Soviet Union and the National Liberation Movement," *International Affairs* (Moscow), no. 7 (July 1971): 20.

6. Gouré and Rothenberg, op. cit., p. 3.

7. S. Mishin, "Latin America: Two Trends of Development," *International Affairs* (Moscow), no. 6 (June 1976): 54.

8. See Nils H. Wessell, "Soviet Views of the Emerging International System" (Paper presented at the Annual meeting of the International Studies Association, Toronto, Canada March, 1976), pp. 1–7.

9. Lozinov, op. cit., p. 39.

10. Regaining state control over raw materials, a part of nationalist trends in the Caribbean today, is a major theme in Soviet thought about Latin America. See A. Matlina, "Latin America: Struggle for Raw Materials," *International Affairs* (Moscow), no. 10 (October 1975): 55–60. Controlling raw materials is one method, the Soviets argue, to control the "ruthless practices of international monopolies"; ibid., p. 55.

11. The Soviets are quick to point out that Caribbean states led in the progressive reentry of Cuba into the diplomatic network of its Latin American neighbors. Barbados, Guyana, Jamaica, and Trinidad and Tobago established diplomatic relations with Cuba in 1972–73, and Panama did the same in 1974. See A. Glinkin, "Changes in Latin America," *International Affairs* (Moscow), no. 1 (January 1975): 51–53.

12. Mishin, op. cit. The other trend is one of disunity, rivalry, and struggle between individual large states for spheres of influence in the region. Ibid. The first trend is "integrational"; the second "disintegrational." The members of SELA included Cuba and twenty-two other Latin American and Caribbean countries. The main aims of SELA are to reinforce regional cooperation and to help coordinate the functions of existing groups such as the Andean Group and the Central American Common Market. The Soviets strongly support SELA.

13. *Ibid.*, p. 57.

14. Lozinov, op. cit., p. 41.

15. Cuba and Jamaica signed a one year economic and technical cooperation agreement in May 1977, as part of their increasingly close relations since 1972–73. See Kingston *Daily Gleaner,* 31 May 1977. And Kingston announced its warming economic long-range plans with the Soviet Union in July 1977. See Kingston *Daily Gleaner,* July 20, 1977. Guyana and the German Democratic Republic (GDR), meanwhile, signed an agreement to develop the bauxite industury in June 1977. See Kingston *Sunday Gleaner,* 12 June 1977. Cuban experts were studying Guyana's sugar industry in June 1977 as sources of possible help (radio broadcast in Spanish from Paris, June 17, 1977). Guyana and the Soviet Union signed a major economic, scientific, and technological agreement in June 1977. See *Granma Weekly Review,* 26 June 1977.

16. The Cubans, for example, continue to criticize sharply the U.S. role in the OAS, which they see as a tool of North American imperialism, despite the rapprochement between Havana and Washington, *Granma Weekly Review,* 10 July 1977, p. 10.

17. James D. Theberge, ed., *Soviet Seapower in the Caribbean: Political and Strategic Implications* (New York: Praeger Publishers, 1972).

18. On the elites in charge of Cuban foreign policy today, and especially their differing perceptions of policy goals, see Gonzalez, op. cit.

19. Ibid.

20. U.S., *Post-Revolutionary Cuba in a Changing World,* a report prepared for the office of the Assistant Secretary of Defense/International Security Affairs, by Edward Gonzalez and David Ronfeldt, Rand Corporation, December 1975, p. 51.

21. Background reading on this point may be found in W. Raymond Duncan, "Problems in Cuban Foreign Policy," in *Latin American Foreign Policies: An Analysis,* ed. Harold E. Davis and Larmon C. Wilson (Baltimore: The Johns Hopkins Press, 1975), esp. pp. 155–60.

22. As the Cubans point out, "The scales are tipping in favor of socialism" in the present balance of forces between socialism and capitalism, and the capitalist system, with the United States at its head, "is sinking deeper and deeper into crises." *Granma Weekly Review,* 22 May 1977, p. 2.

23. Fidel Castro in an interview with Simon Malloy, editor-in-chief of *Afrique-Asie,* reprinted in *Granma Weekly Review,* 22 May 1977, p. 2.

24. On Cuba's perceiving the United States as the main promoter and beneficiary of the emigration of skilled personnel from Latin America, see *Granma Weekly Review,* 5 June 1977, p. 2, and 8 May 1977, p. 10. Juan Mari Bras, General Secretary of the Puerto Rican Socialist Party, visits Havana frequently in order, among other objectives, to gain a larger Caribbean focus for proindependence sentiments, which is not a bad strategy from his point of view. See *Granma Weekly Review,* 9 June 1977, p. 10.

25. On Castro's October 1977 trip to Jamaica and some of the conversations he had with Jamaican leaders, see *Granma Weekly Review,* November 20 1977, pp. 2–4.

26. Gonzalez and Ronfeldt, op. cit., pp. 42–43.

27. Ibid., p. 44, as stated in "Cuba and CEMA," *Latinskaia Amerika,* no. 6 (November–December 1972): 47.

28. *Granma Weekly Review,* 22 January 1978 and 26 February 1978.

13

Foreign Policy and Attitudes
of Elites in Jamaica:
The First Twelve Years of Nationhood

Wendell Bell

On January 22, 1976, *The Jamaican Daily News* carried a banner of red ink on its front page headline: "PLAN FOR RED TAKEOVER HERE." A member of Parliament, dismissed from the Cabinet by Prime Minister Michael Manley, had countered his dismissal with charges that the ruling People's National Party (PNP) was bringing the Cuban Revolution and Communism to Jamaica. In the months that followed, Jamaica reverberated with the repetition and elaboration of these charges as well as with counter-accusations of American intervention in Jamaica, "destabilisation," and rumors of an influx of agents from the Central Intelligence Agency (CIA).

The facts, of course, show a more complicated, less melodramatic, situation as the new state of Jamaica defined its role on the international stage and plotted its relationships with the outside world.

BRIEF DESCRIPTION OF JAMAICA

Jamaica is an island of nearly 2 million people situated in the Caribbean Sea about 90 miles south of Cuba. An English colony since 1655, Jamaica became a politically independent state on August 6, 1962, following a relatively long period of transition to nationhood under British political domination. In November 1944, limited self-government was inaugurated, based upon the Westminster model of government and, for the first time in the history of Jamaica, upon universal adult suffrage. Until full political independence was obtained, there were periodic constitutional changes—each carried out with the cooperation of the British—granting more and more self-government. For a few years, from 1958 to late 1961, it appeared as if Jamaica would achieve independence as part of the West Indies Federation. A referendum held in September 1961, however, resulted in a "go it alone" decision for Jamaica. The federation collapsed and Jamaica became a separate nation-state.

Jamaica's population is mostly black, between 90 and 95 percent having some degree of African ancestry. The correlation between race and social class is high. There is widespread poverty, a high rate of unemployment, and considerable economic inequality. Bauxite mining has become increasingly important since the 1950s, but the sugar plantation remains an important part of the economy. Bananas and tourists are also important to the economy. In 1976 the Jamaican economy was in trouble, with foreign exchange reserves falling into the minus column, and economic recovery had not yet arrived by 1978.

The bare facts of much of independent Jamaica's foreign affairs can be briefly stated. At the end of 1972, Jamaica had thirteen missions or embassies abroad. These were to the United Kingdom, Canada, the United States, Trinidad and Tobago, Ethiopia, West Germany, the Dominican Republic and Haiti (joint), the United Nations (New York), the United Nations (Geneva), Switzerland, Mexico, the Bahamas, and the European Economic Community (EEC). In addition, consulates numbered fifteen, four of which were in the United States. Also, there were a number of multiple accreditations.[1] Diplomatic relations had been initiated with thirty-eight nations, including the People's Republic of China and six Black African states.[2] Twenty-four nations had consular missions in Jamaica.

After 1972, embassies were established in France and Belgium, and diplomatic relations began with Cuba, Australia, Bangladesh, and in March 1975, with the Soviet Union.[3] Jamaica joined the United Nations after political independence and the Organization of American States (OAS) in 1969. It remained a member of the Commonwealth.

FIVE MAJOR FEATURES OF INDEPENDENT JAMAICA'S FOREIGN POLICY

Five interrelated features of Jamaica's foreign policy behavior since achieving independent statehood stand out.

Perpetuation of the Colonial Past

In the early years of political independence, Jamaica's foreign policy was to some extent a carry-over from the colonial past. It "consisted mainly in petitioning the British, U.S., Canadian, and other Western governments for commodity price-supports and markets, outlets for surplus populations and for steady supplies of capital with which to develop its economy."[4] A major diplomatic focus, for example, was on "Britain's entering the European Common Market," which threatened to disrupt Jamaica's traditional relationships, "unless Britain succeed[ed] in persuading the E.E.C. members to grant favourable concessions to Commonwealth members."[5]

Pro-Western, Christian, and anti-Communist was how then-Prime Minister Alexander Bustamante described the new state, and, on the day after Independence Day, he announced that the United States was free to establish a military base on the island without offering any aid in return.[6]

With respect to patterns of trade, Jamaica's relationships had been changing from dominance by the United Kingdom to dominance by the United States for several decades before independence. The United Kingdom was Jamaica's major trading partner in 1938, taking 59.2 percent of its domestic exports and supplying 32.5 percent of the imports. Canada ranked second, taking 26.6 percent of the exports and supplying 15.6 percent of the imports. The United States took only 3.7 percent of the exports, but supplied 21.0 percent of the imports.[7]

Although this pattern was disrupted by the Second World War, by 1950 it returned to approximate the 1938 percentages, with increased imports from the United Kingdom at the expense of Canada and the United States.

After 1950, however, dramatic changes took place and by 1962 the United States had surpassed the United Kingdom in share of exports and nearly equalled it in share of imports. By 1973 the United States was Jamaica's chief trading partner, taking 41.2 percent of exports and supplying 38.6 percent of imports compared to 23.1 and 16.7 percent respectively for the United Kingdom. Although Canada showed a relative decline in its share of exports and imports, it had an absolute increase in both.[8] The growth of the bauxite and alumina industry, of course, was partly responsible for the shift away from the United Kingdom, since it was owned by American, and to a lesser extent Canadian, interests and linked to those markets. The United States assumed even more importance if the foreign earnings of tourism are included, since 80 percent of the tourists were Americans. The United Kingdom retained importance, however, in such traditional Jamaican exports as sugar and bananas.

There were signs of other changes. By 1973, Venezuela, West Germany, and Japan with respect to imports and Ghana, the USSR, and Sweden with respect to exports stood out among other trading partners of Jamaica. And, of course, other Commonwealth Caribbean countries entered the picture.

Caribbean Integration

Although the 1961 Jamaican referendum was responsible for ending the West Indies Federation, Jamaica nonetheless pursued policies after independence aimed at regional cooperation and integration, primarily of an economic nature. Jamaica's view of the region has become a broad one, including all countries whose shores are washed by the Caribbean and the Guyanas and Bahamas, countries of cultural and historical affinity.[9] Thus it includes, in addition to the islands, Mexico and the states of Central America as well as Colombia, Venezuela, Guyana, and Surinam.

Formal association proceeded most rapidly among the Commonwealth Caribbean states themselves that already shared a number of regional institutions, such as the University of the West Indies and the Caribbean Development Bank. The Caribbean Free Trade Association (CARIFTA) was established in 1968. It aimed to remove tariffs, quantitative restrictions, and other limitations on trade among the participating countries. By 1973, exports to other Commonwealth Caribbean countries were 7.7 percent of Jamaica's total while imports were 5.4 percent, although there was an unfavorable balance of visible trade with nearly J\$5 million excess of imports over exports. Jamaica's exports to CARIFTA countries increased nearly threefold since 1969 when they amounted to J\$7.6. By 1973 they had reached J\$20.1.

A Caribbean Community (CARICOM) was formed in 1973 between Guyana, Trinidad and Tobago, Barbados, and Jamaica, to establish a common market and go beyond CARIFTA in pursuing economic integration. CARICOM was enlarged when some of the less developed territories, including the new state of Grenada, joined. Also, wider links with Latin American countries of the circum Caribbean were being explored. For example, Colombia, Costa Rica, Cuba, Jamaica, Nicaragua, Panama, Venezuela, and Mexico cooperated in establishing a Caribbean shipping line. Additionally, a number of exchanges and agreements between Jamaica and Mexico, as well as between Jamaica and Venezuela, took place, including joint plans for aluminum smelters in Mexico and Venezuela.

Of particular interest, both because of possible implication for internal developments within Jamaica and because of its impact on other Caribbean countries, is Cuba's reach south. At the close of 1972, diplomatic relations opened between Cuba and Jamaica. Relationships between Cuba and Jamaica have grown since. Jamaica's prime minister visited Cuba on July 9, 1975 and Fidel Castro visited Jamaica in mid-October of 1977. A number of technical exchanges and reciprocal visits of delegations occurred. For example, by the end of March 1976, there were a total of eighty-three Cubans on official projects in Jamaica. Twenty were engaged on micro-dams projects, 55 on a school construction project, and 8 on a housing project.[10] Cuban medical teams and other groups have since arrived in Jamaica. Also of note was the fact that a delegation from Jamaica with expenses paid by the PNP attended the First Congress of the Communist Part of Cuba held in December 1975.[11]

In 1974, 83 of Jamaica's top political, labor, economic, mass media, civil service, educational, religious, and other leaders were asked the following question:

Do you think that Jamaica should make any changes in its economic relationships with other countries *in the Caribbean?*

	Percent
Yes, increase relationships	67
No, they should stay about the same	32
Yes, relationships should be decreased	1
Total	100%

Two-thirds of the leaders wanted to increase economic relationships with other countries in the Caribbean, but a rather sizeable minority, nearly a third, did not. Considering that the Jamaican leadership with a few notable exceptions had been largely against federation with the other Commonwealth Caribbean territories and that even more culturally different territories, such as Haiti and Cuba, are included *"in the Caribbean,"* it is noteworthy that so many top leaders were now prepared to seek to strengthen ties in the Caribbean. Such ties, however, given the broad definition of the Caribbean held by Jamaican leaders, already may have weakened CARIFTA and CARICOM.

Black Africa, AntiColonialism, and Antiracism

Consciousness of black Africa, anticolonialism, and antiracism are linked together in the minds of many Jamaicans and were manifest in Jamaica's foreign policies after independence. There was a "recognition of the relationship between different racial elements in the country's social structure, and the need to have foreign policy reflect a proper balance between these elements. Thus, the policy began to reflect an emphasis on Jamaica's connection with Africa and international questions with which Africa was closely involved."[12] Not only had diplomatic relations been opened with black African states in 1968, but also in 1969 both the then-prime minister of Jamaica (Hugh Shearer) and the then-leader of the opposition (Michael Manley) took extended tours of the African continent. "Both included a visit to Haile Selassie I in Addis Ababa in an effort to identify themselves with a figure who is venerated by some Jamaicans."[13]

In his study of voting in the seventeenth to twenty-fourth sessions of the UN Matthews found that Jamaica and other Caribbean new states, compared to non-Caribbean Commonwealth members, were part of the pro-African and nonwhite cluster of countries on four racial, African, or colonial issues: apartheid in South Africa, Southern Rhodesia, Namibia, and African territories under Portuguese administration.[14] Jamaica in the UN "placed much emphasis upon race as a fundamental question of human rights" and took a fairly radical stand on such issues, spearheading, for example, the designation of 1968 as International Year for Human Rights.[15] In 1976, Jamaica signed the International Convention on the Suppression and Punishment of the Crime of Apartheid. In general, Jamaica supported African aspirations, decolonization, and antiracism. And it did so in the early years of its participation in the UN, while it was still being cautious on economic issues so as to maximize the chances for private foreign investment, loans, and aid from Western captialist countries, especially from the United States, and while it was still leaning to the U.S. view on admission of the People's Republic of China to the UN and on cold war issues generally.

Paralleling the new diplomatic relations with Africa were changes in the cultural identities of Jamaican elite. Both in 1962, just prior to political independence,[16] and in 1974 comparable samples of top Jamaican leaders were asked,[17] "In regard to your own taste, do you find yourself more comfortable with the food, music, entertainment, and literature of the West Indies and Jamaica or with that of Great Britain, Europe or the United States?" Their answers were:

	1962	1974
West Indian (totally Jamaican or West Indian)	12%	61%
West Indian-Anglo-European mixed	25	28
West Indian-cosmopolitan and other European	0	4
Anglo-European (rejects Jamaica and the West Indies)	63	7
Total	100%	100%
Number of cases	(24)	(81)

The change in twelve years is remarkable. Just before independence, 63 percent of the leaders claimed life styles that were exclusively Anglo-European, explicitly rejecting Jamaican and West Indian culture, while only 12 percent identified with West Indian life styles. By 1974, the situation had reversed. Then, 61 percent of the leaders claimed totally Jamaican or West Indian life styles while only 7 percent identified exclusively with Anglo-Europe.

At least part of this emergent consensus concerning a West Indian identity is linked to the African heritage; for example, 69 percent of the leaders in 1974 who mentioned the African heritage did so favorably.[18] Yet despite the overwhelming evidence of African ancestry among the

Jamaican people, some Jamaican leaders, even when claiming West Indian identities, remained largely identified with the European elements of Creole culture while minimizing the importance of the African elements.

Growing Independence on Cold War Issues

Based on its roll call votes in the eighteenth General Assembly of the UN, which commenced in the autumn of 1963, Jamaica received a relatively high, pro-Western, factor loading (.59) on cold war issues, the most important factor, in a factor analysis.[19] This compares, for example, with .81 for the United States and −.42 for the Soviet Union. In 1965, Jamaica moved out of the U.S. camp for the first time on the issue of admission of the People's Republic of China to the UN and abstained from voting. In 1971, Jamaica voted for China's admission.

According to Schneider and Russett's analysis of alignment on the cold war issue, drawing on roll call votes in the UN from 1946 through 1970, Jamaica became visibly less pro-West in 1965–66, although returning somewhat after 1966. Jamaica's average score on the cold war factor for all the years it was in the UN through 1970 was .36, less than the .59 for 1963 alone. The average for the United States was .95 and for the Soviet Union it was −2.09. Sixty-one countries had higher averages, meaning more pro-U.S. voting records, and sixty-two countries had lower averages, meaning less pro-U.S. voting records.[20]

Jamaica's decline in pro-Western voting on cold war issues was, in the first instance, a growing opposition to the "politics of hegemony," that is, opposition to the domination by either the United States or the Soviet Union.[21] But it was accelerated by détente, which not only reduced the priority of the cold war for smaller states such as Jamaica, but also underscored the perceived need among smaller states to act in concert in order to preserve their autonomy against possible superpower agreements that might negatively affect them.[22] Thus, the "nonaligned" movement that began in relation to the system of American-Soviet bipolarity continued as a countervailing power to peaceful coexistence among superpowers. Furthermore, Jamaica increasingly sought new relationships of trade, technical assistance, loans, and direct aid from Communist countries in the mid-1970s. Jamaica, like other small states, no longer felt that it must stay in one superpower's orbit or the other's.

Nonaligned and Third World Policies

Jamaica's move to a more activist and promotive diplomacy can be seen clearly in its increased participation in nonaligned and third world groups of states. Jamaica was merely an observer to the Heads of States Conference of nonaligned countries in Cairo in 1964. By the time of the Belgrade Conference in 1968, Jamaica was a full member. In 1973 Jamaica sent high-level representatives to Algiers with Prime Minister Michael Manley himself attending, traveling by air with Fidel Castro of Cuba. This is significant, since, as Lewis says, active involvement in the nonaligned group requires the adoption of radical postures with respect to Western domination of the international economic system.[23]

Jamaica participated as one of the forty-six African, Caribbean, and Pacific (ACP) countries in negotiating participation in the European Economic Community. In 1974, Donald O. Mills, Jamaica's permanent representative to the UN, signed the Declaration of the New World Economic Order, favoring, among other things, the right to full compensation for colonialist exploitation for all countries and the regulation of multinational corporations, more active producer-nation associations, and the encouragement by the UN of the nationalization of the means of production.[24] Furthermore, Prime Minister Manley stated that Jamaica must push the Third World case in order to get reasonable returns from industrial countries. The avowed aim of government was to widen and deepen Jamaica's relationships with Latin America and Africa.

In May 1976, Jamaica's Minister of Industry, Tourism, and Foreign Trade attended the Fourth UN Conference on Trade and Development in Nairobi, Kenya. Jamaica gave vigorous support for action to implement the aims of a "new international economic order" including "indexation" whereby prices of exports from developing to developed countries would be made contingent on prices of imports from developed to developing countries.[25]

Bearing on both cold war and Third World policies are the results of two surveys of Jamaican leaders. In 1962, just prior to independence, 24 Jamaican leaders were asked:[26]

When Jamaica becomes fully independent, with which group should Jamaica align itself: the Western nations, the Communist countries, or the neutralist countries?

Western nations		71%
Neutralist countries		25
Communist countries		4
	Total	100%

By 1974, however, attitudes of Jamaican leaders had changed drastically. The data for 1974 are roughly comparable to the data for 1962, since the samples of leaders were drawn in identical ways, and the questions, given the changed circumstances of 12 years of actual nationhood, for all practical purposes are the same. Eighty-three leaders were asked:[27]

Looking at the world situation today with respect to international relations, with which group do you think Jamaica should be associating itself, the Western nations, the Communist countries, or the neutralist countries?

Western nations		36%
Neutralist countries		7
Jamaica's self-interest		27
Third World countries		29
Communist countries		1
	Total	100%

Preference for Western alignment or association was reduced from 71 to 36 percent of the leaders responding. Two additional categories were introduced as a result of volunteered responses of the leaders, "Jamaica's self-interest," that is, "Jamaica should associate itself with any country as long as its self-interest is served," and "Third World countries." The percentage of leaders preferring the "neutralist countries" had gone down, from 25 to 7 percent, indicating a reduction of cold war thinking and the reactive nature of "nonalignment" to it as the new and less developed states began to formulate goals and interests generated out of their own needs and world views. Although only one of the leaders interviewed in 1974 preferred alignment with the Communist countries as his major answer, association with Communist countries was to some extent included in the responses regarding Jamaica's self-interest and Third World countries.

Foreign policy preferences, of course, are not necessarily uniform among elites and may reflect considerable conflict. Such conflict, when it exists, is an important manifestation of the differentiation of elite roles and values. This appeared to be the case in Jamaica. For example, in 1962 (see the total effect in Table 13.1), Western alignment was most preferred by elitemen who were wealthy, conservative or reactionary in economic ideology, relatively old, economic leaders, inegalitarian in attitude, and white, while elite men who rejected Western alignment tended to be less wealthy, radical and liberal, relatively young, political and labor leaders, favorable to the value of equality, and brown skinned. Together, the six independent variables shown in Table 13.1 explained 54 percent of the variation in elite attitudes toward foreign affairs in 1962.

Looking at the direct effects for 1962, one sees that economic ideology (–.596) was the most important variable followed by wealth (.372). Furthermore, there were important indirect effects through economic ideologies in the case of attitudes toward equality (egalitarians tended to oppose the West only because they were radical or liberal), wealth (some of the opposition of the wealthy to the West was because they tended to be reactionaries and conservatives), color (to some extent

TABLE 13.1: Decomposition of Effect in a Path Model Explaining Attitudes toward Foreign Affairs among Top Jamaican Leaders, 1962 and 1974

Dependent Variable	Predetermined Variable	Total Effect	Sector	Wealth	Attitudes Toward Equality	Economic Ideologies	Direct Effect	Multiple R
1962								
Attitudes toward foreign affairs (Western nations)*	Age (old)	.390	.084	-.044	.026	.197	.127	
	Color (white)	.155	.107	.377	.023	-.198	-.114	
	Sector (political, labor, et al.)	-.279	—	-.298	-.020	-.086	.125	
	Wealth (rich)	.648	—	—	.054	.222	.372	
	Attitudes toward equality (egalitarian)	-.178	—	—	—	-.248	.070	
	Economic ideologies (radical)	-.596	—	—	—	—	-.596	.738
1974								
Attitudes toward foreign affairs (Western nations)	Age (old)	.214	.068	.024	.026	.105	-.009	
	Color (white)	.253	.211	.087	.013	.017	-.075	
	Sector (political, labor, et al.)	-.504	—	-.033	-.008	-.101	-.362	
	Wealth (rich)	.189	—	—	.028	.069	.092	
	Attitudes toward equality (egalitarian)	-.131	—	—	-.050	-.050	-.081	
	Economic ideologies (radical)	-.353	—	—	—	—	-.353	.653

*The pole of each variable defined as the high end is given in parentheses.

Source: Wendell Bell and J. William Gibson, Jr., "Independent Jamaica Faces the Outside World: Attitudes of Elites After Twelve Years of Nationhood," International Studies Quarterly 22 (1978): 4–49.

whites—other things controlled—opposed the West because they tended to be radical or liberal), and age (part of the reason the older elites favored the West was because they tended to be reactionary or conservative).

Additionally, in 1962 there were two important reversals of direct and total effects. The first is the institutional sector of leader's major occupation which has a direct effect of .125, showing a slight tendency for political and labor leaders to prefer the West. But, mainly because they are among the less wealthy elite, the total effect (–.279) shows that, in fact, political and labor leaders tended to reject Western alignment.

The second reversal is color, whose total positive effect of .155 is the result of a large positive path through wealth of .337 (whites tended to be wealthy) and a small path through sector of .107 (whites tended to be economic dominants) that overcome a negative direct effect of –.114 (in their own right—other things controlled—whites tended to reject the West) and a negative path of –.198 through economic ideologies (whites tended to be radical or liberal and this tilted them against the West).

The model works, though not quite as well, for the 1974 data, explaining 43 percent of the variance in foreign policy attitudes. Looking at the total effects, one again finds the tendency for the more entrenched and established elites to prefer the West: the relatively old, the white, the economic leaders, and the relatively rich. And, again, there was an ironic tendency for elites who subscribed to the Western values of equality and liberalism to reject alignment with Western nations.

There was, however, an important change by 1974. The most important independent variable had become institutional sector of major occupation, both in total effect (–.504) and direct effect (–.362), although the direct effect of economic ideology (–.353) was nearly as large. In fact, the sign of the direct effect had reversed from what it had been in 1962, and, by 1974, political and labor leaders, compared to economic leaders, were much more likely than they had been in 1962 to reject the West. This reveals the growing competition among elite groups, especially that between the rising bureaucratic bourgeoisie—not only political and labor leaders but governmental workers and functionaries—and the long-established propertied bourgeoisie. At the same time, the importance of wealth as a causal factor declined dramatically, for example, from a direct effect of .372 in 1962 to .092 in 1974 as some members of the bureaucratic bourgeoisie became wealthier and as some members of the old propertied class penetrated the new political and governmental class. (The zero-order correlation between sector and wealth went from –.64 in 1962 to –.38 in 1974.) By 1974, sector, rather than wealth, had become a better measure of major division among Jamaican elites.

DOMESTIC AND FOREIGN AFFAIRS: SOCIALISM AND FOREIGN OWNERSHIP

Domestic and foreign affairs are, as many students of international relations have pointed out, deeply interrelated.[28] Intrasocietal differentiation and domestic policies are frequently local manifestations of a country's distinctive participation in the larger international system. This is especially true of small and economically penetrated states like Jamaica. Multinational corporations offer a prime example since they rival or exceed in wealth, power, expertise, and maneuverability the governments of many of the states in which they operate. For example, Tate & Lyle, specializing in sugar and related products and activities, had annual sales in 1967–68 totaling US$549.2 million while the entire national income of Jamaica for the same period was US$787.2 million. Moreover, Tate & Lyle, like other such companies, had diverse holdings that included sugar refining, land transport and handling, shipping, molasses trading, engineering, farming, technical consultation, and other miscellaneous activities ranging over more than 25 countries. When leaders of underdeveloped countries do business with such corporate mammoths they are often at the mercy of the world views and self-interests of the companies.[29]

Today in Jamaica it is not sugar but bauxite that offers the best example. By 1956, Jamaica became the leading bauxite producer in the world and remains second only to Australia, accounting for 20 percent of the world production in 1974.[30] Bauxite and alumina exports in 1973, for example, totalled US$252.2 million and together were the largest item (about 65 percent) of Jamaica's total visible exports.[31] Thus, relations with the multinational bauxite and aluminum companies operating in Jamaica became a major part of Jamaican diplomacy, a diplomacy that necessarily involved both internal and external aspects. Involved were six companies which controlled, directly or indirectly, 76 percent of the "free world's" aluminum production in 1974 and were the sole buyers in Jamaica.[32] These were Reynolds, Alcoa, Alcan, Kaiser, Anaconda, and Revere.

In January 1974, the prime minister announced that the government would renegotiate contracts with the bauxite and alumina companies. Part of the impetus was the increase in oil prices that presented the country with a crippling fuel bill of J$177.4 million for 1974, nearly triple the J$65.4 million paid in 1973. But this was more a precipitation event than a cause, because "one of the first acts of the new P.N.P. regime in 1972 was the creation of a National Bauxite Commission" whose functions included making recommendations to increase the contribution of bauxite to the country's development.[33]

The prime minister traveled to Canada and the United States in March 1974 to explain Jamaica's problems and the objectives of the renegotiation. In the same month, talks began with the bauxite and alumina companies which lasted until May 14, 1974. In April 1974 the leader of the opposition had written to each of the bauxite and alumina companies in Jamaica saying that the government had the full support of the opposition in seeking to obtain a higher rate of royalty. The talks failed to reach an agreement and the government decided, according to Prime Minister Manley, "to exercise its sovereign right and declare, unilaterally, a production levy on all bauxite mined in Jamaica."[34] Before the end of May, the deputy prime minister announced that the new bauxite levy earnings would finance the budget and allow relief of import restrictions. It was then "anticipated that such earnings would be increased from J$24.4 million in 1973, to some J$170 million for the fifteenth-month period from January 1974-March 1975," although, in fact, earnings turned out to be more.[35] The House of Representatives passed the bauxite levy act in June 1974.

The initiatives taken by the Jamaican government in the case of bauxite revenue illustrates some of the ways in which foreign and domestic policies are intertwined. First, there was the international context within which Jamaica negotiated with the bauxite and alumina companies. As early as 1972, at a meeting in Surinam, Jamaica took a leading role in organizing the bauxite-producing countries of the world. In the early spring of 1974 another meeting was held in Conakry, Guinea, where Australia, Ghana, Guinea, Guyana, Jamaica, Sierra Leone, Surinam, and Yugoslavia agreed to the formation of the International Bauxite Association (IBA). It was formally launched in July 1974 with headquarters in Jamaica, and with two additional founding countries, the Dominican Republic and Haiti.[36]

The model, clearly, was the Organization of Petroleum Exporting Countries. Although how successful the IBA will be in aiding the bauxite producers in increasing their revenues remained to be seen, its emergence strengthened Jamaica's hand in dealing with the bauxite and alumina companies in Jamaica.

The second example is, the domestic political context provided by the official announcement, also in 1974, that Jamaica was to become a democratic socialist country. At its formation in 1940, the PNP had been identified informally as the socialist party in Jamaica and had publicly stated its socialist commitment in 1942. But the PNP retreated from its socialist aims and a left-wing group was purged from its ranks in the 1950s. It was not until 1974 that the PNP government proclaimed, in a series of widely publicized statements and acts, that a democratic socialist era had arrived. Although compensation for socialized assets substituted for expropriation, government ownership and participation, not only in the bauxite and alumina operations, but in other economic activities as well, began. Amid the proclamations, fearful responses and criticisms, and full and double-page advertisements, Jamaicans received the message that capitalism—which was presumedly at the root of slavery and colonialism—was to be abolished, but that entrepreneurism, private business, and free enterprise would continue. There was no reason, so it was said, why the private sector of the nation should not thrive as well or better under socialism as under *laissez-faire* capitalism.[37] Although this may have been confusing, the militant and radical parts of the rhetoric fit Jamaica's new role as an active Third World country.

The visit of President Julius K. Nyerere of Tanzania to Jamaica in the fall of 1974 was the kickoff for the public announcements and campaign, but although the proclamations had awaited his arrival, the policies had not. The government's purchase of controlling shares in private companies began well before, and continued at an accelerated rate after his visit. Besides bauxite and alumina operations, the economic activities entered into included a flour mill, some sugar plantations, Jamaica Omnibus Services, Radio Jamaica, the Jamaica Public Service Company (electricity), and some hotels. One might take PNP spokesmen at their word: State control eventually would include education, health, and social services; infrastructure, including public utilities, communications, and the more vital elements of public transportation; natural resources; financial institutions; basic elements of food and shelter; some private companies that needed salvaging from insolvency; and clearly identified areas of industry and trade where the private sector is either hesitant or unwilling to undertake development itself.[38]

In the summer of 1974, 83 of the top Jamaican leaders were asked:

Do you think that foreign-owned enterprises, such as the bauxite industry, should be nationalized or brought under more stringent local control by the Jamaican government?

The responses were:

		Percent
No		12%
Yes		88
	there should be:	
	Partnership with private Jamaicans	2
	More local control	37
	Partnership with government	26
	Limited nationalization	14
	Major nationalization	9
	Total	100%

Eighty-eight percent of the leaders agreed and only 12 percent disagreed that there should be "more stringent local control." Yet opinions about how much local control there should be varied, only 14 percent favoring limited nationalization and 9 percent favoring major nationalization. In fact, "more local control" and "partnership with government," the most frequent responses, fairly accurately describe many of the later acts of the government.

The question of nationalization is in part a domestic and in part a foreign policy for Jamaica, since its penetrated economy forces it to face the outside world not only abroad but also at home. Furthermore, it is linked by Jamaican leaders' policy preferences to other aspects of foreign policy, as is revealed by their attitudes toward Western alignment as they related to attitudes toward the control of foreign corporations within Jamaica. The relationship is great. Seventy percent of the leaders who did not want any more local control of foreign-owned enterprises preferred alignment with the Western nations compared to only 30 percent of those who wanted more local control. Moreover, except for the two cases who wanted partnership with private Jamaicans, there was a steady reduction in preference for Western alignment as the preference for more stringent local control increased. None of the leaders wanting major nationalization preferred alignment with the West.

SUMMARY AND CONCLUSION

Independent Jamaica's foreign policy has been characterized by five major features: (1) The perpetuation of the colonial past, especially in the early days of independence, but continuing up to the present in trading patterns, for example, even though new elements were being added; (2) regional integration, based especially on increasing economic relationships among Caribbean countries and, from an initial nucleus of Commonwealth Caribbean countries, further economic cooperation within the wider circum-Caribbean region; (3) an intensification of support in the UN and elsewhere for antiracism and black African countries, especially with the purpose of bringing about decolonization and an end to racial discrimination; (4) growing independence with respect to cold war issues, diminishing importance of cold war ideology in defining Jamaica's world views, and increasing diversity and intricacy in dealing with the international system, the latter including the establishment of new international ties with Third World and Communist countries without ceasing relations with Western countries; and (5), increased participation in the nonaligned and Third World groups of states and emergence of a robust Third World identity.

The later included not only a new militant posture with respect to the outside world abroad in efforts to create, among other things, a new international economic order, but also included a new militant posture with respect to the outside world at home. The advent of democratic socialism in 1974 was, to an important degree, an effort of the Jamaican government to control Jamaica's resources and their exploitation by foreign multinational corporations, especially by the bauxite and aluminum companies. On this, as well as other issues, domestic and foreign policies merged as one.

Jamaica's Third World identity involved both practical elements of common circumstance, such as with other bauxite-producing countries, and an emergent ideology linking Jamaica to other countries that were formerly dependent politically, still dependent economically, sources of raw materials, and whose peoples tend to be nonwhite.

Whether the ruling PNP will attempt to bring Cuban-style communism to Jamaica is problematic. What seems obvious is that by 1974 Jamaica's foreign policy was profoundly directed toward Jamaica's own self-interest and emerging identity as a Third World country. Jamaica was —and is—struggling to solve the social questions—unemployment, poverty, illiteracy, low educational levels, poor health services, high birth rates and overpopulations, and other threats to human welfare and happiness—as well as the social psychological question of national identity, pride, and dignity. These aims were reflected both in foreign policies and in democratic socialism at home.

NOTES

1. *Statistical Yearbook of Jamaica, 1973* (Jamaica: Department of Statistics, 1974), pp. 117–22.

2. The Jamaican *Weekly Gleaner,* 27 February 1974, p. 9.

3. Ibid.; and The Jamaican *Weekly Gleaner,* 18 March 1975, p. 1.

4. Locksley G. E. Edmondson and Peter D. Phillips, "The Commonwealth Caribbean and Africa: Aspects of Third World Racial Interactions, Linkages and Challenges," in *International Relations of the Caribbean,* ed. Basil Ince (Trinidad: Institute of International Relations, University of the West Indies, 1977), ms. p. 17.

5. Basil Ince, "The Caribbean in World Politics," in *International Relations in the Caribbean* (Trinidad: Institute of International Relations, University of the West Indies; Curaçao: Hogeschool van de Nederlandse Antillen, 1974), p. 37.

6. Edward W. Chester, *The United States and Jamaica* (forthcoming)

7. Owen Jefferson, *The Post-War Economic Development of Jamaica* (Jamaica: Institute of Social and Economic Research, University of the West Indies, 1972).

8. *Statistical Abstract, 1973* (Jamaica: Department of Statistics, 1974), pp. 174–77.

9. Vaughan A. Lewis, "Thinking About Jamaican Foreign Policy—A Primer" (Jamaica: Institute of Social and Economic Research, University of the West Indies, n.d.), unpublished.

10. The Jamaican *Weekly Gleaner,* 23 March 1976. p. 9.

11. The *Daily Gleaner,* 12 January 1976, p. 2.

12. Vaughan A. Lewis, "The Commonwealth Caribbean Policy of Non-Alignment: A Note," in *International Relations of the Caribbean,* op. cit., ms. p. 8.

13. Edmondson and Phillips, op. cit., ms. p. 19.

14. Harry G. Matthews, "Racial Dimensions of United Nations Behavior: The Commonwealth Caribbean," in *Studies in Race and Nations* (Denver: Center on International Race Relations, University of Denver, 1971–72).

15. Ibid., p. 10.

16. Charles C. Moskos, Jr., *The Sociology of Political Independence* (Cambridge, Mass.: Schenkman, 1967), p. 31.

17. Wendell Bell and Robert V. Robinson, "European Melody, African Rhythm or West Indian Harmony: Cutural Identities of Leaders in a New State," unpublished, ms. p. 11.

18. Ibid., ms. p. 14.

19. Bruce Russett, *International Regions and the International System: A Study in Political Ecology* (Chicago: Rand McNally), p. 70.

20. P. R. Schneider in collaboration with Bruce M. Russett, "Alignment on the Cold War Issue: A Longitudinal Analysis of United Nations Voting," (Paper presented at the Annual Meeting of the International Studies Association, Washington, D.C., February 19–22, 1975).

21. Lewis, "The Commonwealth Caribbean Policy of Non-Alignment," op. cit., ms. p. 15.

22. Vaughn A. Lewis, "The Commonwealth Caribbean and Self-Determination in the International System," in *Size, Self-Determination and International Relations: The Caribbean,* ed. Vaughan A. Lewis (Jamaica: Institute of Socail and Economic Research, University of the West Indies, 1976), pp. 227–47.

23. Lewis, "The Commonwealth Caribbean Policy of Non-Alignment," op. cit.

24. The Jamaican *Weekley Gleaner,* 12 May 1974, p. 9.

25. The Jamaican *Weekly Gleaner,* 11 May 1976, p. 7; 25 May 1976, p. 9; and 1 June 1976, p. 14.

26. Charles C. Moskos, Jr. and Wendel Bell, "Attitudes Toward Global Alignments," in *The Democratic Revolution in the West Indies,* ed. Wendell Bell (Cambridge, Mass.: Schenkman, 1967), p. 89.

27. Wendell Bell and J. William Gibson, Jr., "Independent Jamaica Faces the Outside World: Attitudes of Elites After Twelve Years of Nationhood," *International Studies Quarterly* 22, (1978): 4–49.

28. James N. Rosenau, "Pre-Theories and Theories of Foreign Policy," in *Approaches to Comparative and International Policies,* ed. R. B. Farrell (Evanston, Ill.: Northwestern University Press, 1966), pp. 27–92.

29. George L. Beckford, *Persistent Poverty: Under-Development in Plantation Economies of the Third World* (New York: Oxford University Press, 1972).

30. Edmondson, "Bauxite Diplomacy," op. cit.

31. *Statistical Yearbook of Jamaica, 1974* (Jamaica: Department of Statistics, 1975), pp. 794–95, 906.

32. The Jamaican *Weekly Gleaner,* 10 April 1974, p. 9.

33. Edmondson, "Bauxite Diplomacy," op. cit., p. 15.

34. The Jamaican *Weekly Gleaner,* 30 March 1976, p. 29.

35. Edmondson, "Bauxite Diplomacy," op. cit., p. 1.

36. Ibid.

37. The Sunday *Gleaner,* 24 November 1974, p. 10.

38. The Jamaican *Weekly Gleaner,* 22 October 1974, pp. 6, 14.

14

Perspectives From The Eastern Tier: The Foreign Policies Of Guyana, Trinidad, And Tobago

Basil A. Ince

THE NATURE OF COMMONWEALTH CARIBBEAN FOREIGN POLICY

Any meaningful analysis of foreign policy must be preceded by some knowledge of the political context within which such a policy has been conducted. The independent Commonwealth Caribbean acceded to independence via formal constitutional arrangements. Guyana in 1966 and Trinidad and Tobago in 1962 followed this traditional path, although the former encountered complications, notably, the suspension of its constitution in 1953 and the imposition of a regressive constitution for four years.[1]

The metropolitan connection spawned two divergent types of behavior on the part of these Caribbean Community (CARICOM) states: first, an inheritance of values from the former "mother country," and second, a tendency on the part of these new states to disassociate themselves from the former imperial power. Such disassociational tendencies are manifested in the declaration of nonaligned foreign policies (Guyana, Jamaica, Trinidad and Tobago) and close association with the Third World countries. Most CARICOM states are members of the world-wide nonaligned movement, the Group of 77 at the United Nations, and the African-Caribbean-Pacific (ACP) group.

COMPARING FOREIGN POLICY: GUYANA, TRINIDAD, AND TOBAGO

The fact that Guyana and Trinidad and Tobago each became independent within a period of four years presents no problem for comparing their foreign policies. In addition to their parallel colonial experience and proximate geographic location in the extreme southeast Caribbean, they share other commonalities. Culturally they are both West Indian, although Guyana lies on the South American continent. The composition of their populations is similar. East Indians comprise approximately 52 percent of the total population in Guyana and 35 percent in Trinidad and Tobago, while their African populations are 34 and 43 percent respectively. Race, therefore, is a factor in both the national politics and the foreign relations of these states.[2] This is evidenced in attempts to establish a joint mission in India. Both countries also rely heavily on extractive industries for the bulk of their national income—oil in Trinidad and Tobago and bauxite in Guyana. Both have disputes with Venezuela: Guyana has a long-standing boundary dispute, now temporarily shelved; Trinidad and Tobago has a dispute with respect to fishing boundaries. Finally, both countries have experienced the continuous leadership of only one prime minister since independence, Forbes Burnham in Guyana and Eric Williams in Trinidad and Tobago.

Trinidad and Tobago and Guyana, however, have not pursued identical foreign policies. One reason for this is the leadership in each country. Both leaders have been firmly entrenched with no serious challenges to their leadership within their respective political parties. They both held the portfolio of Minister of External Affairs and have exercised firm control over foreign policy.

Williams and Burnham differ in their political philosophies, in both domestic and foreign arenas. Burnham has consistently projected visions of establishing a socialist state while Williams, a nationalist and pragmatist, has never declared any such intention. Williams has been harshly critical of the Cuban economy and has rejected it as a model for Trinidad and Tobago.[3] Burnham has been less critical of Castro; indeed his People's National Congress (PNC) now has a fraternal arm in Cuba. The Guyanese government has pursued a policy of nationalization to a much greater extent than has Williams.

The leaders of both countries have been influenced by their domestic environments. The Marxist-oriented People's Progressive Party (PPP) led by Cheddi Jagan has been an influential force on Guyana's governing party, the PNC, and there has been no serious opposition emanating from right or center since the independence period. This facilitated Guyana's leftward moves in the 1970–76 period.

A similar environment did not prevail in Trinidad and Tobago. Until 1976, no leftist party could give meaningful opposition to the ruling People's National Movement (PNM), and the recently established United Labour Front is badly fragmented. As a result, the PNM has virtually set its own pace in foreign policy.

One final dissimilarity should be noted—the politics of oil and baux-ite. Trinidad and Tobago's revenues were greatly increased and the country experienced a healthy balance of payments situation following the 1973 oil crisis. On the other hand, by 1976 Guyana was experiencing an economic depression as a result of declining bauxite prices and in-creasing energy costs. These factors influenced the foreign policies of both countries, inducing Guyana toward rapprochement with the United States, while permitting Trinidad and Tobago to expand economic rela-tions with the United States, Europe, and Japan.

Guyana's Foreign Relations

Guyana's foreign relations can logically be divided into three peri-ods: (1) independence to the demise of the coalition government, 1966–69; (2) Lusaka to involvement in the Angolan Civil War, 1970–76; and (3) Ambassador Andrew Young's visit and after, 1977–. With each time frame, Guyana seems to have made new departures in foreign policy.

At the very inception of independence, Guyana enunciated a policy of nonalignment, but the nature of this nonalignment was such that Guyana leaned toward the West. Factors instrumental in this policy were as follows: (1) The manner in which Guyana achieved its independence, that is, the intervention of the CIA on behalf of the PNC or, to be more precise, its toppling of Jagan's PPP regime which has been well docu-mented,[4] as has been the pressure exerted by the U.S. government to delay Guyana's independence until the removal of the Jagan regime,[5] (2) the sad economic plight in which the PNC-UF (United Force) coalition found Guyana as a result of the tremendous financial losses incurred during the struggle for independence. During the Jagan regime, financial assistance and loans from the United States and U.S.-dominated institu-tions were not forthcoming, and (3) the nature of the PNC-UF coalition which formed the first independent Guyanese government. The rightist inclination of the UF was a restraining factor on both internal and exter-nal PNC initiatives.

Once the PNC rid itself of the UF albatross in the general elections of 1968, it implemented what it considered a truly nonaligned and dy-namic foreign policy, beginning with attendance at the Lusaka Summit Conference of Non-Aligned Countries in September 1970. Its outstand-ing role at this conference led to Guyana's hosting in 1972 of the first nonaligned conference in the Western Hemisphere. In that same year, Guyana, along with the independent CARICOM states of Jamaica, Bar-bados, and Trinidad and Tobago, established diplomatic relations with Cuba. This was a bold diplomatic step. Guyanese-Cuban ties became so close that Jagan lent critical support to the PNC regime after returning from representing the PPP at the Havana Conference of Communist Parties of Latin America and the Caribbean (1975). Ties were also forged with Eastern European countries, a move other CARICOM states initially avoided.

Relations with the United States cooled, then plunged to new lows in 1976 with the transshipment of Cuban troops to Angola via Georgetown and the Guyanese charge of U.S. involvement in the explosion of a Georgetown-Havana Cubana aircraft near Barbados. Both governments recalled their ambassadors. This ended the second phase of Guyanese foreign policy.

Recognition of the MPLA as the legitimate government of Angola prior to its military victory was a further indicator that the Guyanese government was pursuing a truly nonaligned foreign policy. At home Guyana was in full pursuit of "cooperative" socialism.

In 1970, Guyana forfeited the monarchy and became the Cooperative Republic of Guyana. Several features of the Cooperative Republic were aimed at terminating external economic domination.[6] In addition to pursuing a policy of meaningful participation in the economy, the government proceeded to nationalize Alcan Bauxite Company (1971), Reynolds Aluminum (1975), Jessel (1975), and Bookers (1976).[7]

Inauguration of the Carter administration saw Guyanese-U.S. relations on the mend and constitutes the third phase of Guyanese foreign policy. Dismayed by dwindling foreign reserves and an unfavorable balance of payments position, in addition to an inability to secure substantial loans from U.S. or international lending institutions, Prime Minister Forbes Burnham took the initiative in improving U.S.-Guyanese relations by returning his ambassador to Washington. The Carter administration reciprocated. In the summer of 1977, President Carter sent Ambassador Andrew Young on a mission to the Caribbean. A Task Force for the Caribbean was established which indicated a $13 million economic pledge for Guyana. Harsh Guyanese verbal assaults on the United States ceased and Prime Minister Burnham admitted there was an improvement in U.S.-Guyanese relations. Some Guyanese now became suspicious not only of renewed American interest in Guyana but also of Guyana's commitment to socialism.

Trinidad and Tobago's Foreign Relations

We can divide Trinidad and Tobago's foreign relations into two periods: (1) independence to the February revolution, 1962 to February 1970, and (2) post-February revolution to the present, March 1970–. The demarcation between periods is based primarily on changes in economic strategy.

From the early 1950s until 1970, Trinidad and Tobago practiced a policy of industrialization by invitation, although this policy weakened in the late 1960s as the government began to take a more active role in the development of the country's economy. In addition, the government encouraged a policy of import substitution in the mid-1960s, in order to provide the manufacturing sector with basic capitalization needs and technical and physical infrastructure. These policies placed heavy reliance on foreign capital. A Caribbean economist has argued that this policy

> posits that the way to develop a manufacturing sector in a small country is to attract metropolitan business which brings not only capital, but also technology, organisation and market conceptions. In addition it was hoped that such industry would use some local raw materials. In exchange for creating employment, generating local income and earning foreign exchange, the industrialists were to be offered a period free from income tax, duty rebates on their imports of equipment, machinery and raw materials, accelerated depreciation allowances, subsidised industrial sites provisioned with water and electricity, and the services of an Industrial Development Corporation.[8]

Although the manufacturing sector expanded through the late 1960s, this policy did not stimulate economic development as expected, and some fifteen years later the population was still contending "with large scale and chronic unemployment, and the government with widespread disenchantment."[9] A question of unequal income distribution was also confronting the government. Such problems, according to economist-politician Lloyd Best, were principal factors in Black Power disturbances soon to engulf the country.

During the 1962–70 period, Trinidad and Tobago pursued a pro-Western policy that continued to manifest itself until the advent of the Black power uprising. This was a continuation of preindependence policy in which Prime Minister Williams had declared himself "West of the Iron Curtain" and had expressed a desire that Trinidad and Tobago join the OAS. When Dr. Williams decided to negotiate the Chaguaramas Naval Base issue, after originally demanding that the United States give up the base in its entirety, many individuals felt he had betrayed the nationalist cause.[10] Williams made it clear, however, that he had gone to the final conference over Chaguaramas with "the problem of the economic needs of Trinidad and Tobago dominant. . . ."[11]

Unlike Guyana, Trinidad and Tobago did not enunciate a policy of nonalignment during this period and contacts with countries of the Communist world were extremely restricted. The entry of the Peking regime into the UN was not supported by the country and Cuba was anathema to the government. What one observer generalizes about the area was especially applicable to Trinidad and Tobago. "Were it not for an occasional visit of a Russian ballet or for a modest trade agreement with Yugoslavia, the existence of Eastern Europe would pass completely unnoticed in the Commonwealth Caribbean."[12]

Trinidad and Tobago now received loans from the United States and from North American-based multinational corporations. However, a loan of $8,850,000 from Texaco designated "solely for purchases in the U.S.A.," moved an opposition member of parliament to conclude that any government that found itself in such a position was susceptible to pressure and could not "dare to call itself independent."[13]

The Black Power uprisings of February 1970 signaled implementation of a new economic policy—that of governmental participation. The inability of previous policy to cope with unemployment and income distribution disturbed Prime Minister Williams to the extent that in 1969 he began advocating the new policy. This middle way, as he saw it, was "an active partnership between Government and major foreign investors in both the formulation and the achievement of Government's development of social objectives."[14] In the wake of the Black Power disturbances, this new philosophy was implemented so speedily that, by 1972, the minister of finance was able to enumerate a large number of governmental investments in petroleum, sugar, banking and finance, air transport, and hotels. In a brochure dated December 1976 the government stated that national ownership could be divided into three categories: (1) companies fully owned by the government (13); (2) those in which the government had majority participation (11); and (3) those in which the government had a minority interest. (9).

Unlike most Caribbean nations, the world energy crisis of the 1970s benefited Trinidad and Tobago. Revenues increased from TT$398 million in 1972 to a projected TT$2,313 million in 1977 and foreign reserves at the end of 1977 stood at TT$3.3 billion. These huge oil revenues led the Trinidad and Tobago government to initiate a new strategy to speed up industrialization and minimize unemployment. Hydrocarbon resources were to be the basis of this strategy, which would establish at Pt. Lisas, in southern Trinidad, a complex of energy-based export-oriented industries, including an ammonia plant, steel and iron plants, and a fertilizer plant. The government hoped dozens of smaller industries would spin-off from this complex. "Screwdriver" and "powder puff" industries were to be a thing of the past. Also, a recent government White Paper set forth a plan to bring together several institutions to form a National Institute of Higher Education, with emphasis on the use of research, science, and technology. An emphasis on marine technology would not be confined solely to energy-based industries, but would also be used for improvement in the agricultural sector.[15]

The disruptions of 1970 did not have effects solely in the economic sector but had a direct impact on foreign policy issues as well. The changing nature of the international system, which permitted small states a certain freedom of action not known in the cold war days, accounted for many of Trinidad and Tobago's actions. In 1970, Prime Minister Williams called for reintegration of Cuba into the fold of Western Hemisphere nations; in 1971 the country voted for the entry of the Peking regime into the United Nations; and, as noted, Trinidad and Tobago joined Guyana, Jamaica, and Barbados in establishing diplomatic relations with Cuba in 1972. Trade relations were initiated with Eastern European countries. Prime Minister Williams made two trips to China and was the first CARICOM leader to send a technical mission to Cuba (to examine the livestock and chemical industries). Trinidad and Tobago joined the Conference of Non-Aligned Nations, and in 1975 declared itself "genuinely non-aligned."[16]

FOREIGN POLICY CONTENT: GUYANA, TRINIDAD, AND TOBAGO, AREA AND ISSUES

United States, United Kingdom, and Western Europe

The United States has always had strong political, ideological, and strategic interests in the Caribbean region and these interests have intensified since the advent of Castro in Cuba.[17] The Caribbean supplies two kinds of bauxite-alumina imports to the United States; 25 percent of U.S. petroleum imports are refined or transshipped in the region; U.S. investment in the Caribbean is estimated at $4.5 billion; and U.S. exports to the region were approximately $2 billion in 1976. Direct U.S. economic interests in Guyana have declined since the nationalization of Reynolds, but U.S. business interests are still strong in Trinidad and Tobago, as evidenced by Texaco and Amoco.

The United States sees the Caribbean as forming a bridge from North to South America and regards it as its "third border." Cuban communism is considered to be infectious to other Caribbean states and U.S. policy has been to thwart Communist expansion in the region. This explains CIA intervention in Guyana in the 1960s and the rapidity with which the United States responded with warships to Trinidad and Tobago's call for assistance during the Black Power disturbances in 1970. The United States displayed its interest in the region again in 1976, when

Washington made it known that it would frown on transshipment of Cuban troops to Angola via Caribbean airports. Guyana incurred the wrath of the United States when it refused to comply.

An improvement in U.S. relations with the Caribbean was evidenced by visits of top-ranking officials to the region in 1977 (including Secretary of State Vance and Ambassador Young). The subsequent creation of a U.S. Task Force for the Caribbean, plus an announced G$30 million in aid for Guyana and intended cooperation with Trinidad and Tobago in a U.S.$200 million consortium for the region, were further indicators of heightened U.S. interest.

Dependence on U.S. capital and technology is evident in Guyana's recent search for financial aid and loans and in the presence of U.S. multinationals in Trinidad and Tobago. In addition, both countries are most interested in the U.S. sugar market and have formally protested the new U.S. Open Sugar Market Policy, which involves import fees. Both countries also have seen fit to peg their currencies to the U.S. dollar.

The United Kingdom, although still influential, no longer possesses the power it once held in the region, maintaining only a reluctant presence. However, the United Kingdom is still constitutionally responsible for the five Eastern Caribbean Associated States (Antigua, Dominica, St. Kitts-Nevis, St. Lucia, and St. Vincent) which, along with Belize on the Central American mainland, are ready to claim their independence. Britain appears willing to oblige.[18] Bookers McConnel Ltd., one of the last bastions of British economic power in Guyana, has now been nationalized, and Britain has sold its oil company, British Petroleum, in Trinidad and Tobago.

Another recently severed Commonwealth linkage is the Commonwealth Sugar Agreement whereby Guyana and Trinidad and Tobago, plus other Caribbean countries, received preferential treatment within the U.K. market. This agreement was replaced by ACP-European Economic Community (EEC) arrangements for sugar under the Lomé Convention, which came into force in April 1976. With the EEC encouraging increased production of beet sugar and the recent decline in sugar prices, negotiations between the metropole and individual West Indian states such as Guyana and Trinidad and Tobago have become very arduous and protracted.

But any nation that has been so deeply involved in a region's history cannot lose its influence overnight, even if it wishes to do so. Despite recent constitutional changes to a republican form of government (Guyana 1970 and Trinidad and Tobago 1976), both forms are based on the Westminster model of parliamentary government. Many other institutions also bear the British imprint. Both Guyana and Trinidad and Tobago are still members of the Commonwealth.

Western European links were natural for countries like Trinidad and Tobago and Guyana whose foreign policies originated with pro-Western inclinations. Europe became increasingly important after negotiations between Britain and the EEC were underway. Listening posts were needed in Brussels and it was not unusual for the former Guyanese Minister of Foreign Affairs, Sridath Ramphal, to be conducting negotiations in Geneva for the Commonwealth Caribbean. While Western European contacts with Guyana may have declined in the post-1970 period, these same contacts with Trinidad and Tobago have been widened in the last year as the latter pursues its new strategy of industrialization.

The Communist World

When the middle road to development was adopted by Trinidad and Tobago in the post-1970 period, economic relationships were established with Yugoslavia, Rumania, and Czechoslovakia. But it was not until 1975 that Trinidad and Tobago established diplomatic ties with the Soviet Union. These ties do not seem to have progressed beyond the formal level. While Prime Minister Williams has yet to visit the Soviet Union, he has visited China, as noted, on two occasions. Such visits came after the thawing of U.S.-China relations and they have been reciprocated by a Chinese Mission which observed the operation of Trinidad's oil industry. Discussions in Peking explored trade, cultural and educational exchange, and technical assistance. An initial trade relationship has begun.

Unlike Trinidad and Tobago, with no declared Marxist in the government or opposition, Guyana's opposition leader Cheddi Jagan has been a declared Marxist for years. In 1969 he enrolled the PPP as a member of the International Communist Movement in Moscow. A Soviet Embassy was opened in Georgetown in the post-1970 period under the Burnham government. Such actions and the efforts of the Cuban Communist Party were persuasive factors that led the PPP to offer "critical support" to the PNC in 1975. (According to one government official, the PPP is a marxist-Leninist party with allegiance to Moscow; the PNC is also Marxist-Leninist but nonaligned.)[19] Two years later the PPP initiated a plan that called for a "national patriotic front government" to work in the interest of national unity. That plan was labeled "superficially attractive" by Prime Minister Burnham. In any case, Guyana, along with Jamaica, became the first countries in the English-speaking Caribbean to seek links with the Communist economic grouping, COMECON.

The interplay of local and international politics—PPP's alignment with Moscow and the Moscow-Peking rivalry—was influential in the establishment of a good working relationship between China and the PNC.

A 1975 article entitled "China is Guyana's Most Generous Socialist Ally," argues that "soft loans, lucrative trade deals, technical assistance through scores of experts, equipment and outright gifts have helped cement China-Guyana relations."[20] Chinese-Guyanese rapprochement has cooled since 1976, however, as a result of three factors: (1) China's support of the "wrong side" in the Angolan conflict; (2) China's alleged support of the U.S. blockade against Cuba; and (3) Chinese opposition to the return of Guantanamo to Cuba.

In sum, while Trinidad and Tobago's relations with Communist countries extend little further than formal trade relations, Guyanese relations with those countries go beyond formality both in trade (COMECON) and in political interaction.

Latin America and the Caribbean

Until recent times, a feature of the Latin American subordinate system has been the paucity of interaction between it and its Caribbean regional subsystem. Even today, interaction takes place primarily with specific states, namely Venezuela, Brazil, and Mexico. Interaction with most other nations in the Southern Hemisphere is limited to international and regional organizations such as the UN, OAS, and the Systema Economica Latino Americana (SELA). Guyana and Trinidad and Tobago belong to all of these organizations except the OAS, from which Guyana is excluded because of its boundary dispute with Venezuela. Most bilateral interactions among members of the CARICOM states and Latin American states fall in the area of economic issues. Conflictual issues such as the Venezuela-Guyana dispute and the Guatemala-Belize territorial dispute have been discussed in UN and OAS forums.

Venezuela

Relations between Venezuela and the states of Trinidad and Tobago and Guyana have characterized by discord and collaboration. Discord between Trinidad and Tobago and Venezuela has evolved from issues such as the Venezuelan surtax (abolished in 1965); illegal immigration to Venezuela; smuggling of goods to Venezuela; and fishing and boundary conflicts in the Gulf of Paria. The latter issue is a particularly vexatious matter for Trinidadian fishermen. Dr. Williams' recent charge of recolonization of the Caribbean by Venezuela has also strained relations.[21]

In the case of Guyana, the perennial issue constitutes Venezuela's claim to five-eighths of Guyana's territory—an issue temporarily shelved until 1982.[22] Before the Protocol of Port-of-Spain was signed in 1970, there had been a series of conflicts on that issue, and Guyana's proclivities, and its assistance to Cuban troops on the way to Angola in 1976, apparently were sufficient to attract Venezuelan troops to the Guyanese border.

There have also been periods of collaboration. In the case of Guyana, some collaboration has grown out of efforts to settle the boundary dispute with Venezuela. There have been no final settlements but a temporary settlement has been found, the Protocol of Port-of-Spain, which will expire in 1982. The Trinidad and Tobago prime Minister played a major role in settlement of this dispute. Trinidad and Tobago purchase crude oil from Venezuela and there have been joint commissions to explore economic collaboration. In 1970, the Trinidad and Tobago government also called on Venezuela for arms to quell its military uprising.

Brazil

Guyanese-Trinidadian relations with Brazil have been much less acrimonious than the relationship with Venezuela. For example, a problem between Brazil and Trinidad and Tobago was solved by a 1974 agreement, recently renewed, giving Trinidad fishermen the right to fish and shrimp adjacent to the coast of Brazil in a 200-mile territorial circuit. Ties also exist in the fields of science, technology, and culture.

Brazilian-Guyanese relations have been fairly cordial. Between 1966 and 1974 a series of mutually beneficial agreements were concluded. Guyana exports bauxite to Brazil and the latter exports manufactured goods to Guyana. Tensions surfaced and relations cooled between the countries in 1976, however, when Brazilian troops were reported to be massing for an attack on Guyana because of Brazilian reports that Chinese and Cuban troops were in the country. A subsequent visit by the Guyanese foreign minister diffused tensions and Brazil declared it had no claims to Guyanese territory since border disputes with Guyana had been settled in 1926 and 1938.

Mexico

Relations between Mexico and the CARICOM states have been minimal, but in 1975 Mexican President Echeverria visited both Guyana and Trinidad and Tobago. Communiques issued at the end of the visits stressed that the countries would work immediately toward expansion of trade, plus economic and cultural ties. Trinidad and Tobago expressed special interest in Mexican experience and knowledge in the transfer of technology and petrochemicals. The demise of a multination aluminum smelter project involving Mexico has apparently slowed down any incipient ties.[23]

The Caribbean

Various schemes for federating the West Indian territories have been advanced by British colonial administrators since the seventeenth century. It was not until the interwar years of the twentieth century, however, that West Indians themselves began to consider this option. Federation became a reality in 1958, but just four years later was relegated to the archives of West Indian history. Since then, integration movements have been the order of the day. Trinidad and Tobago has been a member of all integrative movements, from the federal venture through CARICOM, while Guyana, only an observer during federal negotiations, has been a member of all subsequent movements. Like motherhood, everyone is for it.

Guyana has the distinction of being a prime mover, along with Barbados, in the formation of CARIFTA, via the Dickenson Bay agreement in 1965. Six years later, Guyana was involved in the Declaration of Grenada, which attempted to forge a new state in the Caribbean. Both Guyana and Trinidad and Tobago are major participants in CARICOM and have been principal beneficiaries of the arrangement, along with other area MDCs, Barbados and Jamaica. This has been true from the very inception of the organization, as the following figures indicate. The sum total of intra-CARIFTA imports by the area's more developed countries (MDCs) in 1965 was TT$58,769,000 while that of the lesser developed countries (LDCs) was TT$25,900,000. Four years later the figures were TT$88,882,000 and TT$45,976,000 for MDCs and LDCs respectively. The disparity with respect to intra-CARIFTA exports is even greater for the same time frames. In 1965, total intra-CARIFTA exports for MDCs was TT$77,567,000, LDCs TT$8,233,000. Four years later the figures were MDCs TT$134,767,000, LDCs TT$7,034,000. The comments of Austin Bramble, Chief Minister of Montserrat, are characteristic of sentiments felt by leaders of the LDCs. Bramble not only declares that CARICOM has contributed little to the LDCs but that "it would make no difference if CARICOM were to break-up."[24]

Available figures for imports and exports between Guyana and Trinidad and Tobago suggest that Trinidad and Tobago certainly has held its own. Excluding petroleum trade, Trinidad and Tobago experienced a TT$10 million favorable balance in its 1973 trade with Guyana. There was a sharp decline in trade between these countries in 1977 but the balance has been consistently in Trinidad and Tobago's favor when petroleum is included. For example, in 1977, with petroleum excluded, Trinidad and Tobago experienced a TT$945,000 deficit; with petroleum included, this became a TT$56 million surplus. The trade balance is such that in mid-1977 the Guyanese opposition leader accused Trinidad and Tobago's oil companies of plundering the region, declaring that "foreign oil monopolies in Trinidad. . . . are bleeding the Guyanese and the West Indian working class."[25]

Declining CARICOM trade with Trinidad and Tobago can be explained primarily by two factors: (1) the poor balance of payments position MDCs Guyana and Jamaica have experienced in recent periods (due to world inflation and high oil prices); and (2) Guyana and Jamaica's policy of imposing quantitative restrictions on imports from Trinidad and Tobago. The Jamaican foreign minister stated the position of both Jamaica and Guyana as follows: "We do not have the Foreign Exchange to permit the unlimited importation of Caricom goods."[26]

Jamaica and Guyana's decision to impose quantitative restrictions does not go against the letter of the Treaty of Chaguaramas since Article 28 was inserted as a relief measure for those countries encountering balance of payments difficulties. However, the CARICOM spirit has suffered and the Trinidad and Tobago government has responded to Jamaica and Guyana's restrictions by creating a "tit-for-tat" committee to consider the operation of a system of selective controls on competitive imports into their country. This committee has recommended restriction of 23 items from Guyana, Jamaica, and Barbados.

Such behavior is symptomatic of the widening cracks in CARICOM. Recent relations among CARICOM states have been characterized more by discord than collaboration. Open disenchantment by the LDCs over the lack of economic benefits has now spread to some of the MDCs. Issues on which CARICOM states have had differing positions are as follows: the smelter debacle noted earlier; landing of Cuban planes enroute to Angola; recognition of the Luanda government in Angola; apartheid and sports; a regional aid policy for Mozambique; et al. Frequently Jamaica and Guyana have been on one side of these issues, with Trinidad and Tobago and Barbados on the other.

The socialist ideology pursued by Guyana and Jamaica, and their close relations with Cuba, have not been helpful in drawing the four area MDCs into a closer relationship. There is CARICOM cooperation, as was recently indicated by the financial assistance Trinidad and Tobago extended not only to the LDCs but also to Jamaica and Guyana. On the whole, the CARICOM pledge of foreign policy cooperation has been overshadowed by prevailing discord and has extended little beyond their collective diplomatic recognition of Cuba in 1972. CARICOM integration is probably at its lowest at the time of this writing, and the question of CARICOM survival has been posed by intellectuals and government officials of the region. Prime Minister Williams's words are not without significance. At the Fifteenth Annual Convention of the PNM, barely two months after the signing of the Treaty of Chaguaramas, he intoned: "It is now clear beyond any possibility of doubt that Caribbean integration will not be achieved in the foreseeable future and that the reality is continued Caribbean disunity and perhaps the reaffirmation of colonialism."[27]

CONCLUSION

This comparative study of two MDC CARICOM countries is suggestive of changing international relations patterns throughout the region. One related pattern is a decline in regional integration, in CARICOM in particular. Unilateral self-interest becomes more and more the pattern of Caribbean relations.

These two nations represent diverse approaches to relationships outside the Caribbean: Guyana is easily the most consistently nonaligned nation in CARICOM while Trinidad and Tobago continues its centrist politics. Both Guyana and Trinidad and Tobago, on the other hand, now appear at the forefront of those West Indian nations willing to pursue unilateral and bilateral policies outside the CARICOM framework. The demise of this integrative movement could prove the most debilitating West Indian experience since the Federation failure of 1958–62.

NOTES

1. The catalysts for the British suspension of the Waddington constitution were four pieces of legislation which had been passed by "ministers largely dominated by communist ideas." For background on the 1953 suspension see Cheddi Jagan, *Forbidden Freedom* (London: Laurence and Wishart, 1954); Cheddi Jagan, *The West on Trial: My Struggle for Guyana's Freedom* (London: Michael Joseph, 1966), pp. 145–69. Also see Leo Despres, *Cultural Pluralism and Nationalist Politics in British Guiana* (Chicago: Rand McNally and Company, 1967), pp. 202–20; Basil A. Ince, *Decolonization and Conflict in the United Nations: Guyana's Struggle for Independence* (Cambridge, Mass.: Schenkman, 1974); Raymond T. Smith, *British Guiana* (London: Oxford University Press, 1962), pp. 172–78.

2. In addition to the above works on Guyana which throw some light on the role of race in national politics, see also J. Edward Greene, *Race vs. Politics in Guyana: Political Cleavages and Political Mobilisation in the 1968 General Election* (Kingston, Jamaica: Institute of Social and Economic Research, University of the West Indies, 1974). For the racial factor in national politics in Trinidad and Tobago, see Krishna Bahadoorsingh, "Trinidad Electoral Politics: The Persistence of the Race Factor" (Ph.D. diss., Indiana University, 1966); and Yogendra Malik, *East Indians in Trinidad: A Study in Minority Politics* (London: Oxford University Press, 1971). For articles on the impact of the racial factor in the foreign relations

of these countries, see Basil A. Ince, "Race and Ideology in the Foreign Relations of Independent Guyana: The Case of the East Indians," in *Contemporary International Relations of the Caribbean*, ed. Basil A. Ince (St. Augustine, Trinidad: Institute of International Relations, University of the West Indies, 1978); and Basil A. Ince, "The Racial Factor in the Foreign Relations of Trinidad/Tobago," *Caribbean Studies* 16, nos. 3, 4 (October 1976, January 1977).

3. Eric Williams, "International Perspective for Trinidad/Tobago," in *Documents on International Relations in the Caribbean*, ed. Roy Preiswerk (Rio Piedras, Puerto Rico: Institute of Caribbean Studies, University of Puerto Rico Press, 1970), p. 66.

4. A few of these are Stanley Meisler, "The Dubious Role of AFL-CIO Meddling in Latin America," *The Nation*, 10 February 1964; The New York *Times*, 23 February 1967, 10 June 1963, 10 July 1963; *Times* London, 29 June 1963; *Sunday Times* (London), 16 April 1967.

5. Arthur M. Schlesinger, Jr., *A Thousand Days: John F. Kennedy in the White House* (New York: Fawcett Crest, 1967), pp. 712–13.

6. For the full aims of the cooperative republic, see Harold Lutchman, "The Cooperative Republic of Guyana," *Caribbean Studies* 10, no. 3 (October 1970): 97–115. For a more critical view, see Miles Fitzpatrick, "Guyana: The Corrup-rative Republic," *Tapia*, August 1971.

7. Caribbean governments have given three reasons to justify nationalization: (1) economic nationalization—a desire for greater economic independence; (2) ownership and control of the country's resources; (3) the socialist ideal. Odle, in an illuminating article, advances another viewpoint: (1) nationalization was motivated by moves on the part of the property-owning class to get rid of undertakings that were no longer proving to be viable; (2) nationalization was motivated by the continuous state of economic and social crisis in which CARICOM states found themselves. Odle views such moves as "a series of ad hoc responses to crisis rather than part of a planned programme of socialist response." See Maurice A. Odle, "Toward Understanding the Dynamics of Nationalization in the Caribbean," in *Contemporary International Relations of the Caribbean*, ed. Basil A. Ince, op. cit.

8. Edwin Carrington, "Industrialization by Invitation in Trinidad/Tobago since 1950," in *Readings in the Political Economy of the Caribbean*, eds. Norman Girvan and Owen Jefferson (Kingston, Jamaica: New World Group, 1969), p. 143.

9. Ibid., p. 149.

10. See, for example, Lloyd Best, "From Chaguaramas to Slavery," *New World Quarterly* (Dead Season 1965): 43–70.

11. Trinidad *Guardian*, 17 December 1960.

12. Roy Preiswerk, "The New Regional Dimensions of the Foreign Policies of Commonwealth Caribbean States," in *Regionalism and the Commonwealth Caribbean*, ed. Roy Preiswerk (Trinidad: Institute of International Relations, University of the West Indies, 1969), p. 9.

13. Hansard (House), vol. 4, 4 December 1964, col. 453.

14. See Eric Williams, "International Perspectives for Trinidad/Tobago," in *Documents on International Relations in the Caribbean*, ed. Roy Preiswerk, op. cit., p. 66. This definition had been given as early as 1963, but no effort at implementation was made until 1969 when industrial unrest increased.

15. For full details see *White Paper on National Institute of Higher Education (Research, Science and Technology)* (Port-of-Spain, Trinidad: Government Printery, 1977).

16. Trinidad *Guardian*, 7 July 1975.

17. For an amplification, including quantification of U.S. economic interests, see Robert Crassweller, *The Caribbean Community: Changing Societies and U.S. Policy* (New York: Praeger Publishers, 1972), pp. 44–45.

18. Regarding special problems facing British Caribbean policy and the diplomatic role of Caribbean states in the Anguilla crisis see Basil A. Ince, "The Diplomacy of New States: The Commonwealth Caribbean and the Case of Anguilla," *South Atlantic Quarterly* 69, no. 3 (Summer 1970): 382–96.

19. The *Chronicle,* 12 August 1977. Also, the PNC regards the "cooperative" as the highest form of ownership; the PPP regards this as heresy.

20. Trinidad *Guardian,* 25 October 1975. For an extended discussion of the growing ties between China and Guyana in the 1971–72 period, see Cynthia Enloe, "Guyana's Foreign Policy Process: The Search for Trade, Aid and Identity," in *Selected Issues in Guyanese Politics,* eds. Harold Lutchman, Perry Mars, and Herb Addo (Georgetown, Guyana: University of Guyana, 1976), pp. 241–50.

21. Eric Williams, "The Threat to the Caribbean Community," Speech to the PNM General Council (Port-of-Spain, Trinidad: PNM Publishing Company, 1973).

22. For studies on the Venezuela-Guyana boundary dispute, see Basil A. Ince, "The Venezuela-Guyana Boundary Dispute in the United Nations," *Caribbean Studies* 9, no. 4 (January 1970): 5–26; Cedric L. Joseph, "The Venezuela-Guyana Boundary Arbitration of 1889: An Appraisal," Part I, *Caribbean Studies* 10, no. 2 (July 1970): 56–89. For Part II of this article see *Caribbean Studies* 10, no. 4 (January 1971): 35–74.

23. Clive Thomas believes that the smelter was to be located in Trinidad because it is the "price the other territories have had to pay for balance of payments support." See his article "Neo-Colonialism and Caribbean Integration," in *Contemporary International Relations of the Caribbean,* ed. Basil A. Ince, op. cit.

24. The *Express,* 16 April 1977.

25. The *Express,* 6 June 1977.

26. Trinidad *Guardian,* 22 July 1977.

27. Quoted in an article by Clive Thomas, "The Community is a Paper Tiger," *Caribbean Contact* (July 1977): 15.

15

The Dominican Republic and Haiti: The Limitations of Foreign Policies

Georges A. Fauriol

The Dominican Republic and Haiti share more than just the island of Hispaniola. To varying degrees, both also share a continuing history of national self-abuse characterized by a debilitating approach to political enterprise and a disheartening inventory of international involvement. Their tormented, often painful, and definitively intermingled records as independent countries distinguishes them from the majority of less-developed and smaller states, and particularly from their younger Caribbean neighbors.

With a foreign policy experience dating back well into the nineteenth century (Haiti acquired independence in 1804, the Dominican Republic in 1844), both states have been often unable to develop more viable and effective courses of action, and have, at times, simply defaulted on national priorities. Both share with all modern states a broad set of national policy goals—the desire to preserve the national territory, its limited wealth, and perhaps the national culture. Yet, their record has remained less than distinguished. Haiti and the Dominican Republic evolved out of the nineteenth century bitter and underdeveloped. Since then, the scope of their policies has remained both geographically and substantially restricted.

Contemporary Dominican foreign relations may be best characterized by the observance of a low international political profile, accompanied by a strong disinclination to be visibly associated with North-South disputes or with nonaligned blocs. Conversely, this orientation is in great part dictated by the chosen mode of economic development, which demands the maintenance of a favorable foreign investment climate.

Haitian posture may tentatively be perceived as having an analogous partiality but with a greatly more pronounced preference to restrict the intensity and, at times, the overall coherency of its external interactions.[1] Both states operate by means of restricted ideological and economic criteria, which has led some observers to characterize them as pariah states. More accurately, their overall international behavior has suffered from a serious case of alienation.[2]

THE SETTING OF DOMINICAN AND HAITIAN FOREIGN RELATIONS

External behavior has been influenced by two overpowering factors: the nature of the international environment and internal capabilities. The occasional voracious interest of the former coupled with the under-developed nature of the latter has heightened the significance of these factors to a singular degree. Although nominally sovereign since the last century, both countries have been unable to exclude the prominent influence of external actors—particularly the United States, and, to a more limited extent, France. Paradoxically, even the relations between the Dominican Republic and Haiti have been similarly predisposed, as illustrated by a series of serious military incursions, border disputes, and more generally, continuous meddling in each other's affairs. In addition, the vicissitudes of the Dominican and, particularly, the Haitian polity have produced foreign relations marked by periods of direct foreign entanglements followed by leaner years of relative isolation, and in the case of Haiti, near quarantine from the mainstream of international political life.

Unlike the Commonwealth Caribbean, where independence has been achieved through formal constitutional arrangements and a reform-oriented inheritance, Haiti and the Dominican Republic acceded to political sovereignty through the toils of conflict.[3] Hispaniola, an island which in colonial days may have seemed to be materially the most favored of all the territories of the Caribbean, never completely recovered from the decade of intermittent warfare that preceded Haitian independence.[4] The commercially profitable characteristics of the colonial period concealed an explosive society. In the initial years of independence, improvements in the welfare of the average Haitian and Dominican remained illusory at best. What followed was a long period of political and economic turmoil, featuring unreliable political leadership and spiraling squalor.

Haiti managed to stumble forward without any foreign sponsor or ally for roughly the first fifty years of its political independence. Long regarded as an anomaly, an outcast, and a threat to the established international order of the nineteenth century,[5] Haiti first broke out of this diplomatic isolation in the 1830s; however, as the price of recognition

France imposed a humiliating payment of a substantial sum of money, which Haiti had no inherent way of generating. This compounded Haiti's financial burden without substantially relieving its isolated position. The United States, a trading partner since the 1780s, grudgingly granted diplomatic recognition in 1862.

If the perceived threat of a French return had now disappeared, the collapse of the Haitian-led initiative to sustain political presence in Santo Domingo brought to fruition long-held Haitian fears of an eastern threat. Dominican troubles in Haiti led to the succession of Spanish-Haiti in 1844, twenty-two years after having been overrun by President Boyer's armies. Like Haiti, the Dominican Republic embarked upon an independent political career, plagued with political and economic difficulties and singular foreign policy problems. In an effort to placate, if not nullify, the danger of Haitian invasions, Dominican leaders attempted to encourage support (and annexation) from the European powers and the United States. As it turned out, conflicting motives led to a temporary and futile reassertion of Spanish rule during the 1860s. Belated Dominican resistance, Spanish ineptitude, and the United States' unhappiness with the venture brought this episode to an end.[6]

These events were paralleled by significant alterations in the international environment, namely the development of modern capitalism and the liberalization of international trade (coming some twenty years after the abolition of slavery). During the second half of the nineteenth century and well into the contemporary period, the Dominican Republic and Haiti were drawn into the garrotte of foreign commercial and economic rivalries, and eventually political and military intervention. The United States dominated the Dominican economy to the exclusion of all other powers. By the late 1890s, Americans operated an economic device called the San Domingo Improvement Company (designed to collect debts owed to foreign bondholders) and by 1905 the U.S. government controlled the Dominican customs house. This paved the way for direct American intervention in 1916. Meanwhile, Haiti's feudal economy, originally predominated by France, was increasingly in debt to Germany and U.S. financial interests. France had underwritten all Haitian loans between 1825 and 1896 and owned the National Bank of Haiti, the only bank in the country. The start of the twentieth century gradually saw a shift towards German trading interests and American banking groups. By 1911, a restructured National Bank came under the control of the National City Bank of New York; meanwhile, the United States was reinforcing its position as Haiti's main supplier of goods.[7]

American military intervention in Haiti (1915) and the Dominican Republic (1916) brought to an abrupt end this period of economic bankruptcy and political chaos. With the possible exception of Ulises Heureaux, the cunning tyrant of the 1880s and 1890s, Dominicans had been ruled by a succession of presidential nonentities. In Haiti, conditions had been virtually the same. Surprisingly, both states held on to their confined degrees of autonomy. At the minimum, territorial integrity had been retained.[8]

The rationale for the occupation of Haiti (1915–34) and the Dominican Republic (1916–24) has been adequately recounted elsewhere.[9] Intervention was predicated on the assumption that the way to improve political and economic conditions and make way for the introduction of a democratic policy was to rectify the deficiencies in financial administration. The execution of such a noble plan proved difficult. A minimum of financial order was established, the national debts were reduced, and great efforts were dispensed toward building up a basic economic infrastructure. By 1924, growing American disinterest led to a negotiated withdrawal from the Dominican Republic. In Haiti, however, that presence remained for another decade in the midst of growing social frustrations and mounting political opposition. Haiti became known as America's least successful experiment in imperialism.

American presence failed to produce a strong vein of democratic zeal and financial capabilities in the governing elites. Economically, the decline of agricultural exports after 1928 and the world depression knocked out any pretence of latent prosperity. Politically, the return to the practices of constitutional manipulation were perhaps ironically erected on the institutional foundations of the American occupations. The national security apparatus sustained the rise to power of Leonidas Trujillo who, between 1930 and 1961, ran a ruthless dictatorship.[10] In recent years, particularly after the "Dominican Crisis" of 1965, a somewhat more sophisticated political milieu has been fostered, although the disharmonious aftermath of the 1978 presidential elections is a recall to debilitating legacies.

In Haiti, social and political initiatives were never given a real chance. A period of relative prosperity during the 1940s was followed by a return to the personalist style of authoritarian governmental control. Contemporary Haiti is dominated by the paternalistic ideology of the Duvalier regime (François and Jean-Claude)—a stifling cult of personalism during the elder Duvalier's rule succeeded in eliminating all real and potential sources of competition.[11]

INTERNAL AND EXTERNAL LINKAGES

By most standards of the international system, the human and material profiles of the Dominican Republic and Haiti characterize them as less developed and small states. In addition, socio-economic legacies have effectively localized the importance of foreign relations in the policy of each state.[12]

The saliency of foreign policy issues in political life is low, brought to the fore only in crisis or within the context of ideological preferences. For example, the foreign policy question generating most emotion in the 1978 Dominican presidential campaign dealt with the nature of relations with Cuba. While both major candidates (Joaquin Balaguer and Antonio Guzman) opposed immediate recognition of the Castro government, public opinion continued to hold otherwise. In an even more trenchant contrast, however, Haitian foreign policy decisions are hardly a matter of public debate. The inward-looking Duvalier ideology has made it difficult for a proper forum to develop. It is more accurate to note that in both states (to greatly different degrees) discussion has centered around issues of social development and potentially intimate foreign policy associations derived from them. Significantly, perhaps, the respective ministries of foreign affairs have had only very limited influence over most economic and security questions.

Styles of conduct are therefore more significant than the contents of policy. In the Dominican Republic, the centralized and personalized process of executive control is sensitive to the existence of counter-elites (principally among segments of the armed forces and the wealthy gentry, and also in various fringe groups such as student organizations) that can compete for power. In contrast, there is a total absence of such groups in Haiti. This facilitated François Duvalier's rule, although his son has attempted to give the political process some substance.

Beyond these varying political limitations, active participation in international relations is, in any event, restricted by the administrative costs of diplomacy. This has been particularly acute in Haiti, where the competence of the ministry's supporting staff and its diplomatic corps compares unfavorably with that of any of its Caribbean counterparts. Throughout the 1960s and into the early 1970s, the occupational hazards for Haitian diplomats were not only characterized by uncertain lengths of tenure, but by political disgrace and dismissal, if not worse. In the mid-1970s, Haitian foreign representation is limited to 24 countries, including 6 in Europe, 7 in Latin America, and 4 in Africa, which reflects Haiti's main foreign policy axes.

If the interplay of political components remains limited, the often problematical nature of economic development has a significant bearing on foreign relations. With the Dominican Republic occupying the eastern two-thirds of Hispaniola and Haiti the rest, with each having roughly equal levels of population (respectively 5 and 4.7 to 5.5 million), human and material assets have combined to produce contrasting results. The

Dominican economy has been able to sustain continuous real economic growth (5 to 10 percent annual GNP growth between 1965 and 1974), although the benefits from this have not been well distributed. This has been fueled by an expansion of the mining, manufacturing, and construction sectors. Haiti, on the other hand, is attempting to disengage itself from the economic stagnation of the 1960s, a long-term task highlighted by the nation's presence on the UN's least economically developed list. A GNP per capita of roughly $125 to $150 and an 80 percent illiteracy rate comprise the worst social welfare statistics of the entire hemisphere.

Both countries are dominated by an essentially rural structure, which is reflected in the continued dominance of agricultural products in the export sector. Coffee continues to dominate Haitian foreign trade (50 percent) as does sugar for the Dominican Republic (35 to 40 percent). Investments in mining have substantially altered the composition of Dominican exports (ferronickel leading the way, followed by gold and silver), while bauxite continues to make its limited contribution to the Haitian trade balance. Agricultural and mineral exports have been vulnerable to exogenous forces, from unpredictable weather conditions (severe drought in Haiti) to the fluctuations in international commodity prices.* Likewise, in recent years, both countries have been affected by the slowdown of the world economy and the increase in prices of imports. As bauxite producers, they have joined the International Bauxite Association, without reaping particularly significant benefits.

THE SCOPE OF FOREIGN RELATIONS

A synthesis of Dominican foreign policy brings out two major centers of attention—the United States, and, to a much lesser extent, Haiti. The former has an overwhelming political and economic dimension, while the latter remains a political and security concern and is best dealt with in the context of Haitian-Dominican legacies.

Dominican exposure to external influence has been almost the exclusive domain of the United States. Attempting to promote political stability and economic progress, Washington has at varying intervals both imposed sanctions and granted its support. This intimate relationship has resulted in a pragmatic policy on the part of Santo Domingo that takes into account the overwhelming nature of American interests.[13] Trujillo induced American friendship and consequently received economic and military aid in exchange for support of U.S. foreign policy in international

---

*Raw sugar prices fell from about 27 cents per pound in 1975 to roughly 8 to 9 cents in 1977, whereby they sank below the average Dominican cost of production.

forums. If the Generalissimo's excesses by the late 1950s placed a temporary damper on the relationship, his successors have maintained the shadows of American presence. The opening of Dominican politics after Trujillo's death in 1961 led to a sudden rise in expectations without adequate institutions to channel frustrations and demands. Not surprisingly, the United States kept a close watch over this void, first by supporting Juan Bosch's ill-fated liberal experiment,[14] then his uncharismatic successor, Donald Reid Cabral. The least that could be said about the latter is that by the spring of 1965 troubles were so severe that a major blowup was not to be considered a surprise. Still, the subsequent American intervention was indeed a surprise and remains quite controversial.[15] Suffice it to say that by operating within a policy perception of "no more Cubas," American reaction was both swift and confused. Certainly, considerable diplomatic damage was done. The United States belatedly appealed to the OAS, and the marines were integrated into an Inter-American Peace Force. On June 1, 1966, elections ironically brought in Joaquin Balaguer, a remnant of the Trujillo period.

The twin features of capitalism and dependence were given a substantial boost after 1966 by renewed American economic support, both official and private. In practice, the major goal of the Dominican Republic has been to sustain favorable economic and political relations with the United States. By the same token, the Dominican Republic maintains what is probably the most favorable climate for U.S. investments in the entire region. The years immediately following the 1965 crisis witnessed an investment flow amounting to some $500 million. Total U.S. economic and military assistance amounted to over $67 million in 1968. By 1975–76 this hovered around $20 to 30 million per year, most of it being economic aid. The Peace Corps, with 153 volunteers in 1969, has maintained some presence throughout.

The United States is the Dominican Republic's leading trade partner —70 percent of Dominican exports and 55 percent of its imports. Its principal foreign currency earner and prime export, raw sugar, has historically been sustained through a favorable American import quota. The demise of this system, added to recent Dominican concerns with U.S. protectionist attacks on sugar import quotes, is a continuing concern for the export sector.* American interest remains considerable. Gulf & Western's holdings include some of the largest sugar mill installations in the world. This American economic presence has occasionally resulted in political frictions. Throughout 1974 and 1975, new contract negotiations

---

*With about 1.3 million tons in 1977–78, the Dominican Republic is the fifth most important member of GEPLACEA, the Latin American and Caribbean sugar exporters' group.

with ALCOA (which began domestic operations in the country in 1945) proved difficult. More severe incidents have involved Gulf & Western's illegal financial operations to benefit both itself and the Balaguer government. The spreading of such information on the front page of the *New York Times* proved costly to all parties involved.[16]

The Dominican Republic's other major trading partners include Canada, with whom it has had a growing flow of interactions (over $40 million in trade since 1976),* Japan (which ranks second in Dominican trade),† plus the Netherlands, Belgium, Spain, and, recently, Switzerland. Significantly, the Dominican Republic has no political ties with the Communist world, and consequently entertains minimal trade with those nations.

The principal paths of Dominican and Haitian foreign relations not only pass through each others's capitals, but pass through Washington as well. In addition, the Haitian cultural median lies somewhere between its French and African heritage. Indicative of the political nature of relations on the island of Hispaniola, economic ties between its countries have remained residual at best. Both countries have had major security concerns, leading to reckless military and political episodes. The result has been a high-strung relationship furthered by a good dose of paranoid and racial perceptions and an inclination toward mutual distrust.[17]

Antagonism between the two countries built up throughout the nineteenth century and has continued well into the contemporary period. The most serious incident to date has been the 1937 Dominican massacre of an undetermined number of Haitian seasonal agricultural workers, an episode in which Trujillo appears to have had a key part.[18] Tension also erupted within the framework of Trujillo's conspiracies and invasions (1947–1951), which in return led to an anti-Dominican propaganda campaign on the part of Haiti.

Needless to say, Haitian-American relations have operated within an unfavorable climate. Haiti's pretensions are akin to those of its Dominican neighbor, yet historical legacies, reinforced by an unfortunate inclination towards autarky throughout the 1960s has resulted in a posture that is probably pragmatic under the circumstances but otherwise remains lethargic. The United States learned to live with François Duvalier, although after 1963 relations became minimal. An adverse internal politi-

---

*The ferronickel industry, centered around the Falconbridge Dominicana mine and smelter at Bonao, is largely owned by Toronto interests, although it provides the Dominican government with a negotiated share of the profits. Politically, within the context of Canadian-Latin American policy, the Dominican Republic has not become a target for special consideration.

†During the 1950s a plan was set up to foster Japanese immigration to the Dominican Republic. It was a failure.

cal and economic situation only compounded the difficulties of an essentially regressive policy.[19] With Jean-Claude Duvalier, Haiti's image has improved. The result has been a new wave of American aid ($23 million in economic assistance for 1976, as opposed to a total of $32 million for the 1962–69 period), although success in attracting private U.S. investment has been limited.

Haitian-U.S. relations continue to be nagged by minor episodes. In 1973, the U.S. ambassador and an associate were kidnapped and exchanged the next day for fifteen imprisoned Haitians and $75,000. More recently, Jack Anderson's columns regarding the conflicting nature of President Carter's human rights policy and support of the Duvalier regime, and damaging allegations involving U.S. aid and Representative Daniel Flood of Pennsylvania are indicative of latent complications in future relations.

On the positive side there is now a substantial multinational aid effort, which includes a conglomerate of international agencies ($60 million for 1974–76 from the Inter-American Development Bank, $35 million from the International Development Association) as well as assistance from a diverse group of other UN and private agencies and individual governments (France, Canada, West Germany, and, to a lesser degree, Israel, and Taiwan).* On the basis of its past relationship, France has been actively involved in Haitian development schemes. At times there may seem to be a minor rivalry with U.S. interests. French assistance is now being channeled through two entities, one dealing with the funding of agricultural, health, and transportation projects, and the other devoted to educational matters. As of 1977 there were about 100 French teachers and experts in the education sector.

A singular aspect of both Dominican and Haitian foreign relations has been continued relative isolation from their Caribbean neighbors. Neither state entertains relations with Cuba, although contacts have been established at both the private level (cultural and sporting events), as well as through regional groupings, such as the Caribbean Development and Co-operation Committee (the first meeting of which was held in Havana in December 1975). Relations with the Commonwealth Caribbean have remained both politically and economically restrained. Indicative of these attitudes has been the hesitancy with which both states have approached possible association with CARICOM. Haiti applied in 1974 and its application is still pending. Haiti's presentation of its case was both uncoordinated and badly argued. The Dominican Republic has been interested,

---

*During the same period the Dominican Republic received close to $120 million from the IDB.

yet has made no serious moves in the direction of CARICOM. There is no doubt, however, that formal applications from these two countries, with their larger populations and cultural differences, would create serious conceptual problems for the existing members of CARICOM.

As long as the rule of the Duvalier family in Haiti continues, there is little reason to expect any major change in the pattern of that nation's foreign policies. The possibilities for change in the Dominican Republic, following the victory of Antonio Guzman and the PRD in the 1978 elections, are somewhat greater, but the combination of external and internal restraints will probably serve to seriously constrain the new administration's freedom of action in the international arena.

NOTES

1. A balanced and comprehensive account of Dominican and Haitian foreign relations remains to be written. For a cursory review, see Larman C. Wilson, "The Dominican Republic and Haiti," in *Latin American Foreign Policies,* eds. Harold E. Davis and Larman C. Wilson (Baltimore, Md.: Johns Hopkins University Press, 1975). See also the sections on foreign relations in the various editions (current editions date back to 1973) of *Area Handbook for the Dominican Republic* (Washington, D.C.: Government Printing Office) and its equivalent for Haiti. A characterization of Haitian foreign policy is found in Georges A. Fauriol, "Foreign Policy Behavior and the Smaller and Less Developed States: Guyana, Haiti and Jamaica" (Ph.D. diss., University of Pennsylvania, 1978). Useful documentation is available from the Dominican government, but the same cannot always be said of Haiti.

2. See Robert E. Harkavy, "The Pariah State Syndrome," *Orbis* 21 (Fall 1977); and Yehezkel Dror, *Crazy States* (Lexington, Mass.: D. C. Heath & Co., 1971) for varying definitional problems.

3. See J. P. Nettl and Roland Robertson, *International Systems and the Modernization of Societies* (London: Faber, 1968).

4. Saint-Domingue (Haiti) was the jewel of France's prerevolutionary colonial empire, while the Spanish portion of the island remained a colonial backwater. See Thomas O. Ott, *The Haitian Revolution, 1789–1804* (Knoxville, Tennessee: University of Tennessee Press, 1973).

5. See Rayford W. Logan, *The Diplomatic Relations of the United States with Haiti* (Chapel Hill, N.C.: University of North Carolina Press, 1941), chap. 5–7.

6. See C. S. Tansill, *The United States and Santo Domingo, 1798–1873* (Baltimore: Johns Hopkins University Press, 1938).

7. For detailed accounts, see Dana G. Munro (who later took part in the conduct of U.S. Caribbean policy) for an authoritative if somewhat pro-American treatment of this period, *Intervention and Dollar Diplomacy in the Caribbean, 1900–1921* (Princeton, N.J.: Princeton University Press, 1964). See also Sumner Welles, *Naboth's Vineyard: The Dominican Republic, 1844–1924* (New York: Payson and Clarke, 1928); and Leslie Manigat, "Haiti: the shift from French hegemony to the American sphere of influence at the beginning of the 20th century: the 'conjuncture' of 1910–1911," in *The Caribbean Yearbook of International Relations, 1975,* ed. Leslie Manigat (Leyden, Netherlands: A. W. Sijthoff; St. Augustine, Trinidad: Institute of International Relations, University of the West Indies, Trinidad and Tobago, 1976).

8. Samaná Bay (Dominican Republic) and the Môle St. Nicholas (Haiti) were coveted pieces of real estate; yet through conflicting diplomatic maneuvers and changing American strategic postures after 1900, no plans ever came to fruition.

9. See Munro, op. cit., as well as Dana G. Munro, *The United States and the Caribbean Republics, 1921–1933* (Princeton, N.J.: Princeton University Press, 1974); Hans Schmidt, *The United States Occupation of Haiti, 1915–1934* (New Brunswick, N.J.: Rutgers University Press, 1971). There is unfortunately no equivalent of the latter for the Dominican Republic.

10. See Howard J. Wiarda, *Dictatorship and Development, The Methods of Control in Trujillo's Dominican Republic* (Gainesville, Fla.: University of Florida Press, 1968).

11. See Robert I. Rotberg, *Haiti, The Politics of Squalor* (Boston, Mass.: Houghton Mifflin Co., 1971).

12. The relationships between material weakness, size, and foreign policy behavior have been explored by only a handful of writers. An analysis of relevant factors, focusing on the Caribbean region is found in Fauriol, op. cit.; see also P. J. Boyce, *Foreign Affairs for New States* (New York: St. Martin's Press, 1978); and Marshall Singer, *Weak States in a World of Powers* (New York: The Free Press, 1972).

13. For examples see Welles, op. cit.; and John B. Martin, *Overtaken by Events* (New York: Doubleday and Co., 1967).

14. See his own account in Juan Bosch, *The Unfinished Experiment: Democracy in the Dominican Republic* (New York: Praeger Publishers, 1965).

15. For a key analysis, see Abraham F. Lowenthal, *The Dominican Intervention* (Cambridge, Mass.: Harvard University Press, 1972).

16. Interestingly enough, President Carter's pressures regarding human rights and open politics may have had its first test case with the embroiled 1978 Dominican presidential elections. See *New York Times,* 26 July 1977.

17. See Jean Price-Mars, *La République d'Haiti et la République Dominicaine,* 2 vols. (Port-au-Prince, Haiti: Collection du tricinquantenaire de l'independance d'Haiti, 1953).

18. See R. Michael Malek, "Rafael Leonidas Trujillo Molina: The Rise of a Caribbean Dictator" (Ph.D. diss., University of California, Santa Barbara, 1971).

19. Although hardly favorable, see the well-informed account by Bernard Diederich and Al Burt, *Papa Doc: The Truth about Haiti Today* (New York: McGraw-Hill, Inc., 1969).

16

Oil and Caribbean Influence: The Role of Venezuela

Winfield J. Burggraaff

Since the mid-1970s, Venezuela has emerged as a Caribbean leader, acting not only as a spokesman for the islands in international forums but also providing them with large-scale financial assistance. The quintupling of world oil prices since 1973 and the consequent sharp increase in the market value of Venezuela's leading export have been largely responsible for that country's new role as a Caribbean power.

This chapter examines the effects of the oil price rise on Venezuela's relations with its Caribbean neighbors and discusses how this fiscal revolution, in combination with strong and assertive leadership, has permitted Venezuela to take a much more dynamic part in Caribbean affairs. Inasmuch as the country traditionally played a largely passive role in regional affairs, Venezuela's recent activities represent one important aspect of this volume's subtitle: changing patterns of international relations.

VENEZUELA AND THE CARIBBEAN ENVIRONMENT

Venezuela's place in Caribbean history has been ambivalent, for despite historic ties to the islands and the fact that it has 1,750 miles of Caribbean coastline—more than any other country in the basin—Venezuelans, owing to common bonds of language, culture, religion, and history, have identified more with the mainland Spanish-speaking republics than with the largely non-Spanish-speaking islands of the Caribbean. This can be seen even today when Venezuela, while expanding its influence in the Caribbean, is also exerting leadership in the Andean Group in particular and in Spanish America in general.

To understand the significance of Venezuela's newly acquired role, one must understand its place in the region since the late colonial period. The Independence era was the most glorious period in the nation's history, and Venezuelans today are justifiably proud of the role that their armies and soldiers played in the liberation of five South American countries and of the fact that Francisco de Miranda and Simón Bolívar are continental as well as national heroes. After independence had been won, Bolívar led movements for political federation and integration, such as Gran Colombia and the Panama Congress of 1826.

In the century and a half after independence, however, Venezuela played a weak, passive role in Caribbean and world affairs and generally subordinated its foreign policy to domestic concerns.[1] In the international arena what mattered most was the country's relationship to the major powers; beyond that, the foreign ministry busied itself with sporadic verbal exchanges with Colombia and British Guiana over boundaries. Although various political and military figures became involved in Caribbean political intrigues, Venezuela never developed a coherent official policy toward the Caribbean until the 1970s.

NEW DIRECTIONS

Beginning with the establishment of the present democratic system in 1959, however, Venezuela became more assertive internationally. Under Rómulo Betancourt (1959–64), Venezuela fought Caribbean dictators such as the Dominican Republic's Rafael Trujillo, while throwing its support behind civilian democratic leaders such as Dominican President Juan Bosch. By the early 1960s, it had also turned against Fidel Castro's left-wing dictatorship and maintained an aggressively anti-Castro position until the early 1970s. From the viewpoint of the leaders of Venezuela's shaky democracy, this foreign policy was perfectly logical: it was the policy that they felt could best keep secure their country's own fledgling democratic system.[2]

The objective of Betancourt's policy, and that of his successor Raúl Leoni (1964–69), was clearly political, but the emphasis of the country's international policy changed significantly when the Social Christian regime of Rafael Caldera came to power. Caldera (1969–74) gave the nation's foreign policy a new economic emphasis. He spoke out against U.S. trade policy, hastened the nationalization of the foreign-owned petroleum properties, and acted as a spokesman for the developing world in general.

Before the end of the Caldera regime it would have been unrealistic for Venezuela to aspire to a leadership role. Until 1973, the price of its industrial imports was increasing substantially while oil prices were declining. A barrel of crude that sold for $2.09 in 1950 brought $1.86 in 1970.[3] The situation changed dramatically in 1973–74 when the average price of crude quintupled. Although the Caldera administration did not enjoy the oil revenues of the successor regime, it nonetheless laid the philosophical basis for Venezuela's current position as a Third World leader.[4]

THE EXTERNAL POLITICS OF OIL

The effects of the price increase were immediate and profound. Between 1972 and 1974 Treasury receipts tripled, and in the first year of the price rise (1973), revenues grew from $3.82 billion to $9.95 billion the following year.[5] During the 1976–80 period, income from oil will probably exceed the total oil earnings from 1921 to 1973.[6] Similarly, the country's international reserves soared from $1.023 billion in 1970 to $8.953 billion in 1975.[7] Even though Venezuela devoted billions of this petrodollar windfall to an extremely ambitious domestic Five Year Plan, there was still too much "hot" money from oil sales to put into circulation in the local economy without producing acute inflationary pressures. The inability to invest these dollars rapidly enough internally induced Venezuela to recycle them abroad.

Venezuela now had the economic muscle to bring it the regional and international influence and status it had long been seeking. In the words of one journalist, "after decades as a silent walk-on in the theater of international affairs, Venezuela . . . has transformed itself into a leading actor."[8] Yet vastly increased income is not the only reason for this newly found international prestige. Another reason is that the government has been using this money in a statesmanlike way. Much of the credit for this enlightened policy goes to President Carlos Andrés Pérez (1974–79).

This strengthened economic position coincided with the coming to power of a president who sought to establish himself as a forceful, but responsible, leader of the developing world. Pérez, who "more than any past president, has put Venezuela on the world map," has been described as "one of the most eloquent spokesmen of the Third World."[9] He and his able team of foreign policy advisers have consciously linked leadership in economic liberation and integration in the 1970s to their country's leadership in political liberation and integration in the 1820s.[10]

Although unprecedented revenues and strong leadership are the keys to Perez's ambitious policy, other factors also facilitated its implementation. Caldera had already laid the ideological foundations. In addition, OPEC as an organization and individual OPEC member states were launching similar aid programs. Furthermore, Péez could turn his attention to international affairs because his country's relative prosperity kept the lid on internal unrest.

Although Venezuela contributed to OPEC's recently established Special Fund designed to aid non-oil-producing Third World countries, made major investments in the World Bank, and gained a stronger voice in the International Monetary Fund (IMF) and other international organizations, it was natural for it to seek to exert the greatest influence in its own hemisphere and, in particular, the Caribbean. The latter area includes a score of countries much smaller and poorer; lacking foreign exchange and development capital, they need to borrow money for a host of development projects. Moreover, these countries, which import almost all their oil, were dealt a severe blow by the price rise. Venezuela grasped the opportunity to fill their need for development capital, build up good will by helping to mitigate the effects of accelerated energy costs, and, at the same time, make productive use of excess petrodollars.

It is important to note that Venezuela's push into the Caribbean is merely one significant manifestation of its global policy of advocating international economic justice through the creation of the New International Economic Order. To establish its credibility and legitimacy as a leader of the developing world, Venezuela had to come forward with dollars as well as rhetoric. As Pérez stated, "we will not have moral authority to request a new deal for our region from the industrial and socialist world if, at the same time, we fail to do the same with regard to those countries not yet at our levels of income."[11] Since 1974, Venezuela has displayed "surprising generosity in foreign development assistance."[12] In 1975, for example, it was devoting about 12 percent of its Gross Domestic Product to development assistance abroad, while the industrialized countries allotted less than one percent.[13]

The principal agency established to disburse the petrodollars is the Venezuelan Investment Fund (Fondo de Inversiones de Venezuela— FIV). Created in 1974, its purpose is to syphon off excess petrodollars in order to prevent massive currency injections from causing serious inflationary pressures. Although it has put some of its funds in international capital markets, it has also invested heavily in development loans to Third World countries. Endowed initially with $3.09 billion, by the end of 1975 its reserves were up to almost $6 billion.[14]

Through the FIV and other agencies, the Pérez government has been channeling a significant portion of its oil wealth into the hands of the poorer Third World countries. For example, Venezuela has pledged $100 million of the total $800 million OPEC Special Fund created in 1976 to alleviate the effects of higher prices on nonproducing developing countries. Within the hemisphere, the Caracas government has contributed almost $200 million to Inter-American Development Bank trust funds earmarked for development projects in the Bank's relatively less developed member nations and has also been a major contributor to the Andean Development Corporation.

Some of the most intensive efforts, however, have been directed toward the Caribbean which, as Pérez acknowledged, was the obvious place to begin.[15] The technical cooperation and assistance program "was conceived to promote Venezuela's integral presence in the Caribbean through cooperation with the area's economic and social development, and establishment of closer ties" to other Caribbean nations.[16] To implement the program the FIV and other Venezuelan agencies have been studying the most urgent socioeconomic problems of the countries involved, particularly in the fields of health care, social welfare, education, and infrastructure.

This largesse comes at a most propitious time for the Caribbean, where many countries are suffering from serious balance-of-payments deficits, low commodity prices, soaring rates of unemployment, and severe population pressures. Even more fundamental is the very limited resource base of most of these countries. With the exception of Trinidad and Tobago, they have little or no oil production. Since no major alternate energy sources are available, the rise in oil prices has hit them especially hard. As one of the countries responsible for the higher prices, Venezuela has tried to offset this added burden on Caribbean economies.

The Pérez administration has disbursed development funds multilaterally and bilaterally. Multilateral funds have been channelled into the Caribbean Development Bank, the Commonwealth Caribbean's lending arm. By the end of 1975, Venezuela, the first non-English-speaking member to be admitted, had extended a $10 million loan to the Bank's Special Development Fund and had created a $25 million trust fund to be used for development projects in several countries.[17] In addition, Venezuela, along with Colombia, Mexico, the United States, Canada, and Great Britain, has been negotiating a multimillion dollar aid package for the Caribbean. Other important Venezuelan initiatives include:

1. A $5 million loan in 1974 to the smaller CARICOM countries to purchase their financially troubled regional airline (LIAT).[18]

2. Partnership in a projected shipping venture, the Caribbean Merchant Fleet, is to be owned jointly by Venezuela, Mexico, and other Central American and Caribbean countries.[19]

3. Aid is given for a wide variety of projects in the Eastern Caribbean. The Public Works Ministry has been involved in water resources and aviation studies on St. Lucia, Dominica, Montserrat, St. Kitts, and Antigua. It also has experts in those islands consulting on programs in health care and sanitation. For Dominica, the Ministry of Mines and

Hydrocarbons is developing an exploration plan designed to detect mineral deposits and is evaluating geothermal potential. A scholarship program now under consideration would award grants to students from these islands to study Spanish, tourism and hostelry, and a variety of industrial, agricultural, and service fields.[20]

4. An agreement was made in 1976 with the Dominican Republic, whereby Venezuela will finance, in part, that country's purchase of Venezuelan oil up to $60 million for 1977. The loan, repayable in four years, carries an 8 percent annual interest rate. In 1976 the two countries also signed a joint declaration advocating the creation of the organization of Latin American and Caribbean Sugar-Exporting Countries (GEPLACEA).[21]

5. An agreement was made with Surinam in 1977, giving a Venezuelan oil company a contract to explore for and exploit petroleum deposits within Surinam, and also agreeing, if feasible, to build a refinery to process the oil extracted.[22]

An especially close relationship has been developing between Venezuela and Jamaica, facilitated by a natural ideological affinity between President Pérez and Prime Minister Michael Manley, both social democrats.[23] Manley, like Pérez, has been described as "an articulate spokesman for all underdeveloped nations"[24] In addition, Jamaica desperately needs financial assistance since, principally owing to oil price rises, it is facing balance of payments deficits of $200 million per year through the late 1970s. It has a $100 million deficit in international reserves, bauxite prices are down, the tourist industry is in a slump, and the unemployment rate is almost 25 percent. The FIV has come forward to help alleviate these problems in several ways. It made a $50 million loan to the Bank of Jamaica for long-term financing of programs aimed at developing Jamaica's natural resources and foreign trade, with additional loans to develop the paper industry, infrastructure, and housing. Also under discussion has been the bartering of Venezuelan oil for Jamaican bauxite. The two countries have negotiated a series of deals involving the construction of aluminum smelters and the purchase by Venezuela of large orders of Jamaican aluminum and bauxite. Venezuela also pledged to sell Jamaican oil at 50 percent of the world price, with the balance to be met in local currency for investment in basic development projects.[25]

POLICY ASSESSMENTS

To date, Venezuela's Caribbean policy has been largely successful. From the viewpoint of Caracas, it has largely done what it was designed to do. Excess petrodollars have been invested in worthwhile development projects in oil-poor countries that badly need such assistance, thus winning the country the gratitude of the recipient countries as well as fostering Venezuelan economic and trade interests there. Venezuela's firm commitment to democratic principles and practices has further enhanced its prestige in democratic circles abroad.

This new assertiveness has not, of course, gone unopposed. To date, the most serious attack on its Caribbean offensive has come from Eric Williams of Trinidad and Tobago. The prime minister's alarm became public in a series of political speeches in mid-1975, when he attacked Venezuelan policy on several grounds.[26] He contended that, historically, Venezuela has not been regarded as primarily a Caribbean country. Being traditionally more oriented toward Spanish America, it was really an outsider to the Caribbean community and had no legitimate right to assume a leadership role. Williams also charged that Venezuela was trying to buy influence in the Caribbean with petrodollars and thereby dislocating traditional economic and trade patterns within CARICOM. In addition, the many bilateral agreements with Caribbean countries, especially with Jamaica, worried Williams, who expressed fear that Venezuela would become the economic arbiter of the Caribbean, taking over one industry after another: "fish is going, oil is going, aluminium is going, now the tourist trade is going. . . . What next? Will we all be speaking Spanish in the future, with Venezuela's lavish grant of scholarships, left, right and center?"[27] The prime minister expressed concern too over his neighbor's ambitious oil development program, which included a plan to establish a refinery in Surinam and possibly in Guyana and Antigua as well. He even hinted that Venezuela might be manuevering to gain partial control over the giant refineries on Aruba and Curaçao. Finally, Williams accused Venezuela of not negotiating in good faith over fishing rights in the Gulf of Paria, which separates the two countries.

Both Venezuelan authorities and the press rejected these charges of "imperialist pretensions," as did Michael Manley and other CARICOM leaders.[28] The prevailing view was that Williams wanted to cast aspersions on Venezuela's leadership pretensions in order to bolster his own ambitions to become the leader of the Commonwealth Caribbean. By discrediting Venezuela, he would rid himself of the only other realistic claimant.[29] What undoubtedly concerned him most in terms of Trinidad's economic interests was that Venezuelan oil agreements with the British Caribbean would cut into his country's traditional position as major supplier of refined products in that area.[30]

It is true that Trinidad and Tobago, on account of its large oil and natural gas reserves, is the only other logical leader in the area. As the State Department noted, "Trinidad has achieved significant influence in the Caribbean. . . . *and* has been generous in using its oil revenues to help less fortunate islands."[31] But Venezuelan revenues and resource potential are many times greater than those of this far smaller country, and there is little that Williams can do about this. Since 1976, therefore, the prime minister has largely abandoned his verbal warfare against his mainland neighbor. Indeed, in 1978 Trinidad and Venezuela signed an agreement amicably settling the fishing rights controversy in the Gulf of Paria.

LEADERSHIP PROSPECTS

What are Venezuela's prospects for maintaining its leadership role in the Caribbean? Some signs augur well for its continuing prominence. Most important is its tremendous resource base; it has 20 to 25 years of conventional oil remaining (at current production levels), as well as considerable petroleum potential on the continental shelf. In addition, the Orinoco "bituminous belt" contains at least 700 billion barrels of "heavy" oil that could be recovered profitably if prices hold at sufficiently high levels. Added to oil resources are tremendous reserves of natural gas, hydroelectric power in abundance, and major deposits of bauxite.

Second, we may assume that the gap between oil-rich Venezuela and the oil-poor countries of the Caribbean will, if anything, grow wider. The needs of the latter will continue to be enormous. With British influence on the wane and with U.S. motives increasingly suspect, Venezuela would appear to be a regional leader almost by default.

Nevertheless, Venezuela would do well to heed several warning signs. Eric Williams's sharp attacks, although seemingly isolated, point to the dangers that regional leadership can entail and may anticipate future attacks from other quarters, if Venezuela is perceived as going too far with its leadership pretensions. Indeed, some critical voices have already been raised. For example, Dominican Republic President Joaquín Balaguer, at an Inter-American Development Bank meeting, charged that Venezuela was "in the process of beggaring its neighbors."[32] If Venezuela should secure too tight a hold on the economies of some smaller Caribbean entities, it might run the risk of being charged with imperialism.[33] Growing Venezuelan private investment in the area may intensify such feelings. On top of these new problems, some old ones remain. For example, the long-standing dispute between Venezuela and its eastern neighbor has not been definitively settled. Guyana remains wary of Venezuelan claims over the Essequibo region. Although Venezuela has not taken any provocative action since 1973, the dispute remains a potentially explosive issue in the eastern Caribbean.

More fundamentally, Venezuela will not be able to sustain itself as a regional power if it is not strong internally. Here, there are formidable challenges. Venezuela needs tremendous sums to finance its rapid and sweeping internal development and industrialization program and, despite its record oil revenues, has been borrowing extensively abroad. In 1977 alone, public debt rose over 54 percent, leading to cutbacks in aid programs—the VIF, for example, has been drastically curtailed.[34] Much of the oil wealth is being wasted in an inefficient and graft-ridden administration, with serious mismanagement widespread at all levels, since Venezuela, although rich in natural resources, is unfortunately not so well endowed in human resources. The country still has an acute shortage of skilled workers, technicians, and middle managers.

Given these problems, one may legitimately question Venezuela's capacity to sustain an ambitious foreign aid program for more than five years, if that.[35] Inasmuch as the country's highest priority will most certainly be domestic development, "foreign policy will receive comparatively less energy and attention."[36] It may well be that succeeding presidents will not share Pérez's personal commitment to making their nation a regional and Third World leader. Indeed, internal political pressures may force Venezuelan leaders to focus on structural problems at home, particularly if Venezuela continues its relatively disappointing record of "sowing" the oil or if it fails to distribute the oil wealth more equitably.

External factors will also enter into play. Venezuela's interest in strengthening its ties to the Caribbean will necessarily be limited by its commitments to OPEC and the Andean Group, among others, and by its newly acquired interest in improving relations with Brazil. In summary, Venezuela can be expected to continue as a strong, but not dominant, force in Caribbean affairs, a position appropriate to its role as a "middle power" in Latin America and as a developing country intent on forging a post-petroleum Venezuela.

NOTES

1. Charles D. Ameringer, "The Foreign Policy of Venezuelan Democracy," in *Venezuela: The Democratic Experience*, ed. John D. Martz and David J. Myers (New York: Praeger Publishers, 1977), p. 335; Alberto Micheo, "Política exterior," *SIC* [Caracas] 38 (December 1975): 460.

2. Ameringer, op. cit., pp. 335–356, esp. p. 354.

3. Luis Vallenilla *Oil: The Making of a New Economic Order—Venezuelan Oil and OPEC* (New York: McGraw-Hill, 1975), p. 175.

4. Jean-Pierre Clerc, "Using Solidarity Wisely," *Le Monde Diplomatique*, reprinted in *Venezuela Now: Documentación (Caracas/New York), 30 May 1977, p. 137.*

5. New York *Times*, 16 October 1976.

6. Franklin Tugwell, "Petroleum Policy and the Political Process," in *Venezuela: The Democratic Experience*, op. cit., p. 252.

7. Gumersindo Rodríguez, "The Development of Human Resources: Crucial to Third World Growth," in *Venezuela Now: Documentación*, 15 October 1976, p. 26.

8. Joseph Mann, "Venezuela, Strong Voice of World's Poor," New York *Times*, 15 August 1976.

9. Richard Gott, "Venezuela: Calm Civilian Oasis," *A Guardian Special Report*, 10 March 1977.

10. See, for example, Carlos Andrés Pérez, "Latin America's Future: The Quest for Consciousness and Authentic Community," *Venezuela Now: Documentación*, April 30, 1976, p. 86; Carlos Andrés Peréz, "After 150 Years: Bolívar's Universal Vision of Integration," *Venezuela Now: Documentacíon*, July 30, 1976, p. 5.

11. Carlos Andrés Peréz, "President Pérez Calls for Unity in Third World Development; Address Before the U.N. General Assembly," November 16, 1976, in *Venezuela Now: Documentacíon*, 30 November 1976, p. 49.

12. Tugwell, op. cit., p. 252.

13. Mikel Viana, "Guerra del petróleo y crisis económica mundial," *SIC*, 38 (April 1975): 161.

14. Vallenilla, op. cit., p. 256.

15. See Clerc, op. cit., p. 138.

16. Carlos Andrés Peréz, "1976: Year of Uncertainty for Third World Economies; Excerpts from State of the Nation Address to Congress," March 11, 1977, in *Venezuela Now: Documentación*, 31 August 1977, p. 28.

17. John D. Martz, "Venezuelan Foreign Policy Toward Latin America," in *Contemporary Venezuela and Its Role in International Affairs*, ed. Robert D. Bond (New York: New York University Press, a Council on Foreign Relations Book, 1977), p. 176.

18. Ibid.

19. Ibid., pp. 179–180.

20. Pérez, "1976: Year of Uncertainty," op. cit., pp. 28–29.

221. Ibid., pp. 30, 38.

22. *Caribbean Monthly Bulletin*, June 1977, pp. 41–42.

23. "Contactos Jamaica-Venezuela," *SIC* 40 (February 1977): 87–88.

24. Graham Hovey, "U.S. Paying New Heed to Caribbean Region," New York *Times*, 7 December 1977.

25. "Contactos Jamaica-Venezuela," op. cit., pp. 87–88; Pérez, "1976: Year of Uncertainty," op. cit., p. 37; *Venezuela Now*, 30 January 1977, p. 87; "Venezuela Loan Aids Jamaica," *Venezuela Now*, 30 October 1977, p. 54; U.S., Department of State, "U.S. Relations in the Caribbeans" Assistant Secretary for Inter-American Affairs Terence A. Todman Before the Subcommittee on Inter-American Affairs of the House International Relations Committee, p. 3; *Caribbean Monthly Bulletin*, April–May 1977, p. 11; Martz, "Venezuelan Foreign Policy," op. cit., p. 177; "La ayuda de Venezuela," *Visión*, 22 April 1977, p. 8.

26. Speeches Delivered by the Hon. Dr. Eric Williams, Prime Minister of Trinidad and Tobago: "The Threat to the Caribbean Community," Political Leader's Speech to the People's National Movement General Council, May 4, 1975, and "The threat to the Caribbean Community," Political Leader's Speech at the Special Convention of the PNM, June 15, 1975, in Supplement to the *Caribbean Monthly Bulletin*.

27. Williams, "The Threat to the Caribbean Community," Political Leader's Speech at the Special Convention of the PNM, ibid., p. 37.

28. Martz, "Venezuelan Foreign Policy," op. cit., p. 178.

29. "Las declaraciones de Mr. Eric Williams," *SIC* 38 (July–August 1975): 326.

30. See Martz, "Venezuelan Foreign Policy," op. cit., pp. 177–178.

31. U.S., Department of State, op. cit., p. 3.

32. Martz, "Venezuelan Foreign Policy," op. cit., p. 189; see also Robert D. Bond, "Venezuela's Role in International Affairs," in *Contemporary Venezuela,* op. cit., p. 251; "La ayuda de Venezuela," op. cit., p. 8.

33. Bond, "Venezuela's Role," op. cit.; "La ayuda de Venezuela," op. cit.

34. Everett G. Martin, "Uneasy Croesus," *Wall Street Journal,* 2 May 1978.

35. See, for example, Pedro-Pablo Kuczynski, "The Impact of the Higher Oil Prices on the LDC's: The Case of Latin America," in *Latin America: The Search for a New International Role,* ed. Ronald G. Hellman and H. Jon Rosenbaum (New York: John Wiley & sons, 1975), p. 288.

36. Martz, "Venezuelan Foreign Policy," op. cit., p. 190.

17

Changing Patterns of Caribbean International Relations: Britain and the "British" Caribbean

Sir Kenneth Blackburne

INTRODUCTION

As the late Charles W. Taussig, co-chairman of the Anglo-American Caribbean Commission of World War II, said to a British colleague, "All an American knows when he hears the word 'colony' is that it's somewhere that ought to be freed immediately." He was preaching to the converted. Britain was anxious to relieve herself of her burdensome overseas responsibilities; and the British West Indian colonies were as ready as anyone for independence, with locally born politicians and professional men as good as anywhere in the empire. But the British had a problem that was not fully shared by the other "colonial" powers in the Caribbean. How could viable independence be possible for 15 colonies, each with its own legislature and government, spread over 1.75 million square miles of sea, when 10 had populations of under 100,000 people, and 7 required annual grants from Britain to enable them to meet their day-to-day expenditures?

Many hoped that the West Indies Federation of 1958 would provide the answer. It was joined by all the territories except the Bahamas, British Honduras, Guyana, and the three tiny groups—the British Virgin Islands, the Cayman Islands, and the Turks and Caicos Islands. Within four years it collapsed due to internal political dissension and the withdrawal of Jamaica. Efforts to form a unitary state or a smaller federation in the eastern Caribbean failed, and all the former members of the federation decided to "go it alone." In full accord with Britain, the larger territories became independent nations within the Commonwealth—Jamaica and Trinidad and Tobago in 1962, Barbados and Guyana in 1966, and the Bahamas (which had never regarded itself as an integral part of the British West Indies) in 1973.

The problem of eliminating colonialism in the remaining small islands was temporarily resolved by the grant of internal self-government as seven independent "states," with the United Kingdom retaining responsibility for external affairs and defense. This limited association with Britain can be terminated at any time on a local majority vote. Grenada has already adopted this course, becoming independent and a member of the Commonwealth and of the UN in 1974.

British colonialism is not yet ended in the Caribbean, because the people of the smallest territories have opted to retain their links with the United Kingdom. They comprise Montserrat, the British Virgin Islands, the Cayman Islands, the Turks and Caicos Islands, and Anguilla—which has seceded from St. Kitts-Nevis-Anguilla and been taken under British protection.

The former colony of British Honduras (now Belize) is a special case. With an area of nearly 9,000 square miles, a population of over 140,000, a well-established form of government, and a steadily growing economy which compares well with many Latin American countries, there is only one reason why it has not received its rightful independence. Despite prolonged discussions with Guatemala and the overwhelming support of the UN, Guatemala has refused to withdraw its claim to part of the territory of Belize. British military protection—on land and sea and in the air—has to be maintained to secure the integrity of its boundaries. In the meantime, it still has a British governor with responsibility for defense, external affairs, and for the expenditure of the financial aid provided by Britain.

Despite this varied picture of the status of the former British Caribbean colonies, some regional collaboration survives. The Caribbean Free Trade Area (CARIFTA), established in 1968, consists of all the territories described except the Bahamas. This has become the Caribbean Community and Common Market (CARICOM), designed to promote trade between its members. But the economic plight of Guyana and Jamaica in 1977 has caused them to limit imports from their trading partners and has created such tension that it has for a long time been impossible even to convene a meeting of the heads of government to resolve their differences.

One regional organization—the Caribbean Development Bank—continues to play an important role. Established in 1970, its membership is open to any Caribbean state, and already includes sixteen Commonwealth countries, Venezuela, and Colombia. Britain and Canada are also members, while the United States has made financial contributions. The bank has also received help from the UN.

The historic function of Caribbean territories—British, Dutch, French, and American—was to serve as suppliers of primary products such as sugar to their metropolitan overlords. Most of the investment capital came from these metropolitan countries, from both private and governmental sources. But the position had changed to some degree in the British colonies, even before independence. Trinidad with its oil, and Guyana and Jamaica with their bauxite, had already established close links with the United States and Canada; and all the governments, including the smaller territories, had embarked in the years following World War II on a policy of industrialization for which aid from the British government and investment from companies in Britain, Canada, and the United States was forthcoming. Growing dependence on tourism from North America has produced additional dislocations in many of the islands' economies.

The introduction of independence and "statehood" in the 1960s brought about a dramatic change in the pattern of trade and external investment. As the 1973 Report of the British-North American Committee states:

> In 1960 Trinidad and Tobago, Jamaica, Barbados and Guyana bought between 30% and 40% of all their requirements from Britain and only between 13% and 24% from the United States. By the end of the sixties the United States had become the leading supplier to Trinidad and Jamaica with the shift to Jamaica being particularly marked. Britain's share of Jamaica's imports dropped form 34% in 1960 to 19% in 1970, while the United States' share rose from 24% to 43%.

In recent years, Britain's position as a trading partner has declined still further, as the four major independent countries have widened the scope of their trading and their financial contacts with the rest of the world. Imports from Britain in 1975–76 for Barbados, Jamaica, and Trinidad were below 15 percent of their total imports, while their exports to Britain were about 25 percent of their world exports.

The reasons for this change and the widely divergent degrees of economic progress in the "British" Caribbean call for analysis territory by territory, as their governments have in recent years been guided by differing ideologies.

THE "BRITISH" CARIBBEAN

The Commonwealth of the Bahamas

This nation consists of 700 islands and cays with a population of 197,000 (1974). Previously uninhabited, these islands were settled by the British in the seventeenth century. A predominantly white feudal-capitalist group held power until 1967 when the present prime minister (Hon. L. O. Pindling) assumed office. The change has not visibly affected the islands' stability and economic situation. Tourism, for years a mainstay of the economy, continues to grow, increasing from 244,000 arrivals in 1959 to over a million in 1977. Major tax concessions have encouraged the entry of foreign banks and of trust and insurance companies. The investment of foreign capital, traditionally from North America, has made possible such projects as the establishment of Freeport with an oil refinery and one of the largest bunkering installations in the Western Hemisphere. Unfortunately, the Bahamas have also been linked with international financial scandals and with reports of extensive internal involvements by organized crime.

Because of their proximity to North America, the Bahamas present a quite different picture than that of most of the Commonwealth Caribbean territories. They require little British financial aid, their trade with the United Kingdom is minimal, and their comparative prosperity makes it unnecessary for them to seek aid from all quarters of the globe. Their major problem, creating and maintaining a healthy social, economic, and political system in the face of the flood of North American tourists and residents, with their dollars and influence, is largely outside the scope of British policies.

Barbados

This small island of 166 square miles with a population of 251,272 (1976) constitutes an oft-cited example of stability in the Caribbean. Settled by the British in the seventeenth century, it has had parliamentary institutions since 1627. With two main political parties—not based on race but both using the word "Labour" in their titles—there has been a continuing pattern of moderate, limited socialism. The present prime minister (Hon. Tom Adams) has stated: "Socialist methods to obtain full employment would mean no wage increases and a lowering in the present standard of living."

The economy of Barbados depended in the past on the production of sugar, molasses, and rum. These accounted for over 50 percent of exports in 1975. Unlike the other sugar-producing countries that have assumed total or partial government control of this industry, Barbados has maintained private ownership, although the plethora of private sugar factories has been combined under a single company in which the majority of the plantation owners hold shares. But sugar is a vulnerable crop; in 1975 Barbados had a record balance of payments of B$33.6 million, which was converted in the following year into a record deficit of B$39.2 million due mainly to a drop in the world sugar price.

Of momentous importance for present development, steps had been taken after World War II to stimulate tourism and the growth of local industry. Between 1966 and 1976, income from tourism increased sixfold and provides some much-needed employment for an ever-growing number of workers. Industrial development is also progressing, with the establishment of factories by a number of American and some Canadian companies. An American company has found petroleum in Barbadian waters, which now meets 12 percent of local needs, and further exploration is being continued. The economic results of Barbadian tourism and incentive-industry policies, however, have not fulfilled original expectations.

In the ten years from 1967 to 1976, Barbados received British financial aid of £6 million, together with loans from international sources; and the present financial position is reasonably stable. Population pressures are severe and have been aggravated by British immigration policies. An interesting development is a possible liaison with the OPEC countries, where there is a hope of finding an outlet for the excellent and ever-growing work force, now that traditional migration to Britain is restricted.

Guyana

Guyana, with an area of 83,000 square miles and a population of 714,000 (1970), became a Cooperative Republic four years after the independence of 1966, but remained within the Commonwealth. In the past, it had a domestic problem not shared to the same degree by other Caribbean territories—a sharp division between its two equally divided races. The black half of the population dominated the urban areas, while the descendants of the East Indians, who had come as indentured labor in the last century, still worked mainly in agriculture and lived in the rural areas. Although neither of the two main political parties are exclusively of racial origin, the present prime minister (Hon. Forbes Burnham), who has been in power since 1963, gains much of his support from black voters. The leader of the opposition, Cheddi Jagan (an East Indian and a former premier), is an avowed Marxist and heads the trade union in the sugar industry.

Like all the Caribbean countries, Guyana has serious unemployment problems and is in need of outside aid for economic development. Unlike most of them, however, it has pursued a determined policy of nationalization. The former holdings of two North American bauxite companies and of the powerful British sugar producer—Booker Bros. McConnell Ltd.—

are now owned by the state. The financial result has not been encouraging; there was a balance of payments deficit of G$242.5 million at the end of 1976 and the foreign reserves stood at –£14 million, while the public debt had soared from G$5 million in 1961 to G$878 million in 1976.

Over the years 1967–76, the British government has contributed £ 20 million in grants and loans for budget support and development. Far more is needed; one major project alone—a hydro-power complex, aluminum smelter, and industrial area in the Upper Mazaruni basin—calls for expenditure of at least G$2,000 million. It is not surprising that Guyana, more than any country except Jamaica, has been forced to seek outside financial aid. It is even possible that foreign private enterprise, virtually anathema in the past, may yet be cautiously welcomed back.

The general tendency appears to have been a shift in trading relations from North America and Britain to the East, but relations with the United States have shown recent improvement, and temporary financial aid has come from there as well as from Canada and the European Economic Community (EEC).

Jamaica

With an area of 4,411 square miles and a population approaching 2 million, Jamaica seemed well fitted for independence in 1962. It had two balanced political parties, each backed by a powerful trade union and headed by a leader of international repute. The economy was expanding, thanks to Jamaica's world lead in bauxite production, to tourism, and to the growth of manufacturing. There were, however, grave problems, with unemployment at 13 percent or more and a widening gap between rich and poor.

At first prosperity continued. Income from bauxite and tourism roughly doubled within the next ten years and agricultural production was maintained. Economic difficulties increased in 1972, the same year that the Peoples' National Party, now led by its founder's son (Hon. Michael Manley), returned to power with a program of "democratic socialism." Manley was retained in power in 1976, just when the world recession had accelerated a decline in the economy.

From the outset, Manley's policies were directed at increased state control of the economy and at finding new trading outlets. On winning his second election he declared,

> the diversification of international trading relationships will be the
> main thrust of Jamaica's foreign relations. To realise this, the fullest

exploration of trading possibilities with the Soviet Union, the socialist COMECON bloc, and the development of initiatives with the People's Republic of China will be undertaken.

Manley's policies weakened the links with Jamaica's traditional friends overseas, notably Britain, the United States, and Canada. External capital investment was discouraged by the nationalization of the properties of the British-owned West Indies Sugar Company, of the United Fruit Company, and of two banks, Barclays and the Bank of Montreal Jamaica Ltd. The government also acquired a 51 percent holding in the bauxite companies.

Local business confidence was undermined by the introduction of state trading corporations, which controlled virtually all imports, leaving business at the mercy of the state in regard to selection and sources of goods. Conservative elements were also concerned by the developing rapport with Cuba, even though this resulted in significant aid in such areas as water supplies, education, and health.

These recent political and economic changes have produced some seriously unfavorable results. Large numbers of the professional classes emigrated to North America, even though export of their assets was prohibited. Sugar production fell from a peak of 500,000 tons in 1966 to under 300,000 in 1976. This was due to a combination of adverse weather and labor unrest, even among the cooperatives set up in nationalized estates. A depressing event in 1978 was the importation of 5,000 tons of sugar from Cuba to meet local consumption needs. Citrus and livestock industries have also declined, but other agricultural products such as coffee (now shipped mainly to Japan), cocoa, and cigars have done well. Exaggerated reports of internal violence had an adverse effect on tourism. North American and British groups, which had financed hotel development since the 1960s, pulled out. There was a 20 percent drop in tourist arrivals in 1975, followed by the termination of services by two U.S. airlines and the cancellation of several cruise ship visits to Montego Bay in 1977. Fortunately, 1978 shows signs of a revival in this sector of the economy.

As a result of these problems the public debt increased from J$60 million in 1962 to J$961 million in 1972. By late 1977, the Central Bank of Jamaica had lent 89 percent of its assets to the government and there had been three devaluations of the currency. In November 1977, foreign exchange reserves stood at minus J$201 million. International Monetary Fund (IMF) pressures for further austerity measures reflect continued economic weaknesses.

Britain has only been able to help minimally, with grants and loans totaling £27 million from 1967 to 1976 and a recent credit of J$20 million to enable Jamaica to purchase goods from the United Kingdom. Her CARICOM partners, Barbados, Guyana, and Trinidad, have assisted with a single loan, but are unable or unwilling to do more. Jamaica has sought additional aid from every quarter of the globe, obtaining loans from the World Bank, the IMF, the United States, Canada, Venezuela, and Norway. Recently, Hungary provided a credit of J$22 million for the purchase of capital and consumer goods.

Further change may be on the way. The present government is looking toward the establishment of a republic, but has extended the period of public debate to four years due to lack of local enthusiasm. Recent public opinion polls suggest that the middle class and the rural population retain much of their traditional conservatism, an attitude which caused the fall of the present ruling party and Jamaica's secession from the federation in 1962.

Trinidad and Tobago

In contrast to the problems faced by other Caribbean countries, Trinidad and its associated island, Tobago, present a relatively encouraging picture. With an area of 1,980 square miles and a population of 1,170,300 (1977) almost equally divided between peoples of African and East Indian origin, it has developed into a united and prosperous country. It possesses important oil and natural gas resources, extensive industrial undertakings, and produces sugar, coffee, cocoa, and fertilizers. Above all, it has been led since 1956 by an outstanding political leader —Dr. Eric Williams—who charted the country's future course as an independent country in 1962 by calling for discipline, production, and confidence.

Trinidad has pursued a middle course between state ownership and private enterprise. Part of the oil industry has been taken over by the state and foreign banks have agreed to place a majority of their shares in Trinidadian hands. Private investment is welcomed and the government is sponsoring the development of a major new industrial complex at Point Lisas. The government hopes to raise TT$500 million in loan capital in 1978 from foreign money markets and local banks. It should have no difficulty; in contrast to the visits overseas by the other Caribbean countries in search of aid, private bankers visit Trinidad in search of business.

Dr. Williams has long felt that Britain did not do enough to help her Caribbean territories, and it was no surprise when Trinidad decided in 1976 to become a republic, though still remaining in the Commonwealth. Its trade and contacts with Britain have inevitably declined, but Trinidad has spread her trade and financial contacts worldwide, almost all in the sphere of Western influence.

Grenada

With an area (including the outlying islands of the Grenadines) of 133 square miles and a population of 104,000 (1976), Grenada is the smallest of the Caribbean territories to gain independence. It did so in 1974—a year of considerable unrest and economic difficulty—under the leadership of a colorful yet controversial prime minister, Sir Eric Gairy. Grenada is a lush island which has traditionally produced most of the crops indigenous to the Caribbean. It is also poor and, like other eastern Caribbean territories, has attempted to exploit its climate, beaches, and semi-tropical beauty as a tourist attraction. Its emerging tourist industry has been financed by private overseas investment. Tourism, primarily from North America and Europe, now provide the main source of income and employment. One impact of this industry has been the tremendous pressure placed on Grenada's few roads and picturesque but limited port facilities, severely pressing the government for improvement.

It is yet too soon to assess Grenada's future world relationship; but its needs for external capital and its tourist relationships with North America and Western Europe suggest what these directions will be. Close links are still maintained with Britain, which has supplied substantial aid considering the size of the territory (£6.5 million over the years 1967–76), mainly in the form of grants to support the local budget.

The Associated States

In the eastern Caribbean there are now five "associated states" with full internal self-government—Antigua, Dominica, St. Kitts-Nevis-Anguilla, St. Lucia, and St. Vincent. All are small, with areas of between 130 and 290 square miles, and with populations ranging from 55,000 to 100,000. In the past they depended exclusively on agricultural production, though in recent years tourism has played an increasing part in their economies.

From the earliest days of British settlement, each of these states had its own government and legislature—an expense which could readily be met when sugar and other tropical products produced much wealth. Now the wealth has vanished, and yet these states retain their system of government, and their intense insular pride. The result has been that all of them, at one time or another, have been able to survive only with the aid of grants from the British government, not merely for development, but just to meet their day-to-day expenditure.

In these circumstances, they rely on Britain for their trade and economic survival far more than the independent countries. Although Britain is still officially responsible for their external affairs, no obstacle has been placed in their way when they have sought development aid and investment from other parts of the world. Up to now that investment has been provided from the United States, Canada, and some of the countries of Western Europe. Amounts invested have generally been disappointing and disproportionately directed to serving the desires of tourists.

Four of these island "states" have expressed a desire for full independence at an early date, not least because it will give them access to help from international agencies. Only the present premier of Antigua has intimated that he wishes to see greater economic development before independence—and is taking active steps to this end. There may be difficulties in the case of St. Kitts-Nevis-Anguilla, which has experienced not only the secession of Anguilla, but also the reluctance of many Nevisians to retain their association with St. Kitts.

The attainment of independence is unlikely to make any material change in the nature of their international relationships. Even the present premier of Dominica, perhaps the most likely to follow an independent course, has stated that his government would seek a socialism in which the economy would be divided into three parts—the public, the private, and the cooperative sectors.

The state of Belize has great resources of timber and a well-developed agricultural economy. Whereas it formerly needed regular grants from Britain, it has in recent years balanced its budget, but it has received British aid for development totaling £21.5 million over the ten years 1967–76.

As the only former British colony in Central America, the future of Belize will probably lie mainly in relationships with North America and with those members of the Organization of American States (OAS) that support her resistance to the territorial claims of Guatemala—support which is endorsed by the other former British Caribbean territories, although none of them are in a position to take over Britain's responsibility for the country's defense.

The British Colonies

The future of the five remaining British colonies is complicated by the facts that they are scattered over 300,000 square miles of sea, and that their size and populations make independence problematical. They are as follows:

	Area (sq. miles)	Population (approx.)
Anguilla	35	6,500
Br. Virgin Islands	59	10,000
Cayman Islands	100	10,600

Montserrat	39	13,000
Turks and Caicos Is.	192	7,000

The economy of all, except Anguilla, depends mainly on tourism and on remittances from overseas workers. In the Cayman Islands (by far the most prosperous), world finance is the main asset, with some 200 banks and trust companies, and registered offices for over 7,000 companies. Tourism in the Caymans has also increased dramatically—from a trickle of visitors in the 1960s, the arrivals had risen to 60,000 in 1976, while cruise ships brought day visitors who increased from 2,500 in 1974 to 40,000 in 1977. A C$4 million harbor improvement scheme is nearing completion, while a multimillion oil transshipment port for Little Cayman is planned. The extent to which benefits from all this activity actually reaches the majority of the population, however, is debatable.

Although the majority of tourists to these colonies come from North America, their ties with Britain remain strong, and they have received British government aid of £53 million over the years 1967–76—mainly (except in the Cayman Islands) to balance their budgets. Typical of the attitude of most of their inhabitants is the response of the Caymanians to a visit in 1977 by the UN Committee for Decolonialization who were firmly told at public meetings: "We in the Cayman Islands are proud to be a Colony of Britain; we want no change."

Anguilla is a special case. After its secession from St. Kitts in 1967, Britain had no option but to assume responsibility for its people by providing money and staff. But the premier of St. Kitts-Nevis still maintains that the island belongs to his territory. The future remains in doubt, and Britain finds itself saddled with responsibility in a dispute from which it can gain no advantages.

PAST AND PRESENT RELATIONSHIPS WITH BRITAIN

Since the start of the movement towards independence in 1962, Britain has continued its long-established policy of giving financial aid to both her past and present Caribbean colonies; and, for the past 12 years the British Ministry of Overseas Development has maintained an office in Barbados to provide close liaison between London and the Caribbean territories in the field of development. In the years between 1962 and 1976 the ministry has made available £187 million in grants and loans to the former and existing British Caribbean territories, of which £124 million were provided as outright grants, mainly to meet budget deficits. In addition, the Commonwealth Development Corporation (whose main source of funds is the British Exchequer) has invested in the same period

£58 million (£27 million in Jamaica alone) for developments often undertaken in concert with commercial interests.

It is noteworthy that this aid from Britain has, despite her own economic and financial problems, increased in recent years. Whereas the average annual disbursement over the fifteen years 1962–76 amounted to just over £16 million, the actual disbursement in 1976 amounted to £22 million—or over £4 per head of the population of some five million people.

In addition, until the Lomé Convention of 1976, when the European Economic Community accepted joint responsibility for trading arrangements in favor of the fifty-two developing countries of Africa, the Caribbean, and the Pacific, the British government and the British public had alone shouldered the responsibility of aiding the sugar industry in the British Caribbean. This was done through the Commonwealth Sugar Agreement which normally involved the payment of higher than world prices.

It is also noteworthy that, despite a growing feeling of concern among some sections of the British public at the rapid increase in immigration to Britain from the West Indies and elsewhere, the government has over the years experienced no difficulty in securing funds from parliament for substantial aid to her former colonies. There is general acceptance of Britain's responsibility for providing assistance in their new role as independent nations.

There are, of course, practical reasons for this financial aid. Until World War II, Britain found a ready market for her exports in the Caribbean. Although imports to the region have come in recent years increasingly from North America, British imports are still of some importance. British-based companies, despite nationalization in Guyana and Jamaica, still exist in the area, and British commercial investment remains at a fairly high level.

Above all—after 350 years of British settlement—human links are still strong. All the territories have parliamentary institutions, a legal service, and government organizations based on the British model; and all the self-governing countries are members of the Commonwealth Parliamentary Association, which provides regular contacts between the legislators from all parts of the world. These links exist through all strata of West Indian society—from the senior civil servants trained in the United Kingdom to the simple country folk such as the elderly Jamaican who, when asked what she thought of the recent problems facing her country, replied: "I don't worry; I know that if things get too bad, Missus Queen will send her soldiers—and then we'll be all right." While the Queen is not about to "send her soldiers," attitudes like this demonstrate that the colonial heritage of looking to Britain for solutions to insular problems still exists.

Finally, there is the important link provided by the fact that all the new independent "British" countries in the Caribbean have opted to become members of the Commonwealth. They play an ever-increasing role at the regular meetings of Commonwealth Prime Ministers, whose central secretariat is based in London. Links between Canada and the Caribbean have been close for many years, but valuable relationships are now developing between the Caribbean territories and Australia, New Zealand, and the former British countries in Africa.

THE FUTURE

All of these links between Britain and her former Caribbean colonies may vanish sooner or later in an ever-changing world. But the past history of these territories provides at least a possible indication of future tendencies in their relations with Britain.

In the years since World War II, political power throughout the Caribbean has shifted rapidly from the descendants of British settlers and businessmen to those of African, East Indian, and mixed descent. The unfortunate legacy of slavery which remains ingrained in the West Indian peoples today has produced a growing tendency to loosen links with Britain through denigration of British traditions, through education in schools, and through efforts to revive their African heritage. Coupled with this is the decline in the economic and military power of Britain in the world as a whole. Even the 300-year-old traditions of British parliamentary government and the British legal system are threatened. The switch of foreign relations to new world partners is only to be expected. Already Guyana and Jamaica have developed close links with Cuba and are looking to the Soviet Union for aid. Their relationships with the Eastern bloc must affect their contacts with the West and with Britain, although it is not beyond the bounds of possibility that, particularly in the case of Jamaica, public opinion may bring about a change of course. Trinidad and Tobago, with its natural wealth and conservative leadership, and also Barbados and the smaller islands, acutely aware of the problems of the economies of Guyana and Jamaica, should insure a strong following for traditional British political practices, but even here, relationships with Britain will inevitably lessen as they search elsewhere for new trading and financial partners.

The five remaining British colonies present a very different picture —also for historical reasons. Their economies, with a partial exception in Montserrat, have not been based on the plantation system; there is no legacy of slavery; and all their peoples, apart from those in the tiny islands of Grand Turk and South Caicos (with their former Bermuda-founded salt industry), show a sturdy independence of spirit based on long-standing land ownership. But their tiny size, their distance from Britain, and their limited resources must in time make it necessary for them to look elsewhere than Britain for aid and protection.

One factor in Britain itself may conceivably have some bearing on future relationships with the Caribbean—the effect of immigration from the West Indies and elsewhere on the British public. After World War II (when many West Indians played a notable part in the British Army and Royal Air Force), the rapidly increasing populations of the British West Indian territories caused a large flow of immigrants to Britain, most of whom rapidly established themselves in jobs for which British workers could not be found. They made, and are still making, a great contribution to British life—in public transport, in hospitals, in factories, and in the higher echelons of British society ranging up to the chairman of the Greater London Council and the House of Lords. But rising unemployment in the United Kingdom has led to a move in some quarters for stricter control over immigration—the repetition of a movement which sparked off considerable unrest and anti-British feeling in the Caribbean some eighteen years ago. Any growth of color discrimination in Britain could do major damage to relationships with the Caribbean countries.

Despite these problems, there is still hope for a secure and more prosperous future for the former British territories in the Caribbean provided that the importance of this region to world peace is fully recognized by the Western powers.

The importance of the Caribbean should not be underrated. The region is important strategically and is a source of raw materials needed by the world as a whole. Although Trinidad and Tobago, Barbados, and the Bahamas, and, to some extent, the smaller island "states" and Belize, can readily find help from overseas investors and governments, Guyana and Jamaica—because of their internal policies—are likely to rely increasingly on relationships with the Eastern bloc. Their possible association with COMECON could deeply divide the Commonwealth Caribbean.

Any solution to these problems demands cooperative international action by the West. Money has been poured into the former British territories in recent years not only by Britain, but also by the international agencies, by the United States, and by Canada. But there has been little coordination between them. As long ago as 1973, the British North-American Committee urged that there sould be regular inter-governmental consultation and coordination of policies—at least by the United States, Canada, and Britain.

The prime minister of Trinidad and Tobago, concerned over requests from Guyana and Jamaica for even more financial aid than his country had provided, recently suggested to the United States that they should participate in a foreign exchange rescue operation for these economically-troubled countries. This suggestion appears to have blossomed into the establishment of the Caribbean Group for Economic Aid, following a meeting called by the World Bank in December 1977. The Dominican Republic, Haiti, the Netherlands Antilles, the French territories, and Surinam will come within the purview of the group, which may well open new prospects for the future well-being of the area. It could buttress the political stability that exists in most of the former British territories; and it could perhaps even restore much-needed confidence in those nations whose economies have been disrupted by internal and external responses to changes in their political and economic ideologies.

The group might slowly go further and provide some simple form of international supervision under which Britain could still play a part in the administration of those of her tiny colonies which still wished to preserve their direct links with the United Kingdom.

If a rapprochement between the United States and Cuba should become possible, the Caribbean might then become—as it should be—a peaceful and prosperous part of the western world instead of a divided region split in its allegiance to the conflicting world powers of the West and the East.

But, whatever steps are taken to this end, it would seem that Britain's role in the Caribbean must inevitably grow less and less with the passage of time. The last vestiges of British authority may vanish; but there is reason to hope that Britain's legacy of democracy will endure.

REFERENCES

Bank of Jamaica. *Annual Report.* 1961, 1976.

Commonwealth. London: Royal Commonwealth Society.

Great Britain. Ministry of Overseas Development. Statistics of British financial aid to the Caribbean. 1961–76.

Insight. London: West India Committee. 1977–78.

Mitchell, Sir Harold, Bt. *Caribbean Patterns.* Edinburgh and London: W. and R. Chambers, 1967.

Powell, David. *Problems of Economic Development in the Caribbean.* London: British-North American Committee, 1973.

West Indies Chronicle. London: West Indies Committee

Whitaker's *Almanac.* 1964, 1978.

18

Continental Europe and the Caribbean: The French and Dutch Experience

Albert L. Gastmann

FRANCE AND THE CARIBBEAN

Even though the first nation to achieve independence in the Caribbean was the French colony of Saint Dominque (now the Republic of Haiti) in 1804, the Caribbean community still has, in its midst, territories that are departments of France, remnants of France's former vast overseas empire. Prior to World War II, decolonization was already an issue for the policy makers of France; however, no elite agreement existed in the Antilles or metropolis.

With the establishment of the Fourth Republic in 1946, the decision was made that some form of decolonization was necessary for French possessions in the Western Hemisphere. They were to become politically an integral part of France if this should meet with the approval of the people in that region. For Guadeloupe and Martinique, this meant that the French government was ready to give each island the status of department; their citizens would have the same rights as the citizens of any department of metropolitan France. A referendum was held in the islands and an overwhelming majority of the electorate voted for departmentalization. When this was instituted on March 19, 1946, the French believed that decolonization of the Antilles had been successfully fulfilled.[1]

The policy of succeeding French governments has been based on the belief that the people of the Antilles are and wish to remain French. In 1946 this idea was shared by all the political parties—from the Left to the Right—in the islands. Today this is no longer true. Aimé Césaire, Martinique's most famous author, and for years Mayor of Fort-de-France, broke with the Communist Party in 1956 and formed his own "Parti Progressiste Martiniquais," the PPM.[2] When the benefits expected from

219

departmentalization did not materialize, PPM members started to agitate for a more autonomous arrangement. There was disappointment with economic and social progress. Departmentalization called for a restructuring of the administration in a manner that would be identical with that of France, integrating the civil service into that of the metropole and adapting the legislation of the islands in labor and other fields to that of France. This political modernization did not trigger change in the social and economic fields. Business and land remained in the hands of those who had always had them. The consequence was a clash between the realities of a political system planned for a modern consumer society and an economic structure designed for an antiquated agrarian one.[3]

Traditionally the islands produced sugar and sugar derivatives, bananas, and pineapples for export. Today these products are not competitive, except in protected markets, because French Antillean labor receives European-level wages and fringe benefits. Cuba and other Caribbean areas produce these products less expensively. This has made the islands very dependent on the French market and those of the European Economic Community (EEC).

To counterbalance the steady decline in the agricultural sector, plans were made to develop the industrial one, but so far there has been no apparent success in this endeavor. Basic materials and markets are lacking. Geographically, Martinique and Guadeloupe may be part of the Caribbean; economically they are not. Most exports go to France and most imports come from there.

The economic stagnation influenced social relationships. The social structure remained unchanged and caused dissatisfaction among well-educated young who were entering the job market. It led to heavy competition for bureaucratic positions. Those who were not successful "expatriated" to France where many became disenchanted intellectuals. Among the educated unemployed or underemployed in the islands, economic and social frustration produced demands for change in the political system. Many came to realize that besides departmentalization there were other possible decolonization schemes such as that which France introduced to her African colonies in 1956,[4] offering these possessions prompt and complete self-government. In the Caribbean, events were also stirring popular imagination. The Netherlands had given self-government to her islands and Britain was promising independence to her West Indian domains.

In the French Antilles parties other than the PPM, notably the Front Antillais et Guianais pour L'autonomie, propagated the idea of greater self-government. These groups soon found themselves on a collision course with French authorities. Decrees of April 26, and October 15, 1960, gave special powers to the prefects to forbid government officials and teachers to remain in the islands if they participated in subversive activities.[5] Shortly thereafter, a number of functionaries were expelled from the Antilles. Attempts by senators and deputies of Guadeloupe and Martinique to have the decree repealed were unsuccessful. The French reaction was that these people were a mere minority. After all, under President de Gaulle the vast majority of the population of the two islands would vote for the Gaullist and Socialist candidates, who were ardent supporters of the departmental solution.

French ministers and secretaries of state for overseas departments and territories have stressed that the Departmentalization Law of 1946 was not a government bill but one introduced before the constituent assembly by representatives of Martinique and Guadeloupe, of Réunion, and of French Guiana.[6] French officials also emphasize that when the Fifth Republic was established, the people of the Antilles reaffirmed their desire to keep their special relationship with France. The Antilleans were told that, as soon as assimilation was completed, they would receive the social and economic benefits that accrued to the inhabitants of the metropolitan area. To hasten this process, the French government placed large financial resources at the disposal of the overseas departments through the "Fonds d'Investissement des Departments d'Outre-Mer (FIDOM)," the major agency in charge of government investment in the local sector.[7]

Since 1958, living standards have improved, but political discontent has remained. The reasons for this are manifold. Improvements in living conditions were due not to a developing economy but to infusions of metropolitan money into such projects as raising old age, unemployment, and other benefits. Housing developments were funded by France and schools were built. People were better housed and fed but the job outlook worsened. Some government plans created work temporarily, but once they were completed unemployment rates again increased.

Another criticism of the departmental system was that the prefect and his civil service were controlled more by France now than the governor and his administrators were in colonial days. The prefect and his staff were directly part of the governmental structure of metropolitan France. As such, they had to obey the orders of the ministries in Paris where decisions were made with little concern as to how they would affect overseas departments. Further aggravation was created because the powers of the elected general council of an overseas department had to conform to that of a metropolitan department. After 1946, therefore, the council lacked many powers that it had in the prewar days of the Third Republic.[8]

Prefects, whose personal authority was limited and whose duties to carry out orders from a host of metropolitan ministries were manifold, were often criticized in an irresponsible manner by council members whose powers were negligible. This was partly remedied in 1959, when a secretary general for overseas departments and territories in Paris was given the task of coordinating policies for these departments.[9] Two years later, the prefect obtained more effective control over all activities in his department and, concurrently, the general council regained, to a degree, the powers it had in colonial days. These changes made it possible for the governments of Guadeloupe and Martinique to concentrate on Antillean problems in a more constructive manner. Several island politicians, however, accused French authorities of having negated the decolonization process which departmentalization had introduced. They asserted that the rhetoric of assimilation was only a myth. The act of April 26, 1960, instilled a measure of dictatorial power in the position of prefect as was seen in the expulsion of government functionaries for subversive activities, as discussed above. The islands were, for all purposes, still a colony. Only autonomy could bring self-government which would produce true equality and freedom. Aimé Césaire addressed this discontent in 1964 when de Gaulle was visiting Martinique.

> We can no longer avoid facing a problem that obsesses our youth: the problem of the necessary remodeling of our institutions (I refer to our local institutions) so that they will be better suited to our Antillean condition; so that they are more respectful of our personality and our obvious peculiarity; so that they are more flexible, less petty, more democratic, giving greater recognition to local initiative, local responsibility; so that we may no longer have the feeling, the most depressing feeling, that a group of poor but proud men can experience, the feeling that they helplessly look upon the unfolding of their own history, the feeling that they submit to history instead of making it; in short, the feeling of being frustrated about their future.[10]

Elections in the 1960s still gave party leaders who expressed satisfaction with the departmental solution the majority of the votes. Toward the end of de Gaulle's rule, however, a shift in attitudes became discernible. With the economy of the French Antilles in a state of stagnation, a new wave of agitation for status reform commenced.

In March 1968, the PPM and the Communists declared that departmentalization had failed and that autonomy was mandatory. This manifesto asserted that,

> contrary to the assertion of the government which boasts of the success of its policy in the West Indies and of the 'prosperity' of our territories, Martinique is going through a profound crisis which effects every aspect of social activity and testifies to the failure of 'departmentalization.' . . . It is in order that we ourselves should adopt the solutions which relate

to our particular problem that we refuse to be deprived of all decision making powers, which are at present concentrated in the hands of the French colonial power. To repeat textually the words of the French Head of State in Quebec, we can say that: what we see emerging in Martinique is not only a popular and political entity that is becoming more and more defined, but it is also a particular economic reality which is growing.[11]

The manifesto continues:

Autonomy will allow the Martiniquan people to assume this political power to decide and execute the measures that are dictated by their own interests.[12]

The statements pronounced by the PPM and the Communists related specifically to Martinique, but the sentiments were shared by many in Guadeloupe as is seen in a speech of Henri Bangou, Mayor of Pointe-à-Pitre, and the leading Communist politician on the island.

The French Government has declared that in Guadeloupe the problem of decolonization was solved as soon as the island became a French Department. One part of the population of Guadeloupe supports this position, while another, to which I belong, opposes it and seeks a status more in line with the interests of the people.[13]

The Guadeloupe National Organization Grouping (GONG) raised the first demands for independence in the islands. According to French authorities, the tragic riots of May 1967, which caused several deaths in Guadeloupe, were the work of malcontents who had close relations with GONG and with the Cubans.[14] GONG members deny responsibility and say that the riots were due to French ill treatment of poor blacks.[15]

On June 26, 1967, in response to growing agitation for autonomy or independence, the French Minister of State for Overseas Departments and Territories, Pierre Billotte, declared that the people of the French West Indies were full citizens of France who are bound to France by "a contract which involves the same consequences as that which bound the Provinces of Ancient France to her." He continued, that for the French West Indians "it is as legitimate" to seek to be free as it is useless "to demand to be independent" because the constitution assimilates them to their compatriots of the metropolis.[16]

This position has remained the official one. When President Valery Giscard d'Estaing was in Martinique in December 1974, he said that no adjustments were necessary in the political status of the French Caribbean, but there was room for progress in the social and economic fields to "further the development of the Antilles."[17] The Secretary of State for Overseas Departments, Oliver Stirn, stated the following year at Fort-de-France that departmentalization had permanently resolved the status issue.[18] The same year Jacques Chirac, the prime minister, during a visit to Martinique and Guadeloupe, advocated a "more complete integration" of the overseas departments economically "into the whole of the French Departmental system," and also "into the European Common Market."[19]

Opposition to these views has increased in the last decade. In 1977, the Socialists joined the Communists, the PPM, and others, to form the Front National Martiniquais pour l'Autonomie (FNMA). This group insists upon autonomy.[20] FNMA and other groups calling for autonomy expect support from left wing parties in France and aid from world opinion. The possibility clearly exists that autonomy may become the goal of the French government in the not-so-distant future. Should this happen, there will be a number of internal problems to be resolved in the Antilles.[21] To discuss these, one must first analyze the social and physical components of the islands.

The Department of Martinique is composed solely of the island of the same name. The population is around 350,000. Several islands form the Department of Guadeloupe; the twin islands of Grande Terre and Basse Terre form Guadeloupe proper. The other islands that comprise the department are Marie-Galante, La Désiderade, Iles des Saintes, Saint Barthélemy or Saint Barts, and the French half of Saint Martin. Marie-Galante, 16 miles from Guadeloupe, has a population of close to 16,000. La Désiderade, also 16 miles from Guadeloupe, has about 1,500 inhabitants. Les Saintes, a group of small islands 6 miles south of Guadeloupe, has a population of about 3,500. Saint Martin and Saint Barthélemy are in the Leeward Islands far to the north of Guadeloupe. The former has around 5,000 and the latter 2,500 inhabitants. The people of Saint Martin, like those of Guadeloupe, Marie-Galante, and La Désiderade, are of African descent, but, unlike those islanders, speak an English dialect. The inhabitants of Saint Barthélemy are French-speaking but, together with those of Les Saintes, are of European ancestry, their forebears being Norman and Breton fishermen. When the issue of autonomy or independence is discussed, these geographic, linguistic, and ethnic differences come into play.[22] Were there to be a new political status, the first question would be, should Martinique and Guadeloupe be joined into one political unit? Second, should Saint Martin and Saint Barthélemy remain part of this new entity or be separate from it? And how should Les Saintes be incorporated into such a community? To the people of these small islands these are issues of grave significance. Should one of the islands refuse to join the new unit, it may well obtain the support of the Parliament in Paris.

At present, neither the French Antilles nor France wants independence. Today, autonomy is as far as the islands want to go. GONG and similar movements have relatively small numbers of followers.

When the Communist Party of Martinique, the PCM, held its sixth congress in 1976, the party again declared itself in favor of autonomy, not independence. Party members from Guadeloupe and other Caribbean lands, such as Venezuela, Guyana, and Cuba, attended this meeting.[23] Cuban support for the islands' autonomy was given by Che Guevara at the UN General Assembly in 1964, when he said, "we must point out that the islands of Guadeloupe and Martinique have been fighting for a long time for their autonomy without obtaining it. This state of affairs must not continue."[24]

Most French authorities believe that the Communist parties of the French Antilles and of other nations want to see a change effected in the islands through peaceful means. Some of the authorities are not so certain about the Cubans. Ever since the previously-mentioned GONG Affair in Guadeloupe, the French authorities have maintained that it was Cuban machinations that created unrest and troubles in the French Antilles. French authorities suspect that when an opportunity presents itself, Castro will do everything to assist his comrades in the French Antilles. The "Cuba question" in the Antilles and in Africa worries the French government. In both places, Castro is attacking the vital national interests of France. In the first, he is attacking the integrity of the French state, in the second, her economic and political security.

In the early 1970s, when France was promoting her foreign policy goal of a "more active friendship" with Latin America, one of the points of focus was Cuba.[25] France's aim was to avoid confrontation and to achieve cooperation. Trade relations were promoted. By 1975, when Cuba was buying three times as much from France as France was from Cuba, a mixed French-Cuban Commission was created to strengthen trade ties. But in July of that year, the growing atmosphere of goodwill and friendship was shattered by the "Carlos Affair." Carlos was the code name of a Venezuelan terrorist who was accused of having killed two policemen and a civilian in Paris.[26] Relations with Cuba cooled when the French authorities expelled two Cuban diplomats who they presumed had given help to Carlos. The increasing aid that Cuba has since been giving to liberation movements in Africa has caused the two countries to grow further apart.

The Caribbean trip of Minister Michel Poniatowski, the special representative of the French president, was seen by many in Paris not only as a goodwill tour to promote trade, but also as an opportunity for discussions in Havana regarding the French-Cuban misunderstandings on such topics as Cuba's expanded African presence and extended Cuban influence in the Caribbean. Castro's influence is no longer isolated from French interests either in the Caribbean or Africa, and this is a major concern for France.[27] Dramatic policy changes are not anticipated but French initiatives must be extended. Perhaps France is advancing re-newed Euro-French presence in the Caribbean as a stabilizing agent between U.S.-Soviet rivalry, similar to the Euro-African Solidarity Pact proposed to Ivory Coast President Felix Houphouet-Boigny by Giscard d'Estaing in January 1978.[28]

The future development of the smaller British West Indian islands also has significance for the French Antilles. Dominica, wedged between Guadeloupe and Martinique, is now entering its era of independence. The same holds true for St. Lucia, south of Martinique. What political role will these islands play on the Caribbean scene? These islands have historically had many links with the French Antilles, especially in culture and language. Already in 1976, Oliver Stirn, the secretary of state for the overseas departments, had visited Prime Minister Patric John of Dominica to discuss the possibility of a treaty of economic cooperation.[29]

The major goals of the present French government seem to be keeping the political status quo in France's overseas departments while favoring progressive changes in their economic systems.[30] Furthermore, while promoting the trade of France and the French Antilles in the Carib-bean, France is most anxious to bring about peaceful cooperation in the area.

THE NETHERLANDS AND THE CARIBBEAN

Like the French, the Dutch, in the post-World War II period, tried to incorporate their Caribbean colonies into the metropolitan political system. This effort, however, encountered numerous obstacles and the Netherlands have abandoned it and moved instead to the granting of independence to their Western Hemisphere possessions.

Policy goals of the Netherlands in the Caribbean area are now three-fold: first, to assist the Netherlands Antilles to become a viable indepen-dent nation; second, to maintain economic and commercial relations; third, to assist this area through bilateral aid programs and through participation in United Nations and regional development schemes.

The second World War sounded the death knell to Dutch colonial-ism, a process that began with their East Indian possessions. After several years of hostilities and negotiations, the Netherlands government reluctantly recognized Indonesia as a sovereign nation in 1949. Since then the Netherlands has followed a policy of decolonization. The Netherlands Antilles in the Caribbean and Surinam on the South American mainland obtained internal self-government in 1950. Four years later, they joined the Netherlands in a Tripartite Kingdom. In this political structure, their autonomy was constitutionally guaranteed and they were afforded the right to participate in the formulation of kingdom policies. The majority of inhabitants of the Antilles and Surinam appear to have accepted this solution which also was accepted by the UN General Assembly in December 1955. Some groups in both territories, however, hoped the new constitutional tie with Holland would soon be upgraded to complete independence, an opinion shared by many members of the Labor Party and other Socialist groups in the metropolitan Netherlands.

The viewpoint that the Netherlands Antilles and Surinam should be sovereign won many adherents in the Dutch business community in the early 1960s. They knew that the Tripartite Kingdom was looked upon as a neo-colonial arrangement by many Third World leaders and therefore adversely affected Dutch commercial relations.

In the meantime, chronic unemployment in Surinam induced many Surinamese to migrate to Holland. By the early 1970s, such arrivals were greeted with less and less enthusiasm. This was due partly to the rise of unemployment in Holland and partly because their presence was considered a contributing factor to the weakening of the social and economic structure of the country. Consequently, Dutch labor union leaders became spokesmen for the severing of political ties with these new world territories. Once independent, the people of these nations would no longer have the right to freely migrate to the Netherlands. It is not surprising that a primary goal of the Dutch Labor Party government, in the early 1970s, was independence for the Antilles and Surinam.

The independence movement accelerated following the May 30, 1969, riots in Curaçao. This disturbance grew out of worker protests against Shell Oil's practice of using subcontractors who paid lower wages while demanding longer hours. To quell the rioting, the Antilles government requested Dutch military assistance. The government in the Hague was obligated to comply by the Charter of the Kingdom but did so with great reluctance because intervention was unpopular at home and because much of the Third World press reported it as a colonial operation —an image Dutch authorities were strenuously trying to avoid.[31]

When Paramaribo, the capital of Surinam, was hit by a general strike two years after these riots, Holland decided that the time had come for complete independence. Holland's Prime Minister, Joop den Uyl, put pressure on the Surinamese government of Prime Minister Henk Arron to accomplish this quickly.[32] Arron, despite much domestic opposition, was an ardent supporter of the idea and Surinam gained its independence in 1975.

Prime Minister Den Uyl suggested that the Antilles should follow the same course as soon as possible. J. Evertsz, prime minister of the Netherlands Antilles, stated that he was in favor of independence but opposed having it forced on his country. He argued that several conditions first had to be met. First, the territorial integrity of the new federal nation would have to be internationally recognized. In practice, this meant there had to be a treaty on the maritime border with Venezuela. Second, there had to be a promise that Dutch financial aid would continue. Third, a settlement with Holland concerning the question of the responsibility of the Antilles government for the debts of the island nation had to be reached. Fourth, an agreement on social, cultural, and judicial cooperation was necessary. Finally, there was the issue of the defense of the islands.

Since the cabinet of Prime Minister S.G.M. Rozendal of the Democratic Party took office in the Antilles in 1978, the first of these conditions has been satisfactorily resolved. On March 31 a treaty with Venezuela was signed at Fort Amsterdam, Curaçao, which resolved the maritime border issue. The ceremony was attended by Carlos Andres Pérez, President of Venezuela, who stated that in the future he hoped to welcome the Antilles as a member of the UN and the Organization of American States.[33]

The present Christian Democratic Prime Minister of the Netherlands, Andreas A. M. Jan van Agt, is not pushing independence with as much vigor as den Uyl, but the goal of his government is the same as that of his predecessor, and van Agt and his cabinet will do everything in their power to resolve the other conditions posed by former Prime Minister Evertsz.

The conditions concerning economic assistance should not be too difficult because the Netherlands will continue funding projects that have been initiated in the Antilles with Dutch aid. Despite this, the future economic viability of these islands is fraught with difficulties. A lack of natural resources and a rapidly increasing population will compound difficulties in attaining a solid economic base. Another question which seems to be an insurmountable obstacle at times is the demand of Aruba for "Status Aparte." To understand these problems, some of the basic facts concerning the Netherlands Antilles have to be understood.

The territory is made up of six islands divided into two groups—the Leeward Islands of Aruba, Curaçao, and Bonaire, off the coast of Venezuela; and the Windward Islands of Saint Martin, Saint Eustatius, and Saba, southeast of Puerto Rico. These two groups are separated by 500 miles. The largest island is Curaçao, with 178 square miles, followed by Bonaire with 112, Aruba with 73, Saint Martin (half of which is French) with 16, Saint Eustatius with 12, and Saba with only 3 square miles. About 240,000 people live in these islands, most on Curaçao and Aruba. A majority of the people in Curaçao are wholly or in part of African descent. There are, however, small groups of Dutch Protestants, Sephardic Jews, and other Europeans. Blacks and mulattoes constitute the majority on Bonaire, Saint Martin, and Saint Eustatius. Whites are a prominent segment of the population on Saba, while Arubans are mostly mestizos (in part descendants of Amerindians and whites) and whites.

Obviously, the small size of the Netherlands Antilles, its geographic structure, ethnic composition, and weak economic integration create difficulties in forming an integrated nation state. The language issue poses a further problem. The Leeward Islanders speak primarily Papiamento, a language based on Portuguese, Spanish, African tongues, Dutch, and English. The Windward Islanders speak English. The official language for the whole area is Dutch, which is also the language used for instruction. The Leeward and Windward Islands form more an administrative unit than an economic one. In the decades after 1916, when the oil industry was booming, economic integration of the islands was facilitated. Oil refineries in Curaçao and Aruba made these island magnets for labor. In the last few decades, automation has caused a reduction of personnel at the refineries.[34] This increased unemployment and, consequently, an evolving insular outlook was strengthened.

Further economic difficulties stem from the oil politics of Venezuela and the United States. The former, seeking increased control over its oil industry, insists that much of its oil be refined in Venezuela. As the need for refined oil grew in the developed nations and the price of shipping on supertankers declined, the refineries of the Antilles began to refine crude from the Middle East and Africa.[35] Most of the refined oil was for the East Coast of the United States, the only natural geopolitical outlet for the Antillean refineries. Selling on this market was severely restricted in 1973 when the U.S. Congress passed the Emergency Petroleum Act which gave refineries in U.S. territory preferential treatment.[36] Caribbean refineries faced a precarious future.

A viable, independent Netherlands Antilles will need to be assured that its refineries will be permitted to export refined oil to the United States at terms equal to those given to refineries of U.S. possessions in the Caribbean.[37] The Netherlands Antilles government is therefore of the opinion that positive Antillean economic development is contingent with a commercial agreement with the United States. Good ties with the United States are also needed because tourism on the islands, especially Aruba, Curaçao, and Saint Martin, has become important in the last two decades, and most of the tourists are U.S. citizens.[38]

Meaningful independence exists only when the people of a nation feel that its leadership has freedom and power to participate as sovereign partners in relevant international organizations and in the regional subsystem in which the country exists. Antillean leaders would appear to desire an active voice in Caribbean regional policy-making institutions, and financial and economic organizations such as the Caribbean Development Bank,[39] as well as an opportunity to participate in transregional metropole-based systems such as the Andes Pact and the EEC.[40]

Should the Frente Obrero Party of Curaçao gain more influence, it will probably seek closer cooperation with the Socialist-inclined states of the Commonwealth Caribbean—Guyana and Jamaica. The possibility of an accord with Cuba, however, has potential political repercussions with the United States, Venezuela, and other states in the region and metropole.

There are many centrifugal forces that feed Antillean separatism. Currently, Aruba's demand for "Status Aparte" is the major obstacle to unity. Rightly or wrongly, Arubans have always maintained that the central government in Willemstad, Curaçao, favors its own special interests. Betico Croes, leader of the "Movemiento Electoral Di Pueblo," the MEP Party of Aruba, is against any central Antilles government with meaningful federal power, economic or political,[41] and has been toying with the notion of separate independence for Aruba. The Dutch government is opposed to separatism, favoring Antillean independence as an integrated unit. Aruba, with only seventy-three square miles and a population of fewer than 70,000 people, seems too small for viable independence. However, the MEP is the largest party in Aruba and an unofficial referendum indicates majority opposition to Aruban participation in an independent Antilles federation.[42] Solving this issue of "Status Aparte" will be the hardest task facing the Antilles.[43] There are fears that the fate of the abortive West Indies Federation will be repeated.

The Dutch marines will leave the Antilles by the end of 1978 and a national guard will undertake all duties related to internal law and order.[44] A Dutch naval contingent will remain for the time being. Before independence, an Antillean government will want a treaty with the Netherlands concerning defense. The possibility of a bilateral or multilateral agreement is now being discussed,[45] with Holland preferring the latter.

Internationally-oriented trading is "one of the mainstays of Netherlands Foreign Policy"[46] and this is certainly true in relation to Dutch diplomatic activity in the Caribbean. In advancing Holland's economic interests in the Caribbean, the Dutch government always took into consideration that its policy should not impair good relations with the United States. At the same time, much attention was given to creating and maintaining a friendly atmosphere with the Caribbean nations so that commerce could thrive.

In recent years, younger intellectuals have fervently voiced a desire to give Dutch foreign policy a stronger moral and ideological base. The beliefs of this group found concrete expression when den Uyl became prime minister. In his cabinet, the minister for aid for developing countries was Johannes P. Pronk, a chief spokesman for instilling this moral base in Dutch foreign policy. He promoted this by having Holland participate intensively in development programs of the UN. Furthermore, Holland began a program of direct bilateral assistance to developing countries. Three criteria were applied in selecting "target" countries for this assistance: (1) the degree of poverty of the country, (2) the specific assessed need for aid, and (3) the extent to which the aid would benefit major groups of the population.[47] In addition, there were also special target countries, including Surinam. A treaty was concluded between the Netherlands and Surinam providing for an aid program lasting for at least ten years.[48] When the Antilles become independent, it will also be designated a special target country.

Other target countries in the Caribbean area are Colombia, Cuba, and Jamaica. In 1977, Colombia was allotted 20 million Dutch guilders in bilateral aid; Cuba, 18 million; and Jamaica, 15 million.[49] Even though aid to Cuba is small, it causes much argument in Holland. Some groups feel Cuba is a nation where aid can accomplish much because the country is in the process of building new social and economic foundations; others feel that a country which has funds available to send troops to Africa should not be assisted by Dutch taxpayers. Since van Agt became prime minister, criticism of Holland's relations with Cuba have become stronger and the Dutch aid programs have become engulfed in local politics. Nevertheless, it is still the Dutch goal to foster its foreign policy goals of peace and prosperity in the Caribbean through these programs.

NOTES

1. Guy Lasserre and Albert Mabileau, "The French Antilles and their Status as Overseas Departments," in *Patterns of Foreign Influence in the Caribbean*, ed. Emmanuel de Kadt (London: Oxford University Press, 1972), p. 82.

2. Gerard Latortue, "The Political Status of the French Caribbean," in *Politics and Economics in the Caribbean*, ed. T. G. Matthews, et al., Institute of Caribbean Studies Special Study no. 8 (Rio Piedras, Puerto Rico: University of Puerto Rico, 1971), p. 177; see also Michael M. Horowitz, *Morne-Paysan Peasant Village in Martinique* (New York: Holt, Rinehart & Winston, 1967), p. 88.

3. T. G. Matthews, et al., *Politics and Economics in the Caribbean*, Institute of Caribbean Studies Special Study no. 3 (Rio Piedras, Puerto Rico: University of Puerto Rico, 1966), p. 105.

4. Lasserre and Mabileau, op. cit., p. 97.

5. Ibid., pp. 93–94.

6. Latortue, op. cit., p. 179. See also "Speech on 26th June 1967 by Pierre Billotte," in *Documents on International Relations in the Caribbean,* ed. Roy Preiswerk, (Rio Piedras, Puerto Rico: Institute of Caribbean Studies, University of Puerto Rico, 1970), p. 579.

7. Lasserre and Mabileau, op. cit., pp. 92, 94; André Volait, "La Situation des DOM au Sein de la CEE," *Bulletin d'information du Cenaddom,* 5, no. 25 (Talence, France: Centre National de Documentation des Départements d'Outre Mer, 1975), pp. 8–11.

8. Lasserre and Mabileau, op. cit., p. 92.

9. Arvin Murch, *Black Frenchmen* (Cambridge, Mass: Schenkman, 1971), pp. 24–26.

10. Quoted in Latortue, op. cit., pp. 177–78; see also Horowitz, op. cit., p. 88.

11. "memoire on the Real Situation in Martinique, Presented by the Communist Party of Martinique and the Parti Progressiste Martiniquais, March, 1968," Preiswerk, op. cit., p. 585.

12. Ibid., p. 587.

13. "Speech of 18th May, 1965 by the Mayor of Pointe-à-Pitre, Henri Bangou," Preiswerk, op. cit., p. 584.

14. Laurent Farrugia, *Le Fait National Guadeloupéen* (Paris: Ivry sur Seine, 34 Rue Barbes, 1968), p. 51; and "Speech by Pierre Billotte," Preiswerk, op. cit., p. 581.

15. Farrugia, op. cit., pp. 42–45.

16. Preiswerk, op. cit., pp. 579–80.

17. "Press Meeting by Valery Giscard d'Estaing, Fort-de-France, December 15, 1974," press release (New York: French Embassy Press Service, 1974).

18. "M. Stirn: Les Martiniquais sont des Francaise comme Les Autres," *Le Monde* (France), 31 July 1975.

19. "Le Départementalisation est la seule voie de l'expansion et de la stabilité," *Le Monde* (France), 23 December 1975; see also "Press Meeting Report, 24 October 1975," press release (New York: French Embassy Press Service, 1974).

20. "Martinique," *Le Monde* (France), 27 October 1977.

21. Guy Lasserre, et al., *Antilles Francaises Guyane, Haiti* (Paris: Hachette, les guides bleus, 1973), pp. 118–260.

22. Michel Leiris, *Contacts De Civilisations En Martinique Et En Guadeloupe* (Paris: UNESCO, Gallimard, 1955), pp. 31–44.

23. Sixth Congress of the PCM, held at Morne Rouge, 1976.

24. Jay Mallin, ed., *"Che" Guevara on Revolution—A Documentary Overview* (Coral Gables, Florida: University of Miami Press, 1969), p. 116.

25. "Michel Jobert," *Le Monde* (France), 30 November 1973.

26. "La Visite de Madame Veil," *Le Monde* (France), 12 January 1976.

27. "M. Michel Poniatowski En Visite Officielle Aux Caraibes," *Le Monde* (France), 27 November 1977.

28. "France Bids for a Military Pact with Africa," *African Mirror* 4 (April 1977): 53. This article states that the pact would rest on three basic principles: the right of a state to (1) independence, (2) internal and external security, and (3) self-determination in regard to the type of development it wants. See also Paul Lewis, "Wooing Africa Toward Paris," The New York *Times,* 19 January 1978, p. A4.

29. "Dominica," *Le Monde* (France), 5 February 1976.

30. "M. Barre Announce Des Mesures En Faveur Des DOM," *Le Monde* (France), 2 December 1977.

31. Peter Verton, "Emancipation and Decolonization: The May Revolt and its Aftermath in Curaçao," *Revista Review Interamericana* 6, no. 15 (Spring 1976): 88–101.

32. Henk Doelwijt, "Election Commentary," The *Mini-World News* (Surinam), no. 15, November 1977, pp. 2–24.

33. "Maritiem Verdrag Pleit Voor Behoud Zeemilieu-Venezuela Bedingt Vrije Door-tocht," *Amigoe* (Netherlands Antilles), 1 April 1978, p. 1.

34. E. Lieuwen, *Petroleum in Venezuela: A History* (New York: Russell and Russell, 1954), pp. 46–47.

35. P. R. Odell, *An Economic Geography of Oil* (New York: Praeger Publishers, 1963), pp. 109–44.

36. U.S., *Emergency Petroleum Allocation Act, U.S. Code,* vol. 1, sec. 752(7) (1970, suppl. 3 [1973]). This act defines the United States as "the States, the District of Columbia, Puerto Rico, and the territories and possessions of the U.S."

37. *Notes on the Caribbean Refining Industry and its Structural Dependence upon U.S. Energy Needs* (Willemstad, Curaçao: Office for Oil Affairs, Government of the Netherlands Antilles, 1977), pp. 26–29.

38. "Netherlands Antilles Illustrates Difficulties: A Small Country Faces Trying to Diversity," *IMF Survey,* August 2, 1976, pp. 238–40.

39. Herbert Corkran, Jr., *Patterns of International Cooperation in the Caribbean* (Dallas: Southern Methodist University Press, 1970), p. 205.

40. Harry Hoetink, "The Dutch Caribbean and its Metropolis," in *Patterns of Foreign Influence in the Caribbean,* ed. Emanuel De Kadt (New York: Oxford University Press, 1972), p. 105; "Conclusions of the Charpentier Report on the Dutch and French speaking Carib-bean Territories linked with the European Community and Draft Resolution submitted to the European Parliament, 1964," in *Documents on International Relations in the Caribbean,* ed. Roy Preiswerk, op. cit., pp. 152–64.

41. John Jansen Van Galen, "Aruba Tropisch Texel Wil Een Kolonie Blijven," *Haagse Post* (Netherlands), 27 August 1977, pp. 10–11; see also Bas de Gaay Fortman, "Wat Betekent Onafhankelijkheid," *Haarlems Dagblad* (Netherlands), 19 November 1977, p. 1.

42. "Het Referendum op Aruba," *Beurs-En Nieuws Berichten* (Netherlands Antilles), 26 March 1977, p. 1. This article stated that 59 percent of the voters of Aruba voted for independence on March 25, 1977.

43. "In Voorjaar Conferentie Over Structuur Antillen," *De Volkskrant* (Netherlands), November 22, 1977, p. 1.

44. "Mariniers Verlaten Eind '78 Antillen," *Telegraaf* (Netherlands), 7 February 1978, p. 1; see also Marga Van Dieten and Leo Maduro, *De Nederlandse Antillen, Workdocument Van Het Instituut Voor Ontwikkelingsvraagstukken* (Tilburg: Katholieke Hogeschool, 1977), p. 114.

45. "Mariniers Verlaten Eind '78 Antillen," op. cit., p. 1; and Dieten and Maduro, op. cit., p. 105.

46. Netherlands, Ministry of Foreign Affairs, "Foreign Policy," *The Kingdom of the Netherlands,* no. 15 (The Hague: Ministry of Foreign Affairs, n.d.), p. 3.

47. Ibid., p. 10; Bernard H. M. Blekke, *Evolution of the Dutch Nations* (New York: Roy Publishers, 1945), p. 327.

48. "Foreign Policy," op. cit., p. 10.

49. "Hulpbijdragen, 1978 Voor Concentratielanden," *Internationale Samenwerking* (Netherlands) 10, no. 1 (13 January 1978): pp. 9–11.

19

The Islands and the Littoral: New Relationships

Anthony T. Bryan

Active political and economic linkages between the islands of the Caribbean Sea and the states of the littoral are fairly recent. The colonial history of the circum-Caribbean area (and the resulting variety of linguistic, historical, socio-cultural, economic, and institutional traditions) is primarily responsible for the varied character of the region's countries. The majority of the Latin American nations in the circum-Caribbean area have enjoyed formal political sovereignty since the nineteenth century, while comparative status for countries of the Commonwealth Caribbean is of very recent vintage. In places such as Belize, Puerto Rico, and some smaller islands, the debate over political self-determination is still unresolved. The changes in constitutional status represented by Jamaica, Trinidad and Tobago, Barbados, Guyana, the Bahamas, and most recently, Grenada, has meant the emergence of English-speaking nations, with predominant African or East Indian-descended populations, governed by remnants or adaptations of the Westminster model, and enjoying some preferential links with the larger (British) Commonwealth of Nations and the European Economic Community. They are sufficiently distinct from their Latin American neighbors to bring an added dimension to international relations in the area.

The Caribbean is emerging as an "interest area" in global international relations, and geopolitics and economics are potent factors in this evolution. In examinations of the contemporary international system, little emphasis has been accorded the interactions between states of the periphery, of which the Caribbean region is a part. Given the diversity of states in the region, with respect to their cultural affinities, varied colonial links, constitutional forms, and levels of political development, some framework is desirable for putting into perspective such relationships—

as in this case between mainland states and the island nations of the Caribbean area. Such a framework must of necessity confront the problems of area definition, analysis of the nature and content of interactions, and examinations of pertinent issue areas.

THE PROBLEM OF DEFINITION

A suitable definition of the Caribbean region is a matter of continuing controversy among heads of state, technocrats, and the general public within the region. The constituent elements of the Commonwealth Caribbean may not be in doubt, since it is the functional term adopted in the region to designate the English-speaking countries, whatever their constitutional status. However, the "archipelago" culture area definition voiced publicly by the prime minister of Trinidad and Tobago, and adopted by the Caribbean Development and Cooperation Committee (CDCC) in Havana in December 1975, is in conflict with the geopolitical "Caribbean Basin" argument currently advanced by the Venezuelan government. The "archipelago" culture area definition includes all the islands of the Caribbean Sea, Guyana, and Belize, but explicitly omits Venezuela, Colombia, Central America and Mexico. The "Caribbean Basin" concept includes the islands and mainland littoral countries. While the recent debate over definition is more precisely a debate between independent actors (Trinidad and Tobago and Venezuela) pursuing autonomous self-interests in the area, clearly, failure to agree on the boundaries of a specific Caribbean region means that the circum-Caribbean area is characterized by fluid levels of cohesion. This has implications not only for interactions between states but also for efforts at economic and political integration, as well as the level of cohesion of a regional subsystem. It should be noted, however, that the colonial experience of the circum-Caribbean region reveals the evolution of centripetal traits, in which the commonalities of today still exceed the differences— as important as the latter may be.

Analyses of the management of domestic matters and the conduct of foreign policy in the circum Caribbean should proceed with the recognition that the states of the region are constituents of a weak, dependent, and externally penetrated subsystem, in which powerful nations and transnational corporations exercise strength and influence. When the geopolitical definition of the Caribbean is taken at its widest, the subsystemic framework is made increasingly complex. First, there already exists the notion of a diplomatic community pertaining to the Spanish-speaking countries of the archipelago and the littoral. They belong to a larger Latin American subsystem whose authenticity in international affairs can hardly be denied. Second, while we can now speak of an emerging Caribbean subsystem in which the states of the Commonwealth Caribbean appear as prominent actors, the central characteristic of the Commonwealth Caribbean is the lack of definition and awareness of a diplomatic zone or theater and, consequently, no definition of an indigenous diplomatic community. In the attempts to revitalize intra-regional and extraregional functional and diplomatic cooperation and to restructure the traditional problems of multilateral diplomacy, the Commonwealth Caribbean states will often interact constructively with nations of the wider Latin American region. Notably, these interactions may themselves contain the seeds of both conflict and coherence and have both positive and negative repercussions on regional coherence. In the circum Caribbean, therefore, the emergence of Venezuela, in particular, and Mexico (mainland nations), as influential actors and pivotal states in regional affairs has brought about renewed discussions by statesmen and planners about a suitable definition of the caribbean diplomatic theater and integration zone.[1]

INTERACTIONS BETWEEN THE ISLAND NATIONS AND MEXICO, COLOMBIA, AND CENTRAL AMERICA

Recent interactions between the islands and the littoral in the Caribbean region are motivated primarily by economics and by some political issues. At present, increased ties between states of the region are facilitated through membership in regional organizations. The Organization of American States (OAS) is the main vehicle in formalizing closer identification and cooperation, while the Inter-American Development Bank (IDB) and the Economic Commission for Latin America (ECLA) provide additional levels of contact. Efforts to accelearate autonomous regional economic development are visible in common market arrangements, such as the Central American Common Market (CACM); the Caribbean Community and Common Market (CARICOM); and the Caribbean Development Bank (CDB), which complements CARICOM as a Caribbean regional financial institution and a subregional financial institution of Latin America in which Venezuela and Colombia participate as nonborrowing members and donors of soft funds. More recently, collaboration by some Latin American and Caribbean states to create a new regional economic system resulted in the formal launching of the Sistema Económico Latinoamericano (SELA), the establishment of a multinational Caribbean maritime transport enterprise (NAMUCAR), and a Latin American Energy Organization (OLADE). Most states of the Caribbean region participate in these multilateral institutional efforts to confront problems common to the entire area.[2]

Mexico

Of the many bilateral interactions in the circum-Caribbean area, the most noticeable have been those inspired by Venezuela and Mexico.* In recent years Mexico has displayed an active foreign policy in Third World forums concerned with development and the evolution of the new International Economic Order. During the presidency of Luis Echeverría (1970–76), the Mexican government began to demonstrate interest in the Caribbean as part of a larger policy of Third World identification. Mexican interest in the Caribbean advanced noticeably with the visit of the Mexican president to Jamaica in July 1974. Echeverría signed an agreement between Mexico and CARICOM in which a joint commission was established to explore the possibilities for strengthening economic, technological, and cultural relations. On the same occasion, Echeverría and Prime Minister Michael Manley signed an accord in which the two countries agreed to undertake the joint production of alumina, aluminium, and aluminium manufactures in Mexico and Jamaica.[3] A formal Jamaica-Mexico agreement signed in November 1974 envisaged the construction of an alumina plant in Jamaica (JAVEMEX) having a capacity of 900,000 short tons per year and an aluminium smelter (JALUMEX) with an annual capacity of 120,000 tons, sited in Mexico. The Mexican smelter would be supplied with Jamaican alumina. It was also agreed that each government would own 51 percent of the enterprise located in its territory, with 29 percent of the remaining shares going to the partner and the rest of the 20 percent divided between privately owned companies, other governments, or foreign investors.[†] In addition, the government of Jamaica guaranteed these enterprises a 30-year supply of bauxite. Other joint enterprises included the setting up of light industries based on aluminium in both countries, and the building of a caustic soda plant in Jamaica. During a visit to Mexico in July 1975 by the Jamaican prime minister, the two countries also pledged to undertake the creation of a

---

*Venezuelan and Cuban initiatives in the Caribbean are the subject of other major essays in this collection and are not discussed in detail in this chapter.

†This Jamaica-Mexico agreement should also be viewed in the perspective of Jamaica's 1975 agreement to supply Venezuela with 200,000 tons of alumina a year for ten years and 400,000 tons of bauxite a year for three years, increasing to 500,000 tons for the remaining seven years. In return, Venezuela agreed to provide Jamaica with all the crude petroleum needed to satisfy its industrial requirements at a pre-1973 price, the difference to be deposited in the Central Bank of Jamaica to be used for the financing of programs and investment projects contributing to the development of natural resources and the promotion of exports. In a separate agreement, Venezuela agreed to hold 10 percent of the shares in JAVEMEX. Subsequently these Jamaica-Venezuela arrangements would become the subject of much political controversy in the Caribbean.

Jamaican Merchant Marine Fleet utilizing the expertise of the Transportación Marítima Mexicana. The Jamaican government would have a 75 percent share participation and the Mexican company the remainder.

The second phase in Mexico's initiatives toward the Caribbean was indicated by Echeverría's visits to Guyana and Trinidad and Tobago (and afterward Cuba) as part of a journey to some fourteen countries in the Americas, Africa, and Asia during mid-1975. Cumulatively, no extensive functional agreements were reached with Guyana and Trinidad and Tobago; instead discussions centered on broad issues of concern to the economic and foreign policies of hemispheric countries and of the Third World. Caribbean support was expressed through communiques for the Latin American Economic System (SELA), and for the Charter of Economic Rights and Duties of States approved by the UN in 1974—both of which had their origins as Mexican initiatives. The Mexican president also expressed his support for the effort by Trinidad and Tobago to achieve a special equitable regime for the Caribbean Sea within the ECLA framework. Finally, a permanent Joint Commission was established to promote cooperation and trade between Mexico and Trinidad and Tobago.[4]

On April 28, 1978, the Mexican government of Jose López Portillo formally notified the Jamaican government that it was withdrawing from the proposed aluminium smelter project (JALUMEX) in Mexico. Also implied, though not stated, was that Mexico was withdrawing its interest in JAVEMEX and JAMEX, companion projects for alumina processing and bauxite mining respectively. According to the Jamaican mining minister, the reason cited by the government for its decision not to proceed with the project is the lower return on investment anticipated (than when the project was originally conceived), arising largely from the devaluation of the Mexican peso and the increased costs in energy, machinery, equipment, and technology over the period since it was initiated.[5]

The Mexican withdrawal may be explained in part by a stabilization of that nation's internal economy and a consequent shift in its foreign policy direction. During the Echeverría regime, the Mexican government had embarked on a long-range policy to make it a more important and dynamic economic force within Latin America and in the global system. The policy was prompted by an unprecedented deficit in Mexico's balance of payments account in 1970, and a need to diversify the nation's external commerce, which had depended traditionally on a "special relationship" with the United States. Such diversification also involved the nation's foreign relations, with the objective of developing new export markets, securing vital raw materials for further industrialization efforts, and finding new trading partners. President Echeverría undertook to cultivate these relationships as part of his greater obsession with a leadership role for Mexico in the Third World.

One objective of such foreign policy activism included the creation of an economic subzone comprised of member countries in CARICOM and CACM and a Mexican and Venezuelan bid for Latin American leadership in interclient regional cooperation through SELA. While Echeverría's *tercermundista* rhetoric set the stage for his country's economic expansion throughout the Caribbean and Central America, and its intended leadership of the Latin American and Third World countries in complex bargaining with the world's leading industrialized centers, one of its major objectives also was the utilization of international relations themes for the legitimization of the internal "institutionalized" revolutionary environment. The nexus between domestic politics and foreign policy produced serious internal conflict in the final months of Echeverría's tenure, because of determined opposition from the Mexican business elite who had opted for their transitional dependent relationship with the United States. The adoption of a less radical and low-key foreign policy towards the Third World, including the Caribbean, has been so far characteristic of the López Portillo administration.[6]

The Mexican-Jamaican-Venezuelan projects with respect to bauxite and aluminium had evoked heavy public criticism from Trinidad and Tobago's prime minister in 1975 because he saw them as counterproductive to a proposed aluminium project agreed to by the governments of Trinidad and Tobago, Jamaica, and Guyana in June 1974. Most of his accusations were directed toward Venezuela's efforts to "recolonise the Caribbean" through petrodollar politics; but his verbal attacks implied that he was concerned that perhaps both Venezuela and Mexico were attempting to play pivotal roles in the Commonwealth Caribbean region which might have been reserved for Trinidad and Tobago.[7] His response was to withdraw his government's participation in the planned smelter project with Jamaica and Guyana. The entire issue produced a malaise in relations between Jamaica and Trinidad and Tobago and between the latter and its major partners in CARICOM. The Mexican withdrawal has, however, left open the possibility that a revival of the 1974 Caribbean smelter project is possible.[8]

In light of the smelter controversy, the issue has been raised about the effects of bilateral arrangements (by CARICOM member states with nonmember countries) on the integration movement in the Caribbean. Also, since 1975, the deepening economic crises in Jamaica and Guyana have led those countries to look outside of the confines of the regional integration system in order to obtain new sources of finance for the improvement of their balance of payments positions. Concomitantly, Trinidad and Tobago has been inclined to abandon the regional economic ethos and to use its petroleum wealth and its program of semiindustrialization to attempt the penetration of metropolitan markets. The possibility of further extraregional systemic relations may have negative effects on regional coherence. On the other hand, the debate between government leaders in the circum-Caribbean countries on the question of what constitutes the Caribbean integration zone and diplomatic theater should indicate the need for mechanisms and frameworks of a functional nature that can enhance the possibility of bilateral or multilateral economic relations between member states of CARICOM and nonmember states in geographical proximity.[9]

Colombia

One mainland state that is actively, yet discreetly exploring avenues of interaction with Caribbean island nations is Colombia. Its most noteworthy recent bilateral initiatives have included normalization of diplomatic relations with Cuba (1974) and reinauguration of commercial relations with that country (1976), as well as the mounting of floating trade exhibitions to major Caribbean islands (1976).[10] But Colombia's most significant Caribbean role is multilateral in scope. It is a contributor to, but nonborrowing member of, the Caribbean Development Bank (CDB).

Economic relations with Trinidad and Tobago will probably emerge as one of the notable aspects of Colombia's interest in the Caribbean. Trinidad and Tobago, utilizing its financial returns from petroleum and natural gas production, is embarking on a series of energy-based industries and Colombia is regarded as a market and as a supplier of certain raw materials and commodities.[11] In general, Colombia's interest in the Caribbean islands is more subtle than that of its neighbor, Venezuela, and its pace of economic relations much slower.

Central America

Interactions between the Central American nations and the Caribbean island states are represented by two issue areas: the Panama Canal controversy and the Anglo-Guatemala-Belize territorial dispute. Caribbean and Latin American support for Panama, in its recently concluded negotiations with the United States on jurisdiction over the canal, was widespread.[12] The Anglo-Belize-Guatemala dispute, on the other hand, has contributed to a consistent scenario of circum-Caribbean diplomatic tensions.

The problem between Belize and Guatemala is more than a boundary dispute. It is a territorial dispute in which Guatemala claims the entire territory of Belize, on the basis of controversial historical arrangements formulated more than a century ago.[13]

Strong reassertion of the Guatemalan claim began in the late 1950s, when the possibility of independence for Belize (then British Honduras) began to be considered by Britain and the Peoples' United Party government of George Price, which had come to power in Belize in March 1957. Guatemala broke relations with Britain in July 1963, anticipating the granting of full internal self-government to Belize on January 1, 1964. Nevertheless, both Britain and Guatemala continued to hold talks about the future of Belize (in Miami, 1964, and London, 1965). Efforts to resume talks in March 1972 were broken off because of a British display of military prowess, but they were eventually held in July 1975. At these talks, the Guatemalan government proposed that the southern portion of Belize should be ceded in return for the renunciation of its claim to the remainder of the country. The Belizeans considered this proposal so "preposterous" that the British rejected the proposal and the talks were terminated.[14] During October and November 1975, because of increased Guatemalan activity on the border, Belize requested and received British military assistance. Subsequent Anglo-Guatemalan meetings (in New York, Panama City, and Washington, during 1976) to arrive at a resolution of the conflict have proved futile.

The territorial dispute is part of the unfinished process of political decolonization in the Caribbean region. Eager to obtain its constitutional independence from Britain, but fearful of Guatemalan invasion once British military protection is removed, Belize has engaged in an intense campaign to gather international support for its right to self-determination. Guatemala, which is intent on the "reintegration" of Belize into its national territory, has also tried to justify its case before international forums. In recent times, the campaign on the part of both countries has produced some remarkable changes in perspectives on the dispute held by some leading nations in the hemisphere.

The diplomatic offensive embarked on by Belize has been quite successful. When the Thirty-second Sesson of the United Nations General Assembly entertained a motion on November 28, 1977, calling for the self-determination and independence of Belize, the final vote revealed that 126 countries supported Belize, with only 4 opposed—the Central American states of Nicaragua, El Salvador, Costa Rica, and Honduras.[15] The vote was highly significant because it revealed that a number of influential Latin American states had shifted their support from Guatemala to Belize. The evolution of support offered by Venezuela, Cuba, Mexico, and Panama clearly undermined Guatemala's case. Fragmentation in the previously almost unanimous Latin American block support for Guatemala is linked to the announced diplomatic position of the Commonwealth Caribbean states. Jamaica, Guyana, and Trinidad and Tobago at various times between 1972 and 1976 had raised the matter of Belizean independence at the UN—but their influence was felt in other ways as well.

In December 1974, the leaders of Venezuela, the five Central American Republics, and Panama met at Puerto Ordaz, Venezuela, and issued the Declaration of Guyana. While agreeing to promote new forms of economic cooperation within the Central American isthmus and the Caribbean Basin, the signatories also committed themselves to support Panama in its dispute with the United States over the canal and to support Guatemala in its claim to Belize.[16] The latter article caused great concern in the Commonwealth Caribbean, given Venezuela's vigorous efforts to court the friendship of island nations which were committed to support Belize. Venezuela's stance was perhaps motivated by the need for future Central American support in its border disputes with Guyana and Colombia, but during 1975, a rapid sequence of events may have caused Venezuela to reconsider its position on the issue.

During May and June 1975, the prime minister of Trinidad and Tobago publicly denounced the Guyana Declaration as an attack on the territorial integrity of CARICOM and as evidence of Venezuela's attempt to recolonize the Caribbean.[17] At the Sixteenth Session of ECLA held in Port-of-Spain in May, the Premier of Belize, George Price, pleaded his country's case and Dr. Williams, in his capacity as chairman, appealed for an amicable settlement of the dispute. Support for the Belizean cause was also provided by the release of a joint communique (known as the Kingston Accord), signed by the representatives of thirty-five member nations attending the Commonwealth Heads of Government Conference in Jamaica, in which full support for the early independence of Belize was declared. In July, in Havana, Prime Ministers Manley of Jamaica and Castro of Cuba issued a joint communiqué affirming the right of the Belizean people to self-determination. In August, at the Fifth Conference of Foreign Ministers of Non-Aligned Nations in Lima, Guyana and Jamaica were the principal proponents of a declaration of unconditional support for Belize which emerged from the conference.[18] Finally, during 1975, the Cuban government began lending active support to the Belizean cause at the UN and seemed willing to offer military assistance to Belize when it appeared that Guatemala was preparing an invasion for October.

On October 8, 1975, President Carlos Andrés Pérez announced that Venezuela was withdrawing its support for Guatemala's claim which had been pledged in the Guyana Declaration. Publicly it was conjectured that Venezuela feared the loss of its new Caribbean sphere of influence over the issue.[19] It is also possible that Cuba's decision to support Belize, and the repeated declarations made by Commonwealth Caribbean countries that they would not compromise on the issue, encouraged the Venezuelan government to reexamine its position. In view of Venezuela's growing importance as an influential actor in the international affairs of the Caribbean region, and its active policy of rapprochement and functional cooperation with the Commonwealth Caribbean, the specter of neo-imperialist encroachment once raised had to be denied. Even before Venezuela altered its position, however, it was evident that support for the Guatemalan claim was beginning to erode.

Mexico's stand on the Anglo-Guatemalan conflict over the future of Belize also altered significantly during 1975. Several public statements made by President Echeverría early in 1975 implied that Mexico had abandoned its own claims to the northern section of Belize and was moving towards support of Guatemala's demands. Previously, Mexico's position on the dispute had never been accurately stated, although the prevailing impression in the region was that if the whole of Belize passed involuntarily to Guatemala, Mexico would then enforce its claim. The apparent contradiction in the Mexican view was unexpectedly rectified during a visit to Guatemala by Echeverría in November. He reiterated the long dormant Mexican claim to Belizean territory and on his return to Mexico withdrew a settlement proposal (conciliatory to Guatemala) which had been submitted by his government to the UN. The effect was to counterbalance Guatemala's claims and to indicate support for Belize's right of self-determination. The pro-Belizean stand of Mexico reflected the adoption of a posture more akin to that of the Caribbean nations and a growing number of Latin American and Third World countries.[20]

The Guatemalan government's response to dwindling support was to send its vice-president, in October 1975, on tours of Europe, North America, and the Middle East to clarify its case. The following month, the six presidents of the Central American nations and Panama convened in Guatemala City to reiterate their support of Guatemala.[21] Their efforts were at best counter-productive. On May 8, 1976, the Panamanian Head of State, General Omar Torrijos, declared his country's support for Belize—soon after returning from an official visit to Jamaica where he had gained Manley's support for Panama's aspirations over the Canal Zone.* Torrijos's defection crucially weakened the Guatemalan stance and the government immediately severed relations with Panama. In the meantime, the Commonwealth Caribbean countries maintained their efforts in favor of Belize in the UN during 1975 and 1976. The Barbadian government intercepted and seized a planeload of arms bound for Guatemala in late June 1977. At the Seventh General Assembly Session of the OAS, held in Grenada in June 1977, the Commonwealth Caribbean countries issued a joint communiqué supporting Belize.[22] Finally, the historic vote in the UN General Assembly in favor of Belizean self-determination,

---

*The Communiqué of April 21 studiously avoided any mention of Belize.

registered in November 1977, successfully climaxed the round of diplomatic activity.

The Anglo-Guatemala-Belize dispute is the one issue area that illustrates the nature of conflictual relations between Central America and the Caribbean island states. While the Commonwealth Caribbean states have been consistent in their support of Belize, the Central American Republics have been equally loyal to Guatemala. The dispute has served to strengthen Commonwealth Caribbean attempts at coordination of foreign policy objectives. Obtaining support for the Belizean cause from Venezuela, Mexico, Cuba, and Panama is one of the more positive aspects, then, of the current interactions between Caribbean island states and those of the littoral.

The dispute is far from being resolved, however. It is evident that Britain is anxious to grant independence to Belize, though not to militarily guarantee its territoral integrity after independence. Furthermore, Britain has demonstrated its willingness to compromise with the Guatemalans while theoretically upholding the principle of Belize's right to self-determination. The continuing impasse in negotiations could undermine some of the gains made by Belize, particularly since the British government seems prepared to concede some Belizean territory to Guatemala in order to resolve the issue. Britain would like to provide Guatemala with a ten-mile-wide corridor to the Caribbean Sea, through the southern portion of Belize,[23] but such an arrangement would effectively deprive an independent Belize of a portion of its territory, which is supposed to contain large oil reserves.

The Commonwealth Caribbean nations recognize that the territorial dispute is an obstacle to the full involvement of Belize in current plans for Caribbean regional development and economic integration. In the past, the People's United Party, headed by George Price, had agitated for regional alliance with Central America rather than with the Commonwealth Caribbean, placing emphasis on the country's Mayan and Latin heritage. Realistically, and in view of the nature of the dispute, Belize has since opted for membership in CARICOM rather than CACM. As C. H. Grant points out, Belize, though Spanish-speaking to some extent, is not now regarded as a bona fide Latin American state.[24] Belize seems to have chosen the direction of its economic and political destiny and it requires the continued support of the Commonwealth Caribbean toward this end. In this context, it was recently reported that Jamaica, Guyana, and one unspecified Spanish-speaking Latin American country have agreed to participate in multilateral security arrangements which would defend the territorial integrity of an independent Belize.[25] Although the gesture may provoke even further discord among some CARICOM states, it does indicate the extent to which some nations of the circum-Caribbean region are prepared to go, in order to resist territorial cession. In the event that diplomatic or military support for Belize does not make the situation less intractable, the dispute will continue to act as a constraint on the development of harmonious relations between states in the Central American and Caribbean regions.

SUMMARY AND FUTURE PROSPECTS

The status of current island-littoral relationships, as examined in this chapter, reveals that multiple orientations and initiatives are desirable for individual states which adhere to the Caribbean Basin concept. The archipelago culture area definition, on the other hand, serves mainly the Anglophobe countries of the region in their acceptance of the CARICOM integration zone. As demonstrated in the Belize question, constructive interaction and cooperation between island states and some littoral nations over an issue area is possible; but the relationships may also debilitate regional coherence as illustrated by the smelter controversy and the consequent charges of middle-power recolonization. Theoretically, a strong and viable integration system in the Commonwealth Caribbean community could guarantee, through appropriate functional mechanisms, certain bilateral or multilateral relationships between individual member states and nonmember countries of the mainland. Even the Guatemala-Belize impasse might be susceptible to resolve if the capabilities for coordinated Caribbean diplomatic and military efforts were institutionalized.

One scenario for the future is the emergence of Mexico, Venezuela, and Cuba as regional centers of power, with the ability to manipulate clients in the circum-Caribbean region. So far, these potential middle powers have exercised caution lest they encourage further economic or political fragmentation in the Caribbean archipelago. But their approach may change. The scenario will also be influenced by the role of the United States (the intrusive power) in the observance or nonobservance of regional aspirations and regional subsystemic objectives.* United States' action and reaction should be sufficiently flexible to accommodate the strengthing of viable regional diplomatic and economic zones in the Caribbean area.

---

*In the Anglo-Belize-Guatemala dispute for example, the United States seems not to care whether Belize becomes independent, since Guatemala is a client state of the United States and its economic interests in Belize would remain intact in case of territorial absorption.

In sum, the regulation of relations within the Caribbean archipelago and the interactions between that region and countries of the littoral should be based on mutual respect for deliberate regional choice and coherence. However, the current demise of regional integration experiments in the Caribbean Basin does not indicate that the necessary resolve required for establishing regional autonomy or enhancing the problem-solving capacity of the area yet exists.

NOTES

1. On the matter of the definition of a diplomatic zone, see Vaughan A. Lewis, "The Architecture of Political Regionalism in the Caribbean" (Paper presented at the Conference on Contemporary Trends and Issues in Caribbean International Affairs, Port-of-Spain, Trinidad, May 23–27, 1977), mimeographed. The Trinidad-Venezuela debate is analyzed in Anthony P. Maingot, "National Responses to External Dependency: The Caribbean as an Interest Area," (Paper presented at the Conference on Contemporary Trends and Issues in Caribbean International Affairs, Port-of-Spain, Trinidad, May 23–27, 1977), mimeographed. An analysis of the emerging subsystems is contained in Anthony T. Bryan, "The Commonwealth Caribbean and the Regional Latin American Subsystem: The Limits of Interaction" (Paper presented at the joint Latin American Studies Association/African Studies Association Meeting, Houston, Texas, November 2–5, 1977), mimeographed.

2. For further description and analysis of formal and informal interactions between the Commonwealth Caribbean and Latin America, see Anthony T. Bryan, "Commonwealth Caribbean-Latin American Relations: Emerging Patterns of Cooperation and Conflict," in *Comtemporary International Relations of the Caribbean*, ed. Basil A. Ince (St. Augustine, Trinidad: Institute of International Relations, University of the West Indies, Trinidad, 1978.

3. Trinidad *Guardian*, 1 August 1974 and 9 August 1974.

4. For details of these activities see "Chronology of Events Related to the International Relations of Countries in and Around the Caribbean for the Year 1976," in *The Caribbean Yearbook of International Relations, 1975*, ed. L. F. Manigat (Leyden: A. W. Sijthoff; St. Augustine, Trinidad: Institute of International Relations, University of the West Indies, Trinidad and Tobago, 1976), pp. 7–48 passim (hereafter, *Caribbean Yearbook, 1975*).

5. Trinidad *Guardian*, 3 May 1978.

6. For various assessments of recent Mexican foreign policy, see the following: Mario Ojeda, *Aliances y limites de la política exterior, de México* (Mexico: El Colegio de México, 1976); Olga Pellicer de Brody, "Cambios recientes de la política exterior Mexicana," *Foro Internacional* 50 (October–December): 139–54; Yoram Shapira, "Mexico's Foreign Policy Under Echeverría: A Retrospect," *Inter-American Economic Affairs* 31, no. 4 (1978): 29–61; and Anthony T. Bryan, "Contemporary Mexico: A Review Essay," in *The Caribbean Yearbook of International Relations, 1976*, ed. L. F. Manigat (Leyden, Netherlands: A. W. Sijthoff; St. Augustine, Trinidad: Institute of International Relations, University of the West Indies, Trinidad and Tobago, 1977), pp. 513–17.

7. See the text of his speech to the PNM General Council, May 4, 1975 in the Trinidad *Guardian*, 13 June 1975 and 14 June 1975; see also *The Threat to the Caribbean Community: Speech of Dr. Eric Williams at the Special Convention of the P.N.M., June 15, 1975*, (pamphlet).

8. Note the comments of the Jamaican Mining Minister reported in the Trinidad *Guardian*, 3 May 1978.

9. See Vaughan A. Lewis, "Dangerous Period for Caricom," *Caribbean Contact*, Trinidad February 1978, and Vaughan A. Lewis, "Concept and Analysis in the Study of Third World Integration," *Social and Economic Studies* 26, no. 1 (March 1977): 1–17.

10. *El Tiempo* (Bogota), 4 June and 10 June, 1975; also *Advocate-News* (Barbados), 20 March 1976 and the *Gleaner* (Jamaica), 19 February 1976.

11. Consult the document *Report of the Caribbean Task Force* (Port-of-Spain, Trinidad: Government Printery, 1975).

12. The Jamaica-Panama Joint Communique (April 21, 1976), in *Caribbean Yearbook 1976*, pp. 259–30, is one example of support.

13. Background to the dispute is available in R. A. Humphreys, *The Diplomatic History of British Honduras 1638–1901* (London: Oxford University Press, 1961), Narda Dobson, *A History of Belize* (Port-of-Spain, Trinidad: Longman Caribbean, 1973), L. M. Bloomfield, *The British Honduras-Guatemala Dispute* (Toronto: Carswell and Co., 1953), and C. H. Grant, *The Making of Modern Belize* (Cambridge: At the University Press, 1976).

14. *Statement made by the Premier of Belize to the Fourth Committee of the U.N.* (Belize: Government Printery, 1975).

15. Trinidad *Guardian*, 1 December 1977.

16. The text of the Guyana Declaration is available in the *Caribbean Yearbook, 1975*, op. cit., pp. 551–53.

17. Consult Williams's speeches of May 4, 1975 and June 15, 1975, previously cited.

18. Extracts from the Kingston Accord, The Joint Communique by the Prime Ministers of Jamaica and Cuba (July 13, 1975), and the Lima Declaration are in the *Caribbean Yearbook, 1975*, op. cit., pp. 624ff.

19. Trinidad *Guardian*, 17 November 1975.

20. The current Mexican position on Belize is summarized in the *Latin American Political Report* 12, no. 5, (3 February 1978); discussions of Echeverría's diplomacy in the matter are presented in Shapira, "Mexico's Foreign Policy," op. cit., pp. 56–57; and Ojeda, *Aleances y limites*, op. cit., pp. 198–202.

21. The text of the Guatemala Declaration, November 19, 1975, is available in the *Caribbean Yearbook, 1975*, op. cit., p. 625.

22. It is available in the *New Belize*, July 1977.

23. *Latin American Political Report*, 27 January 1978.

24. *The Making of Modern Belize*, op. cit., pp. 306–24 passim. He points out that in the event of a wider Caribbean-Central American regional integration effort, Belize may be in a unique position to act in a linkage capacity between the two regional blocs.

25. *Express* (Trinidad), 15 March 1978.

Part IV

Caribbean Nations
and International Organizations

20

Integration in Developing Regions as Competing Systems: CARICOM The Caribbean Experiment

Rosina Wiltshire

INTRODUCTION

The integration process within the world's less developed regions, which experienced tremendous impetus in the late 1960s and early 1970s, now seems to be at a nadir. Even the East African Common Market, whose economic Union seemed likely to withstand sharp regional dissension, has floundered. The Caribbean is no exception. Formal institutionalized regional integration in the 1970s evidently represented drowning men clutching at straws, who, sinking deeper into the sea of general economic crises, have now relinquished these straws to head for tested shores represented by renewed integration into the metropolitan units. What cannot be ignored, however, is the quiet process of regional integration that continues to take place at the technical and cultural levels and which defies institutional stagnation.

Neither the concepts of spill over (automatic expansion of integration), spill back (regression in the level or scope of integration), nor spill around adequately describe what seems to be a dynamic and mutually complementary process at work.[1] This process is best represented as a process of integration at the noninstitutional mass level, feeding into the institutional elite level, which in turn gives a dynamic to the former. However, the institutional formal elite integration is more fragile and can at times disintegrate without much affect on the lower level integration process, which does not encapsulate itself, but gives a further thrust to renewed policy initiatives for integration.

The Caribbean region, characterized by its colonial past, poverty, and dependency, is more or less representative of most developing regions. Integration within this context can be seen as a delicate balance of fragmentation and integration, which takes place on two competing levels: (1) the Caribbean regional subsystem and (2) the metropole-dominated international system.

Metropole linkages with the Caribbean are primarily economic, but there is also competition with the Caribbean subsystemic patterns of interrelationships for dominance in the cultural and political spheres. This competition of systems in the integrative process of dependent countries represents the critical distinguishing feature between integration in the developing world and that in the European Community. The countries that comprise the European Economic Community (EEC) did not belong to a strong external competing system of relationships. Integration within Europe primarily represents a process of rebuilding economic links within an existing framework of shared historical, geographical, cultural, and family linkages—links only temporarily disrupted by World War II.[2] The Caribbean, on the other hand, represents a penetrated subsystem linked to the larger metropole-dominated system the United States, with both system and subsystem competing for dominance.

The phenomenon of metropole penetration limits the effectiveness of integration movements of Third World countries. Systemic-subsystemic competition occurs, in spite of elite perceptions which often view regional integration as congruent with metropole interests. In the Caribbean, economic elites, who actively promoted regional integration, saw it as a means of stabilizing existing metropole relationships, not of challenging them.

In spite of this, once the formal regional integration movement was launched, a dynamic of conflicting forces was set in motion. These forces were nurtured by basic divergencies in mass and elite interests. Mytelka holds that there is a narrow elite structure and a vast gap between mass and elite levels of political awareness with respect to the integration process and its consequences, which gives elites a relatively high degree of freedom to determine scope and direction of policy.[3] While partially true, this seems to be an oversimplification of the issue in the Caribbean. Where there has been an ongoing process of high levels of labor migration as existed in eastern Caribbean countries in the formative phases of these societies, together with strong historical and cultural links, formal elite initiatives are paralleled by a mass level of integration which is also an ongoing process. Deutsch partially captured this element in his concept of transactions.[4] The process that takes place between the elite and mass levels of integration within the subsystem is not one of spill over, spill back, or spill around, but rather a symbiotic or mutually complementary relationship.

Institutions are fed by these ongoing processes, gaining legitimacy from the elite sectors. However, because of the high politicization of issues involving economic policy, institutional integration remains fragile. What in fact occurs is that politicians, through their political thrusts at economic integration, give legitimacy to a process which is ongoing and which forms the base for institutional integration. This process also receives impetus from formal institutional activity, but while such policy-making activity strengthens, it is not essential to the process.

Theorists who see Central American or Caribbean integration in isolation from the regional dynamic and the larger competing system tend to focus on leaders and their perceptions.* This affords only a partial perspective. It is not merely the leadership deal of integration, particular development Strategies, and a desire for economic development that has caused the Latin American territories to make 25 attempts at formal integration, but attempts to conform to the reality of a process in motion.[5] Similarly, The 1958–62 abortive West Indies Federation set in motion a dynamic which manifested itself formally in the Caribbean Free Trade Area (CARIFTA) in 1965 and was upgraded to the Caribbean Community (CARICOM) in 1973. Although these building blocks, or institutional links, within the region continue, the institutions of the Caribbean subsystem seem to have reached a point of stagnation while the larger system linkages that tie the Caribbean to the metropole are being strengthened. What becomes clear is that an analysis of the potential success or failure of the Caribbean integration movement cannot be based on whether formal institutions have broken down, but rather has to be balanced by an assessment of the integrative and disintegrative links at work in the systems. The openness of the Caribbean economies and their extreme dependence on the external system suggests that an adequate assessment of regional integration must be seen in terms of competitive system-subsystem dominance.

The core Caribbean community consists of a number of island units plus mainland Guyana. A shortage of labor in Trinidad and Guyana in the early twentieth century and land scarcity in Barbados, plus a comparative absence of job opportunities in the Windward and Leeward islands, all contributed to considerable intraregion migration and to present familial ties throughout the core area. Jamaica is also considered part of the core even though she was not in the mainstream of the early twenthieth century inter-island population movements, but Belize, although now a member of CARICOM, is excluded from the core group due primarily to

---

*This approach is in keeping with traditional foreign policy analyses of developing countries which has tended to focus on leaders, often to the exclusion of the dynamic societal and external forces which also shape foreign policy.

a lack of family linkages with other CARICOM members and her uncertain role with Latin America.

Among all core islands the African race predominantes, with Trinidad and Guyana having an almost equal mix of people of East Indian and African descent. Their educational and political systems are patterned after the British model and English is the official language, although most islands have local dialects resulting from the influence of African slavery and European colonization. The *core* territories may be grouped into the more developed countries (MDCs), which include Jamaica, Trinidad, Guyana, and Barbados, and the less developed countries (LDCs) or Associated States, which include Grenada (now independent), St. Kitts-Nevis-Aguilla, St. Lucia, Montserrat, Dominica, St. Vincent, and Antigua.[6] The MDCs are larger and more economically viable, accounting for over four million of a total core Caribbean Community population of just under five million and for approximately $5 million of the Gross Domestic Product (GDP) of the region; the LDCs account for less than one-fourth of the total population and less than one-tenth of the GDP.[7] All the core islands and territories are essentially poor colonial monocultures that have engaged in a lengthy search for formal integration and, more recently, in efforts toward regional integration.

Thus, the Caribbean may be characterized as comprising a CARICOM core subsystem (minus Belize), which includes both LDCs and MDCs with the following common characteristics: (1) historical experience, (2) geographic proximity, (3) small size, (4) ethnicity, (5) a political system based on the British Westminster two-party model, (6) shared family ties and culture, and (7) economic dependency.[8]

There is also a peripheral Caribbean sector that includes the English-speaking U.S. Virgin Islands, the Bahamas, and Belize: the French areas of Martinique, Guadeloupe, and French Guiana (or Cayenne); Suriname and the Netherlands Antilles; Haiti and the Spanish-speaking islands of Cuba, the Dominican Republic, and Puerto Rico; plus those countries of the Caribbean basin, Venezuela, Mexico, Colombia, Panama, and the five Central American republics. These countries are designated as peripheral because they are all predominantly part of other subsystems. If one can speak of a North American subsystem that includes the United States and Canada, Puerto Rico and the Bahamas fall more clearly into this category. Linguistically and politically, the French and Dutch territories also fit into other subsystems, while Cuba straddles the Latin American, Caribbean, and socialist subsystems.

The West Indies Federation brought all of the core Caribbean territories except Guyana together in an administrative unit which the governing elite saw as a mechanism for gaining independence in a framework acceptable to the British.[9] The member units did not see themselves as economically viable, however, so in reality the federation became a means of integrating more effectively into the larger metropolitan system. Formalization of the delicate balance between the metropolitan linkage and the Caribbean subsystem had taken place. It is instructive to note that Jamaica, the island whose people were most removed from the other federation members both physically and in terms of family linkages, was the one that initially voted to withdraw from the federation in 1961. When Trinidad followed ("ten minus one-nought"), the federation was dissolved in 1962. At this period, the economy of the region was firmly tied to the metropole. Trade with Britain represented approximately 35 percent of all Caribbean export trade, as compared with an approximate 6 percent in exports to the region. Barbados' exports to Britain comprised 71.3 percent of its total exports in 1960.[10]

In the aftermath of the abortive West Indies Federation, the remaining eastern Caribbean territories attempted to form a Federation of Eight. This administrative scheme also failed to materialize.[11] Then in 1965, Barbados, on the threshold of independence, announced with Guyana and Grenada the intention of forming a Free Trade Area, an idea that developed into the Caribbean Free Trade Association. CARIFTA was subsequently enlarged to encompass all the CARICOM territories. Parallel schemes were also taking place among the LDC members of CARIFTA, including an Eastern Caribbean Common Market and the Petit St. Vincent Agreement. Under the latter, residents of Grenada, St. Lucia, and St. Vincent were permitted freedom to work, reside, and acquire property on a reciprocal basis.[12] A Grenada Declaration which advocated full political union was established in 1971; it floundered.[13]

It is against this background that the chances of success of the CARICOM movement in particular and Caribbean integration in general must be evaluated and the sources of fragmentation and consensus within the system and subsystem need to be examined.

SYSTEMIC SOURCES OF STRESS IN THE CARIBBEAN COMMUNITY

Economic Instability

The Caribbean Community is involved in dependent nonreciprocal trade linkages with the United States and Britain, ties which appropriate increasingly larger shares of the regions' exports and imports. U.S.-based multinationals control the major industries of the region, oil and bauxite.

Sugar, the primary agricultural export, is still linked to the British EEC market through a system of preferential agreements. Thus, international economic crises have tremendous stress repercussions on the system linkages. In the mid-1970s, the world economic crises of inflation, energy, and food, interacting simultaneously, resulted in accelerated inflation in the industrial countries. The rate of price increases was further accelerated by a flourfold increase in the price of oil from its average level in 1973.[14] Consumer prices rose 12.5 percent in the United States and 17.5 percent in the United Kingdom during 1974, leading to unprecedented increases in the import bills of Caribbean countries, whose balance of payments were severely affected. At the same time there were major dislocations in the international monetary and capital markets, partly due to the investment of billions of petrodollars in the world money market at very short term while the demand was for medium- and long-term investment. This caused interest rates on medium- and long-term issues to rise to levels as high as 12 to 14 percent.[15] This instability in the international money market delayed reforms in the International Monetary System. For the Caribbean countries in the sterling area, the Sterling Agreement ended at the close of 1974, after the pound suffered a 22 percent devaluation against other major trading currencies since 1971. Added to this instability was Britain's 1973 entrance into the EEC.

Results were devastating, even for Trinidad and Tobago with its petroleum-based economy. There were unprecedented rates of inflation, ranging from 20 percent to 38 percent, in all countries in the CARICOM region. Balance of payments problems became acute and output declined in critical productive sectors. High interest rates made borrowing on the international market almost prohibitive.[16] The CARICOM countries responded by attempting to reduce the system linkages which were producing such shocks and to strengthen subsystem linkages in the political, economic, and policy-making spheres. In 1973, the MDCs upgraded CARIFTA to CARICOM. The Leeward and Windward islands joined in 1974 at the height of the crisis. Severe import restrictions raised import duties and exchange controls were imposed by the MDCs in 1974. Jamaica imposed a bauxite levy, raising their income to (U.S.) $200 million as against $25 million in 1973. The government of St. Kitts-Nevis-Anguilla also began negotiations to acquire all sugar land in St. Kitts in order to nationalize sugar production.[17] Caribbean countries, along with other developing nations, put forward a proposal for a New International Economic Order. If implemented, this would involve a basic restructuring of the larger system linkages, to create a more equitable balance in those relationships.[18] In short, international systemic stress was attacked from several different fronts and resultant spill over contributed to strengthening of Caribbean subsystem linkages.[19]

Caribbean Strategis Significance to the United States

Because of its geographical proximity, the Caribbean has always enjoyed significant strategic importance to the United States. The emergence of a Socialist-oriented Cuba increased U.S. sensitivity to the region. U.S.-Cuban rapproachement would not imply a lessened perception of Cuba as a threat in the region, since normalization of U.S.-Cuban relations "may imply an unleashing of militant foreign policy directed from Havana and aimed at radicalising regional politics."[20] As Roett points out, U.S. efforts to seek normalization have been aimed in part at "reclaiming part of the lead which the Cuban government is perceived to have assumed in the Caribbean."[21]

The 1972 decision of Jamaica, Barbados, and Trinidad to recognize Cuba, in addition to the emergence of a democratic socialist regime in Jamaica, made a closer evaluation of Caribbean initiatives much more salient to the United States. This has had the effect of lessening the capability of CARICOM policy initiatives in critical areas, such as sectoral integration of key productive resources. It was precisely these initiatives towards sectoral integration that ignited the third source of system-subsystem competition and stress.

External Ownership of Critical Resources of the Region

In order to reduce the worst effects of systemic stress, Caribbean countries took dramatic measures to gain greater control of their natural resources. Trinidad and Tobago nationalized Shell Trinidad Ltd., one of its major oil companies, in 1974.[22] With the help of U.S. diplomatic efforts, multinational corporations in Jamaica attempted to get assurances that their interests would not be threatened.[23] Jamaica's imposition of the bauxite levy elicited attempts by the companies to take the issue to court. Acting as a unit, Jamaica, Trinidad, and Guyana made plans to establish a smelter plant, utilizing the central resources of bauxite and oil in the region. Jamaica even extended its initiative to the periphery, agreeing to bauxite smelter projects with Mexico and Venezuela. The International Bauxite Association, with its headquarters in Jamaica, reinforced attempts to forge new linkages outside of the dominant system framework, a policy which in itself produced tensions.

Attempts to break out of old systemic patterns are met by multinational pressures which further exacerbate dislocations already in process. Because of the divergent interests of the metropolitan countries and dependent Caribbean countries, efforts to create strong Caribbean linkages are often resisted. This helps to retard subsystem integration and maintains formal economic linkages at a most superficial level. Trade takes place in nonessential areas and makes little use of regional resources, thus having little spill over effect.

It has been argued that the dominant countries are the major beneficiaries of the external patterns of ownership because of the high level of export of capital to the metropolis. The flow of gains from investment tend to mitigate against the interests of the recipient territories.[24] Ownership patterns do not give Caribbean nations freedom to manipulate crucial economic policy in their own interests, or in the interests of the region as a whole. This factor is excerbated by the fact that the Caribbean elite is linked more firmly into the dominant system than into the subsystem.

SOURCES OF STRESS IN THE CARIBBEAN SUBSYSTEM

LDC/MDC Conflict

One of the major sources of stress in Caribbean integration has been the perception of unequal gains on the part of the less-developed territories. Similar to integration movements in Central and South America, the less-developed countries of the Caribbean—most of whom also enjoy associated status with Britain—have consistently perceived their rewards from the integration movement as inadequate vis-à-vis the gains of the MDCs within the region.[25] This problem tends to be underrated by economists, who underestimate the importance of the consequences of elite perception as a source of stress. Blake and Hall make the very valid point that while polarization flows might be against the CARICOM LDCs, on the regional and economic plane these weak states could be the most substantive beneficiaries of cooperation at the international, economic, and political levels, since, as essentially nonindependent states, they could not otherwise participate directly in the international system.[26] They see the major benefit of the concept of polarization of production and trade as being a political tool for the negotiation of quick direct benefits to the LDCs, and as a guide to planners to constantly review the benefits of integration. The LDCs no longer see integration into the British EEC framework as associated states as a viable alternative, but they do have to bring their disparate plight sharply into focus. The LDCs, who constitute eight units within the core group, control 10.1 percent of the land area, 13.6 percent of the population, 10 percent of the technical managerial skills, probably none of the known mineral resources and energy potential, and in 1973 contributed 6 percent of the GDP of the region.

The MDCs, who constitute four of the units of the CARICOM movement, account for 89.9 percent of the land area, 86.4 percent of the population, 90 percent of the technically skilled personnel, nearly 100 percent of the mineral resources and energy potential and 94 percent of the GDP in 1973.[27] Although a continuing potential source of disaffection with the region, the special provisions of the CARICOM treaty, which seek to accommodate the reality of LDC problems, have softened the impact of this source of stress. The Caribbean Development Bank (CDB), in coordination with the Caribbean Secretariat, created in 1976 a special fund for Emergency Programme Assistance to LDC territories to help provide pooled services and a common team of experts in critical areas, such as agriculture, education, health, and developmental planning.[28] In 1974, from a total of $41.2 million approved as loans by the CDB, $26.3 million was approved for projects located in the LDCs.[29] In 1971, the MDCs of the region also established a Commonwealth Caribbean Technical Assistance Programme. Under this agreement, the MDCs make technical personnel, including salaries, available to the LDCs. But despite such programs, the region seems incapable of really coming to terms with the deeper problems of regional development. This leads us to the second major source of fragmentation confronting the CARICOM movement—ideological divergences among the major units.

Ideology

The growing ideological differences in the region present a clear source of fragmentation in the CARICOM Movement. The Caribbean is faced with certain problems which need coordinated activity. In 1974, the annual food import bill for CARICOM and the Bahamas was well over EC $1 billion, or U.S. $5 billion. There is significant foreign ownership of natural resources and a policy still largely based on industrialization by invitation. In a region where development planning against the background of long-term development strategy is seen to be a priority, there has to be a common perception of what development entails, what are the forces retarding it, and what are the strategies to be pursued to end the cycle of underdevelopment.[30] Obviously, leaders approaching the problem from different ideological perspectives are likely to see one another's definitions as incompatible. Even if they agree on the nature of the problem, their perceptions of the source of the ills and the strategies for change are likely to diverge significantly. Within the CARICOM experiment, the democratic socialist orientation of the Jamaican ruling People's National Party coupled with the cooperative Socialist thrust of the Guyana ruling party were bound to create problems. The leaders of the

LDCs in particular, and the economic elite of all the territories, have projected the fear that these two territories might have a demonstration effect on the rest of the region. A basic distrust inevitably led to tensions and the lessening effectiveness of collaborated strategies. This factor also exacerbated the competitive trends among the leadership which surfaced so strongly during Caribbean federation.

Leadership Styles

Largely because there are so few areas in which Caribbean leaders can exercise policy initiative, they have been extremely jealous of their limited spheres of dominance. The fact of a wide elite-mass gap as a result of educational incongruities and the absence of a strong core of technicians have led to a predominant type of charismatic leadership in the West Indies. Instead of one DeGaulle, the Caribbean boasts at least five, a situation which could have disastrous effects on collaborative activity.

Trinidad's proposed unilateral action towards the University of the West Indies (UWI) provides us with an interesting example. The university represents one of the oldest regional institutions in existence. The Trinidad and Tobago White Paper on Higher Education reasserts the commitment to Caribbean economic integration, but in fact proposes a structure that belies that commitment.[31] The cumbersome UWI management structure has been the subject of many studies and there is no doubt that the university needs significant reform. However, the proposals that recommend local state responsibility for the unit located in its particular territory—with syllabus, entry requirements, examinations, appointments and promotions (including tenure up to Senior Lecturer level) the province of the local campus—would go far beyond remedying the outmoded management structure and would, in fact, destroy the regional nature of the organization. The university now creates a regional Caribbean intellectual and leadership group committed to the ideal of integration. It has been an important source in integrating Jamaica into the core of the Caribbean region.

Jamaica's position in attempting to unilaterally integrate members of the periphery into the regional movement has been another significant source of stress. Jamaica, Trinidad, and Guyana proposed an aluminum smelter arrangement which was to be jointly owned by the three MDCs. Jamaica's decision to sign a similar agreement with Venezuela was seen as a breach of faith on her part, and the other two territories withdrew from the scheme. Trinidad Prime Minister Williams went as far as to suggest that Venezuela had superpower ambitions in the Caribbean region. Jamaica's smelter agreement with Mexico has also floundered; Mexico announced to Jamaica that the project is no longer considered feasible and therefore they no longer wish to be a part of it.[32] Dr. Williams perceived that these moves would give access to the United States through the back door and would play into the hands of aggressive Hispanic American policies in the Caribbean. The absence of shared expectations, which would have been formed by shared ethnicity, language, culture, political organization, or past historical linkages, led to a distrust of Venezuela's goals and loyalty to the region. In view of these forces of stress, what factors maintain the delicate balance of the integrative movement within the region? These forces operate both on the systemic and subsystemic levels, but have their strongest elements in the subsystem.

SUBSYSTEM SOURCES OF INTEGRATION

CARICOM as a Collective Bargaining Agent

The Caribbean territories, because they remain dependent on system fluctuations, have consistently needed strong unified bargaining to extract the best possible alternatives within the limited constraints. The Caribbean Community movement was largely a response to the need for a cohesive bargaining agent in the light of British entry into the EEC. It has been argued that the major function of CARICOM machinery is as an agent of bargaining and diplomacy.[33] In the area of bargaining, the machinery becomes even more critical for the LDCs, who would not normally participate in international negotiations because of their associated status with the British.

The relative flexibility in the system, and the Third World ability to manipulate the system, given the situation of flux that existed in the late 1960s and 1970s, brought on by great power realignments, no longer obtains. The international system is attaining once more a degree of stability and therefore is not likely to respond as positively to Third World attempts to exploit it. It is, therefore, likely that the successes of the diplomatic function of CARICOM will be considerably curtailed.

Small Size

The reality of the diseconomies of small size become clear when it is shown that the seven core LDCs, operate 47 government ministries and an establishment of over 16,000 employees at a cost of over $55 million. Barbados, although more viable, with a quarter of a million population, budgets for 12-ministries and an establishment of less than 10,000 employees at a cost just under $55 million.[34] The small physical size of the territories, their lack of natural resources, and their high levels of dependency have all gone into shaping a phychology of nonviability shared by both elite and mass. They do not think survival is possible as individual isolated units, and it has become increasingly evident that the metropolitan linkage is based on national interest and not on philanthropy. Once that linkage ceases to be profitable, it becomes burdensome, and the metropolis becomes anxious to shed the ties. The CARICOM territories, in particular, recognize that their old linkage with Britain has become burdensome and that continued reliance on her is no longer a reality. Substitutes for her raw materials have been found but cost of production now makes them unprofitable; therefore survival must come from mutual cooperation.

Strategic importance to the United States has not meant a parallel interest in the level of economic well-being. As Roett points out, of total U.S. economic assistance in millions of dollars for the period 1946–1975, the Latin American region received $13,868.8 billion. Of that, Barbados, Guyana, Jamaica, and Trinidad and Tobago combined received only $243.3 million, while Haiti alone received $138.2 million and the Dominican Republic $523.5 million. Of U.S. Export-Import Bank loans (millions of dollars) for the same period, the CARICOM MDCs received $140.9 million out of a total of $7,217.8 million.[35] Although this assistance merely insures elite stability and does not filter down to improve mass welfare and create development potential, it would give the elite a greater degree of security which the Caribbean leaders are denied. The strength that comes from unity is thus pursued as a major avenue for survival.

Shared Characteristics

The shared characteristics of the region, covering factors of ethnicity, historical experience, political institutions, geography, shared family, and economic status, all give to the Caribbean people a sense of being West Indian. This sense of community has grown since the 1958–62 Federation of the West Indies and, although it does not lead to a mass clamor for integration, the shared needs manifest themselves in obvious ways. It is becoming increasingly clear that the educational needs of the territories can not be met by examinations curriculla set by Oxford and Cambridge. A Caribbean Examinations Council has therefore been established which is revising curricula as well as devising its own examinations.

Meteorology and shipping are areas in which cooperation has continued since the federation. The commonality of mass needs also experts pressure to seek coordinated strategies. The lack of adequate food production remains a problem for the Caribbean territories. The territories have explored strategies of competition, integration into external markets, industrialization by invitation, and yet these development strategies have not affected this continuing crisis of the inability of the region to provide its basic necessities. The Caribbean Food Plan for integrated agricultural strategies has been a regional attempt to tackle this vital problem. As long as the problems remain similar, the leaders of the Caribbean are going to be forced to look to one another for help. Formal integrative structures such as CARICOM may atrophy, but there appears to be a continuing search for more effective methods of cooperation.

PROSPECTS FOR CARIBBEAN INTEGRATION

The prospects for the institutions of CARICOM are not bright. The Caribbean Community, although partially adapted to Caribbean needs, was basically patterned after the experience of the European Economic Community. The sources of stress in the region are at a high point, emanating from both system and subsystem forces, although there are significant consensual forces at work. Stress on the system, external and intra-Caribbean, can be a positive factor, inducing new levels of institutional adaptation leading to stress containment. It is posited, however, that prolonged stress tends to have a reverse effect. In the face of prolonged system crises, incremental integration is unlikely to show significant short-run gains. In the absence of careful economic planning designed to shift individual economies away from dependence on system fluctuations, uncoordinated thrusts at strengthening the regional integration movement are likely to exacerbate stress loads rather than really strengthening the movement. Radical shifts are likely to be strongly resisted. This has been the case in the CARICOM movement, where member territories have ultimately reacted to continued crisis by turning back to the linkages which seem to provide immediate short-term remedies to the critical problems of continuing balance of payments crises and runaway inflation.

It must be noted that some important factors propelling integration are also being undermined; but if there is stagnation or even disintegration of some of the essential institutional forms of CARICOM, the dynamic for long-term integration among the core will still be present. The prospect is that new forms grounded in the Caribbean experience are likely to emerge with even more strength, relevance, and legitimacy than previously existed. With time these can eventually be extended to the periphery from a position of strength.

NOTES

1. See Gary Wynia, "Central American Integration: The Paradox of Success," *International Organization* 24, no. 2 (Spring 1970): 319–34

2. See Stanley Hoffman, "Obstinate or Obsolete? The Fate of the Nation State and the Case of Western Europe," in *International Regionalism,* ed. Joseph Nye (Boston: Little, Brown & Co., 1968), pp. 177–230; and Leon Lindberg, "Integration as a Source of Stress on the European Community System," in *International Regionalism,* ed. Joseph Nye (Boston: Little Brown & Co., 1968), pp. 231–68.

3. Lynn Mytelka, "The Salience of Gains in Third World Integrative Systems," *World Politics* 25, no. 2 (January 1973): 236–50.

4. Karl Deutsch, *Political Community and the North Atlantic Area* (Princeton, N.J.: Princeton University Press, 1968).

5. See Gary Wynia, op. cit., p. 321; and Joseph Nye, "Central American Regional Integration," *International Conciliation* (March 1967): 16.

6. See William G. Demas, *West Indian Nationhood and Caribbean Integration* (Barbados: CCC Publishing House, 1974), p. 28. (Statistics updated in July, 1978, letter from William Demas)

7. *From CARIFTA to Caribbean Community* (Georgetown, Guyana: Commonwealth Caribbean Regional Secretariat, 1971).

8. For an interesting discussion of this concept, see L. Cantori and L. Spiegel, "The International Relations of Regions," in *Regional Politics & World Order,* eds. R. Falk and Saul Mendlovitz (San Francisco: Freeman & Co., 1973).

9. J. S. Mordecai, *The West Indies: The Federal Negotiations* (London: George Allen & Unwin Ltd., 1968).

10. *From CARIFTA to Caribbean Community,* op. cit.

11. Arthur Lewis, *The Agony of the Eight* (Bridgetown, Barbados: Advocate Printery, 1965).

12. Peter Emmanuel, Vaughan Lewis, and Alister McIntyre, "The Political Economy: Independence for the Leeward and Windward Islands" (Mona, Jamaica, February 1975), mimeographed, p. 44.

13. See Rosina Wiltshire, "Mini States, Dependency and Regional Integration," in *Size, Self Determination and International Relations: The Caribbean,* ed. Vaughan Lewis (Mona, Jamaica: Institute of Social and Economic Research, 1976).

14. Caribbean Development Bank Report, 1974.

15. Ibid., p. 7.

16. Ibid.

17. Ibid., p. 12

18. "Towards a New International Economic Order," Final Report by the Commonwealth Experts Group (London: Commonwealth Secretariat, 1977).

19. I have argued elsewhere that there were, in fact, conflicting tendencies at play. The Caribbean countries were actually seeking to shape new dependent linkages using the strengthened Caribbean movement as a diplomatic negotiating tool. See Rosina Wiltshire, "Caribbean Integration and Dependency" (Paper presented at Conference on Contemporary Trends and Issues in Caribbean International Affairs, Institute of International Relations, University of the West Indies, St. Augustine, Trinidad, May 1977).

20. For a most insightful discussion of the Caribbean strategies as seen from an American perspective, see Riordan Roett, "The New Realities of Caribbean Geopolitics" (Paper presented at Conference on Contemporary Trends and Issues in Caribbean International Affairs, Institute of International Relations, University of the West Indies, St. Augustine, Trinidad, May 1977).

21. Ibid., p. 11.

22. Trevor Farrell, " 'In Whose Interest'? Nationalization and Bargaining with the Petroleum Multinationals: The Trinidad and Tobago Experience" (Paper presented at Conference on Contemporary Trends and Issues in Carribean International Affairs, Institute of International Relations, University of the West Indies, St. Augustine, Trinidad, May 1977).

23. U.S., Congress, Senate, Committee on Foreign Relations, Subcommittee on Multinational Corporations, *Multinational Corporations and U.S. Foreign Policy, Hearings,* 93rd Cong., 1973, Part 3, pp. 116–18.

24. Alister McIntyre and B. Watson, *Foreign Investment in the Commonwealth Caribbean* (Mona, Jamaica: Institute of Social and Economic Research, University of the West Indies, 1970); see also H. Magdoff, *The Development of Underdevelopment* (New York: Monthly Review Press, 1969).

25. See Wiltshire, "Mini States."

26. Byron Blake and Kenneth Hall, "Polarization Problems in CARICOM: A Critique" (Paper presented at Conference on Contemporary Trends and Issues in Caribbean International Affairs, Institute of International Relations, University of the West Indies, St. Augustine, Trinidad, May 1977), esp. p. 9.

27. Byron Blake and Kenneth Hall, "Institutional Approach to the LDC/MDC Problems in CARICOM," mimeographed, 1977.

28. Ibid., p. 7.

29. Caribbean Development Bank, *Annual Report,* (Bridgetown, Barbados), p. 15.

30. William G. Demas, Address to the Fifth Annual Meeting of the Board of Governors, Caribbean Development Bank Bridgetown, Barbados, May 1975, esp. pp. 6–8.

31. Trinidad and Tobago White Paper on Higher Education (Port-of-Spain, Trinidad: Government Printery, 1977).

32. Jamaica *Daily Gleaner,* 3 March 1978.

33. Wiltshire, "Caribbean Integration and Dependency," op. cit.

34. Emmanuel, Lewis, and McIntyre, op. cit., p. 44.

35. Riordan Roett, op. cit., p. 5.

21

The Caribbean States and International Organization: The United Nations, Organization of American States, and Inter-American Development Bank

Larman C. Wilson

INTRODUCTION

A study of the participation in the three international organizations by the nine states considered here (see Table 21.1) will indicate lack of a common and special Caribbean-wide policy, and limited, collective influence by these states with the notable exception of a group of them in the Organization of American States (OAS). Although these states have common needs and interests, they do not perform as a bloc. There does not exist even a Latin American bloc in the area composed of Cuba, the Dominican Republic, and Haiti; this was true even before Castro came to power in the late 1950s.* There does exist, however, a bloc within the Caribbean family: the Commonwealth Caribbean states (hereafter CWC) —the Bahamas, Barbados, Grenada, Guyana, Jamaica, and Trinidad and Tobago. The CWC states perform as a bloc, particularly in the OAS, which is of mounting concern to the Latin American members. A good example of the CWC states as a bloc concerns the issue of Castro's Cuba, an issue that divides the Caribbean. While the Latin American republics supported OAS sanctions against Cuba within the context of the Cold War, the CWC nations played an important role in ending these constraints.

The Caribbean states have two main goals that are shared with other developing Third World countries: becoming economically developed and reducing or ending foreign dependency. Even though the nations in

---

*In this chapter, the term Latin American will refer to those countries which were originally colonies of France, Portugal or Spain, whereas Commonwealth means those colonies of England.

the Caribbean differ among each other concerning the means for pursuing these goals, they generally have great interest in export diversification, trade with Latin America, regional integration (e.g., the Caribbean Community—CARICOM), joint ventures, commodity agreements (e.g., bauxite and sugar), special access of their exports to the markets of developed countries (e.g., Canada, the United States, and the European Economic Community), private investment, and economic and technical assistance from the OAS, Inter-American Development Bank, and UN. As far as these means are concerned, especially through international organizations, the Caribbean states exercise influence by virtue of their membership and participation in blocs or coordinating groups. This is best illustrated by the UN, where influence, although very limited, is enhanced via the Latin American Group (LAG) which operates in the Group of 77 (G 77) in the UN Conference on Trade and Development (UNCTAD), and in the Third UN Law of the Sea Conference (LOS III). In addition to considerable and mounting CWC influence in the OAS, it also applies to the linkage between the OAS and IADB in the requirement—later excepted in a few cases—that a hemisphere state would have to be a member of the OAS before it could join the IADB. This is the primary reason CWC nations joined the OAS.

As a result of the previous characterization of the Caribbean countries, three Latin American and six CWC, the designation of the Caribbean as a regional subsystem seems premature,[1] although it has some validity if limited to the CWC states. The concept of a Latin American subordinate system in which the Caribbean nations constitute the "periphery" is much more useful.[2] The terminology used in this chapter, however, will be that of the Inter-American System (IAS), whose major institutional components are the OAS and IADB and which includes the CWC nations (present and future) once they become members of the OAS or IADB or both.[3] These states will be included in the IAS and particularly as a bloc in the OAS despite their micro-state, dependent, and penetrated status.[4] This chapter, employing the archipelago or island approach to the Caribbean (with Guyana as the one exception), will use a modified chronological method within the contexts of the East-West (cold war) and North-South demarcations.

THE COLD WAR: THE UN AND THE OAS

This section will trace the relationship between the UN and OAS, the use of these two forums by the United States and Latin America, and the U.S. preoccupation with security and the Latin American concern with economic development.

TABLE 21.1:   Profile and Memberships in International Organizations

					OAS		LADB		
Country	Independence Date	Population (in millions)	Major Exports & Commercial Activities	Party to Rio Treaty	Year Joined	Budget Quota (%)	Year Joined	Shares of Cap. Stock	Percent of Votes
Bahamas	1973	.205	banking tourism	no			1977	1,520	.22
Barbados	1966	.260	sugar tourism	no	1967	.08	1969	1,060	.16
Canada	1867	22	lumber oil food machinery	no			1972	35,090	4.7
Cuba	1902	8.7	sugar minerals	1948+	1952**		no		
Dominican Republic	1844	5	sugar coffee minerals	1947	1949	.18	1959	4,748	.65
Grenada	1974	.112	sugar tourism	no	1975	.03	no		
Guyana	1966	.780	sugar rice bauxite	no	no		1976	1,540	.22
Haiti	1804	6	sugar coffee	1948	1951	.18	1959	3,556	.49
Jamaica	1962	2.2	bauxite sugar	no	1969	.18	1969	4,748	.65
Trinidad/ Tobago	1962	1.3	oil sugar	1967	1967	.18	1967	3,556	.49
United States	1776	208	manuf. goods	1947	1951	66.0	1959	266,020	35.32

*Trusteeship Council has decreased in size from 24 members in 1946 to 5 members in 1978.
**Suspended from participation in 1962.
+Castro renounced the treaty in 1960.
Sources: (Chart prepared by Kathryn W. Stammer.) Chamberlin, Waldo; Havet, Thomas, Jr.; and Hovet, Erica. *A Chronology and Fact Book of The United Nations 1941–1976.* (Dobbs Ferry, New York: Oceana Publications, Inc., 1976).

TABLE 21.1: (Continued)

| | | United Nations | | | IBRD | | IMF | |
| | | SC | ECOSOC | TC* | | | | |
Year Joined	Budget Quota (%)	Non-Permanent Members President of	Member President of		Capital Sub- (in thousands)	Percent of Votes	Quotas in millions of SOR's	Percent of Votes
1973	.02				17,100	.15	20.00	.07
1966	.02		1973 Pres.– 1977–78		11,100	.13	13.00	.04
orig. member	3.18	1948 1949 1958 1959 1967 1968	1946–48 1950–52 1956–58 1965–67 1974 to present pres.– 1958		941,800	3.36	1,100.0	3.76
orig. member	0.11	1949 1950 1956 1957	1946–47 1952–54 1976		no		no	
orig. member	.02		1955–57	1950–53 Pres.– 1950	14,300	.14	43.00	.15
1974	.02				1,700	.09	2.00	.01
1966	.02	1975 1976			17,100	.15	20.00	.07
orig. member	.02		1971–72	1954–59 Pres.– 1959	15,000	.14	19.00	.07
1962	.02	1977 1978 Pres.	1969 1971 1973 1976		44,600	.24	53.00	.18
1962	.02		1973–74		53,500	.27	63.00	.22
orig. member	25.0		1947 to present	1947 to present Pres.– 1947 1955–56 1962 1968 1972	6,473,000	22.55	6,700	22.93

Inter-American Development Bank. *Economic and Social Progress in Latin America.* 1976 Report. Library of Congress, Foreign Affairs Division. *The United States and the Multilateral Development Ranks.* (U.S. Government Printing Office, 1974). Organization of American States. "Asamblea General Actas Y Documentos," Volume I. Session held December 12–15, 1977. World Bank. *Annual Report — 1977.*

OAS

Before turning to the cold war issues in the UN and their regional corollary in the OAS, the laying of the permanent bases of the IAS should be mentioned. The first was the Inter-American Treaty of Reciprocal Assistance (Rio Treaty) which was drawn up at the Rio Conference (1947). The treaty, effective in 1948, provided the basis for collective action and measures by the OAS, subsequently applied against Castro.* (For individual ratification dates, see Table 20.1) The second treaty, the Charter of the OAS, was prepared at the Bogotá Conference (1948); it went into effect in 1951 (see Table 20.1). The charter provided for a complete regional system, created the machinery for increasing the system's effectiveness, and established the principle of nonintervention as the cornerstone. A number of resolutions were also passed, including one on "The Preservation and Defense of Democracy in America," which was the first inter-American resolution to mention "communism."

UN

As the cold war transcended the UN in the late 1940s and 1950s, the members of the Latin American Group, especially Cuba, the Dominican Republic, and Haiti, regularly and strongly supported the United States on political and security issues. This included, among other things, the admission of "Communist" (mainland) China, the Korean War, the Uniting for Peace resolution, nonintervention, and the autonomy of regional organizations (the OAS) in the settlement of disputes.[5] (At the same time, the Latin American representatives strongly supported a number of emerging North-South issues: decolonization and selfdetermination, sovereignty and nonintervention, human rights, and economic development.)[6]

OAS and the U.S.

The cold war also intruded into the IAS where the response of the U.S. was a major effort to convert the OAS into an "anti-communist alliance."[7] At the same time the Latin Americans were bargaining for

---

*Article 6 provided for a meeting of the Organ of Consultation to decide upon collective measures if any American state was "affected by an aggression which is not an armed attack or by an extra-continental or intra-continental conflict, or by any other fact or situation that might endanger the peace of America." Article 8 indicated the range of "measures" or "sanctions" to be applied, from "recall of . . . diplomatic missions" to the "use of armed force."

economic assistance from the United States. The Caracas Conference (1954) illustrated the differing security and economic priorities. There the United States wanted a commitment to collective action versus the "international communist conspiracy" that she believed had gained control in Guatemala, whereas the Latin American delegates desired U.S. economic aid, for which they were willing to exchange their votes. The controversial U.S. resolution for action against Guatemala (she was not specified) upon the basis of the Rio Treaty was passed by a large margin, including the votes of the Caribbean nations. During this dispute, Guatemala, not a party to either the Rio Treaty or OAS Charter, appealed to the UN Security Council. Her appeal provoked a debate in which the U.S., supported by Brazil and Colombia, argued the primacy of the OAS in dispute settlement under article 52 of the UN Charter while the Soviet Union argued the primacy of the UN. The U.S. position prevailed.[8]

IADB

While the United States was preoccupied with communism in the Americas, the Latin American nations were increasingly critical in their demands for economic help. The United States resisted their demands, including one for the creation of an inter-American bank, at economic conferences in Rio (1954) and in Buenos Aires (1957). However, the United States soon reversed its stand and came out in favor of a bank. Perhaps the most important factor in this change was the rise to power of Castro in Cuba. An OAS committee drafted proposals for an IADB which were approved in 1959.

CUBA AND THE OAS: COLD WAR TO NORTH-SOUTH AXIS

Castro's ascendancy was a turning point in inter-American relations. In the Caribbean, it meant that Cuba, a former supporter of the United States on cold war issues, had left the fold and become an ally of the USSR. It also meant that Cuba had become a base for Communist intervention and influence in the Americas. (It is well-known that the Kennedy Administration's Alliance for Progress, an idea borrowed from Latin America, was a response to Castro.)

Once firmly in power, Castro became increasingly dependent upon the USSR economically and militarily. The United States worked through the OAS in an effort to isolate and bring down Castro. This effort received the strong backing of most Latin American republics, particularly Cuba's small and proximate neighbors in Central America and in the Caribbean.

OAS Sanctions

The actions of the OAS under the Rio Treaty demonstrated the role of the former as an anti-Communist alliance and the U.S. preoccupation with communism; they also evidenced a concomitant and growing clash between two preoccupations: the United States with communism and Latin America with economic development. This situation continued until the latter began transcending the former in the late 1960s and early 1970s. It also laid the basis for a regional version of the transition from the cold war to the North-South context.

The three major OAS actions against Cuba in the 1960s had certain common features: they were based upon Articles 6 and 8 of the Rio Treaty (the Dominican Republic and Haiti voted with the required ⅔ majority), and they provoked debates in the UN about the linkage between the OAS and UN.

First, at the Punta del Este Conference in early 1962, Cuba's participation in the OAS was suspended because her ties with the USSR were deemed "incompatible with the principles and standards that govern the regional system," and a ban on arms to Cuba was imposed. (The "exclusion" resolution received the bare ⅔ vote—made possible by Haiti's switch in position—and six states abstained.) Castro appealed to the UN on the ground that the action was illegal since the Security Council had not approved it under Article 53. The U.S.-Latin American view prevailed, that Article 53 did not apply to nonforcible action by the OAS.[9] (In the UN, the LAG responded to Cuba's suspension by meeting informally and not inviting Cuba to participate.)[10]

Second, the discovery of Soviet missiles in Cuba in late 1962 prompted President John F. Kennedy to announce that the United States would impose on October 23 a "quarantine" of all "offensive missiles" being brought into Cuba. At an emergency session, the OAS Council approved overwhelmingly the "quarantine" as a counter to Soviet intervention in the Americas. Although the UN debated the crisis, no resolutions were passed by the Security Council. The missiles were withdrawn after a bilateral agreement in which the United States pledged not to invade Cuba.

Third, the Ninth Meeting of Consultation was held in 1964 after a cache of Cuban arms with plans for insurrection was found in Venezuela. Venezuela's charges of "acts of intervention and aggression" by Cuba were corroborated and sanctions were approved, including the severance of relations and the termination of all trade.[11] The four states that still had relations with Cuba—three South American states and Mexico—voted against the sanctions; however, all but Mexico later complied with the resolution. In 1967, the OAS expanded its sanctions against Cuba.

In 1965, another crisis occurred in the Caribbean, this time in the Dominican Republic. The United States charged that Cuba was involved in the Dominican civil conflict and (in the words of President Lyndon Johnson) intervened militarily to prevent a "second Cuba." This unilateral action provoked strong criticism by certain Latin American states and resulted in undermining the autonomy of the OAS vis-à-vis the UN. At the Tenth Meeting of Consultation, four Latin American countries introduced a resolution condemning the United States and requesting withdrawal from the Dominican Republic. The U.S. approach to get the endorsement of the OAS through the creation of an Inter-American Peace Force was successful after much debate and by the bare ⅔ majority vote (the Dominican Republic and Haiti voted in favor, five states were opposed, and one abstained). But this time the United States was unable to keep the UN out, on account of Latin American opposition. The Security Council discussed the crisis at many sessions, with Cuba participating, and passed a resolution empowering the secretary-general to send a representative and military observer to the Dominican Republic.[12]

OAS Amendments

The Third Special Inter-American Conference (1967) was the culmination of a Latin American drive to amend the OAS Charter by incorporating the commitments of the Alliance for Progress and thus making the OAS a more useful instrument for economic and social development. This effort could also be viewed as an emerging North-South axis within the IAS. The amendments, designed to expand the multilateral activities of the OAS by getting the OAS to accept long-term and additional economic obligations, had the effect of strengthening the economic and social side of the OAS and weakening the political side—for example, the powers of the council which it was believed the U.S. dominated. In short, the changes reflected a shift in OAS emphasis from political-security (cold war) to economic-social (North-South) affairs and concerns, and also a shift to the primacy of Latin America over U.S. interests.[13]

THE NEW CARIBBEAN STATES

Starting in the early 1960s and continuing into the 1970s, an increasing number of former British dependencies became independent, joined the UN, and later the OAS. Their independence has had a marked impact upon the Caribbean and their entry into the OAS, beginning with Trinidad and Tobago, has been a turning point in that organization. The CWC states soon constituted a bloc in the OAS, one that will continue to increase in size and influence as other dependencies gain independence and join the OAS in the late 1970s and in the 1980s. Although these nations have only limited influence in the UN, they first established their identity there as members of the LAG.

Jamaica and Trinidad and Tobago became independent in 1962, joined the UN the same year, and a few years later joined the OAS. Barbados and Guyana joined the UN in 1966, immediately following independence, and applied for OAS membership. Guyana, however, was turned down. The Bahamas and Grenada became independent and joined the UN in 1973 and 1974 respectively, but only the latter has joined the OAS (see Table 21.1).

UN Membership

The CWC countries were interested in joining the UN as a matter of prestige and as a means of obtaining economic and technical aid from the UN Development Program (UNDP), and they also valued for economic reasons membership in two specialized agencies—the International Bank for Reconstruction and Development (BANK) and International Monetary Fund (FUND). In the UN, the Caribbean states have very limited influence, for they do not constitute a bloc. Their limited influence, like that of most other small, developing nations, is partly indicated by Table 21.1 in terms of budget quotas and votes in the BANK and FUND. It is also suggested by the fact that only three states —two CWC—have served as nonpermanent members of the Security Council (SC) and only two have been in the Trusteeship Council (TC), and not one has held one of the two Latin American seats in the International Court of Justice. This lack of influence, however, is being modified by the increasing practice in the UN of drawing committee and subcommittee heads from the Third World.

The Caribbean nations do exercise influence, however, by virtue of membership in certain UN blocs. Besides the Commonwealth Group, a good example is in the LAG which operates within the Group of 77 (G 77) either as a part of the UN Conference on Trade and Development (UNCTAD) or the Third UN Conference on the Law of the Sea (LOS III).* As far as the LAG and CWC states are concerned, a case can be made that the latter operate increasingly as a subbloc in the former. (It is interesting to recall that at the time the first two CWC nations—Jamaica and Trinidad and Tobago—wanted to join the LAG, Guatemala raised objections and unsuccessfully argued that their admission should require

---

*G 77 was the number of countries that signed the Joint Declaration at UNCTAD I in 1964; the number of developing countries in the group now exceeds 100.

100 percent approval of the LAG members.)[14] This results in less cohesion among the LAG members, especially between the Latin American and CWC countries. However, on some issues, as, for example, the vote on zionism, a split occurred among Latin American as well as CWC states.

In general, the Caribbean states have voted consistently in favor of issues from the Third World perspective. For example, they favor self-determination (e.g., of Rhodesia, Namibia, and Belize) and the end of racial discrimination, they favor voting based upon sovereign equality instead of being weighted, and they are in strong support of the New International Economic Order (NIEO). A few specific UN actions are worth noting.[15]

At UNCTAD III (1972), the Caribbean nations were among the 90 voting in favor of a resolution to create a set of obligations on the rights and duties of states, as proposed by President Luis Echeverría of Mexico. (Two years later the UN General Assembly approved overwhelmingly—120 to 6 with 10 abstentions—the resultant UN Charter of Economic Rights and Duties of States, CERDS). The Sixth Special Session (1974) passed a resolution on the Program of Action on the Establishment of a New International Economic Order, again with strong Latin American and Caribbean support. Also passed at the Twenty-Ninth General Assembly, along with the CERDS, was a definition of aggression, which was later incorporated into Article 9 of the amended Rio Treaty in 1975 (noted below). The LOS III provided another case of a common front among the LAG as a part of the Third World. The 28-member LAG maintained its unity on most issues, including the creation of an International Seabed Authority with the jurisdiction to conduct operations and to control the exploitation of the mineral resources in the seabed. At one stage of negotiation, three CWC states—Barbados, Jamaica, and Trinidad and Tobago—warned that the price of their continued LAG support was the right of access to the living resources in the economic zones of other states in the region.[16]

The 1975 General Assembly vote on zionism as a form of racism indicated a division among the Latin American as well as CWC nations. While Cuba, Grenada, and Guyana were among the 5 hemisphere countries voting with the majority of 72, 4 Caribbean states—the Bahamas, Barbados, the Dominican Republic, and Haiti—were among the 35 in opposition; 8 Latin American republics abstained, as did Jamaica and Trinidad and Tobago.[17]

OAS and IADB Membership

Joining the OAS was a carefully considered subject and was primarily economically motivated—in order to have access to the funds of the

IADB as a member, a state was required to be an OAS member. (The IADB requirement of OAS membership as a prerequisite was provided in article II of its original agreement. However, a later amendment permitted three nonmembers of the OAS to become members of the IADB: Canada in 1972, Guyana in 1976, and the Bahamas in 1977. While Canada has no interest in becoming an OAS member and Guyana is correctly barred as a result of Article 8 of the OAS Charter.)* Joining the OAS as a channel to the IADB was one of the alternatives that the CWC states felt compelled to pursue by virtue of British withdrawal from the Caribbean and entry into the EEC.[18] In addition, they were convinced that they would need to turn to Latin America for trade, stress regional integration, and greatly expand their economic relations with the United States and Canada.[19]

At the same time, however, the new nations had misgivings about joining the OAS. They were concerned about an organization with such a strong orientation toward Latin America, a group of countries with which they had little contact, they feared that they would be associated with Latin American instability and practices so contrary to the English legal and political tradition. There was also concern about the defense and security requirements of the Rio Treaty, as they did not share the Latin American view that OAS membership required becoming a party to the Rio Treaty. The Rio Treaty was acceptable against outside aggression but not by one OAS member against another; there was a fear that Venezuela might use it against Guyana. Another worry involved becoming a part of the bureaucracy headquartered in Washington, D.C., and joining an organization dominated by the United States and preoccupied with communism.[20]

In the early 1960s, the OAS considered the question of the admission of new members in anticipation of the applications of Guyana, Jamaica, and Trinidad and Tobago. During these deliberations before the council in 1963 and at the First Special Inter-American Conference in 1964, Guatemala again raised some objections and favored a restrictive admission process, as she had as a member of the UN LAG. At the former meeting, the representative of Uruguay also raised questions about the CWC states altering the political, cultural, juridical, and sociological composition of the OAS, and pointed to their ties with England and mini-state status. At the 1964 conference, there was a debate about OAS

---

*Article 8: "The Permanent Council shall not make any recommendation nor shall the General Assembly take any decision with respect to a request for admission on the part of a political entity whose territory became subject, . . . prior to December 18, 1964, . . . to litigation or claim between an extracontinental country and one or more Member States . . ., until the dispute has been ended by some peaceful procedure." Guyana is a permanent observer of the OAS along with Canada, Japan, Israel, and eight European states.

membership and the Rio Treaty, for the Latin American nations held that the two were linked. The U.S. view prevailed that, although it was difficult to see a state as an effective OAS member without being a party to the Rio Treaty, the latter could not be established as a prior condition. Finally, the Act of Washington was adopted in late 1964, which defined for the first time the rules for admission.[21]

Common Policies

The English speaking Caribbean has certain organs that may be used for working out or coordinating common foreign policy positions. One is the Standing Committee of Ministers of Foreign Affairs which can approve nonbinding recommendations by a ⅔ vote and binding ones by consensus. The Conference of the Heads of Government of the Commonwealth Caribbean Countries is another body that formulates common positions. To a certain extent, the Secretariat of CWC develops common positions concerning monetary and trade matters by means of the preparation of papers and their circulation. A few common positions will be noted below: exclusion from OAS membership, Cuba, LOS, and restructuring the IAS.

Exclusion from OAS Membership

The CWC states believe that all independent states in the hemisphere are entitled to membership in the OAS. They objected very strongly to the exclusion of Guyana under Article 8 of the OAS Charter and feel the same way about Guatemala's position vis-à-vis Belize should the latter become independent. (The independence of Belize is one issue supported by all Caribbean states.) At the Seventh Conference of the Heads of Government of the Commonwealth Countries (1972), a statement was approved and issued by Prime Minister Michael Manley of Jamaica that the governments of Barbados, Guyana, and Trinidad and Tobago "will therefore adopt all necessary measures in order to bring this exclusion of Commonwealth countries from the . . . [IAS] to an end."[22] As a result, these states advocate the repeal of article 8 of the OAS Charter.

Cuba

The sanctions imposed upon Cuba by the OAS in the 1960s, as discussed earlier, occurred prior to the entry into the OAS of the CWC nations and prior to the ratification of the Rio Treaty by Trinidad and Tobago. Therefore, these states were not bound by the sanctions and considered themselves to be free to enter into diplomatic and economic relations with Cuba. In fact, they considered Cuba to be an integral part of the Caribbean and opposed her isolation; they also had legal objections to Cuba's suspension from participation in the OAS, and Mexico believed that it was a dangerous precedent to exclude a state for ideological reasons. Consequently, CWC states, once they became OAS members, strongly supported the movement to establish the right of ideological pluralism and to lift the Cuban sanctions, although only Trinidad and Tobago could legally vote for the latter.

The English-speaking nations have generally welcomed Cuba back into the Caribbean community and have established diplomatic ties and trade relations. Barbados, Guyana, Jamaica, and Trinidad and Tobago entered into diplomatic relations in late 1972; the Bahamas did so in late 1974. The nature of relations has varied from extremely close (Guyana) to cordial (Jamaica), to cool but circumspect (the Bahamas). With the exception of Guyana, these new states have not been in favor of Cuban involvement of Africa.

The lifting of the OAS sanctions against Cuba was another item of CWC interest. At the 1972 General Assembly of the OAS, the United States blocked a proposal calling for a conference to consider lifting sanctions against Cuba, which Barbados, Jamaica, and Trinidad and Tobago supported, but the Dominican Republic and Haiti did not. The next year the OAS General Assembly adopted a resolution accepting the concept of a "plurality of ideologies," which paved the way for the subsequent OAS decision to call a Meeting of Consultation to consider lifting of Cuban sanctions. Meeting in Quito in late 1974, the resolution for reversing the OAS position received only 12 votes (including the Dominican Republic), 2 short of the required ⅔ vote. Three South American states voted against it and 6 abstained, including Haiti and the United States. Four states voting in favor of the resolution, including Venezuela, announced that they would go ahead anyway and establish relations with Cuba.

At the Sixteenth Meeting of Consultation, held in Costa Rica during the summer of 1975, a "Freedom of Action" resolution was passed by a vote of 16 to 3 with 2 abstentions.[23] (Included in the majority were the United States, the Dominican Republic, Haiti, and Trinidad and Tobago.) Even though the United States and the 2 Latin American Caribbean countries voted in favor, they have not normalized relations with Cuba.

LOS

A crisis developed between Ecuador and the United States over fishing in the early 1970s that brought the Latin American and Caribbean countries together against the United States. The issue involved the 200 mile limit, a claim advanced by an increasing number of Latin American states. When Ecuador began enforcing her claim by seizing and fining U.S. private fishing boats, the United States invoked the Pelly Amendment and cut off aid to Ecuador. The response of Ecuador, in this so-called Tuna War, was to accuse the United States of "coercion" and "aggression," charging intervention and requesting a meeting of the Organ of Consultation. The Council approved overwhelmingly (the Caribbean states were included) Ecuador's request and the Fourteenth Meeting of Consultation discussed the problem and then passed a resolution urging the disputants to resume negotiations.

In 1972, a number of states in Central America, northern South America, and the Caribbean met in the Dominican Republic in order to consider a subregional approach to maritime problems, since many of them in the Caribbean area had not claimed a 200 mile limit. Preferring an approach built upon traditional law but reluctant to create a regional organization for maritime questions, the resultant Declaration of Santo Domingo was signed by only 10 of the 15 states that sent formal delegations. The 10 included the Dominican Republic, Haiti, and Trinidad and Tobago, but not Barbados, Guyana, or Jamaica.[24]

Restructuring the IAS

The Latin American movement—Peru, Ecuador, and Venezuela were the prime movers—to amend the Rio Treaty and to amend the OAS Charter again, was one in which the CWC nations played somewhat of an intermediary role between Latin America and the United States. On the issues of ideological pluralism, lifting the sanctions against Cuba, multilateralizing the Inter-American Committee for the Alliance for Progress (CIAP), and revising the Rio Treaty, the CWC states sided with those of Latin America; but on issues of amending the OAS Charter, incorporating and establishing the concepts of integral development and collective economic security for development, particularly the concepts' operationalization, they supported and shared many of the concerns of the United States. This was especially true of Barbados, Jamaica, and Trinidad and Tobago.[25]

At the Third General Assembly (1973), a resolution was passed noting that "there is general dissatisfaction with the functioning and results of the inter-American system" and then creating a Special Committee to Study the Inter-American system and to Propose Measures for Restructuring It (the committee was called CEESI after the Spanish initials). CEESI held a number of sessions until 1975 and produced a set of amendments to the Rio Treaty and to the OAS Charter. In addition, draft conventions on collective economic security and integral development were approved, to be considered and approved as treaties at a special OAS General Assembly in 1977 (later postponed indefinitely because an impasse existed on the conventions between the United States and Latin America).[26] The amendments to the Rio Treaty, which weakened its former collective security nature and incorporated the new concept of collective economic security (a concept strongly opposed by the United States), were approved by the Conference of Plenipotentiaries in Costa Rica in 1975. The amendments to the OAS Charter, including expanded and new commitments in the social and economic development areas, were approved by the council in late 1976. When the council considered the draft conventions on cooperation for development and collective economic security in April 1977, the former was approved unanimously; the latter was passed with one dissent (the United States) and three abstentions—Jamaica alone among the Caribbean states.[27]

IADB

One of the major complaints that the Commonwealth Caribbean countries have voiced for several years is the fact that they did not have their own executive director on the Board of Executive Directors, that is, one among the seven elected by groups of Latin American states; in fact, they had to wait until every third year to serve as alternate director. Instead, they were assigned to a group headed by a director from Venezuela. However, the IADB has responded to this complaint and has approved, starting in 1978, a "Caribbean Group" of five states—Barbados, the Bahamas, Guyana, Jamaica, Trinidad and Tobago—with their own elected director and alternate.

The amount of money loaned to the Caribbean members of the IADB is worth summarizing (see Table 20.1 for the dates of entry). The totals, with the main sector in parentheses, are given in millions of dollars, as follows: Barbados—33 (education); the Dominican Republic—240 (agriculture); Guyana—50 (agriculture; also .8 in grants); Haiti—107 (transportation and communications); Jamaica—107 (agriculture); and Trinidad and Tobago—36 (sanitation).[28]

CONCLUSION

This study of nine Caribbean states—three Latin American joined by six CWC nations in the 1960s and 1970s—has indicated that they do not constitute a bloc or have a separate identity in either the UN or OAS. Although the former regularly supported the United States on cold war issues in both organizations until Castro came to power, thereafter these countries were divided between the former and the latter groups over the issue of Cuba. Nonetheless, the Caribbean nations share two common goals with other Third World members: to become economically developed and to end or moderate their economic dependency. They have differed, however, over the means of achieving these goals, including among other things, regional integration (the Dominican Republic and Haiti would like CARICOM membership).

As the result of the nonexistence of a Caribbean bloc, these states exercise very limited influence in the UN. However, there does exist a subbloc in the Caribbean, the CWC nations. This bloc is active as a part of the LAG in the UN and is of particular—and growing—significance in the OAS, which is causing concern on the part of the Latin American members.

The importance of this subbloc in the OAS will increase as other CWC entities become independent and join.[29] There is, however, ambivalence on the part of the CWC states in their approach to the OAS which they joined because it was a prerequisite for IADB membership and loans. Notwithstanding their growing influence in the OAS, they feel that their membership has been overshadowed by certain outside links. One of these is the special status given to the products of forty-odd African, Caribbean, and Pacific (ACP) states, including the Bahamas, Barbados, Grenada, Jamaica, and Trinidad and Tobago, in the EEC by the Lomé Accord of 1975.[30] This agreement has not only maintained but has increased ties with Europe. Two other external ties are provided by the Commonwealth Conference and the services of its secretariat (this also involves the sterling tie), and by the Non-Aligned Group, which is of far lesser importance.* The Commonwealth Caribbean nations also consider the IADB to be far more important than the OAS, particularly since the IADB is increasingly globalized with fifteen nonhemisphere developed countries as members and contributors.

Finally, the steady increase in the number of CWC states and the subbloc's influence in the OAS is bringing about growing Latin American concern about the future of the organization. This concern will become more acute if the Commonwealth Caribbean nations begin to act as an intermediary bloc between the United States and Latin America or as a bloc which shifts back and forth between the two.

NOTES

1. Leslie Manigat, "The Year 1975 in Perspective (From the late 1950s to 1975: The Emergence of the Caribbean on the International Scene)," in *The Caribbean Yearbook of*

---

*Guyana has been an active member and hosted a conference in 1970. Barbados, Grenada, Jamaica, and Trinidad and Tobago are observers.

International Relations, 1975, ed. Leslie Manigat (Leyden: Sijthoff, 1976), pp. 79–80. This scholarly series is the best on the subject.

2. Louis J. Cantori and Steven L. Spiegel, *The International Politics of Regions: A Comparative Approach* (Englewood Cliffs, N.J.: Prentice-Hall, 1970), pp. 1–8. The Dominican Republic is placed in the "core" while Cuba is considered to be a potential member.

3. Professor John Dreier's distinction between the IAS and the OAS is accepted, in which the former refers to "the broad complex of juridical principles, political policies, and administrative arrangements that has grown up among the American republics over the years" and the latter to "the principal multilateral organization through which the system operates." John Dreier, *The Organization of American States and the Hemisphere Crisis* (New York: Praeger, 1962), p. 11.

4. Cyril Hamshere, *The British in the Caribbean* (Cambridge, Ma.: Harvard University Press, 1972); Emanuel de Kadt, ed., *Patterns of Foreign Influence in the Caribbean* (London: Royal Institute of International Affairs, 1972); and Harold Paton Mitchell, *Europe in the Caribbean;* (Edinburgh: W and R Chambers, 1963).

5. John A. Houston, *Latin America in the United Nations* (New York: Carnegie Endowment for International Peace, 1956); Thomas Hovet, Jr., *Bloc Policies in the United Nations* (Cambridge: Harvard University Press, 1960); and Gaston de Prat Gay, *Politica Internacional del Grupo Latinoamericano* (Buenos Aires: Abeledo-Perrot, 1967), pp. 103–19.

6. Houston, op. cit.; Hovet, op. cit.; de Prat Gay, op. cit.

7. Jerome Slater, *The OAS and United States Foreign Policy* (Columbus: Ohio State University Press, 1967), chaps. 3 and 4.

8. Larman C. Wilson, "The Settlement of Conflicts within the Framework of Relations between Regional Organizations and the United Nations: The Case of Cuba," *Netherlands International Law Review* 22 (1975): 289–92.

9. Ibid., pp. 298–300. Article 53 provided that "no enforcement action shall be taken under regional arrangements . . . without the authorization of the Security Council. . . ."

10. de Prat Gay, op. cit., pp. 46–48.

11. Pan American Union, *Ninth Meeting of Consultation . . .: Final Act* (Washington, D.C.: PAU, 1964).

12. Larman C. Wilson, "Multilateral Policy and the OAS: . . .," in *Latin American Foreign Policies: An Analysis,* Harold E. Davis and Larman C. Wilson (Baltimore: John Hopkins University Press, 1975), pp. 68–69.

13. Dreier, "New Wine and Old Bottles: The Changing Inter-American Scene," *International Organization* 22 (1968): 491.

14. de Prat Gay, op. cit., pp. 48–51.

15. A valuable source is U.S., Department of State, Bureau of International Organization Affairs, *Votes at the Twenty-Seventh* [etc.] *Session of the General Assembly* (Washington, D.C.: 1972–).

16. Edward Miles, "The Structure and Effects of the Decision Process in the Seabed Committee and the Third United Nations Conference on the Law of the Sea," *International Organization* 31 (1977): 161–62.

17. The Washington *Post,* 12 November 1975.

18. Basil Buchanan, "Commonwealth Caribbean Countries and the Organization of American States" (Ph.D diss., The American University, 1976); interviews with Ambassador Valerie T. McComie, January 3, 1978; and Roy Preiswerk, "The Relevance of Latin America to the Foreign Policy of Commonwealth Caribbean States," *Journal of Inter-American Studies* 11 (1969): 245–71.

19. McComie interview; Neville Linton, "Regional Diplomacy of the Commonwealth Caribbean," *International Journal* 26 (1970–71): 401–17; and Preiswerk, op. cit., pp. 246–47, 256.

20. Buchanan, op. cit., p. 45.

21. Buchanan, op. cit., pp. 16–18, 23–35.

22. Quoted in ibid., p. 146.

23. *The OAS Chronicle* 10 (August 1975): 4.

24. E. D. Brown, "Latin America and the International Law of the Sea," in *Latin America: The Search for a New International Role* eds. Ronald G. Hellman and H. Jon Rosenbaum (New York: John Wiley & Sons, 1975), pp. 251–56.

25. Larman C. Wilson, "The Concept of 'Collective Economic Security for Development' and Contemporary Latin American-U.S. Relations," *Towson State Journal of International Affairs* 12 (1977): 28.

26. ibid., pp. 40–41.

27. OAS, *Draft Report of the Permanent Council on the Study of the Texts Prepared by CEESI on the Subjects of Collective Economic Security and Cooperation for Development* (Washington, D.C.: OAS, April 28, 1977), pp. 17, 36.

28. IADB, *Annual Report 1977* (Washington, D.C.: IADB, 1978), pp. 42, 53, 59–60, 63, 73. The total for Trinidad and Tobago is through 1974, since she has not applied for any loans since 1975.

29. Elmer Plischke, *Microstates in World Affairs: Policy Problems and Options* (Washington, D.C.: American Enterprise Institute, 1977), has identified 12 CWC entities as potential members (pp. 145–46).

30. The Lomé accord gives these states duty-free access for their industrial products and for 96 percent of their agricultural exports, provides for a fixed purchase of sugar for seven years, and establishes a stabilization program for exporters' revenues. "The Lomé Convention," *The European Community* (March 1975), pp. 5–8.

Index

About the Editors and Contributors

RICHARD L. MILLETT (Ph.D., University of New Mexico) is Professor of History and Chairman of the Latin American Studies Committee, Southern Illinois University at Edwardsville. From 1976 through 1978 he served as Chairman of the Committee on Central American and Caribbean Studies of the Conference on Latin American History. A specialist on U.S.-Latin American Relations and on the military in Latin America, he has published numerous articles dealing with the Hispanic Caribbean and is the author of *Guardians of the Dynasty: A History of the U.S. Created Guardia Nacional de Nicaragua* (1977).

W. MARVIN WILL (Ph.D., University of Missouri) is Associate Professor of Political Science at the University of Tulsa and has served as Director of the St. Louis based Civic Education Center. His research interests focus upon the Commonwealth Caribbean, but he also teaches Latin American politics and international development. He has conducted research throughout the Caribbean and has written on numerous aspects of both internal development and international relations within the region.

WENDELL BELL (Ph.D., UCLA) is Professor of Sociology and Director of Undergraduate Studies at Yale. President of the Caribbean Studies Association, Dr. Bell has published widely on the Caribbean and in the area of political sociology. He is author of *Jamaican Leaders: Political Attitudes in a New Nation* (1964).

JAN K. BLACK (Ph.D., American University) is a Senior Research Associate of the Division of Inter-American Affairs, University of New Mexico. Formerly a team chairperson in foreign area studies at American University, her publications include *United States Penetration of Brazil* (1977).

SIR KENNETH BLACKBURNE, G.C.M.G., G.B.E., was educated at Clare College, Cambridge. He has served as a member of the Development and Welfare organization of the West Indies, as Governor of the Leeward Islands and as Governor General of Jamaica. Now residing on the Isle of Man, U.K., he is the author of *Lasting Legacy: A Story of British Colonialism.*

KEN I. BOODHOO (Ph.D., University of the West Indies–Mona, Jamaica) is Chairperson of the Department of International Relations, Florida International University, and Associate Professor. A specialist in Caribbean Studies and in the activities of multi-national corporations, he has authored numerous articles in leading journals.

ANTHONY BRYAN (Ph.D., University of Nebraska) is presently Senior Lecturer on International Relations (Latin America) at the Institute of International Relations, University of the West Indies–St. Augustine, Trinidad. Previously on the History faculty at the University of Rhode Island, he has published widely on both Mexican and Caribbean topics.

WINFIELD J. BURGGRAAFF (Ph.D., University of New Mexico) is Associate Professor and Chairman of the History Department, University of Missouri–Columbia. A specialist on Venezuela and on Latin American petroleum policies, he has published *The Venezuelan Armed Forces in Politics, 1935–1959* (1972).

ELSA MAE CHANEY (Ph.D., University of Wisconsin) is Deputy Coordinator of Women in Development for the Agency for International Development (A.I.D.). Her publications include several articles dealing with migration and with development and a forthcoming book *Supermadre: Women in Politics in Latin America* (University of Texas).

WILLIAM G. DEMAS is Director of the Caribbean Development Bank, Barbados. From 1970 to 1974 he was Secretary General of the Caribbean Community (CARICOM) Secretariat. Among his many publications are *Economics of Development in Small Countries* and *Essays on Caribbean Integration and Development.*

W. RAYMOND DUNCAN is Professor of Political Science at SUNY–Brockport. His publications include numerous articles on Latin American politics and on Cuban and Soviet policies in the western hemisphere. Professor Duncan's latest book is *Latin American Politics: A Developmental Approach* (1976).

JUDITH EWELL (Ph.D., University of New Mexico) is Associate Professor of History, William and Mary. She has published articles in the *Journal of Latin American Studies* and the *Revista/Review Interamericana* and is currently doing research on Law of the Sea issues, especially as they relate to Latin America.

GEORGE FAURIOL (Ph.D., University of Pennsylvania) is a research fellow and Director of the Population Program at the Georgetown University Center for Strategic and International Studies. He has done research on Haiti, the Dominican Republic, and Canadian-Caribbean relations and has published in the *Revista/Review Interamericana*.

ALBERT L. GASTMANN (Ph.D., Columbia) has done research and teaching in both Suriname and the Netherlands Antilles. Professor of Political Science at Trinity College, Hartford, Connecticut, he has recently authored the *Historical Dictionary of the French and Netherlands Antilles*.

HERBERT L. HILLER, former Executive Director of the Caribbean Tourism Association and Instructor at Florida International University, is a lecturer, consultant and writer on tourism and travel—and is a contributing editor of the *Caribbean Review*.

BASIL INCE (Ph.d., New York University) is Senior Lecturer in International Relations, University of the West Indies, St. Augustine, Trinidad. He is the author of *The Decolonization Conflict in the United Nations* and editior of *Contemporary International Relations in the Caribbean.*.

ROBERTA JOHNSON (Ph.D., Harvard) is Associate Professor of Political Science at the University of San Francisco. She has also taught at the University of Missouri–Kansas City and has published numerous articles on the status of Puerto Rico, minority politics, and black power.

DAWN MARSHALL (Masters in Social Science, UWI, Mona, Jamaica) is Research Fellow, Institute of Social and Economic Research, University of the West Indies, Cave Hill, Barbados. She has engaged in demographic research in the Caribbean and England and is conducting a major research project on the impact of migration in Barbados.

JOHN PLANK (Ph.D., Harvard) is Professor of Political Science at the University of Connecticut. Formerly Director of Research and Analysis for American Republics, U.S. Department of State and Senior Fellow, The Brooking Institution, he has published numerous articles on Cuba in such journals as *Foreign Affairs* and is the editor of *The United States and Cuba: Long Range Perspectives* (1967).

HARALD M. SANDSTROM (Ph.D., University of Pennsylvania) is Assistant Professor of Political Science at the University of Hartford. A specialist on Caribbean Economic Development, he is also investigating dependency theory and the efforts to develop a new international economic order.

LARMAN C. WILSON (Ph.D., Maryland) is Professor of International Relations at The American University. A specialist on inter-American relations, his publications include co-authorship of *The United States and the Trujillo Regime (1972) and Latin American Foreign Policies* (1975).

ROSINA WILTSHIRE (Ph.D., Michigan) is Lecturer at the University of the West Indies–Mona, Jamaica. A specialist on political integration, she has contributed numerous articles to professional and regional publications.